GODS AND HEROES OF THE GREEKS

Gods and Heroes of the Greeks:

The *Library* of Apollodorus

Translated with introduction and notes by Michael Simpson

Drawings by Leonard Baskin

University of Massachusetts Press   Amherst

For Rachel, Maria, Michael and Robert

CONTENTS

. . . that best of all things, Hellenic—
mankind has no quality more precious:
everything beyond that belongs to the gods.
—C. P. Cavafy

The Library   The *Library* of Apollodorus, a handbook of Greek mythology, alone of the many works of its kind survives antiquity. It is therefore a major source for our knowledge of the myths. Although it was attributed to the Athenian grammarian, Apollodorus (180–120 or 110 B.C.), all of whose writings, except for a few fragments, are lost, modern scholars agree that Apollodorus and the author of the *Library* were not the same man. The latter remains unknown.[1] By convention, however, Apollodorus' name continues to be attached to the work.

The handbook was probably written no earlier than the first century B.C. The most likely date for its composition is the first century A.D.[2] It is composed of three books and an epitome or abridgment of the remainder made by whom we do not know.

The *Library* gives a straightforward account of Greek mythology from the birth of the gods to the death of Odysseus. Sir James G. Frazer calls it "an accurate record of what the Greeks in general believed about the origin and early history of the world and of their race."[3]

The author of the work made no attempt to give literary shape to his handbook. It is not a work of art like Ovid's *Metamorphoses*, but rather a compendium of mythology. The absence of literary artifice, however, enables us to trust Apollodorus' use of his sources.[4]

The most frequently quoted source in the *Library* is Pherecydes, who lived at Athens in the first half of the fifth century B.C. His prose work on Greek mythology (now lost) was consulted as a basic text by writers in the classical, Hellenistic, and Roman periods.[5] Next in importance are Acusilaus, a logographer who lived at the end of the sixth century B.C. and made a paraphrase in prose of Hesiod's genealogical poems; and Hesiod, the eighth-century B.C. Boeotian epic poet, whose *Theogony* and *Works and Days* survive entire. In relying on these early authors the writer of the Library avoids the rationalizing tendency of later mythographers and preserves archaic versions of the myths.[6]

Other sources are the epic poems, including the Epic Cycle and the Returns in addition to the Iliad and the Odyssey of Homer. The Library follows the Argonautica, the Hellenistic epic by Apollonius of Rhodes, for the voyage of Jason and the Argonauts in quest of the golden fleece.[7]

Sources less frequently quoted are Hellanicus, a prolific writer of histories, genealogies, and ethnographic works who lived toward the end of the fifth century B.C., and to whom the author of the Library is indebted for genealogies and for the Trojan history;[8] Herodorus, a late fifth-century B.C. writer who rationalized the fantastic elements in Greek mythology;[9] and Asclepiades, the author in the fourth-century B.C. of a treatise on Greek tragedies.[10] The tragedians were little used: Sophocles is quoted once, alluded to once; Euripides is quoted four times and alluded to three times. Simonides and Pindar are quoted once each.[11]

The most recent edition of the Library, and the one which served as a working text for the translation, is that of Sir James G. Frazer published in the Loeb Library Series in 1921. Frazer based his text on R. Wagner's 1894 Teubner edition, although in doubtful passages he consulted other editions, recording his variations from Wagner's text in an apparatus criticus.[12] Wagner had failed to consult ms. O (Laud. gr. 55 in the Bodleian), which Aubrey Diller believes is "the intermediary between the fourteenth-century archetype and the sixteenth-century apographs."[13] In a reprint of his text issued in 1926 (and misleadingly called a "second edition"), Wagner remedied the earlier defect somewhat by publishing a collation of ms. O in a Supplementum appartus critici.[14] Frazer's text remains the most recent in print.

In order to have translated as sound a Greek text as possible, I thoroughly examined Wagner's Supplementum. I have not thought it necessary to note the few instances in which I have preferred a reading of Wagner or some other editor to one of Frazer.

Myth Myths were for the ancient Greeks the equivalent of the Bible for the ancient Hebrews. The Hebrews have been called "the people of the Book." The Greeks, by contrast, "are the people not of the Book but of the myth."[15] For them, "myth was their great teacher in all matters of the spirit."[16]

Although an awareness of myth as such developed among the Greeks in the latter half of the fifth century B.C. as rational thinking developed, myths continued to retain their value as a source of understanding. At the end of the *Republic* of Plato (c. 429–c. 347) Socrates says, "And so, Glaucon, the *mûthos* was saved and did not perish, and, if we heed it, it may save us" (621b8–c1).

Mûthos, the Greek source of the word "myth," has the general meaning of "word," "speech," and "story." Aristotle in the *Poetics* gives *mûthos* the special technical meaning, "plot." At 1450a 3–5 he says that plot (*mûthos*) is the imitation of an action. He continues, "For by plot [*mûthos*] I mean structure." "Structure" is D. W. Lucas' correct rendition here of the literal Greek "the putting-together of the events." As Lucas says, "The story is a preliminary selection from the stream of events; in the plot the story is organized."[17]

The Greek word *mûthos* and Aristotle's special use of it provide two starting points for defining myth: First, language is its province, and second, it is a structure, a plot, a putting-together of events. To this we add that myths are the product of oral societies, not literate ones, and so it is spoken, not written, language that is the original province of myth. According to Eric Havelock, people in oral cultures think differently from people in literate ones, for whom writing makes possible a new kind of discourse, characterized by the term "conceptual": "Nonliterate speech had favored discourse describing action; the post-literate altered the balance in favor of reflection."[18] Myths are preeminently a discourse of action.

We know Greek myths primarily through Greek literature, which includes oral poetry. Greek literature was composed in and for a society that at first was oral (on its way to becoming literate), and then literate (by the end of the fifth century B.C.), although retaining features of its earlier oral stage. Greek literature thus reflects the tension "between the modes of oral and documented speech."[19] The myths, in fact, are oral society's legacy to Greek literate culture, and that legacy never ceased influencing the thought of these "people of the myth."

Oral societies are traditional societies. They strive to maintain connection with their past, which means that the older generation must create and maintain connection with the younger generation. Telling stories is one way of doing this, stories that the older generation heard when it was young from a still-older generation, and that the present younger generation, when it grows older, will tell to its successor generation. These stories, which link the generations, will be related to all those aspects of the society that it must take into account for its preservation and well-being.

We may now define myth as a "traditional narrative structure" or, more simply, as a "traditional tale."[20] As "traditional" indicates, the origin of a myth is not important, whereas its transmission and preservation are all important. "A tale becomes traditional not by virtue of being created, but by being retold and accepted. . . ." In the process of transmission, a tale can suffer omissions and misinterpretations, yet still retain its identity. This process implies that a tale is independent from a particular text or a particular reality. Its identity must therefore come from "a *structure of sense* within the tale itself." Such structures would be elements of plot or various themes.[21]

A myth applies to something that has collective importance—and that includes almost all aspects of human existence. Institutions of family and society, gods and rituals, the seasons, the availability of food, disease, laws governing marriage and incest, and the order of nature and the universe can all become the subjects of myths.[22]

The relation between myth and ritual remains controversial after almost a century of discussion. Walter Burkert's view of this relation seems the most balanced: although "myth does not grow directly out of ritual," the two are, nevertheless, "closely allied." The function of ritual is "to dramatize the order of life," whereas myth "clarifies the order of life." Moreover, myth "frequently explains and justifies social orders and establishments, and in so doing it is related to ritual, which occurs by means of social interaction."[23]

Myths served as history for the Greeks who, as "traditional" people, used the past to give meaning to the present. Myths were, in a sense, the past preserved, interpreted, and applied to the present. They told the Greeks who they were as a people; they provided, as M. I. Finley says, a "mythical charter" for "Hellenic self-consciousness."[24]

Greek poets, beginning with nameless oral bards, shaped and developed the myths as they retold them, functioning as seers of the past, and it was Homer and Hesiod, Herodotus says (2.53), who created a theogony for the Greeks, gave the gods their epithets, assigned them their prerogatives and functions, and described their forms. For the Greeks, then, myth and literature were inextricably bound together.

Greek myths can be divided into (1) myths describing the origin of the universe, (2) myths describing the birth and development of the gods, (3) myths narrating the early history of human beings, and (4) myths of the heroes.[25] This corpus of traditional tales (particularly those describing the origin of the universe and those describing the birth and development of the gods) can be thought of as a "system of classification, a particular way of ordering and conceptualising the universe."[26] The system classifies powers, for the Greeks conceived of the universe as an elaborate interconnected organization of multiple powers that operate in several areas: in nature, in human society, in individual human beings, and in the other world. These powers—the gods especially, but also other divine and semidivine beings—do not stand outside the universe and the world: They are immanent, not transcendent.[27]

The myths of the origin of the universe (cosmogony) and the birth and development of the gods (theogony), told in Hesiod's *Theogony* and in Apollodorus' *Library,* use the genealogical catalog as their basic ordering device for classifying the powers of the universe. That is, Earth, who comes into being on her own and produces Sky, mates with Sky and gives birth to divine powers. These powers mate in turn to produce the gods whose various unions give rise to yet other divine beings.

We can make the following observations about these myths. First, all life in its particular aspects is charged with divinity. Second, the genealogical catalog conveys the essential relatedness, the connections, among all the phenomena of life. Third, this system of divine powers is conceived, by means of genealogy, as a vast humanlike family, and these powers are modeled on human beings—are anthropomorphic. Finally, their "family relation" instructs us to consider them as a system, rather than singly, in isolation from each other, and, indeed, they cannot otherwise be understood.[28]

G. S. Kirk notes two distinctive characteristics of Greek myths, particularly heroic myths: First, "Fantastic elements—elements not only remote from real life and the actually possible, but also genuinely imaginative in conception—are few"; and second, Greek myths are concise and formally neat: "They do not sprawl or indulge in irrelevant detail or complication."[29] Moreover, the very number of heroic myths in comparison to myths of gods or other supernatural beings makes Greece unique: "No other ancient culture is similar."[30]

According to Kirk, the "commonest themes" of Greek myths exhibit four preoccupations: with "contests and quests, particularly involving monsters"; with "the relations between men and gods . . ."; with "the presence in the background of the gods themselves"; and with "stresses within the family."[31] While Kirk views the repeated references to family stress in Greek myths as "a broad response to a continuing human characteristic,"[32] Philip Slater thinks Greek myths exhibit a pathology specific to ancient Greek society and the Greek family.[33]

Carrying the structuralist thinking of Kirk and others to its furthest extent, Charles Segal uses the term "megatext" to describe the corpus of Greek myths. By "megatext" he means not only the themes and tales available to oral poets, but also "subconscious patterns or 'deep structures' . . . which tales of a given type share with one another." Within the megatext "specific literary narrations of particular myths

. . . operate as sub-texts, exploiting particular aspects of the megatext, commenting on it, or sometimes making explicit certain networks of interconnection implied but not openly stated in the megatext."[34]

The Notes   The notes aim to serve as a source of information about Greek myths and Greek and Latin literature (where the myths are found), locating for the reader specific versions of various myths in various sources. In addition I frequently present in the notes views other than my own about ancient myth and literature in order to give to the reader something of the broad range of thinking about this aspect of classical antiquity.

The notes also aim to engage the interest of the reader. This purpose is in keeping with my belief, expressed by Huizinga, that "Myth and poetry both come from the play-sphere." In myth (and in literature), he says, "the writer's aim, conscious or unconscious, is to create a tension that will 'enchant' the reader and hold him spellbound." Myth-making, "this tendency to create an imaginary world of living beings, . . . [is] a playing of the mind. . . ."[35]

My chief indebtedness is to Sir James G. Frazer's edition of Apollodorus with its *richesse* of information in his notes. My approach and aims are quite different from Frazer's, but in making my own notes to the *Library*, I gratefully drew upon his time and time again.

To the Reader   The following information is necessary to enable the reader to use the text and the notes with understanding:

1   The Greeks and Romans used different names for their gods and goddesses and for some of their heroes. When referring to Greek literature I use Greek names for divinities; when referring to Latin literature, Roman names. For most heroes or other mythological characters (except rarely mentioned ones) I use their Greek names in Latinized form. Heracles and Athena are always thus (never Hercules and Minerva), while the Latin Ajax is used for references in both literatures.

Divinities

Greek	Latin
Zeus	Jupiter (or Jove)
Hera	Juno
Poseidon	Neptune
Demeter	Ceres
Apollo	Apollo
Artemis	Diana
Ares	Mars
Aphrodite	Venus

Hermes	Mercury
Athena	(Minerva)
Hephaestus	Vulcan
Hestia	Vesta
Dionysus	Dionysus or Bacchus
Hades	Pluto

Demeter's daughter, Persephone, has the Latin name, Proserpina; and the hero Polydeuces, brother of Castor, has the Latin name, Pollux.

2   Anything in the *text* in *single* brackets (often cross references) I have added.

3   The signs, | ... |, set off material in the text written by Apollodorus but which, had he been a modern author, he would have put into footnotes (for example, the catalog of Greek chieftains who went to Troy: Epitome 3. 11–14). The material so demarcated is of various kinds, including lists (as in the example above), but frequently versions of myths which he presents as alternatives or additions to his own. These versions are often preceded by such statements as, "Pherecydes says," or "Acusilaus says." Sometimes Apollodorus presents thus a version longer or more interesting than his own and the signs of demarcation have been omitted. Absolute consistency in their use has not been possible.

4   References to Apollodorus throughout are given only as numbers unaccompanied by his name or the title of the handbook. Thus references such as 2. 3. 5 or Epitome 3. 11 *in text or notes and in or out of parentheses or brackets always refer to the text of Apollodorus.* The former example refers to book 2, chapter 3, paragraph 5 (divisions made in the Greek manuscripts). The running numbers which appear in the left hand margins of the translation represent the third number of such references (or the second in the case of the Epitome).

5   Frazer's edition of Apollodorus is cited by short title throughout the notes. Pindar's *Odes,* in four books: *Olympian, Pythian, Nemean* and *Isthmian,* are referred to respectively as *Ol., Pyth., Nem.* and *Isth.,* with the appropriate poem and line numbers.

February 1986

NOTES

1   C. Robert, *De Apollodori Bibliotheca* (Berlin, 1873), 11–14; see also Sir James George Frazer, ed., *Apollodorus: The Library,* 2 vols. (Cambridge, Mass., and London, 1921), 1. ix–x; M. van der Valk, "On Apollodori *Bibliotheca,*" *Revue des Études grecques* 71 (1958), 100; and

A. Lesky, *A History of Greek Literature*, trans. James Willis and Cornelis de Heer (New York, 1966), 856–57.

2 van der Valk, "On Apollodori *Bibliotheca*," 167; Robert, *De Apollodori Bibliotheca*, 40–41.

3 Frazer, *Apollodorus*, 1. xvii.

4 See van der Valk, "On Apollodori *Bibliotheca*," 101–03, for examples.

5 Ibid., 109; Frazer, *Apollodorus*, 1. xix–xx; and Lesky, *Hist. of Greek Lit.*, 221–22.

6 van der Valk, "On Apollodori *Bibliotheca*," 109 and 154–62; Frazer, *Apollodorus*, 1. xx; and Lesky, *Hist. of Greek Lit.*, 106.

7 van der Valk, "On Apollodori *Bibliotheca*," 109 and 114–17; for the Epic Cycle and *The Returns*, see the *Oxford Classical Dictionary* under "Epic Cycle."

8 van der Valk, "On Apollodori *Bibliotheca*," 134–42; Lesky, *Hist. of Greek Lit.*, 330–32.

9 van der Valk, "On Apollodori *Bibliotheca*," 157–58; Lesky, *Hist. of Greek Lit.*, 329–30.

10 Frazer, *Apollodorus*, 1. xx.

11 van der Valk, "On Apollodori *Bibliotheca*," 162. The work's complete disregard of Rome is striking. For a brief discussion see Frazer, *Apollodorus*, 1. xi–xiii.

12 R. Wagner, ed., *Mythographi Graeci*, vol. 1: *Apollodori Bibliotheca*, . . . (Leipzig, 1894); and Frazer, *Apollodorus*, 1. xl–xli.

13 Aubrey Diller, "The Text History of the Bibliotheca of Pseudo-Apollodorus," *Transactions and Proceedings of the American Philological Association* 66 (1935), 310.

14 R. Wagner, ed., *Mythographi Graeci*, vol. 1: *Apollodori Bibliotheca* . . . , *editio stereotypa editionis alterius* (1926) (Stuttgart, 1965), 262–71.

15 Bernard Knox, *Word and Action: Essays on the Ancient Theater* (Baltimore and London, 1979), 17, 18.

16 M. I. Finley, *The Use and Abuse of History* (New York, 1975), 14.

17 D. W. Lucas, ed., *Aristotle: Poetics* (Oxford, 1968), 100.

18 Eric A. Havelock, *The Literate Revolution in Greece and Its Cultural Consequences* (Princeton, N.J., 1982), 7–8.

19 Ibid., 187.

20 G. S. Kirk, *The Nature of Greek Myths* (Harmondsworth and Baltimore, 1974), 22 ff. There are many other definitions of myth, based on different theories, each of which emphasizes a different aspect of a society or of human beings, or the human mind, to the exclusion of other aspects. Percy Cohen, "Theories of Myth," *Man* 4 (1969),

337–53, identifies seven theories of myth. Kirk, *Nature of Greek Myths*, 38–91, following and amplifying Cohen, discusses the limitations of "five monolithic theories" (myths are nature myths, are aetiological, are charters, evoke a creative era, are associated with rituals) and of several additional theories which view myths as "products of the psyche," i.e., myths express something repressed (Aristotle); fulfill a wish or create an emotional condition and are analogous to dreams or daydreams (Freud and others); reveal the "collective unconscious" and contain "archetypes" (Jung); are symbolic (Cassirer); reflect the workings of the human mind (Lévi-Strauss).

John Peradotto, *Classical Mythology: An Annotated Bibliographical Survey* (Urbana: American Philological Association, 1973), offers an annotated list of works on mythology which covers the field from Greek mythology to French structuralism of the early 1970s.

21 Walter Burkert, *Structure and History in Greek Mythology and Ritual* (Berkeley and Los Angeles, 1979), 2–7.

22 Ibid., 23.

23 Walter Burkert, *Homo Necans* (Berkeley and Los Angeles, 1983), 31, 33.

24 Finley, *Use and Abuse*, 26.

25 Kirk, *Nature of Greek Myths*, 113.

26 Jean-Pierre Vernant, *Myth and Society in Ancient Greece* (Brighton, Eng., and Atlantic Highlands, N.J., 1980), 94.

27 Hugh Lloyd-Jones, *The Justice of Zeus* (Berkeley and Los Angeles, 1971), 160.

28 Vernant, *Myth and Society*, 99.

29 G. S. Kirk, *Myth: Its Meaning and Function in Greek and Other Cultures* (Cambridge, Eng., and Berkeley, 1970), 182, 190.

30 Kirk, *Nature of Greek Myths*, 215.

31 Kirk, *Myth*, 187 ff., 202.

32 Ibid., 194.

33 Philip E. Slater, *The Glory of Hera* (Boston, 1968); and "The Greek Family in History and Myth," *Arethusa* 7 (1974).

34 Charles Segal, "Greek Myth as a Semiotic and Structural System and the Problem of Tragedy," *Arethusa* 16 (1983), 176.

35 J. Huizinga, *Homo Ludens: A Study of the Play-Element in Culture* (Boston, 1955), 129, 132, 136.

GODS AND HEROES OF THE GREEKS

CHAPTER ONE

*Theogony, the Rape of Persephone, the Battle
of the Gods and Giants (1. 1. 1–1. 6. 3)*

BOOK 1 1 First Sky ruled over the entire world. He married Earth
and produced Briareus, Gyes, and Cottus, the so-called Hundred-
2 Handed, who possessed a hundred hands and fifty heads and were
unsurpassed in size and strength. After these Earth bore to him the
Cyclopes: Arges, Steropes, and Brontes, each of whom had one eye
in his forehead. Sky tied them up and threw them into Tartarus, a dark
3 and gloomy place in Hades, as far from earth as earth is from the sky,
and again had children by Earth, the so-called Titans: Ocean, Coeus,
Hyperion, Crius, Iapetus, and Cronus, the youngest of all. He also had
daughters called Titanides: Tethys, Rhea, Themis, Mnemosyne, Phoebe,
Dione, and Thia.
4   Grieved at the loss of the children who were thrown into Tartarus,
Earth persuaded the Titans to attack their father and gave Cronus a
steel sickle. They all set upon him, except for Ocean, and Cronus cut
off his father's genitals and threw them into the sea. From the drops of
the spurting blood were born the Furies: Alecto, Tisiphone, and
Megaera. Having thus eliminated their father, the Titans brought back
their brothers who had been hurled to Tartarus and gave the rule to
Cronus.[1]
5   But Cronus tied them up and again imprisoned them in Tartarus.
He then married his sister, Rhea. When Earth and Sky foretold that
Cronus would lose the rule to his own son, he devoured his offspring
as they were born. He swallowed down his first-born, Hestia, then
6 Demeter and Hera, and after them Pluto and Poseidon. Angered by
this, Rhea went to Crete when she was pregnant with Zeus and gave
birth to him in a cave on Mount Dicte. She gave him to the Curetes
7 and to the nymphs, Adrastia and Ida, daughters of Melisseus, to nurse.
They fed him Amalthea's milk while the Curetes, guarding the baby in
the cave, beat their spears on their shields to prevent Cronus from

hearing its crying. Rhea, meanwhile wrapped a stone in swaddling clothes and gave it to Cronus to swallow down as though it were the infant which had just been born.

2 When Zeus was full-grown, he sought help from Ocean's daughter, Metis. She gave Cronus a drug to drink which forced him to vomit up first the stone and then the children whom he had swallowed.[2] With their help Zeus made war on Cronus and the Titans.

After they had fought for ten years, Earth prophesied victory for Zeus if he got the Cyclopes who had been thrown into Tartarus as allies. He killed their guard, Campe, and set them free. They then gave thunder, lightning, and a thunderbolt to Zeus, a helmet to Pluto, and a trident to Poseidon. Armed with these weapons they defeated the Titans, imprisoned them in Tartarus and set the Hundred-Handed over them as guards. The three gods then divided the authority among themselves by lot, Zeus receiving heaven to rule, Poseidon, the sea, and Pluto, Hades.[3]

2   To the Titans, Ocean and Tethys, children called Oceanids were born: Asia, Styx, Electra, Doris, Eurynome, Amphitrite, and Metis. Asteria and Leto were born to Coeus and Phoebe; to Hyperion and Thia, Dawn, Sun, and Moon; Astraeus, Pallas and Perses were born to

3 Crius and Eurybia, daughter of Sea. Atlas, who holds the sky on his shoulders, Prometheus, Epimetheus, and Menoetius were all born to

4 Iapetus and Asia. Zeus struck Menoetius with a thunderbolt in the battle against the Titans and hurled him down to Tartarus. Chiron the Centaur, who was part man and part horse, was born to Cronus and Philyra. The winds and the stars were born to Dawn and Astraeus,

5 Hecate to Perses and Asteria, and to Pallas and Styx, Victory, Strength, Rivalry, and Violence. Zeus made the waters of the Styx, which flow from a rock in Hades, the basis for oaths, giving the river this distinction to reward the help she and her children gave him against the Titans.

6   Phorcus, Thaumas, Nereus, Eurybia and Ceto were born to Sea and Earth. Iris and the Harpies, Aello and Ocypete, were born to Thaumas and Electra. Phorcus and Ceto had as offspring the Phorcides and the

7 Gorgons, whom I shall mention when I tell the story of Perseus [2. 4. 2–3]. The Nereids were born to Nereus and Doris. | Their names are: Cymothoe, Spio, Glauconome, Nausithoe, Halie, Erato, Sao, Amphitrite, Eunice, Thetis, Eulimene, Agave, Eudore, Doto, Pherusa, Galatea, Actaea, Pontomedusa, Hippothoe, Lysianassa, Cymo, Eione, Halimede, Plexaure, Eucrante, Proto, Calypso, Panope, Cranto, Neomeris, Hipponoe, Ianira, Polynome, Autonoe, Melite, Dione, Nesaea, Dero, Evagore, Psamathe, Eumolpe, Ione, Dynamene, Ceto, and Limnoria. |

3 Zeus married Hera and by her had Hebe, Ilithyia, and Ares. He

also had intercourse with many other women, mortal and immortal. By Themis, daughter of Sky, he had the Seasons [Horae]: Peace, Order, and Justice, and the Fates: Clotho, Lachesis, and Atropus. By Dione he had Aphrodite; by Eurynome, daughter of Ocean, the Graces: Aglaia, Euphrosyne, and Thalia; by Styx, Persephone; by Mnemosyne, the Muses: first Calliope, then Clio, Melpomene, Euterpe, Erato, Terpsichore, Urania, Thalia, and Polymnia.[4]

2   Now Calliope had a son, Linus, the father of whom was said to be Apollo, although he was in fact Oeagrus. Heracles killed him.[5] She also had Orpheus, the singer and lyre player, who by his singing made stones and trees move. When his wife, Eurydice, died from the bite of a snake, he descended into Hades in order to recover her, and, in fact, persuaded Pluto to let her go. The god promised to release her if Orpheus would not turn around after he left Hades until he reached his own house. But Orpheus did not believe Pluto, turned around and saw his wife, and she (as a result) returned to Hades. Orpheus also invented the mysteries of Dionysus. He was torn apart by the Maenads and lies buried in Pieria.[6]

3   Clio fell in love with Pierus, the son of Magnes, because Aphrodite was angry when Clio reproached her for her passion for Adonis. After making love with him Clio bore him a son, Hyacinthus, who was loved by Thamyris, the son of Philammon and the nymph, Argiope. He was the first to love a male. Apollo later fell in love with Hyacinthus but accidentally killed him while throwing the discus. Thamyris, who was unusually handsome and unexcelled in singing and playing the lyre, challenged the Muses to a contest in music. They agreed that if he won he could have intercourse with them all, but if he lost, they could deprive him of whatever they wished. They won and took away his

4   sight and his ability to sing and play the lyre.[7]

Rhesus, whom Diomedes killed at Troy, was born to Euterpe and the river Strymon.[8] Some say that he was the son of Calliope. The Corybantes were the offspring of Thalia and Apollo; the Sirens, whom I shall speak of in the section on Odysseus [Epitome 7. 18–19], the offspring of Melpomene and Achelous.[9]

5   Hera gave birth to Hephaestus without intercourse. | Although Homer [*Iliad* 1. 571–72, 577–78] says that Zeus was the father. | Zeus threw him from Heaven for helping his mother when she was tied up. For Zeus suspended her from Olympus because she sent a storm upon Heracles at sea after he captured Troy. Hephaestus fell to Lemnos and crippled his legs, but Thetis saved his life.[10]

6   Zeus had intercourse with Metis, although she changed into many shapes to avoid making love with him. While she was pregnant Zeus swallowed her up, for Earth said that after she bore the daughter she

was now carrying she would produce a son who would be ruler over heaven. Fearing this, he swallowed her. Prometheus | or as some say, Hephaestus | struck Zeus' head with an axe when the time came for her to give birth and Athena leaped from it in full armor at the river Triton.[11]

4   Asteria, one of Coeus' daughters, threw herself into the sea in the form of a quail to escape intercourse with Zeus. The city, Asteria, formerly named for her, was later called Delos. Leto made love with Zeus and was afterwards driven by Hera over the earth until she came to Delos. There she gave birth to Artemis and then, with Artemis acting as midwife, to Apollo.[12]

Artemis became a huntress and remained a virgin, while Apollo learned prophecy from Pan, the son of Zeus and Hybris. He went to Delphi where Themis was the oracle at that time. When the snake, Python, who was guarding the shrine prevented him from coming near the opening (where the priestess delivered oracles), he killed it and seized the shrine.[13] Not long afterwards he also killed Tityus, the son of Zeus and Elare, the daughter of Orchomenus. After Zeus made love with Elare he hid her under the earth because he feared Hera. He brought up into the light Tityus, the child with whom she had been pregnant and who was huge in size. Tityus saw Leto on her way to Pytho, and being filled with desire, attacked her. She called to her children to help her, and they shot him down with arrows. He was also punished after death, for in Hades vultures perpetually eat his heart.[14]

2   Apollo also killed Marsyas, the son of Olympus. For he found the pipes which Athena had thrown away (because they made her face ugly when she blew on them) and challenged Apollo to a contest in music. They agreed that the winner could do as he wished to the loser. During the contest, Apollo played the lyre upside down and ordered Marsyas to do the same [with the pipes]. Because he could not, Apollo won. He then hanged Marsyas from a tall pine tree and killed him by stripping off his skin.[15]

3   Artemis killed Orion in Delos. | They say that he was born from the earth and had a huge body. Pherecydes says that he was the son of Poseidon and Euryale. | Poseidon had given him the power of walking on the sea. His first wife was Side, whom Hera threw into Hades for claiming to be more beautiful than she. He later came to Chios where he sought to marry Merope, the daughter of Oenopion. Oenopion made him drunk, then blinded him after he went to sleep and cast him on the shore. But Orion went to the forge of Hephaestus, and seizing a boy there, set him on his shoulders and ordered him to guide him to the sunrise. When he arrived there his eyes were kindled by

4   the sun's rays and he recovered his sight. He then hurried back to Oenopion, but Poseidon had prepared an underground house for him, built by Hephaestus. Dawn then fell in love with Orion and carried him off to Delos. Aphrodite had caused her to be continually in love
5   because she had slept with Ares. | Now Orion, as some say, was killed when he challenged Artemis to a contest with the discus, but others say that he was shot by Artemis after attacking Opis, one of the virgins who had come from the Hyperboreans. | [16] Poseidon married Amphitrite, the daughter of Ocean, who bore him a son, Triton, and a daughter, Rhode, whom the Sun married.[17]

5   Pluto fell in love with Persephone and carried her off secretly with the help of Zeus. Carrying a torch, Demeter looked for her over all the earth both day and night. When she learned from the inhabitants of Hermion that Pluto had abducted her, she left heaven in anger at the gods, and came to Eleusis in the form of a mortal woman. First she sat down upon a rock called (after her) Unlaughing, beside the well named Callichorus, then went to Celeus, the king at that time of the Eleusinians. When the women in the palace told her to sit beside them, an old crone named Iambe told a joke and made the goddess smile. | For this reason they say that women make jokes at the Thesmophoria. |

Metanira, the wife of Celeus, had a child whom Demeter took to nurse. Wishing to make the baby immortal, she would put it on the fire at night and strip off its flesh. Metanira observed Demophon (for that was the baby's name) growing prodigiously during the day. When she found him buried in the fire she cried out. The baby thereupon was
2   burned up and the goddess revealed herself.

Demeter made a chariot drawn by winged dragons for Triptolemus, the older of Metanira's sons, and gave him wheat which he sowed from the sky over the entire inhabited world. | Panyasis says that Triptolemus was a son of Eleusis, for he says that Demeter came to him. Pherecydes, however, says that he was a son of Ocean and Earth. |

3   When Zeus ordered Pluto to return Kore, he gave her a pomegranate seed to eat to prevent her from remaining with her mother. Unaware of its effect, she swallowed it. Because Ascalaphus, the son of Acheron and Gorgyra, told on her, Demeter placed a heavy rock on him in Hades. Persephone was compelled to spend a third of each year with Pluto and the rest with the gods.[18]

6   This is the story of Demeter.

Angry because of the Titans, Earth bore the Giants to Sky.[19] They had enormous bodies, were invincible in their power and of fearful appearance. Thick hair hung from their heads and chins, and their feet had scales like snakes. | Some say they were born in Phlegrae, but others in Pallene. | They hurled rocks and burning oak trees into the sky.[20] Porphyrion and Alcyoneus were the most powerful of them all, and the latter was even immortal whenever he fought in the land where he was born. He stole from Erythia the cattle of the Sun. There was an oracle which said that it was impossible for the gods to kill any of the Giants, although they could be killed with the aid of a mortal. When Earth learned this, she sought a drug which would protect the Giants, even from a mortal. But Zeus, forbidding the Dawn, Moon, and Sun to appear, got possession of the drug first and, through Athena, summoned Heracles as an ally. Heracles first shot Alcyoneus with an arrow, but he revived as he fell upon the ground. At Athena's sugges-

2 tion he dragged him outside Pallene and so he died.[21] Porphyrion attacked Heracles and Hera. Zeus then filled him with desire for Hera, but when he tore off her robe and tried to rape her she cried out for help. Zeus struck him with a thunderbolt and Heracles shot him with an arrow, and he was killed. Of the Giants remaining, Apollo blinded Ephialtes in his left eye, Heracles in the right; Dionysus killed Eurytus with his wand; Hecate killed Clytius with torches. Hephaestus threw red-hot iron from the forge at Mimas, and Athena hurled Sicily at Enceladus. She then skinned Pallas and covered her own body with his skin for protection in battle. Poseidon chased Polybotes across the sea to Cos and there broke off that part of the island called Nisyrum and threw it at him. Hermes, wearing Hades' helmet in the battle, killed Hippolytus, and Artemis killed Gration.[22] The Fates attacked Agrius and Thoas with bronze clubs and killed them. Zeus destroyed the other Giants with thunderbolts, and Heracles shot them all with arrows as they lay dying.

3 When the gods had defeated the Giants, Earth was angrier still. She had intercourse with Tartarus and gave birth in Cilicia to Typhon, who was half man and half wild beast. He was the largest and most powerful of all Earth's offspring, so huge up to his thighs (which were of human form), that he towered above all mountains. His head touched the stars and his hands, when outstretched, reached the one to the west, the other to the east. From his shoulders extended a hundred snake heads. From his thighs down he had huge coils of vipers which, when stretched out, reached all the way to his head and hissed loudly. His entire body was covered with wings and his hair and beard were unkempt and blew in the wind. Fire flashed from his eyes. Such was Typhon as he hurled fiery rocks at heaven itself and rushed at it with hissing and shouting. From his mouth he spewed out a great stream of fire. When the gods saw him attacking heaven, they quickly fled to Egypt and in the course of their flight changed themselves into animals. Zeus hurled thunderbolts at Typhon while he was yet at a distance

from him. When Zeus drew nearer, he struck him with a steel sickle and chased him as far as Mount Casius in Syria. Seeing that he was wounded, he fought him with his bare hands. Typhon wound his coils around him and held him fast. Then, taking the sickle from him, he cut out tendons from his hands and feet, lifted him on his shoulders, and carried him over the sea to Cilicia where he left him in the Corycian cave. He put the tendons in the cave, too, hidden in a bearskin, and placed the she-dragon, Delphyne, as a guard over them. She was half girl and half wild animal.

Hermes and Aegipan, however, stole the tendons and secretly replaced them in Zeus' hands and feet. With his strength now restored, the god suddenly threw thunderbolts at Typhon from the sky, where he had been carried in a chariot with winged horses, and chased him to the mountain called Nysa. There the Fates tricked him, for he tasted the fruit called "ephemeral," persuaded that it would make him stronger. He was again driven to Thrace and hurled entire mountains at Zeus in a battle around Mount Haemus. When these bounced back upon him under the force of the thunderbolt, blood gushed out on the mountain. From this, they say, the mountain is called Haemus ["bloody"]. As he started to flee across the Sicilian sea, Zeus threw Mount Aetna in Sicily upon him. It is a large mountain and they say that fire erupts from the thunderbolts which were thrown into it up to the present time.[23] This is the extent of my remarks on this subject.

NOTES

(1. 1. 1–1. 6. 3)

1   Apollodorus begins his mythology with a theogony ("birth of the gods"). Although much abbreviated, it is probably derived from Hesiod's *Theogony*, a poem a little more than a thousand lines long and to be dated toward the latter part of the eighth century B.C. In addition to differences in conception—Apollodorus' theogony is short and reportorial, Hesiod's poem is a long and carefully planned work of art—there are many differences in detail. Hesiod, for example, begins (116 ff.) with Chaos (literally "Emptiness"), followed by Earth and then by Eros ("Desire"), which plays an important part in further creation. In Hesiod's *Theogony* Earth produces Sky by virgin birth (126–27), and he then conceives with her the various offspring named by Apollodorus.

A significant difference between the two theogonies is the account of the castration of Sky. Apollodorus relates the event in the shortest possible space, although he notes, as does Hesiod, that Sky's genitals were thrown into the sea and that from the drops of spurting blood the Furies were born. In Hesiod's longer dramatic narration (160–206), Earth gives the sickle she made for the purpose of castrating Sky to her son Cronus, the only one of her children she can persuade to enter her plot, and then has him lie in wait for his father. Sky comes to Earth full of desire, and while they are making love, Cronus springs out with the sickle and castrates him. From the drops of spurting blood both Furies and Giants grow. The genitals themselves float in the ocean for a time until they produce a white foam from which the goddess Aphrodite takes shape and is born.

A theogony is a classification system for identifying and ordering phenomena in the natural world. Like all classification systems it embodies a way of looking at the world. The Greek theogony is anthropomorphic: human characteristics are projected onto the nonhuman world; all nonhuman phenomena are humanized. Sky, for example, "marries" Earth and they "produce" offspring. (In neither Apollodorus' nor Hesiod's theogony, however, is the human race specifically created. Its existence is taken for granted.)

The theogony as classification system is hierarchical: Sky rules first, then Cronus rules, then Zeus rules, the first as a "given," the second by force, the third by a combination of force and intelligence. The genealogical catalog, the basic device of such a system, reinforces the hierarchial aspect of the theogony in establishing a chain of cause and effect which, because it is a parent-child chain, implies a "pecking order."

The genealogical catalog also makes possible what Norman O. Brown calls "a pattern of progressive differentiation" represented as "a process of evolutionary proliferation," as generations succeed each other. The direction of the cosmic evolution, Brown notes, is from the natural to the human: "Zeus and the Olympians are essentially anthropocentric, they are deified aspects of the life of man."

Finally, the theogony as classification system is male oriented. The direction of cosmic evolution moves, to quote Brown again, "from the primacy of the female to the primacy of the male." Brown here has reference in Hesiod's *Theogony* to the beginning of creation when Earth produces Sky by virgin birth and then mates with him. For Apollodorus, male primacy is established from the beginning: "First Sky ruled over the entire world. He married Earth, etc." (1. 1. 1).

The best short essay in English on Hesiod's *Theogony* is Norman O. Brown, trans., *Hesiod: Theogony* (Indianapolis and New York, 1953), Introduction, 7–48. The above references to and quotations from Brown are taken from 15–17. The standard scholarly work on the poem, with valuable prolegomena and commentary is M. L. West, ed., *Hesiod: Theogony* (Oxford, 1966).

The Greek theogony was probably influenced by Near Eastern creation stories (as Brown, *Hesiod*, 36 ff., and West, *Hesiod*, 19 ff., note). One such, to which both scholars compare the Greek theogony, is the Babylonian creation epic known as *Enuma Elish*, to be found in J. B. Pritchard, ed., *Ancient Near Eastern Texts Relating to the Old Testament* (Princeton, 1955), 60–72. E. O. James, *Myth and Ritual in the Ancient Near East* (London, 1958), ch. 5, "The Myth and Ritual of Creation," 144–77, discusses various Near Eastern creation stories along with those from Greece.

Ovid's account of creation at the beginning of his *Metamorphoses* (hereafter abbreviated as *Met.*), unlike the Greek accounts, comes to a climax with the creation of mankind, without which the world was incomplete. Man, made in the image of the gods, alone of living creatures is able to stand erect and to behold the heavens. See *Met.* 1. 1–88. For an ancient *antimythic* and deliberately *nonanthropomorphic* view of creation, see Lucretius' account of the origin of the world in book 5 of his *De Rerum Natura*.

2　Hesiod *Theogony* 453–84 says that Zeus was born on Mount Aegeum on Crete, not on Mount Dicte. Amalthea, whose milk the infant Zeus drank, was a goat (Callimachus *Hymn* 1. 47–48, Diodorus Siculus 5. 70. 3). At 2. 7. 5 Apollodorus says that Amalthea (there identified as the daughter of Haemonius) owned a bull's horn which gave forth an endless supply of meat or drink, as one wished—the original Cornucopia or Horn of Plenty. Frazer, *Apollodorus* 1. 257, cites the variant that from one horn of the goat Amalthea ambrosia flowed, from the other, nectar.

The Curetes, who protected Zeus by their noise-making, were semidivine Cretan spirits of youth. (Their name is derived from *kouros*, "young boy.") Apollodorus refers to them also at 2. 1. 3 and 3. 3. 1.

Pausanias, in the second century A.D., saw at Delphi the stone which Rhea wrapped in swaddling clothes and gave to Cronus in place of Zeus. Oil was poured on it daily and on festival days unspun wool was laid on it (Pausanias 10. 24. 6).

3　Zeus' power, Norman O. Brown notes (*Hesiod*, 20), is based on politics, not on personal strength. He defeats the Titans through "political deals" made with the Cyclopes (his armament industry) and the Hundred-Handed (his mercenary army). Earlier he sought the help of Metis ("Cunning Intelligence"), and politics, unlike brute force, requires the use of intelligence.

The relation between the Cyclopes, the sons of Sky and Earth who help Zeus against the Titans, and the crude shepherds whom Odysseus encounters in the famous "Nobody" episode in book 9 of Homer's *Odyssey* is not clear. Later writers seemed to think of them as one group—or at least as inhabiting roughly the same place. Thucydides (6. 2) locates the land of the Odyssean Cyclopes near Mount Aetna on the east coast of Sicily. Virgil (*Aeneid* 8. 416 ff.) places the forge of Vulcan, where the Cyclopes labor as smiths, on the small island to the north of Sicily which he names Vulcania (422; modern Vulcano). Elsewhere, however, Virgil locates the Cyclopes at Mount Aetna in Sicily (*Georgics* 4. 170–73, *Aeneid* 3. 569–71). For further reference to the Cyclopes, and especially to the Cyclops, Polyphemus, see Epitome 7. 4–9 and ch. 13 n. 3.

For the division of heaven, sea, and Hades (or the underworld) among Zeus, Poseidon, and Pluto, see also Homer *Iliad* 15. 187 ff. The method of the lot used in the division was very "political," the lot being a device as important as elections for making choices in fifth century B.C. democratic Athens.

4   The record of births beginning with the offspring of Ocean and Tethys (1. 2. 2) and continuing through the Muses, the daughters of Zeus and Mnemosyne ("Memory"), named at 1. 3. 2. is a further example of the genealogical catalog creating what Norman O. Brown (*Hesiod*, 15) calls "progressive differentiation" or "evolutionary proliferation." Apollodorus does not follow Hesiod's order (and it is pointless to align his list with Hesiod's).

The goddess Styx ("Hateful") lived in Hades apart from the other gods in a huge house with silver columns. Her river (sometimes also called the Acheron) formed the boundary of Hades, and only the properly buried dead were ferried over it by the boatman Charon, described variously by Euripides (*Alcestis* 252–57), Aristophanes (*Frogs* 138–40, 180–269), and Virgil (*Aeneid* 6. 295–330, 384–416). A god who violated an oath taken by the Styx was condemned to a year's unconsciousness and nine years' banishment from the company of the gods (Hesiod *Theogony* 775–806). For a mortal, the penalty for violating an oath taken by the Styx was torture after death (Homer *Iliad* 3. 278–79 and 19. 259–60).

The order of Zeus' consorts, according to Hesiod, was Metis, Themis, then Hera (*Theogony* 886, 901, 921). These matings and subsequent offspring continue the process of the ordering of existence. Themis ("Universal Law") bears the Seasons, personifying originally spring, summer, and winter, and so representing the regularity of the physical world, but as Peace, Order, and Justice they are now transferred to the human world and represent its (ideal) regularity.

The Fates, Clotho ("Spinner"), Lachesis ("Apportioner of Lots"), and

Atropus ("Inflexible") control the events in human lives. They were also known to the Greeks as *Moirae* ("Portions") and to the Romans as *Parcae* ("Bringers Forth"), these names reflecting their functions as giving mankind their lots at the beginning of their lives. They were represented in visual art as spinning, measuring, and cutting the thread of life.

The Graces, Aglaia ("Radiance"), Euphrosyne ("Merriment"), and Thalia ("Good Cheer") embody aspects of human happiness.

The Muses, goddesses of poetry, both produced beautiful music and inspired poets, who could not sing without their inspiration. The Muses were the daughters of Mnemosyne ("Memory"), and memory was the most essential quality needed by oral poets, as early Greek poets were. When the Greek bard, improvising from memory (with thousands of formulae in his head) invokes the Muse(s), he prays not for inspired lyricism but for an inspired memory. Hesiod begins the *Theogony* with a long and rapturous invocation to the Muses (1–115), born in Pieria but living on Mount Helicon, the source of all song, including his, who also perform as a choir on Mount Olympus.

The names of the Muses express aspects of poetry: Calliope means "beautiful voice"; Clio, "celebrate"; Melpomene, "singer-and-dancer"; Euterpe, "happy delight"; Erato, "lovely"; Terpsichore, "enjoyment of dancing"; Urania, "heavenly"; Thalia, "good cheer" (also the name of one of the Graces); and Polymnia (also Polyhymnia), "many songs."

The Sirens once challenged the Muses in singing, were defeated, and had their feathers plucked by the Muses who used them to make crowns for themselves (Pausanias 9. 34. 3–4). Apollodorus tells us (3. 5. 8) that the Sphinx which threatened Thebes learned its riddle from the Muses.

The Muses sang for mortals as well as for the gods, performing at the weddings of Cadmus and Harmonia and Peleus and Thetis (Pindar *Pyth.* 3. 88–95), and at the funeral of Achilles (Pindar *Isth.* 8. 57–58).

5   Heracles killed the celebrated poet-musician Linus with a blow from the lyre when the latter, apparently teaching him to play that instrument, struck him (for inattentiveness?): see 2. 4. 9. (At Theocritus *Idyll* 24. 105 Linus teaches Heracles to read.) According to Pausanias 9. 29. 6–7 Linus was killed by Apollo for competing with him in music. A dirge, the Linus song, was sung for him at harvest time (Homer *Iliad* 18. 561–72). It carried the refrain, *ailinon, ailinon,* "Ah me for Linus!" (Aeschylus *Agamemnon* 121). He was mourned widely: Herodotus 2.79 reports that the Linus song was sung in Egypt, Phoenicia, Cyprus, and elsewhere.

6   By the song he sings in Hades, Orpheus wins Eurydice's release from the world of the dead in the two best known ancient versions of the myth, Virgil *Fourth Georgic* 453–527 and Ovid *Met.* 10. 1–85. (For the death of Orpheus in Ovid, see *Met.* 11. 1–66). The climax of the myth, the second loss of Eurydice, each poet tells in his own way. For Virgil, some mad impulse suddenly seizes Orpheus—a forgivable impulse, if only the shades of death knew how to forgive! At the very edge of the light of day he loses control and turns to look at his beloved. At that instant their laborious effort is ruined, the agreement with death broken. As she recedes from his sight Eurydice cries, "What madness destroyed me and you, Orpheus? Farewell, I am carried back to night. Though I stretch my helpless hands to you, I am no longer yours." Virgil here tries to show, says Brooks Otis, *Virgil: A Study in Civilized Poetry* (Oxford, 1963), 201, "the tragedy of human passion. . . . Orpheus can actually conquer death by his poetic genius, by a song. Yet he cannot conquer his own impulses which destroy him in the very moment of triumph. And this is the real reason why death conquers him at last."

Ovid's treatment is that of a poet who seems more worldly wise: As they near the upper world Orpheus, fearful of losing Eurydice and greedy for the sight of her (*avidus videndi*), looks at her. She begins to fall back, but Orpheus will not give up without a fight and engages in a kind of wrestling match to hold on to Eurydice (*prendique et prendere certans*). But back to Hell she goes, uttering only "Farewell!" and uncomplaining. Although, while on their way up, Orpheus seems merely sexually eager, after he loses Eurydice he is stunned (Ovid *Met.* 10. 64 ff.). For seven days he sits on the bank of the river Styx, motionless, weeping. Finally he wanders on, and it is now that trees uproot themselves to come to hear his singing. By this juxtaposition Ovid conveys a major theme of the *Metamorphoses*, that poets are "hurt into poetry" as Auden said of Yeats. This theme is graphically expressed in Ovid's version of the myth of Tereus, Procne, and Philomela (*Met.* 6. 424–674).

For references to Orpheus as inventor of the mysteries of Dionysus, see Frazer, *Apollodorus* 1. 18. On the mystery religion of Orphism (or the Orphics), see W. K. C. Guthrie, *The Greeks and their Gods* (London, 1950), ch. 11, "The Orphics," 307–32, and G. S. Kirk and J. E. Raven, eds., *The Presocratic Philosophers* (Cambridge, Eng., 1963), 37–48.

The myth of Orpheus has fascinated many creative minds because, according to Elizabeth Sewell, *The Orphic Voice* (New Haven, 1960) "Language and mind, poetry and biology meet and bear on one another in the figure of Orpheus" (5). In addition, she says, "In the Orpheus story, myth is looking at its own self. This is the reflection of myth in its own mirror" (41).

7   As to Thamyris' love for Hyacinthus: the Scholiast on Euripides *Phoenissae* 1760 attributes the invention of homosexuality to Laius, the abductor of Chrysippus. See 3. 5. 5 and ch. 6, n. 24.

Ovid *Met.* 10. 162–219 tells of Hyacinthus' accidental death from the discus thrown by his lover, Apollo. Apollo decrees that the dying boy will be reborn as a flower, the marking on which the Greeks read as the letters *ai ai*, Greek for "Alas! Alas!" and also the vocative case for the name of Ajax. At *Met.* 13. 394 ff. Ovid derives the hyacinth (with the marking *ai ai*) from the blood of Ajax, which spilled to the ground when that hero killed himself in grief at the award of Achilles' arms to Odysseus.

According to Lucian *Dialogues of the Gods* 14, Zephyr, the West Wind, also in love with Hyacinthus, maliciously blew Apollo's discus into the boy's head.

Homer *Iliad* 2. 594–600 tells of Thamyris' challenge to the Muses and their punishment of him.

8   Homer *Iliad* 10. 474–502 tells of Rhesus, just arrived in Troy, killed in his sleep by Diomedes; and Euripides wrote a play *Rhesus* (if it is genuinely Euripides') in which the hero's death is described at 756 ff.

9   The Corybantes were priests of the Phrygian goddess Cybele (also known simply as the Mother). See E. R. Dodds, *The Greeks and the Irrational* (Berkeley and Los Angeles, 1963), 77–79; and George Thomson, *Aeschylus and Athens*, (London, 1966), 103, 351–58.

At 1. 7. 10 Apollodorus says that Sterope was the mother of the Sirens.

10   Hesiod *Theogony* 927–29 says that Hera gave birth to Hephaestus without benefit of intercourse because she was angry with Zeus.

As for Zeus suspending Hera from heaven for afflicting Heracles (with two anvils tied to her feet), see Homer *Iliad* 15. 18–28. At *Iliad* 1. 590–94 Hephaestus describes how he was thrown from heaven, fell for a day and landed at sunset on Lemnos, where Sintian men cared for him, although at *Iliad* 18. 394–99 he says that he fell into the sea and was saved by Thetis and Eurynome.

11   Hesiod *Theogony* 886–900 tells of Zeus' swallowing Metis in order to eliminate competition, thus adopting the bad practice of his father, Cronus. We may note that two of the most active goddesses in Greek mythology representing, to put it somewhat simplistically, the passion of love and intelligence, were born from males: Aphrodite

from the severed genitals of Cronus (see n. 1) and Athena from the head of Zeus. Moreover, Dionysus, also an important deity and originally carried by Semele, was born from Zeus' thigh (3. 4. 3).

Myths of male parturition, especially with reference to important deities (and running counter to empirical evidence), hint at antagonism between the sexes. For an account of this antagonism, see Philip E. Slater's book, *The Glory of Hera* (Boston, 1968), valuable, but somewhat marred by mishandling of evidence as Sarah B. Pomeroy notes in "Selected Bibliography on Women in Antiquity," *Arethusa* 6. 1 (1973), 137–38.

Pindar *Ol.* 7. 33–37 says that Hephaestus delivered Zeus of Athena over Rhodes, her birth causing a shower of golden snow to fall on the island.

12   According to the Homeric *Hymn 3, to Apollo*, 14–18, Artemis was born on Ortygia, an island near Delos. Apollo was born on Delos under a date palm, which was "one of the most famous sights in antiquity, from Homer to Pliny [first century A.D.]," according to Allen *et al.*, *The Homeric Hymns*, 202 (comment to Homeric *Hymn 3*, 17).

13   The Homeric *Hymn 3, to Apollo* gives a different version of Apollo's establishing himself at Delphi. At 214 ff. he travels over the earth, seeking a place to give oracles to men. He comes to Crisa, beneath Mount Parnassus, and builds a temple there with the help of neighboring men. At a nearby spring he kills a great she-dragon which did great harm to men (300 ff.). After he shoots her (356 ff.), he says, "Rot (*putheu*, 363, from *puthô*, "to make to rot") here," and, lying dead in the hot sun, she did just that. From her rotting the place is called Pytho (*Puthô*) and men call Apollo Pythian (*Puthios*, 373). A later etymology connected the name Pytho and the epithet Pythian to the Greek root *puth-* which forms the verb *punthanô* (past, *eputhon*), "I learn by inquiry," because men went to Delphi to learn from the oracle of Apollo answers to questions.

Ovid *Met.* 1. 438–51 says that Apollo used 1,000 arrows to kill the monster. The Pythian games, second in importance only to the Olympian, were instituted to celebrate Apollo's triumph.

For Apollodorus, the oracular shrine was already established when Apollo came, and Themis was the oracle. Aeschylus *Eumenides* 1–8 gives the order of succession of oracles at Delphi as Earth, Themis, Phoebe (Titanides, daughters of Sky and Earth), then Apollo, who received the office as a birthday present from Phoebe.

Joseph Fontenrose, *Python: A Study of Delphic Myth and its Origins* (Berkeley and Los Angeles, 1959), 13–22, discusses Apollo's combat with the dragon, distinguishing five versions of it (21).

14   The monstrous Tityus, lying stretched over many acres in Hades with vultures perpetually eating his liver, was one of the sights visitors to the underworld saw (Homer *Odyssey* 11. 576–81, Virgil *Aeneid* 6. 595–600). But he was debunked by Lucretius (along with Hell and its inhabitants generally) for whom Tityus-the-liver-gnawed was a metaphor describing those afflicted with the passion of love (Lucretius *De Rerum Natura* 3. 984–94). Prometheus, too, had his liver eaten daily by an eagle (it grew back at night), as punishment from Zeus (1. 7. 1 and Hesiod *Theogony* 521–25).

15   Ovid *Met.* 6. 383–95, in telling briefly the story of Marsyas' fatal contest with Apollo, emphasizes the punishment. As Apollo strips off his skin Marsyas cries, "Why are you tearing me from myself?" One sees him skinless, a living wound (*nec quicquam nisi vulnus erat*) covered with blood, nerves exposed, veins pulsing; one can even count the muscles in his chest: Ovid's portrait of the artist failed. His skin was displayed in historical times in the market place of Celaenae, a town in Asia Minor near the source of the Maeander River (Herodotus 7. 26).

16   Frazer, *Apollodorus* 1. 31, notes that since Side, the name of Orion's first wife, means "pomegranate" in Greek, their marriage expresses mythically the ripening of that fruit when the constellation Orion is visible in the nightly sky. Aratus *Phaenomena* 634–46 says that Orion made a sexual assault on Artemis which was unsuccessful, however, for she set a scorpion after him which attacked and killed him. Hence the constellation Orion forever flees that of the Scorpion.

17   Rhode is the personification of the island (in Greek) *Rhodos*, "Rose." Pindar *Ol.* 7. 54–73 tells the story that when Zeus and the other immortals divided by lot the world among themselves *Rhodos* still lay hidden in the depths of the sea. The Sun was absent from the division and the gods forgot to include him in the distribution. When he complained, Zeus was about to cast the lots again when lo! the island Rose appeared, blossoming on the surface of the sea. The Sun at once claimed her for his own (the other gods agreed). And so the father of bright piercing rays, driver of fire-breathing steeds, took his Rose, they embraced, and she bore him seven brilliant sons.

18   *Kore* means "Maiden" in Greek and is another name for Persephone. The myth of Demeter and her daughter, Persephone, carried off by the god of the underworld, is best represented in ancient literature in Ovid *Met.* 5. 341–571 and the Homeric *Hymn 2, to Demeter.* The latter is by far the fuller and more important telling of the myth, which formed the basis, as Frazer said, "of the most famous and solemn religious rites of ancient Greece," that is, the Eleusinian mysteries

(Theodor H. Gaster, ed., *The New Golden Bough, etc.* [New York, 1964], 426). Apollodorus' version of the myth, although different in a few details, is based on the Homeric hymn.

Demeter and Persephone were vegetation goddesses, personifications of the grain, which Europeans call corn. The harvest of grain was identified with the dying of the year in autumn, but as the year was reborn in spring, seeds newly sown sprouted new grain and the continuation of human life was assured for another year. It was this process which was ritually enacted in the Eleusinian mysteries. A recent thorough discussion of the relation among myth, Homeric hymn, and these mysteries can be found in N. J. Richardson, ed., *The Homeric Hymn to Demeter* (Oxford, 1974), Introduction, especially 12–30.

The most eloquent statement of the meaning for the ancient Greeks of the myth of Demeter and Persephone and the cult associated with it remains that of Frazer: "Above all, the thought of the seed buried in the earth in order to spring up to new and higher life readily suggested a comparison with human destiny and strengthened the hope that for man too the grave may be but the beginning of a better and happier existence in some brighter world unknown. . . . No doubt it is easy for us to discern the flimsiness of the logical foundation on which such high hopes were built. But drowning men clutch at straws, and we need not wonder that the Greeks, like ourselves, with death before them and a great love of life in their hearts, should not have stopped to weigh with too nice a hand the arguments that told for and against the prospect of human immortality. . . . Therefore we do no indignity to the myth of Demeter and Persephone—one of the few myths in which the sunshine and clarity of the Greek genius are crossed by the shadow and mystery of death—when we trace its origin to some of the most familiar, yet eternally affecting aspects of nature, to the melancholy gloom and decay of autumn and to the freshness, the brightness, and the verdure of spring" (Gaster, *The New Golden Bough*, 433–34).

One significance of the pomegranate seed (or seven seeds: Ovid *Met.* 5. 535–38) eaten by Persephone was the ancient belief that the living may visit the underworld and return provided that they eat no food there. (See Allen *et al.*, *The Homeric Hymns* 169.) Ascalaphus (in Apollodorus and Ovid *Met.* 5. 538–50) observed Persephone eating the seeds and revealed it, hence was punished. In Ovid, Persephone turns him into a screech owl.

The pomegranate was also a symbol of marriage and fertility (from the number of its seeds), perhaps an aphrodisiac, and Persephone's eating its seeds may symbolize marriage with Pluto which would, of course, compel her to spend part of her time with him. (See Allen *et al., The Homeric Hymns,* 169–70.)

Lillian Feder, *Ancient Myth in Modern Poetry* (Princeton, 1971), 13–24, discusses the Demeter-Persephone myth in modern poetry.

19   According to Hesiod *Theogony* 183–85, Earth was impregnated by drops of Sky's blood when Cronus castrated him, and in due course gave birth to the Furies and the Giants.

20   And so began the Battle of the Gods and the Giants, which was sculptured on the outside of the Temple of Apollo at Delphi (Euripides *Ion* 206–18). In Ovid's account (*Met.* 1. 151–62) Zeus quickly kills the Giants with his thunderbolts, but their shed blood impregnates Earth who brings forth the first race of men, a savage and violent breed—one can tell that they were born from blood. These Zeus destroys by a Flood (*Met.* 1. 262–312). For similar stories in other mythologies, see Frazer, *Apollodorus* 2, appendix 2, "War of Earth on Heaven," 318–26.

21   Heracles dragged Alcyoneus outside Pallene because, as Apollodorus has just told us, the Giant was immortal in his own homeland.

22   Accounts differ as to which god killed which Giant. Pindar *Pyth.* 8. 12–19, for example, says that Apollo (not Heracles) shot Porphyrion. Euripides *Ion* 212–15 says that Zeus burned up Mimas with a thunderbolt, although according to Apollonius Rhodius *Argonautica* 3. 1226–27, Ares killed him. While Euripides *Ion* 209–11 says that Athena fought Enceladus (agreeing with Apollodorus), Virgil *Aeneid* 3. 578–82 tells of Enceladus, struck by Zeus' thunderbolt, buried beneath the volcano, Mount Aetna, which was hurled upon him. The fire with which he burns erupts from Aetna and when he turns his body from side to side to ease his pain Sicily quakes and rumbles. (But see 1. 6. 3 and n. 23 below for another etiological story about Mount Aetna.)

Hades' helmet, worn by Hermes, made its wearer invisible (Homer *Iliad* 5. 844–45). Perseus wears it when he beheads Medusa and so her sisters cannot pursue him (2. 4. 2–3).

23   For Zeus' struggle with Typhon (known also as Typhoeus), see Hesiod *Theogony* 820–68. Hesiod omits the details of the fight given by Apollodorus, describing it rather as a titanic conflict between two giants, the violence of which shakes the entire world. His might tested as in no other battle, Zeus fatally strikes the monster with his thunderbolt, setting the world on fire in the process, and finally hurls him into Tartarus.

Ovid *Met.* 5. 325–31 names the animals into which the gods, fleeing to Egypt to escape Typhon, changed themselves: Zeus became a ram;

Apollo, a crow; Artemis, a cat; Dionysus, a goat; Hera, a heifer; Venus, a fish; and Mercury, a flamingo. Frazer, *Apollodorus* 1. 49, observes that the story of the gods' metamorphoses into animals in Egypt was probably invented by the Greeks to explain the Egyptian worship of animals.

Pindar *Pyth.* 1. 15–28 tells of Typhon pinioned in Tartarus under Sicily (*sic*) and causing eruptions of Mount Aetna. Next follows a vivid description of an historical eruption (479 B.C.) and (probably) an eyewitness account of brilliant volcanic activity at night from this semidormant volcano. On Typhon under Mount Aetna, see also Aeschylus *Prometheus Bound* 351–72 and Ovid *Met.* 5. 346–56.

CHAPTER TWO

Prometheus, Deucalion, and Pyrrha and Their Children,
the Children and Grandchildren of Aeolus
(1. 7. 1–1. 9. 15)

BOOK 1 7 Prometheus molded men from water and earth and gave them fire which he had hidden in a fennel stalk unknown to Zeus. When Zeus learned of it, he ordered Hephaestus to nail Prometheus to Mount Caucasus in Scythia. Prometheus was pinned there for many years. An eagle swooped down upon him daily and ate his liver, which grew back during the night. This is the penalty Prometheus paid for stealing fire, until Heracles freed him, as I shall relate in the section on Heracles [2. 5. 11].[1]

2   Prometheus had a son, Deucalion, who was king of the region around Phthia. He married Pyrrha, the daughter of Epimetheus and Pandora, who was the first woman and was made by the gods. Now when Zeus wished to destroy the race of bronze, Deucalion, following Prometheus' advice, built an ark, put in provisions, and entered it with Pyrrha. Zeus caused a heavy rain to fall and submerged the greater part of Greece, with the result that all of mankind was drowned except for a few who fled to nearby high mountains. At that time the mountains of Thessaly were separated and all the land outside the Isthmus and the Peloponnese was flooded. Deucalion was carried through the sea in the ark for nine days and nine nights and then came to rest on Parnassus. When the rain stopped he emerged from the ark and sacrificed to Zeus as the god of Escape. Zeus sent Hermes to him and granted him a wish. He asked for mankind to come into being. On Zeus' instructions he and Pyrrha picked up stones and threw them over their heads. The stones he threw became men, the ones Pyrrha threw, women. From this comes the word "people" [*laoi*], metaphorically from "stone" [*laas*].[2]

Deucalion had children by Pyrrha: first, Hellen, | though some say that Zeus was his father, | second, Amphictyon, who was king of Attica
3   after Cranaus, and third, a daughter, Protogenia, who had Aethlius by

Zeus. Dorus, Xuthus, and Aeolus were born to Hellen and the nymph, Orseis. He named the Greeks "Hellenes" after himself and divided their land among his sons.[3] Xuthus received the Peloponnese and by Creusa, daughter of Erectheus, had Achaeus and Ion, after whom the Achaeans and Ionians are named. Dorus received the land opposite the Peloponnese and called its inhabitants Dorians after himself. Aeolus was king of the region around Thessaly and named the people living in it Aeolians. He married Enarete, the daughter of Deimachus, and had by her seven sons and five daughters, | Cretheus, Sisyphus, Athamas, Salmoneus, Deion, Magnes and Perieres; and Canace, Alcyone, Pisidice, Calyce and Perimede | . Hippodamas and Orestes were born

4   to Perimede and Achelous, and Antiphus and Actor to Pisidice and Myrmidon. Ceyx, son of Lucifer, married Alcyone. They died because of their arrogance, for Ceyx said that his wife was Hera, while Alcyone said that her husband was Zeus. For this Zeus turned them into birds, making her a kingfisher [*alcyôn*] and him a tern [*ceyx*].[4]

Canace had Hopleus, Nireus, Epopeus, Aloeus, and Triops by Poseidon. Aloeus married Iphimidia, the daughter of Triops, who was in love with Poseidon. Going continually to the sea's edge she scooped water into her genitals with her hands. Poseidon made love with her and she bore him two sons, Otus and Ephialtes, who are called the Aloads. Each year these grew a foot and a half in width and six feet in height. When they were nine years old and now thirteen and a half feet wide and fifty-four feet tall, they decided to fight against the gods. Piling Ossa upon Olympus and Pelion upon Ossa, they threatened to mount up to heaven. They claimed that by filling up the sea with mountains they were going to make it into dry land and the dry land into sea. Ephialtes made advances to Hera and Otus to Artemis. Moreover, they tied up Ares. Hermes, however, freed him, and Artemis killed the Aloads in Naxos by means of a trick: She changed herself into a deer and bounded between them. Trying to hit the animal they thrust their spears into each other.[5]

5   Calyce and Aethlius had a son, Endymion, who led Aeolians from Thessaly and settled them in Elis. Some say that he was a son of Zeus. The Moon fell in love with him because he was the most handsome of all men, and Zeus granted him a wish. He chose to sleep forever, re-

6   maining deathless and unaging. To Endymion and a river nymph | or as some say, Iphianassa | , Aetolus was born. He killed Apis, son of Phoroneus, and fled into the land of the Curetes where, after killing Dorus, Laodocus, and Polypoetes, the sons of Phthia and Apollo, who had welcomed him, he named the land Aetolia after himself.[6]

7   Aetolus and Pronoe, the daughter of Phorbus, had two sons, Pleuron and Calydon, after whom the cities in Aetolia were named. Pleuron

married Xanthippe, the daughter of Dorus, and had by her a son, Agenor, and daughters, Sterope, Stratonice, and Laophonte. To Calydon and Aeolia, daughter of Amythaon, were born Epicaste and Protogenia, the latter of whom bore Oxlyus to Ares. Agenor, the son of Pleuron, married Epicaste, the daughter of Calydon, and they had a son, Porthaon, and a daughter, Demonice, who bore Evenus, Molus,

8 Pylus, and Thestius to Ares. Evenus had a daughter, Marpessa, who, although Apollo courted her, was carried off by Idas, the son of Aphareus, in a winged chariot which he got from Poseidon. Evenus pursued him in a chariot to the river Lycormas but was unable to overtake him.

9 He slaughtered his horses at the river and threw himself into it. The river is called Evenus after him.[7] Idas arrived in Messene where Apollo happened to meet him and tried to take the girl away from him. Zeus separated them as they were fighting to marry her and allowed the girl herself to choose the one whom she wished to marry. Fearing that Apollo would abandon her when she grew old, she chose Idas as her

10 husband. | Thestius and Eurythemis, the daughter of Cleoboea, had daughters named Althaea, Leda, and Hypermnestra, and sons named Iphiclus, Evippus, Plexippus, and Eurypylus. Porthaon and Euryte, the daughter of Hippodamas, had sons named Oeneus, Agrius, Alcathous, Melas, and Leucopeus, and a daughter, Sterope, who, they say, gave birth to the Sirens by Achelous. |

8 Oeneus, king of Calydon, was the first to receive the grapevine from Dionysus.[8] He married Althaea, the daughter of Thestius, and by her had Toxeus whom he killed for leaping over the ditch which formed the boundary of the town. Oeneus had other sons, Thyreus and Clymenus, and two daughters, Gorge, whom Andraemon married, and Deianira, who, they say, bore Althaea to Dionysus. This Deianira drove the chariot and was accomplished in the art of war. In order to

2 marry her, Heracles wrestled with Achelous [see 2. 7. 5]. Althaea bore another son, Meleager, to Oeneus. | Although others claim that Ares was his father. |

They say that when he was seven days old the Fates, who were present, declared that Meleager would die when the log burning in the fire place was burned up. Hearing this, Althaea snatched out the log and put it in a chest for safekeeping. Meleager grew into a noble and invulnerable man, but died in the following way. Oeneus forgot Artemis when he sacrificed to all the gods the first fruits of the annual harvest in the land. In anger she sent a huge and powerful boar which prevented the fields from being planted, and killed the cattle and people who crossed its path. Oeneus called together the best men from Greece to fight the boar and announced that he would give its skin as a prize to the man who killed it. | The following assembled to hunt the boar:

Meleager, the son of Oeneus, and Dryas, the son of Ares, from Caly-
don; Idas and Lynceus, sons of Aphareus, from Messene; from Lace-
daemon, Castor and Pollux, sons of Zeus and Leda; Theseus, son of
Aegeus, from Athens; Admetus, the son of Pheres, from Pherae; from
Arcadia, Ancaeus and Cepheus, sons of Lycurgus; Jason, the son of
Aeson, from Iolcus; Iphicles, the son of Amphitryon, from Thebes;
Pirithous, the son of Ixion, from Larissa; from Phthia, Peleus; and
from Salamis, Telamon, son of Aeacus; Eurytion, son of Actor, from
Phthia; Atalanta, daughter of Schoeneus, from Arcadia; from Argos,
Amphiaraus, son of Oicles. The sons of Thestius also joined them. |

When they had come together, Oeneus entertained them as his guests
for nine days. On the tenth Cepheus, Ancaeus, and some others complained about hunting with a woman [Atalanta]. Meleager forced them
to go on the hunt, however, because he wanted to have a child by
Atalanta, although he had a wife, Cleopatra, the daughter of Idas and
Marpessa. When they had surrounded the boar it killed Hyleus and
Ancaeus. Peleus accidentally killed Eurytion with a javelin. Atalanta
was the first to hit the boar, shooting it in the back with an arrow,
and then Amphiaraus shot it in the eye. Meleager struck it in the
flank and killed it and gave the skin to Atalanta. The sons of Thestius,
however, insulted that a woman should receive the prize when there
were men to get it, took the skin away from her. They claimed that
they deserved it because of their lineage if Meleager refused to take it.

3   Meleager killed the sons of Thestius in anger and again gave the skin
to Atalanta. Althaea, upset by the killing of her brothers, lit the log
and Meleager suddenly died.[9]

| Others say, however, that Meleager did not die in this way, but
that when the sons of Thestius claimed the skin on the ground that
Iphiclus struck the boar first, war broke out between the Curetes and
the Calydonians. Meleager joined the fighting and killed several of
Thestius' sons, whereupon Althaea cursed him. He then in anger remained at home. When the enemy had drawn near the walls and the
citizens were begging him to help them, he was with difficulty persuaded by his wife to rejoin the battle. After killing the rest of Thestius'
sons he himself died fighting. When Meleager died, Althaea and
Cleopatra hanged themselves, and the women who were weeping over
the dead man were turned into birds. |

4   After Althaea died, Oeneus married Periboea, the daughter of Hippo-
nous. | The author of the *Thebaid* says that when Olenus was captured,
Oeneus received Periboea as a prize. Hesiod, however, says that after
she was seduced by Hippostratus, the son of Amarynceus, Hipponous
sent her from Olenus in Achaia to Oeneus, since he lived far from
5   Greece, and commanded him to kill her.[10] Others say, however, that

MELEAGER'S
BOAR

1975   BASKIN

Hipponous learned that his daughter had been seduced by Oeneus and because she was pregnant sent her away to him. | She bore Tydeus to Oeneus. | Although Pisander says that Gorge was his mother, for Zeus had willed that Oeneus fall in love with his own daughter [Gorge]. |

Tydeus grew up to be a brave man. | Some say that he was exiled for killing Alcathous, the brother of Oeneus. The author of the *Alcmaeonid* says, however, that he killed the sons of Melas who were plotting against Oeneus.[11] They were Pheneus, Euryalus, Hyperlaus, Antiochus, Eumedes, Sternops, Xanthippus, and Sthenelaus. Pherecydes says that it was his own brother, Olenias, whom Tydeus killed. When Agrius brought charges against him, he fled into Argos to Adrastus, and having married his daughter, Deipyle, had Diomedes by her [see 3. 6. 1]. | He accompanied Adrastus on the expedition against Thebes, was

6 wounded by Melanippus and died [see 3. 6. 3–8]. The sons of Agrius | Thersites, Onchestus, Prothous, Celeutor, Lycopeus, and Melanippus | took the kingdom from Oeneus and gave it to their father. In addition to this, they shut up Oeneus alive and tortured him. Later, Diomedes [the son of Tydeus] came secretly from Argos with Alcmaeon and killed all the sons of Agrius except Onchestus and Thersites, who ran away into the Peloponnese before he came. Since Oeneus was old, he gave the kingdom to Andraemon who had married Oeneus' daughter, and brought Oeneus into the Peloponnese. The sons of Agrius who had escaped lay in wait for the old man at the hearth of Telephus in Arcadia and killed him. Diomedes took the body to Argos and buried it where there is now a city, Oenoe, named after him. He then married Aegialia, the daughter of Adrastus, | or as some say, of Aegialeus | and made an expedition against Thebes and Troy.[12]

9 Athamas, one of the sons of Aeolus, ruled over Boeotia and had a son, Phrixus, and a daughter, Helle, by Nephele. His second marriage was to Ino, who bore to him Learchus and Melicertes. Plotting against the children of Nephele, Ino persuaded the women to parch the wheat. They took it without the knowledge of the men and did this. The earth, sown with parched wheat, failed to produce its annual crop. Athamas then sent to Delphi to seek a remedy for the failure of the crops. Ino persuaded the men sent to Delphi to say that the oracle prophesied an end to the barrenness if Phrixus were sacrificed to Zeus. On hearing this, Athamas was forced by his subjects to bring Phrixus to the altar. Nephele, however, snatched him up along with her daughter and gave them a ram with a golden fleece which she had received from Hermes. It carried them through the air over land and sea. But as they crossed the water which lies between Sigeum and the Chersonese, Helle fell off and drowned, and the sea was called Hellespont after her. Phrixus came into Colchis which was ruled by Aeetes, the son of

the Sun and Perseis, and the brother of Circe and Pasiphae, the wife of Minos. Aeetes received him and gave him one of his daughters, Chalciope. Phrixus sacrificed the ram with the golden fleece to Zeus, the god of Escape, and gave its fleece to Aeetes, who nailed it to an oak in a grove of Ares. By Chalciope Phrixus had sons named Argus, Melas, Phrontis, and Cytisorus.[13]

2   Athamas later also lost his children by Ino because of Hera's anger. For he went insane and shot Learchus with an arrow, while Ino threw herself and Melicertes into the sea [see also 3. 4. 3]. Exiled from Boeotia, he asked the oracle where he should live, and the god told him to live wherever he was offered hospitality by wild animals. After traveling through many lands, he came upon wolves devouring the remains of some sheep. When they saw him they ran away, leaving behind the parts on which they had been feeding. Athamas called the country he founded there Athamantia after himself. He married Themisto, the daughter of Hypseus, who bore to him Leucon, Erythrius, Schoeneus, and Ptous.

3   Sisyphus, the son of Aeolus, founded Ephyra, which is now called Corinth, and married Merope, the daughter of Atlas. They had a son, Glaucus, to whom Eurymede bore Bellerophon, the killer of the fire-breathing Chimera [see 2. 3. 2]. Sisyphus is punished in Hades by being made to push a stone with his hands and head. He tries to roll it over the top of a hill, but although he pushes against it, it rolls back down again. He is punished for this reason: When Zeus secretly carried off Aegina, the daughter of Asopus, Sisyphus is said to have revealed this to Asopus, who was looking for her.[14]

4   Deion, the king of Phocis, married Diomede, the daughter of Xuthus, and she bore him a daughter, Asterodia, and sons, Aenetus, Actor, Phylacus, and Cephalus, who married Procris, the daughter of Erechtheus. Dawn later fell in love with Cephalus and carried him off.[15]

5   Perieres got control over Messene and married Gorgophone, the daughter of Perseus, who bore sons named Aphareus, Leucippus, Tyndareus, and Icarius. | Many say that Perieres was not the son of Aeolus, but of Cynortas, the son of Amyclas. Therefore I shall tell the story of the descendants of Perieres in the treatment of Atlas' family [3. 10. 3]. |

6   Magnes married a river nymph who bore to him sons named Polydectes and Dictys. These settled Seriphus.

7   Salmoneus at first lived in Thessaly, but later went to Elis and there built a city. He was arrogant and wished to make himself the equal of Zeus and was punished for this lack of reverence. For he said that he himself was Zeus, removed the god's sacrifice and ordered men to sacrifice to him. Dragging bronze cauldrons behind his chariot with dried skins tied over the tops of them he claimed he made thunder,

and hurling burning torches in the air he said that he made lightning. Zeus struck him with a thunderbolt and utterly destroyed the city he had founded, with all its inhabitants.[16]

8   Tyro, the daughter of Salmoneus and Alcidice, was reared by Cretheus, the brother of Salmoneus, and fell in love with the Enipeus River. She continually visited its flowing stream and lamented there. Poseidon in the form of Enipeus made love with her. She gave birth secretly to two sons and exposed them. As the babies were lying out in the open, some horsemen passed by and a mare grazed one of them with her hoof, making a bruise on its face. One of the horsemen took up the children and reared them, calling the one with the bruise Pelias ["Livid"] and the other Neleus. When they were grown they found their mother and killed their stepmother, Sidero, for they knew that she had mistreated their mother. They set out after her and caught her in the grove of Hera, where she had fled. Pelias slaughtered her at the

9 altars themselves and made a general practice of dishonoring Hera. Later, the brothers quarrelled with each other and Neleus went in exile to Messene, founded Pylos and married Chloris, the daughter of Amphion.[17] | She bore him a daughter, Pero, and sons named Taurus, Asterius, Pylaon, Deimachus, Eurybius, Epilaus, Phrasius, Eurymenes, Evagoras, Alastor, Nestor, and Periclymenus. | Poseidon gave to Periclymenus the ability to change his shape. When Heracles sacked Pylos, Periclymenus changed himself into a lion, into a snake, and then into a bee, but died even so at Heracles' hands with the rest of Neleus' sons. Nestor alone was saved since he was reared among the Gerenians [see also 2. 7. 3.]. He married Anaxibia, the daughter of Cratieus. | By her he had daughters named Pisidice and Polycaste, and sons named Perseus, Stratichus, Aretus, Echephron, Pisistratus, Antilochus, and Thrasymedes. |

10   Pelias settled in Thessaly and married Anaxibia, the daughter of Bias | or as some say, Phylomache, the daughter of Amphion |. By her he had a son, Acastus, and daughters named Pisidice, Pelopia, Hippothoe and Alcestis.

11   Cretheus founded Iolcus and married Tyro, the daughter of Salmoneus, who bore him sons named Aeson, Amythaon, and Pheres. Amythaon lived in Pylos and married Idcmene, the daughter of Pheres, by whom he had sons named Bias and Melampus. Melampus lived in the country. In front of his house there grew a hollow oak which was a lair for snakes. Melampus' servants killed the snakes, but he gathered wood for a fire, burned them, and reared their young. When they were grown they came to him while he slept, one at each shoulder, and cleaned his ears with their tongues. He arose, frightened, but was able to understand the voices of birds flying overhead. Learning the future

from them he foretold it to men.[18] He learned also the art of divination by means of sacrifices and, meeting Apollo at the Alpheus River, was afterwards an excellent seer.

12   Bias sought to marry Pero, the daughter of Neleus. Since many wanted to marry her, Neleus said that he would give her to the man who brought him the cattle of Phylacus. They were in Phylace guarded by a dog which neither man nor animal could approach. When Bias was unable to steal them he asked his brother to help him. Melampus promised his aid and foretold that he would be caught stealing the cattle but would get them after being imprisoned for a year. Melampus then went to Phylace and, as he had foretold, was caught in the act of stealing the cattle and imprisoned in a cell. When nearly a year had passed he heard worms talking in the wood of the ceiling. One asked how much of the beam had been eaten through and the others answered that only a very little of it was left. Melampus immediately demanded to be transferred to another cell. Shortly after this was done, the roof of the first cell collapsed. Phylacus was amazed, and when he learned that Melampus was a famous seer, he freed him and summoned him to tell how his son Iphiclus might have children. Melampus promised to tell him in return for the cattle. After he sacrificed and cut up two bulls he called the birds to himself. He learned from a vulture that once when Phylacus was castrating rams he laid the still bloody knife beside Iphiclus, and that the child became frightened and ran away. Phylacus then stuck the knife in a sacred oak and it was swallowed up and hidden by the bark. The vulture said that if he found the knife, scraped off the rust and gave it to Iphiclus in a mixture to drink for ten days, he would have a son. After he learned this Melampus found the knife, scraped off the rust and gave it to Iphiclus to drink for ten days. Iphiclus then had a son, Podarces. Melampus drove the cattle to Pylos, received the daughter of Neleus and gave her to his brother.[19] He lived in Messene for a time, but when Dionysus drove the women of Argos mad, Melampus restored them to sanity in return for a part of the kingdom and lived there with Bias [see 2. 2. 2].

13   To Bias and Pero a son, Talaus, was born. He married Lysimache, the daughter of Abas, Melampus' son, and by her had Adrastus, Parthenopaeus, Pronax, Mecisteus, Aristomachus, and Eriphyle, whom Amphiaraus married. Parthenopaeus had a son, Promachus, who went with the Epigoni on the expedition against Thebes [see 3. 7. 2], and Mecisteus had a son, Euryalus, who went to Troy. Pronax had a son, Lycurgus, and Adrastus and Amphithea, the daughter of Pronax, had daughters named Argia, Deipyle, and Aegialia, and sons named Aegialius and Cyanippus.

14   Pheres, the son of Cretheus, founded Pherae in Thessaly and had

sons named Admetus and Lycurgus. Lycurgus lived in Nemea and after he married Eurydice | or as some say, Amphithea | had by her a son, Opheltes, later called Archemorus [see 3. 6. 4]. Apollo worked as a laborer for Admetus, king of Pherae [see 3. 10. 4], who sought to marry Alcestis, the daughter of Pelias. Pelias had proclaimed that he would give his daughter to whoever yoked a lion and a boar to a chariot. Apollo yoked them and gave them to Admetus. He, in turn, brought them to Pelias and received Alcestis. While performing sacrifices at his marriage, Admetus forgot to sacrifice to Artemis. For this reason when he opened the marriage bedroom he found it full of coiled snakes. Apollo advised him to propitiate the goddess and asked the Fates, when the time came for Admetus to die, to release him from death, if someone agreed to take his place. When the day appointed for his death came, since neither his father nor his mother wished to die for him, Alcestis died in his stead. Persephone sent her back to earth again or, as some say, Heracles fought Pluto and brought her back to Admetus.[20]

NOTES

(1. 7. 1–1. 9. 15)

1   In Hesiod's versions of the myth (*Works and Days* 47–104 and *Theogony* 521–602), Prometheus is not the creator of mankind, as in Apollodorus (and Ovid *Met.* 1. 76–86), but its benefactor and the indirect cause of all men's troubles. In *Works and Days* Zeus withholds fire from the human race, but Prometheus steals it (hiding it in the hollow stalk of a fennel) and gives it to men. Zeus then punishes them by ordering the Olympian gods to create a woman, named Pandora, whom Prometheus' slow-witted brother, Epimetheus, accepts as a gift, forgetting the former's injunction never to receive anything from Zeus. Pandora opens a jar she has brought with her and from it fly out into the world all the evils which afflict the race of men.

In the *Theogony* Zeus binds Prometheus with chains to a column (perhaps one of the pillars of heaven, as M. L. West, ed., *Hesiod: Theogony* [Oxford, 1966], 313, suggests in a comment to line 522). Zeus also sends an eagle to feed daily upon Prometheus' liver, which grows back each night. Heracles eventually sets him free. Zeus in this way punishes Prometheus for tricking him into choosing as a sacrificial offering inedible ox bones, which Prometheus concealed under a covering of delectable-looking fat. The desirable lean meat and organs Prometheus had stuffed inside the unappetizing stomach of the animal. Angered by this deception, Zeus withholds fire from men, Prometheus steals it for them, and Zeus retaliates by ordering Hephaestus to create woman, that "beautiful evil" (*kalon kakon, Theogony* 585), destructive, a disaster for mankind.

Sex antagonism is nakedly expressed here, although it appears not infrequently in Greek literature (e.g., in the long poem of Semonides of Amorgos and Euripides *Hippolytus* 616–68; see also ch. 1, n. 11). This antagonism is found in other cultures of the ancient Mediterranean world, as one infers from reading Near Eastern and Hebrew mythologies. The large question is Why? Answers have been (and are still being) given from J. J. Bachofen through Hegel and Jung to Erich Neumann and Philip E. Slater.

A smaller, but related, question is this: Why, in Hesiod's versions of the Prometheus myth is man's gaining of fire linked to the advent of that evil, woman? Now fire in the Prometheus myth stands for the technical advances which are the basis for human civilization (see Plato *Protagoras* 320c–322d and George Thomson, *Aeschylus and Athens* [London, 1966], 297–98). To the collective (and presumably male) mythmaker's mind, men received fire (the basis for technology), a good, and woman, an evil, together. How are we to understand in this myth, which both has formed and reflects Western consciousness, the relation between fire and woman? Is the mythmaker saying that woman "seduced" man into (technological) civilization in somewhat the same way that the Harlot Woman in the epic of Gilgamesh seduces (and weakens) Enkidu as a way to bring him from nature to culture? This answer does not satisfy.

The only serious attempt to write a social history of women in antiquity is that of Sarah B. Pomeroy in her book, *Goddesses, Whores, Wives and Slaves: Women in Classical Antiquity* (New York, 1975). The problems of such an undertaking, as she notes, are the scarcity of evidence, the fact that, apart from some fragments of lyric poetry extant classical literature was written by men, and much of that is tainted by misogyny (x).

Her analysis of what evidence there is leads her to conclude that men far outnumbered women in classical antiquity, perhaps by as much as two to one: "Either women were undernumerated when living and undercommemorated after death to an extent that can only be described as startling, or there were actually fewer women than men, or both of these factors operated simultaneously" (227). She cites female infanticide, as well as an inferior diet for females, and child-bearing at a too young age (both leading to a shorter life expectancy for women than for men) as causes of the disproportion between the male and female population in antiquity (228).

Yet the picture is not so neat: Although to the warrior societies of Greece and Rome the primary goals of winning wars and maintaining

empires made women "peripheral" except as "bearers of future soldiers" (228), she says that "The Greeks were the first we know of to
consider and question women's role. This did not happen in other
societies at the time or indeed much later" (230).

It is not Pomeroy's aim to account for sex antagonism in antiquity.
(And as noted above, it existed in other Mediterranean cultures besides
the Greek and Roman.) The question may be unanswerable. Yet her
book, with its careful analysis of such evidence as there is, should be
read by all who wish to know what can be known about the actual
position of women in ancient Greece and Rome.

The interested reader may also consult the periodical *Arethusa* 6. 1
(Spring, 1973), entitled *Women in Antiquity*, and containing a selection
of recent essays on the subject.

Hugh Lloyd-Jones, *Females of the Species: Semonides on Women*
(London, 1975), presents text, translation and commentary of the dia-
tribe against women by the seventh century B.C. iambic poet, Semonides. In addition, Lloyd-Jones offers the text and a translation (not his
own) of the new Archilochus fragment. In the introduction, discussing
the Greek view of women, Lloyd-Jones informs us that "The basic
Greek attitude to women was, like the basic Greek attitude to most per-
manent features of human life, realistic and disillusioned" (28).

Aeschylus' *Prometheus Bound*, the only surviving play of a trilogy,
is perhaps the best known ancient version of the myth. Prometheus
here appears as the hero who suffers for saving mankind. He is chained
to a desolate crag in the Caucasus Mountains (with a stake driven
through his chest) by the minions of a vengeful Zeus whose plan to
destroy mankind Prometheus thwarted. Zeus' claim to right is his new
and hard won power gained from the Titans. His victory, however, is
due in part to Prometheus' help.

Zeus cannot destroy, he can only torture Prometheus. The hero,
moreover, possesses information about Zeus which the god does not
know—only that his ignorance of it may prove fatal. No amount of
pain can force Prometheus to divulge it. From fragments of the lost
plays of the trilogy it seems that the conflict between these opposing
gods is resolved through compromise, the point being that it is a
conflict of right against right.

According to George Thomson, *Aeschylus and Athens*, Aeschylus
presents a religious view of human progress (316) and also dramatizes
the Athenian political revolution of the sixth and fifth centuries B.C.,
after which landowners and merchants, formerly hostile and feuding
with each other, lived in democratic harmony in Athens. The outcome
of the revolution (and Aeschylus' vision of it) is marred by the fact
that there remained in Athens a class which was not free, to which

democracy had not been extended, the slave class (323). For additional discussion, see Anthony J. Podlecki, *The Political Background of Aeschylean Tragedy* (Ann Arbor, 1966), ch. 6, "Prometheus Bound," 101–22.

The fifth century Greek Sophist, Protagoras, in Plato's dialogue of that name (320c–322d) uses the myth of Prometheus as the basis for an anthropological account of the development of mankind. Because of Epimetheus' stupid, unplanned distribution of natural equipment and power to living creatures, the human race was left naked and defenceless. (Epimetheus ran out of gifts to give before he got to men.) So Prometheus gave mankind fire and the technical arts, stolen from Hephaestus and Athena. Men were still without the political skill enabling them to live successfully in organized communities (the only way they could survive against wild beasts), but Zeus supplied this deficiency, and here we are.

The Prometheus myth has fired the imaginations of artists from ancient times to modern, generating many works of literature, art, and music. For a rapid survey of these works, see Mayerson, *Classical Mythology*, 45–54.

2   If there is any certainty that surviving Greek literature (once estimated at 5 percent of the total) gives a fair indication through the myths it preserves of the importance of individual stories to the Greeks, then the ancient myth of the Flood had little meaning to them, for its earliest appearance in extant Greek works is Apollodorus' version of it. (Pindar [518–438 B.C.] *Ol.* 9. 44–53 makes the briefest allusion to it, mentioning Deucalion and Pyrrha as progenitors of a race of stone, and the Flood but indirectly.)

Lucian, a prolific nonnative writer in Greek who lived in the second century A.D., briefly tells the story of Deucalion, Pyrrha and the Flood in his *On the Syrian Goddess* (12). Its omission from early, classical, and Hellenistic Greek literature is to be remarked upon since the flood myth has such an important place in Near Eastern mythologies: Hebrew (Genesis 6:5–9:17), Babylonian (the Gilgamesh epic, the most reliable version of which is in J. B. Pritchard, ed., *Ancient Near Eastern Texts Relating to the Old Testament* [Princeton, 1955], see 93–95) and Sumerian (in Pritchard, 42–44), the Sumerian Deluge story serving as the basis for the Babylonian version in Gilgamesh (see Samuel Noah Kramer, *Sumerian Mythology*, revised edition [New York, Evanston, and London, 1961], 97).

The Greeks had long known the story: Acusilaus and Hellanicus, logographers (= proto-historians) who lived at the beginning and end of the fifth century, respectively, and who were, incidentally, sources for Apollodorus, related the myth as we are told by the Scholiasts on

Pindar *Ol.* 9. 42 and 9. 45. The Greeks *had* a flood myth but (1) it was of little importance if the above remarks are probable and (2) in their flood myth the emphasis was not on an angry deity's destruction of a sinful mankind, but, rather, typically anthropocentric, on human beings (Deucalion and Pyrrha) re-creating the human race.

Ovid, a Roman, on the other hand, conveys in his version of the myth (*Met.* 1. 125–415), the fullest in Greco-Roman literature, a meaning not unlike that of the writer of Genesis. But Ovid does not isolate the Deucalion-Pyrrha myth as a free-standing story to emphasize the sinfulness and deserved destruction of the human race. Rather, he makes it part of "one continuous, coherent narrative" which begins with the creation of the world from Chaos (*Met.* 1. 1 ff.), followed by the Fall (or Downward Slide) of man through four ages—gold, silver, bronze and iron; a council of gods, in which Jove justifies the decision to destroy mankind by telling how he was offered human flesh to eat by Lycaon, the exemplar of human evil; the flood; and, finally, the re-creation of man (see Otis, *Ovid*, 93–94).

Ovid, too, as does the Greek myth, chooses to focus upon Deucalion and Pyrrha, good and decent people (one of the poet's few happy couples), who are lonely for human company, pray to Themis (not to Zeus, as in Apollodorus), eventually puzzle out the goddess' instruction to toss their mother's bones over their shoulders (their "mother" is Earth, her "bones" are stones and—voila!) and re-people the wet and empty world.

3   According to the Parian Marble (a fragment of a stele found on the island of Paros and on which is inscribed a chronology of Greek history from "the beginnings" to 263 B.C.), the change of names from Greeks (*Graikoi*) to Hellenes occurred in 1521 B.C. (see Frazer, *Apollodorus* 1. 57).

4   Ovid *Met.* 11. 410–748 gives a version of the myth of Alcyone and Ceyx, king of Trachis, which is quite different from Apollodorus' brief notice, the theme of the Roman poet's story being the imperishable love between the wife and her husband. Alcyone, unable to endure the death of Ceyx, shipwrecked at sea (and appearing to her as a ghost in a dream), longs to die, goes to the shore to mourn, sees the body of her husband floating in the water a short way out, runs along a stone jetty to reach him and suddenly, as she leaps from the jetty, she flies— a halcyon skimming the waves, crying its haunting cry. She hovers over the corpse of Ceyx, embraces him with her wings, kisses with her bill his cold dead mouth. Does Ceyx feel her touch or is his face merely moved by the tossing of the waves and only seeming to respond? He does feel it! The gods pitied them and bring Ceyx to life again, as a bird, her mate. As halycyons, too, they love each other, never parting.

They breed, produce young, and care for them in a nest on the surface of the sea during fourteen days at the winter solstice when the wind god keeps the winds down for them, the sea is calm and the weather warm and sunny—sailors' halcyon days. (See also Lucian *Halcyon or Concerning Metamorphosis* 1–2 who describes the tender, plaintive cry of the halcyon.)

There was a popular belief among the Greeks, who observed the affection between these birds, that in old age the male halycon (called a ceryl), too feeble for flying, was carried on the wings of the stronger female. Lines from a poem by the lyric poet, Alcman (second half of the seventh century B.C.), seem to support this belief. The poet mourns that he is now too old and feeble to join the young girls when they sing and dance: "O maidens singing strongly, sweetly, / my limbs no longer bear me up. / I wish I were a ceryl, and with halcyons / could skim the surface of the sea, serene in heart, / a sea-purple, holy bird." (Alcman 26 in David A. Campbell, ed., *Greek Lyric Poetry: A Selection* [New York, 1967], 25).

5   Homer *Odyssey* 11. 305–20 tells us that Otus and Ephialtes were much the handsomest (males? Giants?) after Orion. Their assault on heaven would have succeeded had they been a little older and so a little stronger. In Homer it is Apollo, not Artemis, who kills them. W. B. Stanford, ed., *The Odyssey of Homer*, 2 vols. (London and New York, 1959), 2. 393 (comment on 11. 315–16), compares their effort to scale heaven to the Tower of Babel in Genesis 11: 1–9. Virgil *Aeneid* 6. 582–84 mentions them briefly.

According to Homer *Iliad* 5. 385–92, these ancient Katzenjammer Kids once tied up the war god Ares and kept him in a bronze cauldron for thirteen months. Ares would have died had not their stepmother, Periboea, told Hermes, who secretly freed the god, quite weakened and, in fact, nearly dead from the confinement.

6   There are only scattered references to Endymion in ancient litera-ture. Hesiod in the *Great Eoiae*, a catalog of heroines who bore children to the gods (only fragments remain), says that Endymion was carried to heaven by Zeus, but fell in love with Hera in the form of an image which Zeus made to fool him and was then cast into Hades. The story is similar to the myth of Ixion told by Pindar *Pyth.* 2. 21–48.

His eternal sleep gave rise to the proverb, *Endymionis somnum dor-mire*. In one version the Moon, in love with Endymion, lulls him to sleep so that she may kiss him while he slumbers (Cicero *Tusculan Disputations* 1. 38. 92). He must have awakened sometimes in order to beget the fifty daughters which Pausanias 5. 1. 4 attributes to the two of them.

The eternal, moonlit sleep of the forever young, passive Endymion had little appeal to the daylight, bustling Greeks and Romans. Roman children, Cicero says, just cannot keep still. As they grow up they love to play strenuous games, and the desire to lead an active life increases as they get older. "And so, not even if we should think that we would have the happiest dreams would we want Endymion's sleep given to us. If it should be, we would consider it to be like death itself" (*De finibus* 5. 20. 55–56).

The myth of Endymion, like no other ancient story, inspired the imagination of Keats in his *Endymion*, a poem of 4,050 lines in four books, "one of the longest poems on a classic myth in English" (Douglas Bush, *Mythology and the Romantic Tradition in English Poetry*, reissued with a new preface [New York, 1969], 88).

Painters such as Tintoretto, Rubens, and Van Dyck among others have been attracted to the myth. See Mayerson, *Classical Mythology*, 167–69.

7   Evenus seems to have followed the practice of Oenomaus, father of Hippodamia, who forced his daughter's suitors into chariot races with him, killing the losers (they always lost) and nailing their heads to the wall of his house. See Epitome 2. 3–8 and Frazer, *Apollodorus* 1. 62–63.

8   For Oeneus in Apollodorus, see also 1. 8. 4–6, 2. 7. 6 and 3. 7. 5. He is mentioned briefly in Homer *Iliad* 2. 641–42, 6. 216–21 and 14. 115–20 and also in the story of Meleager at 9. 529–99.

9   The story of Meleager, Althaea, and the fire brand was famous throughout Greece, as Pausanias 10. 31. 4–5 tells us. Phrynicus, one of the earliest tragedians (late sixth and early fifth centuries B.C.), dramatized it, as did Sophocles and Euripides (Frazer, *Apollodorus* 1. 64–65). Aeschylus *Choephoroe* 602–11 refers to the myth as an example of powerful female passion.

The earliest account of the myth is Homer *Iliad* 9. 529–99, which includes the Calydonian boar hunt but omits Atalanta and also the burning brand, although it perhaps hints at the latter in referring to the curses Althaea calls down on her son for the death of her brother (9. 566–72). These curses infuriate Meleager and he withdraws from the defense of the city when the Curetes attack it (cf. 1. 8. 3). The tale is part of the lengthy, rambling plea made by Phoenix, Achilles' old tutor, in his effort to persuade his former charge to put aside his wrath and rejoin the hard pressed Greeks. Phoenix cites Meleager as a cautionary example of great anger eased at last, but relaxed too late to allow Meleager to have the gifts promised if he returns to battle. The promise is withdrawn.

This passage shows us something about the way the Greeks used mythology, that is, as a repository of lessons about social behavior and so of especial importance in the education of the young. Phoenix's use of Meleager as a negative example, however, has an effect opposite to the one intended, as Cedric H. Whitman points out in *Homer and the Heroic Tradition* (New York, 1965), 191.

The fullest version of the myth of Meleager is Ovid *Met.* 8. 260–525. His narrative falls into two parts: Meleager and the Calydonian boar hunt (260–444) and Meleager, Althaea, and the burning brand (445–525). In the first part the heroes Meleager has assembled to help him hunt the boar take part in a scene which begins with slapstick and ends in tragedy: Nestor, to avoid the boar, pole vaults into a tree. Telamon, running forward to hurl his spear, trips over a root and falls flat on his face. Theseus grandly casts his spear—and sees it hit a tree branch. Jason launches his spear which, alas, pierces the abdomen of a companion. But these worthies resent the presence at the hunt of a woman, Atalanta (the first actually to hit the boar), and refuse to allow her to keep the prize of the skin and head which Meleager, who finally kills the beast, gives to her. The argument that arises turns into a brawl in which Meleager kills two of his mother's brothers.

In the second part (445–525) pathos contrasts with the earlier slapstick. Ovid concentrates on the agony of Althaea, grief-stricken and angry at the death of her brothers, but unable to bring herself to kill her son in revenge by lighting the brand. Four times she tries to put it on the fire; four times she stays her hand, the mother and the sister in her at war: "I want to and I do not want to. What shall I do? . . . Obligation to my brothers—but I am called a mother—these break my mind" (*Nunc animum pietas maternaque nomina frangunt,* 508). Finally, face averted, with trembling hand she hurls the brand into the flames. Meleager, far away, feels his viscera begin to burn but resists the pain. He worsens, his life ebbing, and he does not know why. In his last breath he calls farewell to his family—and perhaps his mother, too (*forsitan et matrem,* 522). Burning brand and pain blaze up together; together they die down and go out. The breath of life enters the soft air; little by little the white ash covers the dying coal.

For comment on the myth, see Anderson, *Ovid*, 357–78, especially 357–58 and 371–72.

Bacchylides, a lyric poet who was a younger contemporary of Pindar, 5. 56–175 tells the story of Meleager in one of the most poignant renditions of any myth in Greek (or Latin) literature. Heracles in his trip to the underworld to bring back Cerberus encounters Meleager, still in his shining armor, thinks him to be a living person, and draws his bow against him. Meleager tells him to calm himself: He is dead. At Heracles' request he then relates his story, weeping as he does so. He speaks of Artemis' anger at Oeneus for the omission of sacrifice, of the Calydonian boar hunt, and of the battle over the boar's hide in which by chance he killed his mother's brother, for "blind from the hand go the arrows against the souls of enemies, bringing death to whom the god wills" (132–35). But Althaea, refusing to accept an accident of war, lit the brand to end the life of her son. Meleager was in the act of slaying an enemy when he suddenly felt the strength within him draining and the sweet life ebb away. "As my breath grew shorter I wept to leave my sunlit youth" (153–54). That time and that time only tears came to the eyes of Heracles, hearing the fate of the doomed young man.

Frazer saw in the myth of Meleager the idea of the "external soul," other examples of which in Greek mythology are Nisus (with the life-maintaining purple hair on his head: 3. 15. 8) and Pterelaus (with a similarly valuable golden hair on his head: 2. 4. 5 and 7). See Theodor H. Gaster, ed., *The New Golden Bough* (New York, 1964), 680–93.

10   The *Thebaid*, now lost and of unknown authorship, was a poem in the Epic Cycle, a collection of early Greek epics in imitation of Homer and arranged to make a narrative from the beginning of the world to the end of the heroic age. Apart from the *Iliad* and the *Odyssey* only a handful of fragments of these poems remain. The reference to Hesiod is unknown.

11   The *Alcmaeonid* is another lost poem of unknown authorship in the Epic Cycle relating the story of Alcmaeon, son of Amphiaraus, who killed his mother, Eriphyle, to avenge his father (see 3. 6. 2 and 3. 7. 5).

12   Diomedes, one of the greatest Greek chieftains at Troy, appears prominently in Homer's *Iliad* (see especially books 5 and 10) until he is wounded by Paris at 11. 368–400.

13   Herodotus 7. 197, in a different and somewhat elliptical version of the myth, tells us that Athamas and Ino plotted to kill Phrixus and that (as a result) an oracle ordered the Achaeans, his subjects, to forbid the oldest son of the family line ever to enter the town hall, on pain of being sacrificed should he enter and then emerge from it. The reason for the oracle's order, Herodotus says, is this: When the Achaeans were about to sacrifice their king, Athamas, his grandson, Cytisorus (i.e., the son of Phrixus) rescued Athamas and so brought down divine anger on his posterity. To avoid being sacrificed, many descendants of Athamas (or Cytisorus) fled. Frazer, *Apollodorus* 1. 75, concludes from the myth in Apollodorus, from Herodotus' notice and from what we know of Sophocles' play, *Athamas*, that in Athamas' family line the oldest son was "liable to be sacrificed either to prevent or to remedy a failure of the crops," and later "a ram was commonly accepted for the human victim." See Gaster, ed., *The New Golden Bough*, 293–300, especially

296–99. For a discussion of sacrifice of the king and its relation to the idea of the dying and reviving god, which Frazer saw as "the core of human existence and the linchpin of the universe" for primitive people, see John B. Vickery, *The Literary Impact of The Golden Bough* (Princeton, 1973), ch. 2, "The Controlling Ideas of *The Golden Bough*," 38–67 (quotation from 58).

14   Homer *Odyssey* 11. 593–600 describes Sisyphus with sweat dripping from his limbs, head bent so low that dust seems to rise from it, heaving his weight against the stone, straining to budge it. When he manages to push it to the top of the hill, the stone's weight somehow shifts and it rolls back down again. In Homer's line rhythm and sound not only reinforce, they create sense, and even a Greekless reader can hear the stone rumbling back downhill and coming to a stop in: *aûtis epeîta pedónde kulíndeto lâas anaidês* (11. 598).

Only once did Sisyphus get any respite from his endless toil. When Orpheus came to the underworld to recover Eurydice all punishment and torture ceased while Orpheus sang, and Sisyphus sat upon his stone to listen to the poet's song (Ovid *Met.* 10. 44, . . . *inque tuo sedisti, Sisyphe, saxo*).

Apollodorus ignores the mythical tradition characterizing Sisyphus as a cunning "trickster" figure. Hyginus *Fabulae* 201, however, relates how Sisyphus outwitted Autolycus, the master thief, who, supposedly undetectable in theft, was stealing Sisyphus' cattle. Sisyphus, however, branded the hooves of his own cattle and when he visited Autolycus he was able by means of the brands to pick out the animals stolen from his herd.

Hyginus also says that Sisyphus made Anticlia, Autolycus' daughter, pregnant. She married Laertes and gave birth to Odysseus, but he was really Sisyphus' child according to this variant, and inherited his cunning from him.

Sophocles *Ajax* 189 and Euripides *Iphigenia in Aulis* 524 refer to Odysseus as a son of Sisyphus, as does Aeschylus in a lost play (see W. B. Stanford, *The Ulysses Theme* [Ann Arbor, 1968], 103). Hyginus *Fabulae* 60 tells us that Sisyphus hated his brother, Salmoneus, and seduced his daughter, Tyro, to get revenge on him. The story is unfinished, but Hyginus says that Sisyphus is punished in Hades on account of his impiety.

The story of Sisyphus' outwitting Death itself (so that no one died until Ares freed Death and bound Sisyphus over to him) was the theme of lost tragedies by Aeschylus, Sophocles and Euripides (Frazer, *Apollodorus* 1. 78–79).

For Albert Camus, Sisyphus' endless punishment signifies the absurdity of life. Release from the continual struggle toward some height is

impossible. Happiness comes from awareness of one's hopeless condition and of the value of continuing the struggle. See *The Myth of Sisyphus and Other Essays,* trans. Justin O'Brien (New York, 1967).
15   For additional elements in the myth of Cephalus and Procris, see also 2. 4. 7 and 3. 15. 1.

Ovid *Met.* 7. 661–865 tells the myth of Cephalus and Procris as a tragic tale of jealousy arising from the intense love between the young married pair. For comment, see Anderson, *Ovid,* 311–32. Ovid also tells the second part of the myth in his *Ars Amatoria* 3. 667–746.
16   Aeneas saw Salmoneus in the underworld (Virgil *Aeneid* 6. 585–94), although Virgil realizes that Salmoneus' attempt to appear as Zeus by simulating the god's thunder and lightning was a sign that he was mad (*demens,* 590). Salmoneus was the brother of Sisyphus (see n. 14 above).
17   Apollodorus seems to borrow from Homer *Odyssey* 11. 235–59 in relating the myth of Tyro and her passion for the Enipeus River, but he omits the scene of love-making between Tyro and Poseidon (in the form of Enipeus): God and girl lie down together at the mouth of the swirling river where Poseidon arches a huge purple wave over them for privacy. He removes her clothes and "entrances her with his spell." When he finishes the act of love he takes her hand in his and gently says, "Enjoy, woman, our love, for in the coming year you will bear splendid sons: bed with a god and babies always follow. Rear them with care. And now go home, but quiet! do not tell anyone my name. For I, you see, am Poseidon, Shaker-of-Earth."

The myth of Pelias and Neleus has many points of similarity with the legend of Romulus and Remus. As dramatized by Sophocles it was thought to be the source of the Roman story of the founding of Rome by Romulus and Remus. (See Frazer, *Apollodorus* 1. 82–83.) The details of the enmity between Tyro, the mother of Pelias and Neleus, and Sidero, their stepmother, seem otherwise unknown.

Homer *Odyssey* 11. 281–87 relates the marriage of Chloris and Neleus, naming their children as Nestor, Chromios, Periclymenus (sons), and Pero (daughter). Nestor appears in the *Iliad* as the garrulous old chieftain, living in the past, who is also a source of wisdom and often serves as a diplomat, soothing the quarrelsome Greek chieftains.
18   Helenus, a Trojan seer in Homer's *Iliad* and Virgil's *Aeneid,* and Cassandra, the prophetess who appears in Aeschylus' *Agamemnon,* acquired the art of prophecy in the same way as Melampus. (See Frazer, *Apollodorus* 1. 86–87).
19   Homer *Odyssey* 11. 287–97 and 15. 225–38 give versions of the myth of Neleus, Pero, Bias, and Melampus which differ slightly from

Apollodorus (and from each other). The fullest account is probably that of the Scholiast on Homer *Odyssey* 11. 287 for which, with additional variants and discussion of the myth, see Frazer, *Apollodorus* 2, appendix 4, "Melampus and the Kine of Phylacus," 350–55.

20   Euripides creates one of his best known dramas, the *Alcestis*, from the myth of Admetus and Alcestis (although Artemis and Persephone play no role in his version of the myth).

The folk-tale kernel of the story seems to be this: "On the wedding day of a King, Death comes for the bridegroom; Death is willing to accept a substitute, but both the King's parents refuse the sacrifice; finally, the young bride intervenes and follows Death to save the life of her beloved." Variations include a wrestling match between Death and the husband. If he fails, his bride sacrifices herself to save his life. In Euripides, the one device is used to save the husband, the other to save his self-sacrificing wife. Furthermore, in Euripides' play the character who wrestles with Death is an outside agent (Heracles), rather than the husband himself. "Thus, while both ways of foiling death are presented, the husband engages in neither while gaining from both. Already we catch a glimpse of a whole new dimension, full of psychological and ethical possibilities, in Euripides' adaptation" (D. J. Conacher, *Euripidean Drama: Myth, Theme and Structure* [Toronto, 1967], 330–31, following Albin Lesky). The introduction of Heracles, the outside agent, may well be a Euripidean innovation (Conacher, *Euripidean Drama* 332–33).

In the folk-tale kernel of the myth one sees some structural similarity with the Orpheus-Eurydice myth. Euripides makes this similarity explicit: Early in the drama Admetus says, "If I only had Orpheus' voice and song and so could charm Persephone and her husband by my singing and take Alcestis from Hades, I would go down and not let Cerberus nor Charon stop me until I brought her back to life in the light of day" (357–62). He, of course, is no Orpheus and it is Heracles who rescues Alcestis. It is also Heracles who performs as a kind of drunken Orpheus in a blending of these two myth characters which is quite innovative: Heracles stops at Admetus' palace on the way to perform one of his labors, sees that the house is in mourning, but is persuaded by a grieving Admetus to stay, although he is not told who has died.

What might be termed an "Orpheus in the underworld" scene begins with a horrified servant's description of Heracles' bursting noisily into the gloomy household (the "house of death"), where he ignores the lamentation for Alcestis, demands wine, which he guzzles until he is tipsy, crowns his head with a myrtle wreath and, the servant says, then sings at the top of his lungs off-key (the "song of Orpheus"), nearly drowning out the keening in the house for the dead Alcestis (747–72).

Heracles himself then appears onstage, somewhat drunk, and sings his "song." (Eumolpus taught Heracles to sing and play the lyre says Theocritus *Idyll* 24. 109–10.) He berates the servant for his sad and melancholy face: "Come here," he says, "let me tell you something: Do you know what life is like? I don't think so. Listen to me: We are all obliged to die and nobody even knows if he'll be here tomorrow. Things happen, we don't know how, and can't figure out how. That's the truth, let me tell you. So enjoy yourself. Drink, count only the life you have today your own. As for the rest—God only knows. And pay attention to sweet Love. . . . Since we're human beings we might as well act human. If you're always sad and cast down, life isn't life, it's a continual disaster" (773–802).

When he learns that it is Alcestis the house is grieving for, Heracles, sobered, sorrowful, resolves to go to Hades where, if he cannot force Death to give her up, he will make entreaties to Persephone and Pluto and persuade them to let him lead her back to the upper world.

Heracles wrestles with Death and wins and so recovers Alcestis: The play is not the Orpheus-Eurydice myth in disguise. But by using elements of that myth in the way described above Euripides adds an important theme to his drama: We must somehow relieve the despair of our lives, and art, even Heracles' drunken, off-key song, is a way: "gaiety transfiguring all that dread" in Yeats' words.

It is interesting to note that Diodorus Siculus 4. 25–26.1 connects Heracles' descent into the underworld for Cerberus where, he says, Persephone welcomed him like a brother, to the descent of Orpheus. Before going to the underworld, moreover, Heracles was initiated into the Eleusinian mysteries by Musaeus, the son of Orpheus.

For additional treatment of the myth and Euripides' use of it, see A. M. Dale, ed., *Euripides: Alcestis* (Oxford, 1954), Introduction, v–xxix. Two excellent essays on the play by Anne Pippin Burnett deserve special mention: "The Virtues of Admetus," *Classical Philology* 60 (1965), 240–55 (reprinted in Erich Segal, ed., *Euripides: A Collection of Critical Essays* [Englewood Cliffs, N.J., 1968], 51–69) and *Castastrophe Survived* (Oxford, 1971), ch. 2 "*Alcestis*," 22–46.

CHAPTER THREE

Jason, the Argonauts, Medea and the Golden Fleece
(1. 9. 16–1. 9. 28)

BOOK 1 9 Jason was born to Aeson, the son of Cretheus, and Polymede, the daughter of Autolycus. He lived in Iolcus over which Pelias, succeeding Cretheus, ruled. When Pelias consulted the oracle about his kingdom, the god warned him to beware of the man with one sandal. He later understood the oracle, although he failed to at first. For when he was performing a sacrifice to Poseidon by the sea, he summoned among many others Jason, who lived in the country because of his love of farming. Hastening to the sacrifice he emerged from the river Anaurus, which he crossed on the way, with one sandal, having lost the other in the stream. When Pelias saw him he understood the oracle and, going up to him, asked him what he would do, if he had authority, on hearing an oracle which said that he would be murdered by a citizen. Jason replied, "I would command him to bring the golden fleece." Pelias did not honor Hera [see 1. 9. 8–9] and Jason said this either by chance or because of Hera's anger, in order that evil come to Pelias in the form of Medea. When Pelias heard this, he immediately ordered him to go after the fleece. It was in Colchis in a grove of Ares, hanging from an oak and guarded by a serpent which never slept.[1]

Sent on this mission Jason summoned to his side Argus, the son of Phrixus, who, on Athena's advice, built a fifty-oared ship named Argo for its builder. Athena used in its prow a timber from the oak of Dodona which could speak.[2] When the ship was finished Jason consulted the oracle, and the god told him to gather together the nobles of Greece and set sail. | He assembled the following: Tiphys, son of Hagnias, who was the ship's pilot; Orpheus, son of Oeagrus; Zetes and Calais, sons of Boreas; Castor and Pollux, sons of Zeus; Telamon and Peleus, sons of Aeacus; Heracles, son of Zeus; Theseus, son of Aegeus; Idas and Lynceus, sons of Aphareus; Amphiaraus, son of

Oicles; Caeneus, son of Coronus; Palaemon, son of Hephaestus, or
of Aetolus; Cepheus, son of Aleus; Laertes, son of Arcisius; Autolycus,
son of Hermes; Atalanta, daughter of Schoeneus; Menoetius, son of
Actor; Actor, son of Hippasus; Admetus, son of Pheres; Acastus, son
of Pelias; Eurytus, son of Hermes; Meleager, son of Oeneus; An-
caeus, son of Lycurgus; Euphemus, son of Poseidon; Poeas, son of
Thaumacus; Butes, son of Teleon; Phanus and Staphylus, sons of
Dionysus; Erginus, son of Poseidon; Periclymenus, son of Neleus;
Augeas, son of the Sun; Iphiclus, son of Thestius; Argus, son of
Phrixus; Euryalus, son of Mecisteus; Peneleos, son of Hippalmus;
Leitus, son of Alector; Iphitus, son of Naubolus; Ascalaphus and
Ialmenus, sons of Ares; Asterius, son of Cometes; and Polyphemus,
17 son of Elatus. | They sailed out to sea with Jason as captain and put
in at Lemnos. It happened that there were no men on Lemnos at that
time and the island was ruled by Hypsipyle, the daughter of Thoas.
Because the Lemnian women did not honor Aphrodite, she afflicted
them with a bad smell. For this reason their husbands took captive
women from nearby Thrace and went to bed with them. Thus spurned,
the Lemnian women murdered their fathers and husbands. Hypsipyle
alone saved her father, Thoas, by hiding him.[3] The Argonauts, then,
put in at Lemnos which was ruled at that time by a woman and had
intercourse with the women. Hypsipyle went to bed with Jason and
bore sons named Euneus and Nebrophonus.

18   Sailing from Lemnos they touched at the land of the Doliones ruled
by Cyzicus. He welcomed them hospitably. They sailed from there by
night but encountered contrary winds, lost their bearings and returned
to the Doliones. The Doliones, however, thinking that they were a Pe-
lasgian army (for they happened to be continually at war with the
Pelasgians) fought a battle with them at night with neither side aware
of the identity of the other. The Argonauts killed many of them,
including Cyzicus. When day came and they realized what they had
done, they cut their hair in mourning and gave Cyzicus an elaborate
funeral. Afterwards they sailed away and put in at Mysia.

19   There they left Heracles and Polyphemus. For Heracles' lover, Hylas,
the son of Thiodamas, was sent to get water and was seized by nymphs
because he was so handsome. Polyphemus heard him shouting and
drawing his sword, ran after him, thinking that he was being carried
off by pirates. Encountering Heracles he told him this, and while both
were looking for Hylas the ship sailed away. Polyphemus founded in
Mysia a city, Cius, and ruled over it, but Heracles returned to Argos.[4]
| Herodorus, however, says that Heracles did not sail at all at that
time, but worked as a slave in Omphale. Pherecydes says that he was
left behind at Aphetae in Thessaly when the Argo spoke, saying that

she could not endure his weight. Demaratus maintains that Heracles sailed to Colchis, for Dionysius even says that he was the leader of the Argonauts. |

20   From Mysia they came to the land of the Bebryces which was ruled by Amycus, the son of Poseidon, and a Bithynian nymph. Being a powerful man, he compelled strangers who put in at his shores to box, and thus killed them. He approached the Argo at that time and challenged the best man on board to a boxing match. Pollux offered to box with him and, striking him on the elbow, killed him. When the Bebryces attacked him, the chieftains seized their weapons and put them to flight, killing many.[5]

21   Sailing from there they came to Salmydessus in Thrace where Phineus lived, a seer who had lost his sight. | Some say that he was Agenor's son [Apollonius Rhodius *Argonautica* 2. 236–37, 240, and Hyginus *Fabulae* 19], but others claim that he was a son of Poseidon. He was said to have been blinded in various ways: by the gods for prophesying the future to men, by Boreas and the Argonauts for blinding his sons in obedience to their stepmother, by Poseidon for revealing to the sons of Phrixus the way to sail from Colchis to Greece. |[6] The gods also plagued Phineus with the Harpies. They had wings, and when a meal was set out on a table for him, they flew down from the sky and carried off most of the food. What they left smelled so horribly that it was impossible to go near it. The Argonauts wanted to learn the course for sailing, and Phineus said that he would plot it for them if they would free him from the Harpies. They filled a table with food for him, and the Harpies with a cry suddenly swooped down and carried it off. Seeing this, the sons of Boreas, Zetes and Calais, drew their swords and, since they had wings, chased the Harpies through the air. Now death was fated either for the Harpies at the hands of the sons of Boreas, or for the sons of Boreas if they failed to catch them. While being pursued one Harpy fell into the Tigres River in the Peloponnese, which is now named Harpys, after her. She is called Nicothoe by some, Aellopus by others. The other, named Ocypete | or as some say, Ocythoe; Hesiod calls her Ocypode [but Ocypete at *Theogony* 267] |, fled along the Propontis and came to the Echinadian Islands which are now called Strophades after her, for she turned [*estraphê*] when she came to them. As she flew over the shore she fell from exhaustion together with her pursuer.[7] | Apollonius in the *Argonautica* [2. 284–97] says that they were pursued as far as the Strophades and suffered no harm after they swore no longer to plague Phineus. |

22   Freed from the Harpies, Phineus showed the Argonauts the best course for sailing and warned them about the gigantic Clashing Rocks.

When driven against each other by the force of the winds, these rocks barred passage through the sea. A thick mist enveloped them, the sound of crashing filled the air around them and it was impossible even for birds to fly through them. Phineus told them to send a dove between the rocks, and if they saw it pass safely through, to sail through themselves with confidence, but if it perished, not to force their way through. After they heard this they put out to sea, and when they were near the rocks they released a dove from the prow of the ship. As it flew between the rocks, their clashing together cut off the tip of its tail. Watching closely for the rocks to separate, then rowing furiously, they passed through (with Hera's help), although the tip of the ornamented poop was sheared off. From that time the Clashing Rocks have stood still, for they were fated to stop completely after a ship passed through them.[8]

23   The Argonauts now arrived at the land of the Mariandynians and were kindly welcomed by King Lycus. There the seer Idmon died after being gored by a boar. Tiphys also died and Ancaeus took over as pilot of the ship. After they sailed past the Thermodon River and Mount Caucasus, they came to the river Phasis in Colchis. When the ship was brought to anchor, Jason went to Aeetes, told him of the command of Pelias, and called upon him to give him the fleece. Aeetes promised to do so if Jason yoked the bulls with bronze feet. For he had two huge wild bulls, a gift from Hephaestus, which had bronze feet and breathed fire from their mouths. Aeetes ordered him to yoke these and to sow dragon's teeth. (He had received from Athena half of the teeth which Cadmus planted in Thebes.) As Jason pondered how to yoke the bulls, Medea fell in love with him. She was a sorceress, the daughter of Aeetes and Idyia, daughter of Ocean. Fearing that the bulls would kill him, Medea promised to help him yoke them and to get the fleece for him (both without her father's knowledge) if he would swear to marry her and take her with him on the return voyage to Greece. When Jason swore to do these things, she gave him a magic ointment which she instructed him to smear upon himself, his shield, and his spear before he attempted to yoke the bulls. For she said that if he was protected by this, he could not be harmed by fire or by iron for one day. She also told him that when he planted the teeth men would spring up from the ground fully armed and attack him. When he saw them collected in a group, she continued, he was to throw stones into their midst from a distance, and while they as a result fought each other, he was to attack them. After Jason heard this and applied the ointment, he went to the grove of the temple seeking the bulls. Although they attacked him breathing fire, he yoked them. When he planted the teeth

men in armor grew out of the ground. Seeing several together Jason threw stones at them unseen and then drew near and killed them as they fought each other.

Although Jason had yoked the bulls, Aeetes did not give him the fleece. In fact, he wanted to burn the Argo and kill its crew. Medea, however, anticipated his plan and led Jason to the fleece during the night. She drugged the serpent guarding it, stole the fleece, and boarded the Argo with Jason. Her brother, Apsyrtus, went with her. With these they put out to sea during the night. When Aeetes learned what Medea had dared to do, he set off in pursuit of the ship. When she saw him near she murdered her brother and cutting him up, dropped the pieces into the sea. Aeetes stopped to collect the parts of his child and so fell behind. He then turned back and buried as much of his son as he was able to recover, naming the place of burial Tomi.[9] He sent out many Colchians to look for the Argo, threatening them with the punishment which he intended for Medea if they failed to bring her back. They separated and looked for her in various places.

As the Argonauts sailed past the Eridanus River, Zeus, angry because of the murder of Apsyrtus, sent a violent storm upon them and drove them off their course. Just as they sailed past the Apsyrtides Islands the ship spoke, saying that Zeus' anger would not end unless they traveled to Ausonia and were purified by Circe of the murder of Apsyrtus. So they sailed past the Ligurian and Celtic nations, through the Sardinian Sea and past Tyrrhenia to Aeaea where they appealed as suppliants to Circe and were purified. Orpheus sang a song as they sailed past the Sirens in order to drown them out, and so restrained the Argonauts. Butes alone swam over to them and Aphrodite carried him off and settled him in Lilybaeum. After the Sirens the ship came to Charybdis and Scylla and the Wandering Rocks [*Planctae*]. Great fire and smoke were seen rising over the latter. Thetis, however, summoned by Hera, conducted the ship safely through them with the help of the Nereids. Next they sailed past the island, Thrinacia, where the cattle of the Sun lived, and came to Corcyra, the island of the Phaeacians, which was ruled by Alcinous.

When the Colchians were unable to find the ship, some settled in the Ceraunian mountains and others traveled to Illyria and colonized the Apsyrtides Islands. Still others came to the land of the Phaeacians, found the Argo, and demanded Medea from Alcinous. He said that if she had already made love with Jason he would give her to him, but if she were still a virgin he would send her back to her father. Alcinous' wife, Arete, quickly married Medea to Jason. Thereupon the Colchians settled among the Phaeacians and the Argonauts put out to sea with Medea.

26   Sailing at night they encountered a violent storm. Apollo stood upon
the Melantian ridges and made lightning by shooting an arrow into the
sea. Then they saw a nearby island and, anchoring at it, called it
Anaphe ["Appearance"] because it appeared unexpectedly. They built
an altar to Apollo the Radiant, performed sacrifices, and feasted.
Twelve serving girls whom Arete had given to Medea teased and joked
with the chieftains. Therefore it is the custom even now for women to
make jokes at the sacrifice.

       Putting out to sea again, they were prevented by Talos from landing
at Crete. | Some say that he belonged to the race of bronze, but others
that he was given to Minos by Hephaestus. | He was a man of bronze,
| although some say that he was a bull, | and had a single vein extend-
ing from his neck down to his ankles with a bronze nail driven in the
end of it. Talos kept watch over the island by running around it three
times a day. At this time he observed the Argo sailing toward the
island and threw stones at it. He was deceived by Medea and died.[10]
| Some say that she drove him mad by means of drugs. Others say
that having promised to make him immortal, she drew out the bronze
nail and all his *ichor* flowed out. Still others say that he died after being
shot in the ankle with an arrow by Poeas. |

       Remaining there for one night they next put in at Aegina to take on
water, turning this chore into a contest. From there they sailed between
Euboea and Locris to Iolcus, having completed the entire voyage in
four months.[11]

27   Pelias had given up the return of the Argonauts as hopeless and
wanted to kill Aeson, but he asked to be allowed to kill himself. While
performing a sacrifice he drank a large quantity of the blood of the bull
and died. Jason's mother cursed Pelias and hanged herself, leaving
behind a small son, Promachus. Pelias killed him, too. Jason handed
over the fleece on his return and, although he was eager to avenge the
wrongs done to him, he bided his time. He sailed to the Isthmus with
the chieftains and dedicated his ship as an offering to Poseidon. Then
he asked Medea for a way to punish Pelias. She went to the palace
and persuaded Pelias' daughters to cut him up and boil him, promising
to make him young again by means of drugs. To gain their confidence
she cut up a ram and by boiling it made it into a lamb. Trusting her,
they cut up their father and boiled him. Acastus buried his father with
the help of the inhabitants of Iolcus and then drove out Jason and
Medea.

28   They went to Corinth and lived there happily for ten years until
Creon, the king of Corinth, betrothed his daughter, Glauce, to Jason,
who divorced Medea and married her. Medea called on the gods whom
Jason had sworn by, continually cursing him for his ingratitude. She

then sent a robe soaked in poisonous drugs to the bride. When she put it on she was hideously burned to death by a terrible fire, along with her father, who rushed to her rescue. Medea killed her sons, Mermerus and Pheres, and then fled to Athens in a chariot drawn by winged serpents which she had received from the Sun.[12] | It is also said that she left her infant children behind when she fled, placing them on the altar of Hera of the Height as suppliants. The Corinthians, however, removed them and tortured them to death. |

Medea went to Athens, married Aegeus and bore him a son, Medus. Later, after plotting against Theseus, she and her son were expelled from Athens. He conquered many barbarians and called all the land under his power Media. He died on an expedition against the Indians. Medea returned secretly to Colchis, and finding that Aeetes had been removed from power by his brother, Perses, killed Perses and restored the kingdom to her father.[13]

NOTES
(1. 9. 16–1. 9. 28)

1   Apollodorus' version of Jason's quest for the golden fleece (1. 9. 16–26) draws mainly upon the *Argonautica*, a poem in Greek hexameters written by Apollonius Rhodius in the third century B.C. Almost 6,000 lines long and divided into four books, the work is the great epic of the Hellenistic period (336–146 B.C.). More will be said about Apollonius' treatment of the myth of the voyage of Jason and the Argonauts in n. 11.

Apollodorus relies primarily on Euripides' *Medea* for his brief narration of the flight of Jason and Medea from Iolcus to Corinth and of the tragic events which happen there when Jason abandons Medea for the daughter of the king of Corinth (1. 9. 27–28). Versions of the myth appear in surviving Greek and Latin literature which spans a period of more than 500 years: Pindar's *Pyth.* 4, 462 B.C.; Euripides' *Medea*, 431 B.C.; Apollonius Rhodius' *Argonautica*, third century B.C.; Ovid's *Met.* 7. 1–403, first century B.C.; and Seneca's *Medea*, first century A.D.

For Pindar's treatment of the myth (translation of *Pyth.* 4 with introductory essay), see Carl A. P. Ruck and William H. Matheson, transs., *Pindar: Selected Odes* (Ann Arbor, 1968), 16–51. Pindar's Jason, representing "honor, all golden, that can be won if you are good enough . . ." (32), would be unrecognizable to Euripides or Apollonius (see n. 11 and 12 below).

2   After the murder of Medea's brother, Apsyrtus, the Argo (or rather the timber in its prow from the sacred oak at Dodona) does

speak, telling the Argonauts that they must be purified for Apsyrtus' murder or continue to suffer the anger of Zeus (1. 9. 24). Dodona, at Epirus in northwestern Greece, was the seat of the most ancient oracle of Zeus at which a sacred oak was thought to speak the oracular responses. See Homer *Iliad* 16. 233–35, *Odyssey* 14. 327–28, and Herodotus 2. 54–57. According to Plato *Phaedrus* 275b-c the Greeks believed that the oak at Dodona uttered the first prophecies to human beings.

3   The "bad smell" of the Lemnian women, caused by their failure to honor the goddess of love and resulting in their husbands' refusal to cohabit with them, probably signifies a vaginal odor. See Claude Lévi-Strauss, *The Raw and the Cooked*, trans. J. and D. Weightman (New York and Evanston, 1969), 270.

It is interesting to note in this connection that the Greek chieftains on their way to Troy maroon Philoctetes on the same island of Lemnos because of the stench from a wound on his foot which will not heal. (See Sir Richard C. Jebb, ed., *Sophocles: The Philoctetes* [reprinted Amsterdam, 1962], x–xi and comment to lines 1031 ff., 165; see also *Philoctetes* 876). In Sophocles' play Philoctetes has become habituated to and now prefers the complete state of nature which Lemnos represents. The play is concerned with the recovery of Philoctetes to culture: his return to the Greek expedition at Troy, where Heracles promises that his wounded foot will be healed (*Philoctetes* 1424), and hence no longer smell.

4   Theocritus *Idyll* 13 relates the myth of Heracles and Hylas as young love lost (or rather kidnapped). While Heracles frantically searches Mysia for Hylas, whom water nymphs have pulled into the depths of their pool, the Argo sails away. But Heracles makes his way to Colchis on foot, rather than returning to Argos as Apollodorus, following Apollonius Rhodius *Argonautica* 1. 1345–48, says, and is taunted by the Argonauts for jumping ship. Theocritus' poem may have been written as "criticism" of the treatment of the myth in the *Argonautica* (1. 1207–1362) by his contemporary, Apollonius. See A. S. F. Gow, ed., *Theocritus*, 2 vols. (Cambridge, Eng., 1952), 2. 231–32.

5   Theocritus *Idyll* 22. 27–134 narrates the story of the boxing match between Pollux and Amycus probably in "criticism" of Apollonius' version of the myth in *Argonautica* 2. 1–97 (which Apollodorus follows), just as *Idyll* 13 "criticizes" Apollonius' treatment of Heracles and Hylas. See Gow, *Theocritus* 2. 382–83.

6   At 3. 15. 3 Apollodorus gives as the "orthodox" version what he here presents as one of three variants: that Phineus blinded his sons after their stepmother accused them of seducing her and that the Argonauts punished him for it. See also Frazer, *Apollodorus* 2. 106–07.

7   Virgil *Aeneid* 3. 225–58 vividly describes the Trojans' encounter

with the screeching, stinking Harpies, whom he identifies with the Furies. Hesiod *Theogony* 267 calls them "fair haired" (*êukomoi*). At 3. 15. 2 Apollodorus says that Zetes and Calais died in pursuit of the Harpies, but also reports the variant, which he attributes to Acusilaus (and which was followed by Apollonius Rhodius *Argonautica* 1. 1298–1308), that they were killed by Heracles in Tenos.

8   The Clashing Rocks (*Symplêgades*), also called Blue Rocks (*Cyaneae*), are to be distinguished from the Wandering Rocks (*Planctae*). The former were located at the entrance to the Black Sea, the latter at the Straits of Messina or in the Lipari Islands.

9   According to Apollonius Rhodius *Argonautica* 4. 303–481, from whom Apollodorus here departs, Apsyrtus pursued Jason and Medea with a group of Colchians, overtook them, and bottled them up on an island in the Danube, but then was tricked, ambushed, and murdered by Jason (with Medea's help) beside a temple on the island. Apollodorus seems to follow Pherecydes (see Frazer, *Apollodorus* 1. 112–13).

10   In the incidents related in 1. 9. 26 Apollodorus again departs from Apollonius. First, he omits the episode in Libya, to which a storm drives the Argonauts and where they endure much suffering (*Argonautica* 4. 1228–1628). Second, he places the intervention of Apollo and the appearance of the island, Anaphe, before the Argonauts approach, try to land on, and are repulsed from Crete by Talos (*Argonautica* 4. 1636–1730). Third, Apollodorus seems to ignore Apollonius' account of the death of Talos (*Argonautica* 4. 1638–88)—or so abbreviates it as to make it unrecognizable. According to Apollonius, while Talos heaved rocks from Crete at the Argo Medea bewitched him from afar, causing him to graze the vein in his ankle, the one vulnerable spot in his bronze body, against a jagged rock, so that all his *ichor* gushed out and he died. (*Ichor* was what flowed in the veins of gods, that is, their blood.)

11   Apollodorus based his narration of the myth of Jason, Medea, and the quest for the golden fleece primarily upon the *Argonautica* of Apollonius Rhodius. Apollonius was a literate, even erudite, poet who was at one time director of the great library at Alexandria. He was, of course, writing for his own time, but his work (available in a Penguin translation by E. V. Rieu under the title, *The Voyage of Argo* [Baltimore, 1971]) has a direct appeal to the late twentieth century sensibility.

Gilbert Lawall, "Apollonius' *Argonautica*: Jason as Anti-Hero," *Yale Classical Studies* 19 (1966), 121–69, says that Apollonius' Jason stands as a "symbol of the unique predicament and responses of Hellenistic man" (169). The predicament is the quest itself: Jason does not want to go; in fact, the voyage terribly depresses him (162–63). He dislikes everything about it (164). He is "utterly un-heroic" (165; often described as *amêchanos*, "helpless"). Once he is lurching on his way, though, he does want to succeed, and chooses nonheroic means to do so, exploiting love and preferring circumvention to the more usual heroic confrontation (136). Opportunistic when he is not depressed (138), Jason will be pious, if success requires piety, or treacherous, if piety fails (145–47).

What the voyage teaches him is that success must be bought at any price, the key ingredients of success being charm, the power of love, intelligence, and treachery. It is Jason's charm which attracts Medea. By means of her love Jason gets access to her magical powers, enabling him to obtain the golden fleece (148–66). "The price of success is great . . . in terms of the corruption of values and character. Traditional values of heroism, honor, and integrity are jettisoned as Jason puts in motion the machinery of success" (168).

In a later discussion of the epic Charles Rowan Beye, "Jason as Love-Hero in Apollonios' *Argonautika*," *Greek, Roman, and Byzantine Studies* 10 (1969), 31–55, considers the poem itself an "anti-epic," rather than Jason as an "anti-hero" (34). The poem, a "distortion" of the epic tradition is, in fact, "perverse" (34).

Apollonius' Jason is, Beye admits, impotent in every way, but Apollonius deliberately makes him the formal hero of the work (37). Apollonius creates in Jason "a sexual hero, a lover; and this kind of hero is new in epic" (44).

In addition to being a sexual hero, though, "Jason is uniformly portrayed as passive" (48). Beye explains Jason's passivity as "irresolution" (55) on Apollonius' part in using an epic tradition which "could not, even for Apollonius, accommodate itself to the theme of a male exhibiting strong feelings of love and affection for a female" (54).

But it may be that Apollonius recognized controlled passivity as an important element in a sexual hero and that Jason's passivity in the *Argonautica* is deliberate and manipulative, not due to the poet's irresolution.

12   Apollodorus follows Euripides' *Medea* (produced in Athens in 431 B.C.) in his account of the end of Medea's stay in Corinth. Since it is one of Euripides' greatest plays and perhaps the single most important work by which the myth of Jason and Medea is known, some comment on it is in order.

Anne Burnett, "*Medea* and the Tragedy of Revenge," *Classical Philology* 68. 1 (January 1973), 1–24, considering the play a tragedy of revenge, sees Jason, a "hustling, puny man" (16), as guilty not of adultery but of breaking the oath of marriage which he and Medea swore to each other.

Two things must be understood: First, "Oaths . . . were no mere human conveniences, like a business man's contracts; they were absolutely necessary to society, . . . were divinely ordained and magically protected. Oaths stood like the primeval pillar that supports the sky, a link that could at the same time hold off a possibly angry weight" (13). Second, "The alliance of Jason and Medea was not an ordinary marriage, and this fact is central to an understanding of what it is that Medea avenges in the play. The connection between this Greek and this barbarian took its whole substance from its defining, extraordinary oaths. . . . They were united . . . as two members of a secret society might be, bound together by common crimes . . ." (13).

The inference can be drawn from Burnett's analysis of the play that Jason, the Greek, Medea, the barbarian, their connection by oath, and Medea's dependence upon that oath represent for Euripides the psychological reality of marriage between Greek man and woman ("foreign" in a male-dominated society) in fifth-century Athens.

When Jason cuts Medea off, she retaliates with "exactitude" (14): " 'For you I gave up father and home,' she seems to say to him, 'so from you I take a father-in-law and an adopted home. You dissolved my marriage and meant to take my children from me . . . ; I dissolve your marriage now, the old one and the new, and take your children both present and future forever away from you. . . . Because of you I am tainted with crime, an exile, and alien wherever I go . . . ; because of me you too will be tainted now, and no second king will offer refuge and his daughter's hand to you. You meant to give me an abandoned old age; I give one now to you' " (14).

But in the murder of their children, the "last perfection of her private revenge" (21), Medea "simultaneously destroys that female creature, her human self. . . . The murder of the boys is an act of violence against herself with which Medea the erinys [demonic Fury] punishes the woman Medea . . ." (22–23).

The play has an extraordinary preoccupation with children (and parents), from the Chorus' reference to the daughters of Pelias, who killed their father (9–10) to Jason's impossible wish, filled with anguish, that he had never had children at all (1413–14); Eilhard Schlesinger, "On Euripides' *Medea*," briefly notes what he calls "the child motif," in Erich Segal, ed., *Euripides: A Collection of Critical Essays* (Englewood Cliffs, N.J., 1968), 80. Central are the two children of Jason and Medea (referred to *passim*, but see especially 1021–80 and 1236–50, expressing Medea's excruciating pain at killing them) who carry the deadly gift to Glauce, another child (see 1144–1210). Also expressed in the play are the wish for some other way to get children than by women (Jason, 573–75), the pain of child-bearing (Medea, 250–51), the grief of child-rearing (the Chorus, 1090–1115). Aegeus, the childless king of Athens, passes through Corinth after consulting the oracle of

Apollo at Delphi about how to have children (667–69). Medea promises an end to his childlessness if he will give her refuge in Athens (708–18). Near the end of the play Medea is rescued by the chariot of Helios, her "father's father" (1321–22). Thus Medea, too, is a child—who killed her own brother (1134–35). At the end of the play (1317 ff.) Jason and Medea taunt each other and quarrel like children over who is responsible for the death of their two boys (lifeless in the chariot), over who loved them more. Euripides' tragedy of children older and younger killing and destroying each other reveals a vision of Greek society as a Child's Garden of Murder in which someone ought to grow up.

Ovid *Met.* 7. 1–401, realizing that he could not compete with Euripides, presents in Medea "the psychology of love in human beings who are victims of their own passions, not helpless targets of amoral deities." Medea undergoes a change (a metamorphosis?) from a "love-torn girl" into "an accomplished witch, delighting in her powers," and from a "benevolent" witch to a "malevolent" one. See Anderson, *Ovid*, 243–87. Quotations are from 243, 262 and 275.

Seneca's *Medea*, modelled on Euripides' play, is bloodier and more violent, akin to what we call "Gothic" in literature. For a brief discussion of it, see C. D. N. Costa, *Seneca: Medea* (Oxford, 1973), Introduction, 1–13, who also notes the influences of Senecan tragedies on later European drama. For subsequent art and literature making use of the myth of Jason and Medea, see Mayerson, *Classical Mythology*, 352–54. The more interesting works are Robinson Jeffers' loose translation of Euripides' *Medea*, his earlier poem, *Solstice*, and Jean Anouilh's *Médée*.

13   See Epitome 1. 5–6 and Plutarch *Theseus* 12 for Medea at Athens and her thwarted attempt to poison Theseus. Ovid *Met.* 7. 404–24 narrates Theseus' arrival at Athens and vividly describes the poison (aconite = wolfsbane) which Medea brews and beguiles Aegeus into offering to Theseus, unaware that he is his son. As Theseus raises the deadly mixture to his lips Aegeus recognizes the family crest on the hilt of his son's sword and strikes the cup from his hands. Medea then disappears: *effugit illa necem nebulis per carmina motis*, "She escaped death in a cloud conjured by incantation" (424).

CHAPTER FOUR

The Family of Inachus, Including Io,
Bellerophon, and Perseus
(2. 1. 1–2. 4. 8)

BOOK 2   1   Now that I have narrated the story of the line of Deucalion, I shall next speak of that of Inachus.

Ocean and Tethys had a son Inachus, after whom a river in Argos is named. To him and to Melias were born sons named Phoroneus and Aegialeus. After Aegialeus died without offspring, the entire country was called Aegialia. Phoroneus ruled over all the land later called the Peloponnese and had two children, Apis and Niobe, by the nymph Teledice.

Apis converted his power into a tyranny and was a violent despot, naming the Peloponnese Apia after himself. Thelxion and Telchis conspired against him and he died childless. He was believed to be a god and called Sarapis.[1]

Zeus and Niobe had a son Argus. (Niobe was the first mortal woman with whom Zeus had intercourse.) | According to Acusilaus they also had a son Pelasgus after whom the inhabitants of the Peloponnese were 2 called Pelasgians. Hesiod, however, says that Pelasgus was born from the earth. I shall speak of him below [3. 8. 1]. | Argus received the kingship and called the Peloponnese Argos after himself. He married Evadne, the daughter of Strymon and Neaera, and by her had Ecbasus, Piras, Epidaurus, and Criasus, who inherited the kingdom.

Ecbasus had a son Agenor, who had a son Argus, called the All-Seeing One. He had eyes in all parts of his body. Being very strong, he killed the bull which was devastating Arcadia and wore its hide. He also fought and killed Satyr, who was injuring the Arcadians by carrying away their livestock. Echidna, the daughter of Tartarus and Earth, was in the habit of kidnapping passers-by. Argus is said to have killed her after watching for her to go to sleep.[2] He avenged Apis by killing those who murdered him.

3   Argus and Ismene, the daughter of Asopus, had a son Iasus, said to

be the father of Io. | Castor, the writer of chronicles, however, and many of the tragedians claim that Io was the daughter of Inachus. Hesiod and Acusilaus say that she was a daughter of Piren. | Zeus seduced her while she held the priesthood of Hera. Found out by Hera, he changed Io into a white cow by a touch of his hand and swore that he had not made love with her. | Because of this Hesiod says that oaths of lovers do not incur the wrath of the gods. |

Hera asked Zeus for the cow and made Argus the All-Seeing One guard her. | Pherecydes says that Argus was a son of Arestor; Asclepiades, a son of Inachus; Cercops, a son of Argus and Ismene, the daughter of Asopus. Acusilaus says that he was born from the earth. | Hera tied Io to the olive tree which grew in the grove of the Mycenaeans and Zeus ordered Hermes to steal her. He was unable to do it secretly because Hierax gave him away, so he killed Argus with a stone and was thenceforth called Argiphontes [Slayer-of-Argus]. Hera sent a gadfly to sting Io and it drove her first to the Ionian Gulf which is named for her. Next, she traveled through Illyria, crossed Mount Haemus and forded what was then called the Thracian Straits but is now called Bosporus [cow-ford] after her. She entered Scythia and the Cimmerian land, wandering over a large area and swimming through much of the sea both in Europe and in Asia, until she finally came to Egypt, where she regained her original form and gave birth beside the Nile to Epaphus.[3]

Hera asked the Curetes to spirit him off, and they did. When Zeus learned of it, he killed the Curetes and Io began searching for Epaphus. She wandered through all of Syria (for there it was revealed to her that the wife of the king of Byblus was nursing her son) and after she found him she returned to Egypt and married Telegonus, who was at that time king of Egypt. She erected a statue of Demeter | whom the Egyptians call Isis; they also call Io Isis. | [4]

4   Epaphus, now king of the Egyptians, married Memphis, the daughter of the Nile, founded a city and named it Memphis after her. He had a daughter Libya after whom the country Libya is named. Libya and Poseidon had twin sons, Agenor and Belus. Agenor went to Phoenicia, became king, and there founded a great line. I shall for that reason put off telling of him [see 3. 1. 1]. Belus remained in Egypt where he became king, married Anchinoe, the daughter of the Nile, and by her had twin sons named Egyptus and Danaus. | According to Euripides he had two other sons, Cepheus and Phineus. | Belus settled Danaus in Libya and Egyptus in Arabia. The latter conquered the land of the Melampods and named it Egypt after himself. Egyptus had fifty sons and Danaus fifty daughters, each by a number of wives. They later quarrelled over the rule, and Danaus, fearing Egyptus' sons, built a ship on the advice

of Athena (he was the first to make one), put his daughters on board it, and fled. He put in at Rhodes and set up the statue of Lindian Athena. From there he went to Argos where he received the kingship from Gelanor who was then king. He placed the land under his control and called the inhabitants Danai after himself.

Now the land was without water because Poseidon had made the springs dry up in his wrath at Inachus. (He had sworn that the country belonged to Hera.) Danaus, therefore, sent his daughters to get water. One of them, Amymone, while seeking water, threw a spear at a deer and struck a sleeping satyr. He jumped up and was eager to make love with her, but when Poseidon appeared he fled and Amymone made love with him instead. Afterwards Poseidon showed her the springs at Lerna.

5   The sons of Egypt came to Argos, urged Danaus to end his hostility toward them and asked to marry his daughters. Danaus did not trust their offer of friendship and continued to resent his exile, but nevertheless agreed to the marriage proposals and distributed his daughters among them. | Hypermnestra, the oldest, was chosen for Lynceus and Gorgophone for Proteus. These were the sons born to Egyptus by his royal wife Argyphia. Of the rest, Busiris, Enceladus, Lycus, and Daiphron received by lot the daughters born to Danaus by Europe, namely, Automate, Amymone, Agave, and Scaea. Their mother was of royal blood, but Elephantis was the mother of Gorgophone and Hypermnestra.

Istrus married Hippodamia; Chalcodon, Rhodia; Agenor, Cleopatra; Chaetus, Asteria; Diocorystes, Cleodamia; Alces, Glauce; Alcmenor, Hippomedusa; Hippothous, Gorge; Euchenor, Iphimedusa; Hippolytus, Rhode. The mother of these ten was an Arabian woman while the young women were born to Hamadryad nymphs named Atlantia and Phoebe.

Agaptolemus received by lot Pirene; Cercetes, Dorius; Eurydamas, Phartis; Aegius, Mnestra; Argius, Evippe; Archelaus, Anaxibia; Menemachus, Nelo. The seven young men were sons of a Phoenician woman and the young women were daughters of an Ethiopian woman. Without drawing lots the sons of Egyptus by Tyria received as wives the daughters of Memphis because of the similarity of their names: Clitus married Clite; Sthenelus, Sthenele; and Chrysippus, Chrysippe.

Egyptus' twelve sons by the river nymph Caliadne cast lots for Danaus' daughters by the river nymph Polyxo. The sons were Eurylochus, Phantes, Peristhenes, Hermus, Dryas, Potamon, Cisseus, Lixus, Imbrus, Bromius, Polyctor, and Chthonius; and the daughters were Autonoe, Theano, Electra, Cleopatra, Eurydice, Glaucippe, Anthelia, Cleodore, Evippe, Erato, Stygne, and Bryce. Egyptus' sons by Gorgo cast lots for the daughters of Danaus by Pieria, Periphas receiving Actaea; Oeneus, Podarce; Egyptus, Dioxippe; Menalces, Adite; Lampus, Ocypete; and Idmon, Pylarge. Of Egyptus' youngest sons Idas married Hippodice; Daiphron, Adiante (the mother of the two young women was Herse); Pandion, Callidice; Arbelus, Oeme; Hyperbius, Celaeno; and Hippocorystes, Hyperippe. The mother of the men was Hephaestine and the mother of the women was Crino. |

After they had received their brides, Danaus held a banquet and gave daggers to his daughters. All except Hypermnestra killed their husbands while they slept. She spared Lynceus for he allowed her to remain a virgin. For this reason Danaus imprisoned her under guard. The rest of Danaus' daughters buried the heads of the bridegrooms in the ground in Lerna and held funerals for the bodies outside the city. Athena and Hermes purified them on Zeus' orders. Danaus later reunited Hypermnestra and Lynceus and gave his other daughters to the victors in an athletic contest.[5]

Amymone had a son Nauplius by Poseidon. He lived to a great age and sailed the sea luring men to their deaths by means of beacon signals. It happened that he died by a similar kind of death. Before he died he married Clymene, the daughter of Catreus, | according to the tragedians; or Philyra, according to the author of The Returns;[6] or Hesione, according to Cercops. | His children were Palamedes, Oeax, and Nausimedon.

2   Lynceus ruled Argos after Danaus and by Hypermnestra had a son Abas. He and Aglaia, the daughter of Mantineus, had twin sons named Acrisius and Proetus. They quarrelled with each other even in the womb, and when they were grown, fought over the kingship, inventing the shield in the course of their battle. Acrisius won and drove Proetus out of Argos.[7] Proetus went to Lycia to the court of Iobates, | or, as some say, of Amphianax, | and married his daughter who was named Antia | according to Homer [Iliad 6. 160], but Stheneboea according to the tragedians [but see 3. 9. 1]. | His father-in-law with an army of Lycians restored him to his own country and Proetus then seized Tiryns, the walls of which the Cyclopes built for him.[8]

Acrisius and Proetus divided all the Argive land between themselves, the former ruling Argos, the latter Tiryns. Acrisius had Danae by Eurydice, the daughter of Lacedaemon, and Proetus had Lysippe, Iphinoe, and Iphianassa by Stheneboea.

When Proetus' daughters were grown they went mad because they refused to accept the rites of Dionysus, | according to Hesiod, but according to Acusilaus because they mocked the wooden statue of Hera. | After going insane they wandered through all the Argive country, passed through Arcadia and the rest of the Peloponnese, and ran with abandon through the desert. Melampus promised to cure the women in return for a third of the rule. He was the son of Amythaon and Abas' daughter Idomene, a seer and the first to use drugs and cathartics in the practice of medicine. When Proetus refused treatment at such a high price, his daughters became yet more insane and in addition the rest of the women went mad along with them. Moreover, they left their houses, killed their own children, and went to the desert. Not until the situation was at its worst did Proetus agree to the price demanded. Now, however, Melampus promised to cure the madness only on condition that his brother Bias receive as much territory as he. Proetus, fearing that Melampus would exact an even higher price if treatment were delayed, agreed to these terms. Melampus then took with him the strongest of the young men and by means of shouts and a certain inspired dance chased the women from the mountains to Sicyon. During the pursuit Iphinoe, the oldest of Proetus' daughters, died. The two remaining were purified and regained their sanity. Proetus gave them to Melampus and Bias to marry and later had a son Megapenthes.[9]

3   Bellerophon, the son of Glaucus who was the son of Sisyphus, accidentally killed his brother Deliades | or as some say, Piren, or as others say, Alcimenes |, and going to Proetus, was purified. Stheneboea fell in love with him and sent him a message containing a sexual proposition. When he rejected it she told Proetus that Bellerophon had made a proposition to her. Proetus believed her and gave him a letter to deliver to Iobates with instructions to kill Bellerophon. After he read the letter Iobates ordered him to kill the Chimera, thinking that he would be destroyed by the monster, for it was more than a match for many men, let alone one. It had the forepart of a lion and the tail of a serpent, and its third head, in the middle, was that of a goat, through which it breathed fire. It devastated the land and destroyed the livestock. It is said that the Chimera was reared by Amisodarus (Homer agrees [*Iliad* 16. 328–29]) and was the offspring of Typho and Echidna (as Hesiod relates [*Theogony* 304–07, 319–20]). Bellerophon mounted Pegasus, the winged horse born by Medusa to Poseidon, flew up in the sky, and from there shot and killed the Chimera. After this ordeal Iobates ordered him to fight the Solymi. When Bellerophon did that, he next commanded him to engage the Amazons in battle. After he killed these, Iobates chose out the bravest of the Lycians and ordered them to ambush and kill Bellerophon. When he had killed all these, Iobates, in awe of his strength, showed him the letter and asked him to remain with him. He then gave him his daughter Philonoe in marriage and when he died left his kingdom to him.[10]

4   When Acrisius asked the oracle how to have male children the

god replied that his daughter Danae would bear a son who would kill him. Fearing this, Acrisius constructed an underground chamber of bronze in which he guarded his daughter. | Some say that Proetus, however, seduced her (and that from this arose the quarrel between him and Acrisius). Others say that Zeus changed himself into liquid gold and flowed through the roof into Danae's womb, in this way having intercourse with her. | Acrisius later found out about Perseus, the son she gave birth to. He refused to believe that she was seduced by Zeus, so he put her and her son into a chest and cast them into the sea. The chest was carried to Seriphus where Dictys recovered it and reared Perseus.

Polydectes, Dictys' brother and king of Seriphus, fell in love with Danae. Unable to make love with her since Perseus had now reached manhood, he called together his friends, including Perseus, under the pretext that he was soon going to marry Hippodamia, daughter of Oenomaus, and was now soliciting wedding presents. Perseus boldly offered the head of the Gorgon as his gift, so Polydectes ordered him to bring it, although he sought horses from the rest.

Led by Hermes and Athena, Perseus went to the daughters of Phorcus and Ceto, Enyo, Pephredo, and Dino, sisters of the Gorgons and old women from birth. They possessed one eye and one tooth which they shared among themselves. Perseus seized the eye and the tooth and when they asked for them back, said that he would return them if they would show him the way to the nymphs. Now these nymphs possessed winged sandals and the *kibisis*, which, they say, is a leather pouch. They also had the helmet of Hades. After the daughters of Phorcus gave Perseus directions, he gave back the tooth and eye. When he reached the nymphs they gave him the items which he had come for. He threw the leather pouch across his shoulder, fitted the sandals to his feet, and put on the helmet which made him invisible. Hermes gave him a sickle made of steel. He flew to Ocean and found the Gorgons, Stheno, Euryale, and Medusa, asleep. Medusa alone was mortal, and it was for this reason that Perseus went after her head. The Gorgons' heads were encircled by snakes with scales; they had huge teeth, like boars, bronze hands and golden wings, enabling them to fly. They turned those who looked at them to stone.

Perseus stood over them as they slept and, looking at the reflection of the Gorgon in his bronze shield while Athena guided his hand, severed Medusa's head. Thereupon a winged horse, Pegasus, and Chrysaor, the father of Geryon, leaped forth from the Gorgon. She gave birth to these by Poseidon.

Perseus put the head of Medusa into the leather pouch and was retracing his steps when the other two Gorgons, awakened, started in pursuit of him. They were unable to see him, however, because of the helmet which made him invisible.

On his return Perseus came to Ethiopia, over which Cepheus ruled. There he found the king's daughter Andromeda offered as prey to a sea monster, for Cassiepea, Cepheus' wife, claimed that her beauty was superior to that of all the Nereids. The Nereids were enraged. Poseidon was also angry, and sent a flood and a sea monster upon the land. When the oracle Ammon prophesied that the Ethiopians would be saved from these calamities if they offered Cassiepea's daughter Andromeda to the monster, Cepheus, compelled by his subjects, tied his daughter to a rock. On seeing her Perseus fell in love with her and promised to kill the monster if Cepheus would give her to him to be his wife. After they swore oaths to this effect, Perseus fought the monster, killed it, and released Andromeda.

Phineus, Cepheus' brother, plotted against Perseus because Andromeda had first been promised to him. When Perseus learned of the plot, he showed the head of Medusa to Phineus and his cohorts and immediately turned them all to stone.

Perseus returned to Seriphus where he found his mother and Dictys suppliants at the altars because they feared violence from Polydectes. He entered the palace and, averting his eyes, displayed the head of Medusa to Polydectes and his friends who were gathered there. Immediately they were all turned to stone, just as each was at the moment he saw it. Perseus then set up Dictys as king of Seriphus and gave the sandals, leather pouch, and helmet to Hermes, who returned them to the nymphs. He presented the head of Medusa to Athena and she placed it in the middle of her shield. Some say that Medusa was beheaded because of Athena, for she wished to be considered as beautiful as the goddess.

4 Perseus hurried to Argos with Danae and Andromeda to see Acrisius. When he learned that they were coming he left Argos in fear of the oracle [that Danae's son would kill him, 2. 4. 1] and went to the land of the Pelasgians. Teutamides, king of Larissa, held athletic games in honor of his father who had died and Perseus came to participate in them. Competing in the pentathlon he hurled the discus, struck Acrisius on the foot, and killed him instantly. Perseus realized that the prophecy had been fulfilled. He buried Acrisius outside the city but was ashamed to return to Argos to claim the inheritance from his grandfather, so he went instead to Proetus' son Megapenthes at Tiryns and exchanged Argos for Tiryns with him. Megapenthes then ruled

5 Argos and Perseus, Tiryns. He also fortified Midea and Mycenae.[11]

Before Perseus came to Greece, Andromeda bore him a son Perses (whom he left with Cepheus) from whom the kings of Persia are said to be descended.[12] In Mycenae she bore to him sons named Alcaeus, Sthenelus, Heleus, Mester, and Electryon, and a daughter Gorgophone, whom Perieres married.

Alcaeus and Astydamia, the daughter of Pelops, had a son Amphitryon and a daughter Anaxo. | Some say that their mother was Laonome, the daughter of Guneus; others that it was Hipponome, the daughter of Menoeceus. | Mestor and Lysidice, the daughter of Pelops, had a daughter Hippothoe whom Poseidon carried off to the Echinadian Islands. He had intercourse with her there and she gave birth to Taphius, who founded a colony at Taphos and called the people Teleboans because he had traveled far [*têlou ebê*] from his native land. Taphius had a son Pterelaus whom Poseidon made immortal by planting a golden hair on his head.[13] Pterelaus had sons named Chromius, Tyrannus, Antiochus, Chersidamas, Mestor, and Eueres.

Electryon married Alcaeus' daughter Anaxo, and by her had a daughter Alcmena and nine sons: | Stratobates, Gorgophonus, Phylonomus, Celaeneus, Amphimachus, Lysinomus, Chirimachus, Anactor, and Archelaus |. In addition to these he also had an illegitimate son Licymnius by a Phrygian woman Midea.

Sthenelus and Nicippe, the daughter of Pelops, had daughters named Alcyone and Medusa. Later they had a son Eurystheus, who became king of Mycenae in the following way: When Heracles was about to be born, Zeus announced among the gods that the next descendant of Perseus would rule Mycenae. Out of jealousy Hera persuaded the Ilithyiae [the goddesses of childbirth] to delay Alcmena's labor and contrived for Eurystheus to be born two months prematurely.[14]

6   While Electryon was ruling Mycenae, the sons of Pterelaus came with a contingent of Taphians and demanded back the kingdom of their maternal grandfather Mestor. When Electryon ignored their claim, they drove off his cattle. Electryon's sons came to his defence, and the two forces challenged and destroyed each other. Of Electryon's sons Licymnius was saved since he was still young. Of Pterelaus' sons Everes survived, since he had guarded the ships. The Taphians who remained sailed away with the cattle they had stolen and left them with Polyxenus, king of the Eleans. Amphitryon ransomed them from Polyxenus and brought them back to Mycenae.[15]

Wishing to avenge the deaths of his sons, Electryon decided to make war on the Teleboans. He entrusted the kingdom to his nephew Amphitryon, and put his daughter Alcmena in his charge, making him swear to preserve her virginity until he returned. As Electryon's cattle were being returned, a cow charged him and Amphitryon hurled the club in his hand at it. The club bounced off the cow's horns, struck Electryon in the head, and killed him. Using this as a pretext, Sthenelus banished Amphitryon from all of Argos and seized control of Mycenae and Tiryns. He sent for Atreus and Thyestes, the sons of Pelops, and put Midea in their care.

Amphitryon went to Thebes with Alcmena and Licymnius, was purified by Creon [for the killing of Electryon], and gave his sister Perimede to Licymnius. Alcmena said that she would marry Amphitryon if he would avenge the deaths of her brothers. He promised to do so and, summoning Creon to help him, prepared an expedition against the Teleboans. Creon said that he would join Amphitryon if he would rid Cadmus' land of the wild vixen which was preying upon it. Although Amphitryon tried to catch her, she was fated not to be caught. As the country continued to suffer, the Thebans left out for her each month a son of one of the citizens, for otherwise she would have carried off many.

Amphitryon then went to Athens to Cephalus, the son of Deioneus, and, by offering him a share of the spoils taken from the Teleboans, persuaded him to lend the dog which Procris received from Minos and brought from Crete to help catch the vixen. This dog was fated to catch everything which it pursued. As it chased the vixen Zeus turned them both to stone.

Amphitryon raided the islands of the Taphians accompanied by Cephalus from Thoricus in Attica, Panopeus from Phocis, Heleus the son of Perseus from Helos in the Argolid, and Creon from Thebes. As long as Pterelaus continued to live, Amphitryon was unable to capture Taphos. But when Comaetho, the daughter of Pterelaus, who was in love with Amphitryon, plucked the golden hair from her father's head, he died and Amphitryon conquered all the islands. He then killed Comaetho and sailed with the booty to Thebes, giving the islands to Heleus and Cephalus, who founded cities on them and named them for themselves.

Before Amphitryon arrived back at Thebes, Zeus came to Alcmena in the form of Amphitryon on a night which he extended to three times its normal length, went to bed with her, and told her about the war with the Teleboans. When Amphitryon returned and realized that his wife was not responding to his attempt to make love, he asked her the reason. She replied that he had slept with her when he arrived the night before. He then learned from Tiresias that Zeus had made love with her. Alcmena bore two sons: to Zeus, Heracles, who was older by one night, and to Amphitryon, Iphicles.[16]

NOTES
(2. 1. 1–2. 4. 8)

1   According to Frazer, *Apollodorus* 1. 129, Apollodorus identifies
Apis with the Egyptian bull, Apis, which was in turn identified with
Sarapis. Sarapis was another name for the Egyptian god, Osiris, thought
by some to be the god whom the Greeks called *Ploutôn* (Diodorus
Siculus 1. 25. 2).

   At Aeschylus *Suppliants* 260–70 Apis is called a physician, son of
Apollo, who came from Naupactus and as a kind of Greek St. Patrick
cleared the Peloponnese of harmful snakes and is remembered in Argive
prayers for his benefaction.

2   Hesiod *Theogony* 295–314 describes Echidna as a "glancing-eyed
nymph with lovely face" above, below a monstrous snake, "terrible,
enormous and squirming and voracious, there in earth's secret places"
(Lattimore's trans.). One may view her as an image of the Greek male's
ambivalence toward women, the negative aspect of which was "intense fear" and "terror," in the words of Philip E. Slater, *The Glory
of Hera* (Boston, 1968), 8, specifically, fear of female genitalia (20),
which a fearful male might describe as Hesiod describes the lower half
of Echidna. To Typhaon she bore Orthos, Geryon's dog; Cerberus, the
watchdog of Hades; and the hydra which Heracles killed. It will be
of interest to both psychoanalytic and structuralist critics of myth that
Echidna bore the Sphinx which plagued Thebes (Hesiod *Theogony* 326–
27) to her son, Orthos. Oedipus' killing of the Sphinx enabled him to
marry his mother, Jocasta.

3   Apollodorus' account of Io follows more or less closely that of
Aeschylus *Suppliants* 291–315, although the dramatist says that Hera
(not Zeus) changed Io into a cow out of jealousy, and that Zeus, still
enamored, turned himself into a "handsome, cow-mounting" bull, but
was foiled, first by Argus, then by the gadfly. When Io arrives in Egypt
after her wanderings (later described at *Suppliants* 540–89), Zeus, reap-
pearing, by a touch of his hand impregnates her and she gives birth to
Epaphus. See George Thomson, *Aeschylus and Athens* (London, 1966),
136–37 for the idea that Aeschylus' version of the myth is based on a
sacred marriage.

   In Aeschylus *Prometheus Bound* 561–886 Io, in the form of a heifer,
arrives in her wandering at the place in the Caucasus Mountains where
Prometheus has been impaled on a crag by minions of Zeus. Prometheus reveals knowledge of her past wandering and describes that to
come, thus making the future seem even more immediate (Thomson,
Aeschylus and Athens, 309; in this first play of a trilogy the future

has an almost metaphysical importance to a believer in progress such as Aeschylus).

Io in the *Prometheus* has been called "Woman to Prometheus' Man," whose part in the play is to "symbolize affliction as it falls particularly on womankind" (E. A. Havelock, *The Crucifixion of Intellectual Man* [Boston, 1951], 64–65). In Io, Havelock continues, Aeschylus attempts to give the lie to the Pandora myth which blamed mankind's evils on woman (see ch. 2, n. 1). Aeschylus wishes "to make amends to Woman and place blame where it belongs, upon the shoulders of the will to power."

Bacchylides relates the myth in a quick-moving, elliptical poem (19).

Ovid's treatment of the myth of Io (*Met.* 1. 583–746) combines the comic and the serious in a narrative which dramatizes favorite Ovidian themes: The tragic gap between image and inner self and the impossibility of communication between human beings—except through art, inevitably created out of pain.

Jove's seduction of the girl Io is really rape: He runs her down, creats a mist for privacy, *tenuitque fugam rapuitque pudorem* (600), "stops her flight and violates her chastity." Juno spies the mist and, suspicions aroused (for it is a bright and sunny day), investigates. Jove barely has time to change Io into a heifer before Juno arrives. At once aware of the situation, Juno admires the heifer's beauty in spite of herself and then, since confrontation is out of the question, plays the game of civility, asking Jove where he found her. Jove lies; Juno traps him by asking for the heifer as a gift. The god squirms: It is cruel to hand over his beloved to his wife, suspicious to refuse. Fear of being caught battles with love. Fear wins, for Jove thinks that to withhold such a trifle would increase Juno's suspicion (irony: she already knows). So he gives Io to Juno, who at once sets Argus the All-Seeing One to guard her.

Ovid then shifts perspective to Io's feelings in her new strange condition: penned up, chained, eating "bitter" grass, sleeping on the ground, drinking muddy water. Trying to speak, she moos. Frightened by the sound she makes, she sees her image in a pool of water and recoils from it, frightened even more. She meets her sisters and father (Inachus, for Ovid), follows them, allows them to pet her and feed her, not knowing who she is. If only she could speak, she would beg for help and say her name! Unable to communicate she traces in the dust with her hoof her name, the written word serving as *corporis indicium mutati triste* (650), a "sorrowful sign of her changed body." Here Ovid presents for the first time in the work and in its barest form a constant theme: Art forced from pain, art here being the simple letters "I" and "O" which her desperate anguish drives Io, blocked from speaking, to inscribe in the dust.

Jove sends Mercury to kill Argus. Juno sends the gadfly to sting Io and drive her wandering. Finally, in Egypt, she sinks wearily on her forelegs by the Nile, trying with her cow's body to assume a position of prayer, and utters horrible sounds of grief which, though nonhuman, communicate unendurable pain. Jove is finally moved to swear to Juno never again to dally with Io. Juno, mollified, allows Jove to turn Io back into a human being. As she changes form, Io "stands erect and fears to speak, lest she moo like a cow, and timidly tries again her language lost" (745–46).

4   See Herodotus 2. 59 and 156 for the identification of Demeter with Isis, and 2. 41 (and Diodorus Siculus 1. 24. 8) for the identification of Io and Isis.

5   The myth of the daughters of Danaus is the basis for a trilogy by Aeschylus of which one play, the *Suppliants*, survives (463 B.C.?). In the drama Danaus' fifty daughters, descendants of Io, flee from Egypt to Argos to avoid marriage with their cousins, the fifty sons of Egyptus. Pelasgus, king of Argos, at first unwilling to grant them sanctuary, finally agrees, after the people of Argos have been persuaded to give their assent. Danaus sights the sons of Egypt arriving in pursuit and runs to the city for help. A herald from Egypt's sons appears onstage with military attendants to carry off the maidens. Pelasgus, however, returns with an army and the herald, though threatening war, withdraws. Danaus reappears, urges his daughters to be grateful and to live decently in Argos and they enter the city in a procession singing happily of their deliverance.

In the second play of the trilogy the daughters of Danaus are forced to agree to marry their suitors. But they swear an oath to their father to murder their husbands on their wedding night and do in fact behead them, except for Hypermnestra, who spares her husband, Lynceus.

The action of the third play takes place on the morning after the murder of the husbands. Its subject seems to have been Hypermnestra's refusal to kill her husband. She is harshly judged for breaking her oath and is perhaps put on trial, at which she may have been defended by Aphrodite, as a surviving fragment of a speech by the goddess would suggest. Similarly, in the third play of Aeschylus' trilogy, the *Oresteia* (which survives), Apollo defends Orestes in his trial for his mother's murder. Alternately, Aphrodite's speech may have been part of the purification of the maidens and the overcoming of their aversion to marriage (see Albin Lesky, *A History of Greek Literature*, trans.

J. Willis and C. de Heer [New York, 1966], 252–53 for reconstruction of the lost plays).

There is an obvious similarity between the plots of the *Suppliants* and Sophocles' *Oedipus at Colonus* (406 B.C.?), as well as an affinity in theme between the lost third play of the trilogy, as it has been reconstructed, and Sophocles' *Antigone* (440s B.C.). These likenesses suggest a preoccupation in the Greek mind with ideas which at times come into conflict with each other. First, the rightness (or duty) of the state in receiving, sheltering, and protecting the helpless and/or rebellious individual, as Argos receives the daughters of Danaus, perhaps in "revolt against a great law that runs through the divinely ordained world, bidding man and woman come together" (Lesky, *Hist. of Greek Lit.*, 252); and as Athens receives the exile Oedipus, outcast everywhere because of crimes which outrage both the human and the "divinely ordained world." Second, the right of the individual to follow his or her conscience, or to give allegiance to a law higher than the state (as Hypermnestra and Antigone do), even when conscience or allegiance is in conflict with the claims of the state. The Greek imagination dramatizes the relation of state to individual and illuminates an unceasing struggle in the Western mind.

For their crimes the daughters of Danaus are punished in the underworld by perpetually drawing water in vessels with leaky bottoms (Hyginus *Fabulae* 168 and Horace *Odes* 3. 11. 25–32).

Thomson, *Aeschylus and Athens*, 287, notices a resemblance between the crime of the daughters of Danaus and that of the women of Lemnos (see 1. 9. 17) and suggests that "both legends sprang out of the changes in the social status of women."

6   For Nauplius, see Epitome 6. 7–11 and ch. 12, n. 3. He sought to avenge himself on the Greeks returning from Troy because of the death of his son Palamedes through the intrigue of Odysseus.

The Returns was a poem in five books possibly by Agias (or Hagias) of Troezen belonging to the Epic Cycle and describing the return of various Homeric heroes from Troy (except Odysseus, whose return is the subject of Homer's *Odyssey*). It ends with the murder of Agamemnon, his son Orestes' revenge, and the homecoming of Menelaus. A summary by Proclus is preserved. See Hugh G. Evelyn-White, ed., *Hesiod, the Homeric Hymns and Homerica* (Cambridge, Mass. and London, 1936), 524–29.

7   Frazer, *Apollodorus* 1. 145 notes that Jacob and Esau also quarrelled both in the womb and later in life (Genesis 25:22 ff.).

8   Bacchylides 10. 77–79 says that the Cyclopes built a "very fine wall" around Tiryns for Proetus. The stones, unwrought, were so large

that not even a pair of mules could budge the smallest one (Pausanias 2. 25. 8). "Cyclopean" is a term used to describe the masonry of massive stone built during the Mycenean period not only at Tiryns, but also at other citadels such as Mycenae and Athens. See additionally, Emily Vermeule, *Greece in the Bronze Age* (Chicago, 1972), 264–66.

9   At 3. 5. 1–2 Apollodorus narrates Dionysus' attempts to establish his rites in Thrace and Thebes, whose kings, Lycurgus and Pentheus, refused to accept his cult. Dionysus made Lycurgus insane and, in retaliation for Pentheus' opposition, drove the Theban women mad. (See ch. 6, nn. 18 and 19.) At Tiryns, according to Apollodorus, Proetus' daughters go mad because they, not their father the king, reject Dionysus' rites. They are healed by Melampus, an unusual resolution to madness caused by Dionysus. Although Apollodorus says that Melampus was the first to use drugs and cathartics in the practice of medicine, he here cures the daughters of Proetus by other means.

According to Bacchylides 10. 40–109, it is Hera who makes Proetus' daughters insane and drives them from their father's palace at Tiryns, for they once entered her sanctuary in girlish spirits and claimed their father was wealthier than the goddess. (Bacchylides' version has some affinity with the variant of Acusilaus, reported by Apollodorus, that the girls went mad because they mocked Hera's statue.) Hera in anger afflicts them with madness which makes them run shrieking to the mountains and through them to Argos.

The grief-stricken father tries to kill himself, but palace guards restrain him with "gentle myths" (*múthoisi . . . meilichiois*, 90) and by force of hands. After the girls run wild through the woods of Arcadia for thirteen months, Proetus finally comes to the spring called Lousos, washes himself in it, and prays to Artemis to heal his daughters from their insanity, promising her sacrifices. The goddess hears his prayer, persuades Hera to relent, and heals the girls.

The cure Bacchylides describes makes no mention of Melampus. Proetus' daughters, moreover, are maddened by Hera, not by Dionysus. According to Ovid *Met.* 15. 322–28, though, Melampus cures Proetus' daughters by means of a medicine which creates an aversion to wine, making them prefer to drink pure water. He throws the leftover medicine into a spring (the same spring in which Proetus, in Bacchylides' version, bathes before praying to Artemis). Those who drink its waters, Ovid says, ever after avoid wine and prefer to drink pure water. Thus in one of the two versions in which Melampus appears (that of Apollodorus), he cures the girls of madness caused by Dionysus, god of wine. In the other (that of Ovid) he cures Proetus' daughters of what appears to be an addiction to wine. In the former instance part of Melampus' cure seems to be something like shock therapy. In the latter he uses what might be called chemotherapy (along with incantations: Ovid *Met.* 15. 326). See also Virgil *Eclogues* 6. 48–51.

10   The Proetus-Bellerophon-Stheneboea myth belongs to a type which occurs many times in Mediterranean mythologies. The characters in this myth-type are an older man (benefactor, father, or older brother), a younger man (receiver of benefaction, son, or younger brother) and the wife or mistress of the older man (but *not* the mother of the younger man). The wife or mistress falls in love with the younger man and makes him a sexual proposition; he rebuffs her; to protect herself, she accuses him to the husband of attempting to seduce her.

In Greek mythology, in addition to Proetus-Bellerophon-Stheneboea, there are: Acastus-Peleus-Astydamia (3. 13. 3); Amyntor-Phoenix-Amyntor's concubine (unnamed, nor is she said to have made Phoenix a sexual proposition, although she falsely accuses him of seducing her: 3. 13. 8. Apollodorus is at variance with Homer's account at *Iliad* 9. 438–95); Phineus-Plexippus and Pandion-Idaea (3. 15. 3); Theseus-Hippolytus-Phaedra (Epitome 1. 18–19); and Cycnus-Tenes-Philonome (Epitome 3. 24). Demodice's attempted seduction of her nephew Phrixus, who rejected her, is a variation of the pattern. Demodice was the wife of Cretheus, who was Phrixus' uncle. Demodice made her false accusation to her husband and he told his brother, Athamas, father of Phrixus, who tried to kill his son. Phrixus was saved, however, by the ram with the golden fleece (Hyginus *Astronomica* 2. 20).

In Egyptian mythology: "The Story of Two Brothers" in J. B. Pritchard, ed., *Ancient Near Eastern Texts Relating to the Old Testament* (Princeton, 1955), 23–25. In Hebrew mythology: Potiphar–Joseph-Potiphar's wife in Genesis 39.

Each of these narratives, although of the same plot or myth-type, presents individual variations and its own particular denouement. There are at least two important questions to ask: (1) Why does the myth recur? (2) Is the difference in the outcomes of the myths significant and if so, what is that significance?

Edmund Leach's statement (*Claude Lévi-Strauss* [New York, 1970]) that the Theseus-Hippolytus-Phaedra myth is "very close to being the inverse of the Oidipus story . . ." may be valid for the myth-type (80). Instead of son killing father and marrying mother (the Oedipus plot), in each of these myths "mother" desires "son," is rebuffed, accuses him to "father," who punishes or kills "son." A partial answer to the first question is thus implied: The myth-type is about the family, its basic relationships, and its major tensions. It recurs because families recur and, with or without Freud, dominate human experience and attention.

An answer to the second question will have to consider the psy-

chological configurations of different cultures. The "psychological configuration of a culture" is inevitably related to the view and attitudes
(assuming some uniformity) which members of a particular culture have
with regard to its basic unit: the family. That view and those attitudes
will determine the nature (not the fact) of family relationships and of
the tensions engendered by them. Since Proetus-Bellerophon-Stheneboea,
Acastus-Peleus-Astydamia, and Theseus-Hippolytus-Phaedra belong to
the same culture but have different outcomes, it is clear that the "psychological configuration" of Greek culture was not monolithic but varie-
gated. It may be safely said, however, that there is more of a family
resemblance among the Greek versions of the myth-type than between
them and the Egyptian or Hebrew versions.

The earliest reference to the Proetus-Bellerophon-Stheneboea myth is
found in Homer *Iliad* 6. 156–97. (Homer names Proetus' wife Antia;
he does not name her father the king of Lycia, and he makes no mention of Pegasus.) The letter Proetus gives Bellerophon to deliver to the
king of Lycia ("ominous signs," *sêmata lugra, Iliad* 6. 168, i.e., "Kill the
bearer of this letter") is of interest as the only mention of writing in
the *Iliad,* a poem composed, it is thought, orally, and distinctive by the
absence of qualities (good and bad) which writing confers.

Hesiod *Theogony* 325 says that Bellerophon and Pegasus killed the
Chimera. In Pindar *Ol.* 13. 63–90, Bellerophon cannot tame Pegasus
until Athena gives him a golden bit as a "charm" or "drug" by means
of which he controls and mounts the horse. Riding him into the sky he
kills the Amazons, the Chimera, and the Solymi (in that order).

The happy ending of the myth in Apollodorus differentiates it from
the Theseus-Hippolytus-Phaedra and Acastus-Peleus-Astydamia myths,
although it was certainly the intention of Proetus to kill Bellerophon
(but indirectly) as it was of Theseus to kill Hippolytus and Acastus,
Peleus. Note that Proetus attempts murder through language (the letter to Iobates), even as Theseus effects murder through language (the
prayer to Poseidon at Epitome 1. 19, but a curse, which is dramatically
emphasized, in Euripides *Hippolytus* 887–90).

The outcome of the Proetus-Bellerophon-Stheneboea myth makes
it similar to those stories which tell of an ordeal to be undergone or a
price to be paid by a suitor in order to win his bride (e.g., Perseus-
Andromeda: 2. 4. 3; Heracles-Iole: 2. 6. 1; Heracles-Deianira: 2. 7. 5,
cf. 1. 8. 1–2; and Pelops-Hippodamia: Epitome 2. 4–8).

11   The myth of Perseus has engaged many artists and thinkers
from an unnamed Corinthian vase painter in the second half of the
seventh century B.C. to John Barth, Louis MacNeice, and Sylvia Plath,
twentieth century novelist and poets, respectively. Along the way the
myth inspired Simonides, Pindar, Sophocles, Euripides, Ovid, Benve-

nuto Cellini, Sigmund Freud, and other psychoanalytic interpreters of myth. Attention should be called to Benvenuto Cellini's magnificent bronze statue of Perseus holding the severed head of Medusa (sixteenth century, now in Florence; for a photograph of it, see Frederick Hartt, *History of Italian Renaissance Art* [New York, n.d.], 588, fig. 719).

Apollodorus gives perhaps the most complete treatment of the entire myth, which he seems to have taken from Pherecydes (Frazer, *Apollodorus* 1. 153), omitting, however, the detail that Perseus, in an angry quarrel with his father-in-law, Cepheus, flashed Medusa's head at him, but since the old man was blind, it had no effect. Perseus turned the head around to see what was wrong with it and turned himself to stone (Jocelyn M. Woodward, *Perseus: A Study in Greek Art and Legend* [Cambridge, Eng., 1937], 23).

Homer *Iliad* 14. 319–20 claims that Zeus was the father of Perseus. Both Sophocles and Euripides wrote tragedies on Danae (now lost; see the reference to fragments in Frazer, *Apollodorus* 1. 153).

Simonides, a poet of the sixth and fifth centuries B.C. composed a choral lyric poem which included the story of Danae and the infant Perseus put out to sea by her father, Acrisius. This fragment survives:

> . . . when blown by wind through heaving swells
> in the wood-carved chest, frightened, crying,
> she covered Perseus with her hand.
> 'Such horror, my son!' she said, 'and yet you drowse, full of milk,
> so peaceful in this wretched box, in shimmering, night-blue dark.
> You know nothing of the vast sea, of water roaring over your head,
> nor the voice of the moaning wind,
> wrapped in your purple blanket, asleep,
> dear little face. But if you knew the danger,
> and if your tiny ear could hear my cry . . .
> But sleep, my baby. And let the sea sleep, too.
> And let this endless danger sleep! Please, Father Zeus,
> I pray for a sign of help from you.
> But if my prayer is arrogant, or lacks respect,
> forgive me.'

Although psychoanalytic writers have concentrated on the meaning of the beheading of Medusa, the ancient authors pass briefly over this part of the myth. Hesiod *Theogony* 280–81, for example: "When Perseus cut off her [Medusa's] head, out leaped great Chrysaor and Pegasus, a horse." In the *Shield of Heracles* 216–37 Hesiod describes, engraved on Heracles' shield, Perseus' flight from the pursuing Gorgons, whose belts are snakes with flickering tongues, gnashing teeth, and glaring eyes. Perseus runs at full speed, Medusa's head in a silver bag slung over his back.

Pindar *Pyth.* 10. 29–48 (498 B.C.) mentions Perseus' stopping in the never-never land of the Hyperboreans on his return from beheading Medusa: "Breathing courage, Danae's son once came into the company of blessed men (Athena was his guide). He had slain the Gorgon and came bearing the snake-haired head, stone death to the islanders" (44–48).

In *Pyth.* 12, composed some eight years later, Pindar derives Athena's invention of the flute from the lament of the Gorgons at the death of their sister. The poem celebrates the victory of Midas of Acragas (in Sicily) in the flute-playing competition in the Pythian games of 490 B.C.

The art, Pindar says, "Athena once invented, adapting [for the flute] the death-dirge of the angered Gorgons which she heard flowing, anguished woe, from the maidens' horrible serpent-heads when Perseus cried out in triumph and brought the third of the sisters to Seriphos-in-the-sea and its people, as their fate. Yea, he darkly confused the monstrous race of Phorcus and made his wedding gift to Polydectes bitter, and bitter Polydectes' enslavement of his mother, forced into his bed: He drew forth the head of lovely Medusa, Danae's son did, the one we say was born from golden rain" (6–18).

Ovid, whose treatment of the myth is the longest in surviving Greek and Latin literature, nevertheless gives only five lines to the beheading of the Gorgon (*Met.* 4. 782–86): "He gazed on the form of the horrible Medusa reflected in the shield of bronze held in his left hand. And while she and the snakes slept soundly, he ripped her head from her neck, and swift-winged Pegasus and his brother were born from the mother's blood."

The account of the second century A.D. writer, Lucian, is somewhat fuller than that of Ovid and the single sentence in Apollodorus: "Now Athena enabled him to see Medusa's image in her gleaming shield as in a mirror. Then he took her hair in his left hand and, looking at the reflected image and with the sickle in his right hand, he cut off her head and flew away before her sisters awakened" (*Dialogues of the Sea Gods* 14. 2).

Woodward, *Perseus,* 41, notes that Greek artists, too, at least the earlier ones, chose for their subject Perseus' flight from the Gorgons, "rather than the actual beheading of Medusa. . . . One would perhaps have expected the more concrete, graphic scenes to have appealed to the earlier artist's range of ideas."

Psychoanalytic interpretations of the beheading of Medusa begin with Freud, for whom decapitation is castration, and the decapitated head of Medusa represents "the female genitals, . . . and essentially those of [the] mother." The fear inspired by the power of Medusa's head to turn those who look at it to stone is "... a terror of castration...." It grips a boy "... hitherto unwilling to believe the threat of castration" when he "catches sight of the female genitals.... The sight of Medusa's head makes [him] ... stiff with terror, turns him to stone.... [B]ecoming stiff means an erection" so the boy is simultaneously reassured that he still possesses a penis (Sigmund Freud, *Collected Papers*, vol. 5, ed. James Strachey [New York, 1959], 105).

Philip E. Slater, *The Glory of Hera* (Boston, 1968), a contemporary Freudian, says that "The Perseus myth ... reflects a social system in which the father is peripheral in the home, and in which emotional power is seen as residing in the mother. It is she who must be confronted, and when Perseus wishes to vanquish his enemies the only way he can do it is by exposing them to the same maternal bogie which so terrifies him. Like the boys of many primitive societies who live in the women's quarters until puberty ... , he has no paternal model of mastery, and assuming the male role is full of difficulties" (318).

Slater attempts in his lengthy analysis of the myth to accept Freud's interpretation of the meaning of Medusa's head (as maternal genitalia) although he is troubled by that interpretation. Medusa's head represents not the maternal genitalia, Slater says at one point, but fear of these genitalia. The snakes are not penis symbols (as Freud said) but are an "an aspect of the vagina itself." Head and snakes do not represent the mother as castrated, "but rather ... her being experienced as 'castrating'..." (17–20). Elsewhere Slater qualifies what he said earlier and contradicts himself, still attempting to adapt Freud's interpretation of the myth, which he cannot bring himself to accept, to his own (309–10, 321–24, 331).

Freud and his followers seem to have made the unquestioned assumption that Medusa's head, a monstrosity, something awful and fearful, must automatically be thought to represent female (or maternal) genitalia. Can unconscious fear or repugnance toward female genitalia have crept into their interpretations?

Surely it is just as plausible to consider Medusa's head as phallic as well as vaginal. In the ancient world, indeed, the head was thought to be the source of male potency. It contained the "cerebrospinal substance," the seed of life. The head (along with the knees) was associated with the male genitals as the source of life or of generative power (R. B. Onians, *The Origins of European Thought*, ... [Cambridge, Eng., 1951], 108–13, 174–78). Moreover, the stone herms often set up outside Greek houses and possessing articulation only of a head and phallus confirm the connection in the Greek mind between the two

(Adrian Stokes, *Greek Culture and the Ego* [London, 1958], 57–58). To be valid, psychoanalytic interpretation of the myth must accept the phallic aspect of the head. As phallic-vaginal it has an altogether different meaning.

In his treatment of the myth at *Met.* 4. 610–803 (end) and 5. 1–249, a total of 443 lines, Ovid focuses on Perseus' rescue of Andromeda: Perseus returns from the encounter with the Gorgons and from the air sees Ethiopia where Andromeda is set out as prey for a sea monster. Perseus fights and defeats the monster and frees Andromeda. Victory sacrifices and a wedding banquet follow. At the request of the banqueters, Perseus narrates the beheading of Medusa, relates adventures of his return, and explains why Medusa has snaky hair. Phineus, Andromeda's uncle and the rejected suitor, with his cohorts attacks Perseus in the midst of the festivities in the banquet hall. Perseus, exhausted by conventional battle, holds up the head of Medusa, turning to stone Phineus' remaining allies and lastly Phineus himself. Perseus returns home with his bride, makes war on Proetus, and turns Polydectes to stone.

The fact that Perseus in *returning* from his mission stops with the Ethiopians, *narrates* to them at a banquet the story of his adventures; the fact that the banquet is disrupted by a *suitor* who is enraged because he has lost his bride-to-be and who then begins a battle royal *inside the banquet hall*—these are obvious borrowings from Homer's *Odyssey*, although Ovid compresses two of Homer's episodes, Odysseus' stay with the Phaeacians and his later battle with Penelope's suitors in his own palace, into a single episode in his own narrative.

Note, too, that at the climax of Odysseus' battle with the suitors in the *Odyssey* Athena raises the aegis, her shield, to the outer side of which Medusa's head was affixed, and the surviving suitors, beholding it, are maddened by fear and stampede like cattle (*Odyssey* 22. 297 ff.). So Perseus, wearied by his battle with Phineus and his allies (and in danger of losing it), holds aloft the head of Medusa (*Met.* 5. 177 ff.), and turns to stone 200 (one-half) of his remaining opponents (5. 208–09), and so wins the battle.

Ovid has cast his narrative of the myth into the form of a little epic. Brooks Otis, *Ovid as an Epic Poet* (Cambridge, Eng., 1970), though he seems wrong-headed in his analysis of this part of the *Metamorphoses*, calling it a "little *Aeneid* that does not come off" (159) and saying, "Here Ovid is at his worst and his worst is very bad indeed" (164), is right, nevertheless, to compare it to the *Aeneid* ("Ovid's Virgilian epic," 164) with Perseus as Aeneas (159). If Perseus is meant to suggest Aeneas, then one wants to know what Ovid saw in Virgil's Aeneas that is analogous to the head of Medusa. What is Aeneas' chief weapon which, like Medusa's head, destroys friend and foe alike? The answer, of course, is his *pietas* (his sense of duty to his own which is transformed into a sense of mission to found Rome, whatever the cost), the compelling power of which, as it gathers force, corresponds to the power of Medusa's head. Virgil's epic, as readers know, is strewn with victims of Aeneas' *pietas*.

It is worth noting in this connection that Ovid's Medusa, in turning people to stone, creates statues, that is, makes art: All along the fields and roads to the Gorgons, Perseus says, he "saw *simulacra* ["statues"] of men and beasts turned to stone from their living selves after beholding Medusa" (4. 779–81; *simulacrum* is used primarily to refer to works of art: see Lewis and Short, *A Latin Dictionary, sub verbum*. Cf. also *simulacra* at 5. 211 and *marmor* ["marble"] at 5. 214, referring to allies of Phineus turned to stone by Medusa's head).

Much more telling is Ovid's description of Phineus turned to stone by Perseus, who thus ends his battle with Andromeda's former suitor and his allies (5. 210–35). Like Virgil's Turnus, whom Aeneas battles for Lavinia in book 12 of the *Aeneid*, Phineus acknowledges that he is beaten and asks for mercy. They fought not from hatred nor for power, he says, but for a wife. His claim is prior in time, Perseus' superior in merit. Surrender holds no dishonor. He wants nothing for himself except his life; the rest Perseus can have. "After he spoke (nor dared to face him whom he was beseeching), Perseus replied: 'Fearful Phineus, what I can give and what is a great gift for a coward (Fear not, Phineus!), this I give: You will be untouched by sword. Indeed, I grant to you to remain forever a monument, and in my father-in-law's house you will always be visible to my wife so that she can console herself with the image of her fiancé.'" Perseus then shoves the head at Phineus, who frantically turns his face away until Perseus forces him to view it. His twisted neck stiffens; eyes harden. Mouth remains timid, expression begging, hands praying, appearance submissive—fixed in marble (*in marmore . . . mansit*, 5. 234–35).

The following conclusion may be drawn: Ovid's Perseus and Medusa represent Aeneas and his *pietas* (that is, a poem, the *Aeneid*). But Aeneas and his *pietas*, in turn, represent, to put it rather simply, Augustus and his *pax* (actual history). There is a kind of double symbolism in Ovid's Perseus and Medusa: They symbolize Aeneas and his *pietas* in the *Aeneid*, but also Virgil's process of art by means of which he fixed forever in poetry the criminality of Augustus, glossing it with *pietas* and, of course, his own great poetic "charm" (see Pindar *Ol.* 1. 30–32), and creating for Ovid a falsification in art grotesque beyond words. Ovid's Perseus and Medusa mirror Virgil's Aeneas and his *pietas* which freeze in art Augustus and his *pax*.

Otis claims that Ovid's "imitation of Virgil is . . . without the excuse of parody . . ." (163). But if Ovid symbolizes Aeneas' *pietas* (and so Augustus' *pax*) with Perseus' head of Medusa, then his "imitation of Virgil" is the most savage satire imaginable, revealing a profound cynicism with regard to Virgil, his epic, and his motives for writing it (not to mention the Augustan regime).

For Perseus in later art and literature, see Philip Mayerson, *Classical Mythology in Literature, Art, and Music* (Waltham, Mass. and Toronto, 1971), 294–95. John Barth's "Perseid" in his novel, *Chimera* (Greenwich, Conn., 1973) presents the myth as comedy. His description of Perseus' getting the eye and tooth from the Graeae is extremely funny (70–72). Sylvia Plath's strange poem, "Medusa," in *Ariel* (New York, 1966) shows how this myth can grip a literary imagination particularly attuned to the grotesque. Louis MacNeice, in his poem "Perseus," conveys by the myth awareness of death and time's turning to stone.

12   Herodotus 7. 61, writing in the fifth century B.C., says that the Persians took their name from Perses, son of Perseus. At 7. 150 he reports that Xerxes, king of Persia, before he invaded Greece sent a message to Argos invoking Perses, the common ancestor of Argives and Persians, and asked them not to make war on him when he entered their country.

13   For Pterelaus with his golden hair as an example (along with others) of the "external soul," see ch. 2, n. 9.

14   Hera was presumably jealous because Heracles was the son of Zeus by one of his numerous paramours. (But see ch. 5, n. 1 and the reference to Philip E. Slater's *The Glory of Hera.*) Heracles and Eurystheus as descendants of Perseus: the former was his great-grandson (Heracles-Alcmena-Electryon-Perseus); the latter his grandson (Eurystheus-Sthenelus-Perseus). Alcmena and Eurystheus were thus first cousins, making her son, Heracles, and Eurystheus first cousins once removed. The two were further related to each other through Pelops who was Eurystheus' maternal grandfather (Eurystheus-Nicippe-Pelops) and Heracles' maternal great-great-grandfather (Heracles-Alcmena-Anaxo-Astydamia-Pelops).

According to Homer *Iliad* 19. 95–133, on the day that Alcmena was due to give birth to Heracles, Zeus vowed that there would be born that day a descendant of his who would rule all those dwelling near him. Hera, feigning distrust of Zeus' words, persuaded him to swear an oath that he would keep his vow. He did so and was tricked by Hera, for she rushed to Argos and caused the wife of Sthenelus, seven months pregnant, to be delivered prematurely of Eurystheus, while at the same time she held back the birth of Heracles. Zeus was forced to keep his oath and so Eurystheus became lord of the Argives rather than Heracles, as Zeus had intended.

At Ovid *Met.* 9. 285–323 Alcmena tells the story of the birth of Heracles and the trick a servant girl played on the goddess of childbirth who was preventing her from delivering the child. She had been in labor for seven days and prayed to the goddesses of childbirth for relief. Lucina (as Ovid calls the Roman Ilithyia) came in answer to her prayer but, suborned by Juno, sat outside Alcmena's room with knees pressed together and held tightly by hands locked with fingers intertwined, muttering under her breath her inhibiting incantations, all to prevent Heracles' birth. Alcmena's screams brought women to her bedside and one of them, a bright and diligent servant girl named Galanthis, as she went in and out of the room, noticed the woman sitting outside it with arms around her knees held together by interlaced fingers. Suspicious, Galanthis said to her, "Congratulate my mistress! Her baby has come, her prayer is answered!" The goddess leaped up in consternation, thus breaking the spell, Alcmena was able to deliver the baby and Heracles was born. Galanthis laughed at the success of her deception but then was seized by the angry goddess and changed into a weasel.

It was in forced service to Eurystheus that Heracles performed his twelve (originally ten) labors: Hera, still jealous, afflicted him with a fit of insanity during which he murdered his children and those of his brother, Iphicles (2. 4. 12).

15   As Frazer, *Apollodorus* 1. 167–68 points out, Mestor, a son of Perseus and Andromeda, was the great-great-grandfather of the sons of Pterelaus, not their grandfather, as Apollodorus says, and since Electryon was Mestor's brother, it is hard to imagine that he was still ruling Mycenae when Pterelaus' sons made their expedition against it.

16   Hesiod *Shield of Heracles* 1–56 tells differently (and more briefly) the story of Amphitryon and Alcmena, the death of Electryon, Amphitryon's war with the Teleboans, and the births of Heracles and Iphicles. He omits the details of Amphitryon's gathering of allies and the treachery of Pterelaus' daughter, Comaetho (and her reward), which enabled Amphitryon to conquer Taphos.

According to Hesiod, Amphitryon was banished from Mycenae (or Argos) because he killed his father-in-law, Electryon, in an argument over cattle, not by accident, as Apollodorus says, and came to Thebes as a suppliant (Alcmena with him).

Amphitryon and Alcmena were married when they came to Thebes (contrary to Apollodorus) and lived together, but their marriage remained unconsummated and they slept apart until he proved himself by avenging the deaths of her brothers whom the sons of Pterelaus (the Teleboans, also called Taphians; see 2. 4. 6) had killed.

Amphitryon had no little incentive for the task: The wife who was withholding herself from him was the most beautiful and most intelligent of all women, tall, with slender ankles, dark-eyed and scented with the golden aura of Aphrodite (4–8). Moreover, "she honored her husband in her heart as no woman ever had done before" (9–10). Amphitryon rushes off to conquer the Taphians and Teleboans, burn their villages, and so avenge Alcmena's brothers.

Zeus, meanwhile, was plotting a scheme, stealthy seduction in his secret mind (as Hesiod says), and set out from Olympus at night full of desire for Alcmena. Sitting on Mount Phicium (near Thebes) he figured out his happy plan, came to Alcmena, made love with her in Amphitryon's bed, and satisfied his desire.

The same night Amphitryon returned, victorious. Not stopping to greet his tenants and shepherds as was customary, he rushed right home to Alcmena: "As a man relieved to be recovered from a near-fatal disease or released from a strong prison, so Amphitryon eagerly, gladly, entered his house" (42–45). Though Zeus had just left her (or rather, their) bed, "all night long Amphitryon lay with his chaste [sic] wife, delighting himself with the gifts of golden Aphrodite" and none the wiser (46–47). In due course she bore twin sons: Heracles to Zeus and Iphicles to Amphitryon.

Both Sophocles and Euripides wrote plays, now lost, on Zeus' deception of Alcmena (Apollodorus' version of the myth) and it is the theme of the *Amphitryo*, an extant comedy by the Roman playwright Plautus. For additional details, see Frazer, *Apollodorus* 1. 174–75. Jean Giraudoux's modern play, *Amphitryon 38*, supposedly represents the thirty-eighth version of the myth.

CHAPTER FIVE

Heracles and the Sons of Heracles
(2. 4. 8–2. 8. 5)[1]

BOOK 2 When Heracles was eight months old, Hera, wishing to destroy him, sent two huge serpents to his crib. Alcmena cried out for Amphitryon, but Heracles stood up and strangled them to death, one with each hand.[2] | Pherecydes says that Amphitryon put the snakes in the crib because he wanted to find out which of the two babies was his. When Iphicles fled but Heracles stood his ground, he realized that Iphicles was his son. |

9   Amphitryon taught Heracles to drive the chariot, Autolycus taught him to wrestle, Eurytus to shoot the bow, Castor to fight with heavy armor, and Linus to play the lyre. Linus was the brother of Orpheus and became a citizen of Thebes. He once struck Heracles, who then killed him in anger by a blow with his lyre.[3] When Heracles was tried on a murder charge, he quoted a law of Rhadamanthys which said that a person who defends himself against assault shall be considered innocent, and so was acquitted. Amphitryon, fearing that he would do something similar again, sent him away to tend the cattle. Growing up among the herds, he soon excelled all men in size and strength. It was obvious that he was a son of Zeus for he was eight feet tall, never missed with the bow or the javelin, and fire flashed from his eyes. When he was eighteen and still tending the cattle, he killed the lion of
10 Cithaeron which was ravaging the cattle of Amphitryon and Thespius, king of Thespiae. While trying to catch the lion, Heracles stayed with Thespius for fifty days. The king had fifty daughters, all born to him by Megamede, daughter of Arneus. Being eager for them to conceive children by Heracles, he put a different one into Heracles' bed each night that he went out to hunt the lion. Heracles thought it was the same one in his bed each night and slept with them all. After he killed the lion he wore its skin, using its head with gaping mouth as a helmet.[4]

11 Returning from the hunt, he encountered heralds of Erginus on their way to collect the tribute paid by the Thebans. Now the Thebans gave tribute to Erginus for the following reason: Menoeceus' charioteer Perieres struck Clymenus, king of the Minyans, with a stone in a sacred grove of Poseidon at Onchestus. He was brought half dead to Orchomenus, but before he died he ordered his son Erginus to avenge his death. Erginus led an army to Thebes, killed many of the Thebans and made a treaty with them requiring tribute for twenty years at the rate of one hundred cattle per year. Heracles met the heralds traveling to Thebes to collect the tribute, cut off their ears, noses, and hands, hung them around their necks, and told them to take these as tribute to Erginus and the Minyans. Enraged at this, Erginus made an expedition against Thebes. Heracles got weapons from Athena and, taking command of the army, killed Erginus, routed the Minyans, and compelled them to pay the Thebans double the tribute that they had exacted. It happened that Amphitryon died in this battle fighting bravely. As a reward for his courage, Heracles received from Creon his oldest daughter Megara, who bore him three sons, Therimachus, Creontiades, and Deicoon. Creon gave his younger daughter to Iphicles, who already had a son Iolaus by Automedusa, the daughter of Alcathus. After Amphitryon's death, Zeus' son Rhadamanthys married Alcmena and lived as an exile at Ocaleae in Boeotia.[5]

Heracles had already learned from Eurytus how to use the bow. He now received a sword from Hermes, a bow and arrows from Apollo, a golden breastplate from Hephaestus and a robe from Athena. He him-
12 self cut his club at Nemea. After the battle with the Minyans, Hera drove Heracles mad because of her jealousy and he threw his own sons by Megara and two of Iphicles' children into a fire. Condemning himself to exile because of this, he was purified by Thespius and went to Delphi to ask the god where he might live. It was then that he was first called Heracles, by the Pythian priestess. Before this he was called Alcides. She told him to settle in Tiryns and serve Eurystheus [king of Mycenae and overlord of the neighboring town of Tiryns, whose ruler was his vassal] for twelve years by performing the ten labors to be laid upon him. When he had finished them, she said, he would be immortal.[6]

5 When Heracles heard this he went to Tiryns and set about performing the labors which Eurystheus assigned to him.[7] First Eurystheus ordered him to bring to him the skin of the Nemean lion. It was impossible to wound this creature, the offspring of Typhon. On his way to hunt the lion, Heracles came to Cleonae and stayed with a laborer named Molorchus. Molorchus wanted to sacrifice an animal, but Heracles told him to wait for thirty days and if he returned safely from

the hunt, to sacrifice to Zeus the Savior, but if he died, to sacrifice to him as to a hero.

He went to Nemea, found the lion, and first shot an arrow at it. When he realized that he could not wound it he chased it brandishing his club. When the lion ran into a cave with two entrances he blocked up one, entered the other, and cornered it. Grabbing it by the neck he strangled it, then put it onto his shoulders, and carried it to Cleonae. He found Molorchus on the thirtieth day about to sacrifice an animal to him thinking him dead, but Heracles sacrificed instead to Zeus the Savior and brought the lion to Mycenae. Eurystheus, amazed at his courage, forbade him to enter the city and ordered him thereafter to announce the results of his labors at the city gates. They also say that Eurystheus out of fear had a large bronze jar made to hide in underground, and gave orders for the labors through a herald, Copreus, son of Pelops the Elean. Copreus had killed Iphitus and fled to Mycenae, where he lived after being purified by Eurystheus.

2   As a second labor Eurystheus ordered Heracles to kill the Lernaean hydra, a water creature bred in the swamp of Lerna, which invaded dry land destroying livestock and ravaging fields. The hydra had a huge body with nine heads, eight of which were mortal, the one in the middle being immortal. Iolaus drove Heracles to Lerna in a chariot. Heracles found the hydra in its lair on the top of a hill beside the springs of Amymone and shot flaming arrows at it to force it to come out. When it emerged he seized and held it. The hydra, in turn, wrapped itself around one of his feet and clung to it. Heracles was unable to kill it by smashing its heads with his club, for when he struck one head, two others grew up. Moreover, a huge crab was helping the hydra by biting his foot.[8] He killed the crab and called to Iolaus for help. Iolaus set fire to part of the woods nearby and with torches burned the heads as they sprouted, thus preventing them from growing. In this way Heracles overcame the growing heads, then cut off the immortal one, buried it beside the road leading through Lerna to Elaeus and put a heavy rock over it. He ripped open the body of the hydra and dipped his arrows in its bile. Eurystheus said that he ought not to count this as one of the ten labors for he had not conquered the hydra alone but with the help of Iolaus.

3   As a third labor Eurystheus ordered him to bring the Cerynitian deer alive to Mycenae.[9] It lived at Oenoe, had golden horns, and was sacred to Artemis. Because he wished neither to kill it nor wound it Heracles hunted it for an entire year. When the animal, exhausted from running, fled to Mount Artemisius and from there to the Ladon River, Heracles shot an arrow at it as it was about to cross the stream, caught it and, putting it on his shoulders, hurried through Arcadia.

Artemis and Apollo encountered him and tried to take the deer away from him, reproaching him for trying to kill Artemis' sacred creature. As an excuse Heracles claimed that he had been forced to capture it and said that Eurystheus was responsible. He thus calmed the angry goddess and brought the animal alive to Mycenae.

4   The fourth labor Eurystheus assigned him was to bring to him the Erymanthian boar alive. This creature was preying on Psophis from its lair on Mount Erymanthus. When he crossed Pholoe Heracles stayed with the centaur Pholus, the offspring of Silenus and an ash tree nymph. He offered roasted meat to Heracles while he himself ate raw flesh. When Heracles asked for wine Pholus said that he was afraid to open the wine jar because it belonged to all the centaurs jointly. Heracles told him to take courage and opened it himself. Drawn by the smell of the wine, the centaurs appeared soon afterwards at the cave of Pholus, armed with rocks and fir trees. Anchius and Agrius, the first to venture inside the cave, were driven out by Heracles who threw lighted torches at them. Shooting arrows at the rest, he chased them as far as Mount Malea. There they took refuge with Chiron, who had been driven from Mount Pelion by Lapiths and now lived at Malea. As the centaurs crowded around Chiron for protection, Heracles shot an arrow which pierced the arm of Elatus and struck Chiron's knee. Distressed at this, Heracles ran and pulled out the arrow and poured on the knee a medicine which Chiron gave him. The wound refused to heal and Chiron entered his cave, wishing to die. Since he was immortal he could not. Zeus permitted Prometheus to become immortal in his place and so Chiron died. The rest of the centaurs fled in different directions, some going to Mount Malea, Eurytion to Pholoe, and Nessus to the river Evenus. Poseidon received the others at Eleusis and hid them on a mountain.

Pholus drew an arrow from a corpse, amazed that something so small could kill creatures so large. The arrow slipped from his hand, struck his foot, and killed him. When Heracles returned to Pholoe and found Pholus dead, he buried him.[10] He then continued the hunt for the boar. By shouting he drove the animal out from some underbrush and chased it into deep snow. When it was exhausted he caught and tied it and brought it to Mycenae.

5   For his fifth labor Eurystheus ordered Heracles to remove the cattle manure from Augeas' barnyard in one day's time. Now Augeas was king of Elis and son of the Sun | or of Poseidon, or of Phorbas, according to various authorities | . He owned many herds of cattle. Heracles came to him and without revealing Eurystheus' order, said that he would remove the manure in one day if Augeas would give him a tenth of his cattle. Augeas replied that he did not believe him but promised

the cattle. Taking Augeas' son Phyleus as a witness, Heracles dug a channel to the barnyard, diverted the Alpheus and Peneus Rivers (which flowed nearby) through the channel into the yard and dug another channel on the other side of it for the water to run out. When Augeas learned that the task had been accomplished at Eurystheus' command, he refused to pay Heracles for it and even denied ever having promised him anything. In addition, he said that he was ready to submit the matter for judgment. When the judges were in session Heracles called Phyleus who testified against his father, saying that Augeas had agreed to pay him. Augeas in a fit of anger before the verdict was rendered ordered Phyleus and Heracles to leave Elis. Phyleus went to Dulichium and lived there while Heracles went to Olenus to the house of Dexamenus. He found him on the point of unwillingly betrothing his daughter Mnesimache to the centaur Eurytion. Heracles, called upon for help, killed Eurytion when he came for his bride. Eurystheus refused to consider the removal of the manure as one of the ten labors, saying that Heracles had done it for profit.

6   The sixth labor Eurystheus assigned to Heracles was to drive away the Stymphalian birds. In Stymphalus, a city of Arcadia, there was a lake called Stymphalis surrounded by thick woods. Innumerable birds had flocked to it for refuge, fearful of being caught by wolves.[11] Heracles was at a loss how to drive the birds out of the woods, but Athena gave him a brass noise-maker which she got from Hephaestus. By making a noise with this upon a mountain beside the lake, he frightened the birds and then shot them as they flew up in terror, unable to endure the sound.

7   Heracles' seventh labor was to bring to Eurystheus the Cretan bull. | Acusilaus says that this is the bull which carried Europa over the water for Zeus [3. 1. 1], although some say that it is the one which Poseidon sent up from the sea when Minos said that he would sacrifice to Poseidon anything which appeared from the sea. They say that when Minos saw how beautiful the bull was, he sent it to his herds and sacrificed another to Poseidon. The god, angered by this, made the bull wild. | When Heracles came to Crete after the bull and asked Minos for help, he was told to fight it and capture it by himself. So he caught it, returned with it to Eurystheus and after he showed it to him let it go free. It wandered to Sparta and over all Arcadia, and crossing the Isthmus came to Marathon in Attica where it attacked the inhabitants.

8   The eighth labor Eurystheus assigned to Heracles was to bring to Mycenae the mares of Diomedes the Thracian. He was the son of Ares and Cyrene and king of the Bistones, a very warlike Thracian nation. The mares were man-eating. Heracles sailed with volunteers and, having overpowered the men in charge of the stable, led the mares to the

sea. When the Bistones came in arms to the rescue, he turned the mares over to Abderus to guard. He was the son of Hermes from Opus in Locris and was a lover of Heracles. The mares killed him by tearing him apart. Heracles fought the Bistones, killed Diomedes, and forced the rest to flee. He founded the city Abdera beside the tomb of the slain Abderus and brought the mares to Eurystheus. He, however, let them go. They went to Mount Olympus and were killed by wild animals.[12]

9   Heracles' ninth labor was to bring Eurystheus the belt of Hippolyte. She was queen of the Amazons, who were skilled in warfare and lived around the Thermodon River. They engaged only in male activities. If they gave birth after intercourse, they reared the females only. They pinched off their right breasts in order not to be hindered in throwing javelins, but kept their left breasts for nursing. Hippolyte wore the belt of Ares as a sign that she was their leader. Heracles was sent after this belt because Admete, Eurystheus' daughter, wanted it. He took volunteers to help him and sailing in one ship put in at the island of Paros where the sons of Minos, Eurymedon, Chryses, Nephalion, and Philolaus lived. It happened that they killed two men who disembarked from the ship. Angered at this, Heracles killed the sons of Minos. He besieged the rest of the inhabitants until they sent envoys to propose that he take any two of them he wished in return for the two of his men who were killed. He ended the siege and took away Alcaeus and Sthenelus, sons of Androgeus, son of Minos. He arrived in Mysia at the palace of Lycus, the son of Dascylus, who offered him hospitality. Aiding Lycus in an ensuing battle with the king of the Bebryces, Heracles killed many men, including the king Mygdon, brother of Amycus. He detached much of the land of the Bebryces and gave it to Lycus who called it Heraclea.

As Heracles sailed into the harbor at Themiscyra, Hippolyte met him. She promised to give him the belt when she learned why he had come. But Hera, assuming the appearance of one of the Amazons, passed through the crowd saying that the foreigners who had just arrived were carrying off the queen. The Amazons hurried to the ship, armed and on horseback. When Heracles saw them with weapons he suspected a trick, so he killed Hippolyte, took away her belt and, fighting off the rest, sailed away and put in at Troy.[13]

Troy happened just then to be suffering under the wrath of Apollo and Poseidon. For they wanted to test Laomedon to see whether he was arrogant, so they appeared to him as men and offered to build a wall around Troy for pay. When they had built it he refused to pay them. Because of this Apollo infected the city with a plague and Poseidon sent a sea monster on a flood tide which carried off the people on the coastal plain. Since oracles declared that the city would be freed from the monster if Laomedon set out his daughter Hesione as prey for it, he tied her to rocks near the sea. Heracles saw her lying exposed and promised to save her if Laomedon would give him the mares which Zeus gave him to compensate for carrying off Ganymede. Laomedon promised them to him, and Heracles killed the monster and saved Hesione. When Laomedon reneged on his promise, Heracles threatened to make war on Troy and sailed away.[14]

He put in at Aenus where he was a guest of Poltys. As he was sailing away he shot and killed Sarpedon on the beach. Sarpedon was a violent man, a son of Poseidon and brother of Poltys. Heracles came to Thasos and there subdued the Thracians living on the island and gave it to the sons of Androgeus to inhabit. Leaving Thasos for Torone he was there challenged to a wrestling match by Polygonus and Telegonus, sons of Proteus and grandsons of Poseidon. Heracles accepted the challenge and killed them. He then brought the belt to Mycenae and gave it to Eurystheus.

10   The tenth labor assigned to him was to bring the cattle of Geryon from Erythia, an island near the ocean now called Gadira, where Geryon, son of Chrysaor and of Callirrhoe, daughter of Ocean, lived.[15] Geryon had three human bodies from the waist down. He owned red cattle which were tended by Eurytion and guarded by a two-headed dog, Orthus, the offspring of Echidna and Typhon. Going through Europe after Geryon's cattle and killing many wild creatures, Heracles entered Libya and came to Tartessus, where he set up pillars opposite each other at the boundaries of Europe and Libya to mark the limit of his journey.[16] He aimed his bow at the Sun because it made him hot, and the god, admiring his courage, gave him the golden cup in which he crossed the Ocean. When Heracles arrived at Erythia he camped on Mount Abas. The dog Orthus sensed his presence and attacked him, but he struck it with his club and killed the herdsman, Eurytion, who came to help it. Menoetes, who was herding the cattle of Hades there, reported to Geryon what had happened. Geryon met Heracles leading off the cattle beside the Anthemus River and attacked him, but Heracles shot him with an arrow and killed him. Heracles put the cattle into the golden cup and, after sailing across to Tartessus, gave it back to the Sun.[17]

He next passed through Abderia and came to Liguria where Ialebion and Dercynus, sons of Poseidon, tried to rob him of the cattle. Heracles killed them and traveled on through Tyrrhenia. At Rhegium a bull broke away, leaped into the sea and swam across to Sicily. The bull, going through the country nearby (called Italy from that time on because the Tyrrhenian word for bull is *italus*), came to the plain of Eryx who was king of the Elymi. Eryx, a son of Poseidon, bred the bull with his herds. Heracles left the cattle with Hephaestus and hurried to look for it. He found it among the herds of Eryx who refused to give it back to him unless he defeated him at wrestling. Heracles wrestled with him and defeated him three times, killing him in the final match. He then took the bull and drove it and the rest of the cattle to the Ionian Sea. When he arrived at the inlets of the sea, Hera maddened the cattle with gadflies and they stampeded into the foothills of the mountains of Thrace. Heracles chased and caught some of them and drove them to the Hellespont, but those left behind became wild. He blamed the Strymon River for his difficulty in rounding up the cattle and so filled it with rocks, making it impassable, although it was navigable before. He then brought the cattle to Eurystheus who sacrificed them to Hera.[18]

11   Heracles completed his labors in eight years and one month.[19] Eurystheus refused to acknowledge the cleaning of Augeas' barnyard and the killing of the hydra, and as an eleventh labor ordered Heracles to get the golden apples from the Hesperides. These apples were on Mount Atlas in the land of the Hyperboreans | not, as some say, in Lybia | and were a wedding present to Zeus and Hera from Earth. An immortal serpent with a hundred heads and many different voices, the offspring of Typhon and Echidna, guarded them. They were also guarded by the Hesperides: Aegle, Erythia, Hesperia, and Arethusa.[20] Heracles set out on his journey and arrived at the river Echedorus. Cycnus, the son of Ares and Pyrene, challenged him to a fight. Ares joined the combat on his son's side but Zeus hurled a thunderbolt among them, ending the battle.[21] Hurrying on foot through Illyria to the river Eridanus, Heracles came to the nymphs, daughters of Zeus and Themis, who showed him Nereus. Heracles seized him while he slept. Although Nereus changed into every possible shape, Heracles tied him up and refused to set him free until he learned from him the location of the apples and the Hesperides.[22] When he learned where they were he traveled through Libya, then ruled by Antaeus, son of Poseidon, who forced strangers to wrestle with him and killed them. Heracles, compelled to wrestle with him, raised him off the ground (for when he touched earth he became stronger, | hence was said by some to be a son of earth |) and crushed him to death.[23]

After he left Libya Heracles journeyed through Egypt, the king of which was Busiris, son of Poseidon and Lysianassa, daughter of Epaphus, who regularly sacrificed strangers upon an altar of Zeus because of an oracle. For the land of Egypt had been barren for nine years until Phrasius, a skilled seer from Cyprus, said that the barrenness would end if they sacrificed a foreigner to Zeus every year. Busiris promptly sacrificed the seer and continued to sacrifice foreigners who came to Egypt. Heracles too was captured and brought to the altar, but he broke loose from his bonds and killed Busiris and his son Amphidamas.[24]

Crossing Asia, Heracles put in at Thermydrae, the harbor of the Lindians. He unyoked from a wagon one of two bulls belonging to a cattle driver, sacrificed it, and made a meal for himself, while the cattle driver, helpless to do anything, stood upon a mountain and cursed. Therefore even now, when they sacrifice to Heracles, they do so with curses.[25]

Passing by Arabia he killed Emathion, a son of Tithonus. Next he traveled through Libya to the outer sea where he received the golden cup from the Sun. After crossing over to the mainland opposite, he shot the eagle on Mount Caucasus, offspring of Echidna and Typhon, which continually ate Prometheus' liver. He set Prometheus free, taking on himself the symbolic fetter of olive, and to Zeus offered Chiron who, although immortal, was willing to die in Prometheus' place.[26]

Prometheus advised Heracles not to go after the apples himself but to hold up the world for Atlas and send him instead. This he did when he came to the land of the Hyperboreans. Atlas got three apples from the Hesperides and, when he returned to Heracles, told him to continue holding up the world in his place (for he no longer wished to) and he himself would deliver the apples to Eurystheus. Heracles agreed, but then by a trick shifted the world back onto Atlas. For Prometheus suggested that he ask him to take it back long enough for him to put a pad against his head. When Heracles did so Atlas put the apples on the ground and took back the world. Heracles then picked up the apples and left. | Some say that he did not get them from Atlas but picked them himself after killing the serpent guarding them. | He gave them to Eurystheus, but he returned them to him and Heracles then handed them over to Athena who took the apples back to the Hesperides. For it was considered impious for them to be placed anywhere else.

12   As a twelfth labor Heracles was ordered to bring Cerberus from Hades. This creature had three dogs' heads, the tail of a serpent, and heads of different kinds of snakes down its back. Before starting after it Heracles went to Eumolpus at Eleusis, wishing to be initiated into the mysteries. Since he was polluted by the deaths of the centaurs, it was impossible for him to witness them. But Eumolpus purified him and he was initiated. He next went to the entrance of Hades at Taenarum in Laconia and descended. When the souls saw him they all fled, except Meleager and the Gorgon Medusa. Heracles drew his sword at the Gorgon thinking that she was alive, but then learned from Hermes that she was a harmless wraith. Near the gates of Hades he

found Theseus and Pirithous, the latter of whom was bound because he sought to marry Persephone. When they saw Heracles they stretched out their hands to him to be raised from the dead through his power. He grasped Theseus by the hand and restored him, but although he wished to raise up Pirithous, he let him go when the earth began to move. He also rolled away the stone of Ascalaphus. Wishing to offer blood to the souls, he slaughtered one of the cattle of Hades. Their keeper, Menoetes, son of Ceuthonymus, challenged Heracles to wrestle. Heracles grasped him around the waist and crushed his ribs but let him go at the request of Persephone. When he asked Pluto for Cerberus, the god invited him to lead the creature away if he could subdue him without using the weapons he was carrying.

Heracles found Cerberus at the gates of Acheron. Protected by his breastplate and covered by the lion's skin, he seized the monster's head with his hands and held it in a powerful stranglehold until he subdued it, although he was bitten by the serpent in its tail. He ascended with it through Troezen, but Demeter turned Ascalaphus into an owl. Heracles showed Cerberus to Eurystheus and then brought him back to Hades.[27]

6   After the labors, Heracles went to Thebes and gave Megara to Iolaus. Wishing to marry, he learned that Eurytus, ruler of Oechalia, had offered marriage with his daughter Iole as the prize to the one who defeated him and his sons at archery. He then came to Oechalia and proved superior to them at archery, but he did not get the girl, although Iphitus, the elder of the sons, said that they should give Iole to him. Eurytus and the rest, however, refused, saying that they were afraid
2   that if Heracles had children he would kill them again. Shortly afterwards, when Autolycus stole cattle from Euboea, Eurytus thought Heracles had committed the theft. Iphitus, however, did not believe it. He went to Heracles, whom he had met returning from Pherae after restoring the dead Alcestis to Admetus, and asked him to help him look for the cattle.

Heracles promised to do so and offered him hospitality, but again going mad threw him down from the walls of Tiryns. Wishing to be purified of the murder he went to Neleus, the ruler of Pylus. When Neleus refused him out of friendship for Eurytus, Heracles went to Amyclae and was purified by Deiphobus, the son of Hippolytus. He contracted a terrible disease because of the murder of Iphitus and went to Delphi to ask for a cure for it. When the Pythian priestess failed to prophesy for him, he tried to steal the tripod from the temple and set up his own oracle. Apollo fought with him but Zeus hurled a thunderbolt between them. After they were stopped from fighting Heracles received the oracle. It said that he would be cured of his disease if he
3   allowed himself to be sold, worked as a slave for three years, and paid

damages for murder to Eurytus. Upon hearing the oracle Heracles allowed Hermes to put him up for sale and he was bought by Omphale, the daughter of Iardanus and queen of the Lydians, to whom her husband Tmolus left his kingdom when he died. Eurytus did not accept the money for damages when it was offered to him.[28]

As Omphale's slave Heracles captured and tied the Cercopes at Ephesus.[29] Syleus the Lydian forced passing strangers to dig in his vineyard. After pulling up his grapevines by the roots Heracles killed Syleus and his daughter Xenodoce. Sailing to the island Doliche, he found the body of Icarus which had washed up on the shore, buried it, and changed the name of the island from Doliche to Icaria. For this reason Daedalus made a nearly life-size statue of Heracles at Pisa which Heracles, mistaking at night for a living person, struck with a rock. It was while Heracles was indentured to Omphale that the [Argonauts'] voyage to Colchis, the hunt of the Calydonian boar, and Theseus' arrival from Troezen to rid the Isthmus of dangers, were all said to have taken place.[30]

4   After serving Omphale and being cured of his disease, Heracles gathered a volunteer army of nobles and sailed to Ilium in eighteen fifty-oared ships. When he arrived, he left Oicles behind to guard the ships and set out with the rest of the army to attack the city. Laomedon, king of Ilium, attacked the ships with a large number of men, killing Oicles in the battle, but was then driven off by Heracles and his men and put under siege. During the siege Telamon was the first to breach the wall and enter the city. When Heracles, coming in next, saw that Telamon had entered before him, he drew his sword and pursued him because he did not want anyone to be thought more powerful than himself. Seeing him, Telamon began to collect stones lying nearby. When Heracles asked him what he was doing Telamon replied that he was building an altar to Heracles the Fair Victor [*Kallinikos*]. Heracles thanked him and, after capturing the city and killing Laomedon and his sons (except for Podarces), he gave Hesione, the daughter of Laomedon, to Telamon as a war prize, allowing her to take with her whomever she wished from among the war prisoners. When she chose her brother Podarces, Heracles said that he must first become a slave and then be given to her in exchange for something. So when he was put up for sale she took the veil from her head and gave it in exchange for him. Henceforth Podarces was called Priam [*priamai*, "to buy"].[31]

7   When Heracles sailed from Troy, Hera sent violent storms against him and so angered Zeus that he hung her from Olympus. Heracles sailed to Cos but the Coans, thinking that he was the leader of a band of pirates, threw stones at him and prevented him from putting in. He forced his way in at night, however, captured the island, and killed the

king Eurypylus, son of Astypalaea and Poseidon. Heracles was wounded in the battle by Chalcodon, but was snatched up by Zeus. After he sacked Cos he went to Phlegra at Athena's request and helped the gods defeat the Giants.[32]

2   Later he collected an Arcadian army to which he added volunteers from the nobles of Greece and made an expedition against Augeas. Hearing that Heracles was preparing to go to war against him, Augeas appointed Eurytus and Cteatus generals of the Eleans. They were Siamese twins and the strongest men of their generation, being sons of Molione and Actor, the brother of Augeas, | or, as it is said, of Poseidon | . Heracles happened to fall ill on the expedition and therefore made a truce with Eurytus and Cteatus. When they realized that he was ill they attacked the army and killed many. Heracles retreated, but later, during the third Isthmian festival, he ambushed and killed at Cleonae the twins whom the Eleans had sent to the festival to take part in the sacrifices, then marched to Elis and captured the city. He killed Augeas and his sons and restored Phyleus to the kingship. He also instituted the Olympian games, established an altar to Pelops, and built six altars for the twelve gods.[33]

3   After capturing Elis, Heracles marched against Pylus. He captured the city and killed Periclymenus, the bravest of Neleus' sons, who changed into different shapes when fighting. Heracles killed Neleus and his sons except for Nestor, for he was still a youth and was being reared among the Gerenians. In the battle he also wounded Pluto [Hades] who was giving aid to the Pylians.[34]

After he captured Pylus, Heracles made an expedition against Lacedaemon because he wished to avenge himself on the sons of Hippocoon. He was angry with them for allying themselves with Neleus and angrier still because they killed the son of Licymnius. For when Licymnius' son was looking at Hippocoon's palace, a Molossian dog ran out and attacked him. He threw a stone, hitting the dog, and the sons of Hippocoon then rushed out and beat him to death with their cudgels. It was to avenge this death that Heracles gathered an army to attack the Lacedaemonians. He went to Arcadia and asked Cepheus to join him as an ally with his twenty sons. But Cepheus, fearing that the Argives would march against Tegea if he left, refused to go on the expedition. Heracles had received from Athena a lock of the Gorgon's hair in a bronze jar and he now gave it to Sterope, Cepheus' daughter, saying that if an army attacked the city, she was to hold up the lock of hair three times from the walls without looking at it and the enemy would then be routed. Hearing this, Cepheus and his sons joined the expedition. In the battle both he and his sons were killed, as was Iphicles, the brother of Heracles. Heracles killed Hippocoon and his sons and after conquering the city restored Tyndareus to the kingship.

4   Passing by Tegea, Heracles seduced Auge, not knowing that she was Aleus' daughter. She later secretly gave birth to a baby and placed it in a grove sacred to Athena. A plague was ravaging the land and Aleus entered the grove to sacrifice and there discovered his daughter's baby. He exposed the child on Mount Parthenius but it was saved by divine providence, for a doe newly delivered of a fawn suckled it, and shepherds took it up, naming it Telephus. Aleus gave Auge to Nauplius, the son of Poseidon, to sell abroad in a foreign land. Nauplius gave her to Teuthras, the ruler of Teuthrania, who made her his wife.[35]

5   Heracles then went to Calydon where, seeking to marry Deianira, daughter of Oeneus, he wrestled with Achelous in order to win her. Achelous changed himself into a bull and Heracles broke off one of his horns. Heracles married Deianira and Achelous received back his horn, giving in return for it the horn of Amalthea, the daughter of Haemonius. For she possessed the horn of a bull, | which, Pherecydes says, could provide food or drink in abundance as one asked for them | .[36]

6   Heracles made an expedition with the Calydonians against the Thesprotians. After capturing the city Ephyra, the king of which was Phylas, he made love with Astyoche, the king's daughter, and became the father of Tlepolemus. Remaining there for a while, he sent word to Thespius to keep seven of his sons, to send three to Thebes and the remaining forty to the island of Sardinia to form a colony.[37] Later, while dining with Oeneus, Heracles struck with his knuckles and killed Architeles' son Eunomus while the boy was pouring water over his hands. (Eunomus was a relative of Oeneus.) His father pardoned Heracles since the boy's death was accidental.[38] Heracles, however, wanted to undergo exile in accordance with the law and so decided to go to Ceyx in Trachis.

Taking Deianira with him, he came to the river Evenus across which Nessus the centaur ferried travelers for money, claiming that because he was just he had received the right to do this from the gods. Heracles crossed the river by himself but when he was asked for the fare, he allowed Nessus to carry over Deianira. While ferrying her across Nessus tried to rape her. Heracles heard her screaming and shot Nessus in the heart as he emerged from the river. As he lay dying, he called Deianira to him and told her that if she wanted a love potion to use upon Heracles, she should mix the sperm which he had emitted on the ground with blood from the wound made by the arrow head. She did this and preserved the potion.[39]

7   Passing through the land of the Dryopes and in need of food, Heracles met Thiodamas driving a pair of bulls. He unyoked one of them, slaughtered it, and prepared a meal.[40] When he came to Ceyx at Trachis, he was welcomed by him and conquered the Dryopes.

After leaving there he fought as an ally of Aegimius, king of the Dorians, for the Lapiths, under the leadership of Coronus, were at war with him over the boundaries of the country. Being besieged he asked Heracles for help in return for a share of the land. Heracles gave his aid, killing Coronus and others, and delivered the entire country to Aegimius without recompense. He also killed Laogoras, king of the Dryopes, and his children while he was attending a banquet in a grove of Apollo. Laogoras was a violent man and an ally of the Lapiths. While passing by Itonus, Heracles was challenged to a hand to hand fight by Cycnus, son of Ares and Pelopia. Accepting the challenge he fought and killed him.[41] When he came to Ormenium, the king Amyntor tried by force to keep him from passing through, but Heracles, finding his way blocked, also killed him.

When he arrived at Trachis he gathered an army to attack Oechalia, for he wanted to avenge himself on Eurytus. Allied with him were Arcadians, Melians from Trachis, and Epicnemidian Locrians. Heracles killed Eurytus and his sons and captured the city. After burying the dead in his army (Hippasus, son of Ceyx, and Argius and Melas, sons of Licymnius) and after pillaging the city, he led off Iole as a prisoner. He came to anchor at Cenaeum, a promontory of Euboea, and there set up an altar to Zeus Cenaeus. Preparing to make a sacrifice, he sent the herald Lichas to Trachis to bring back a bright colored tunic for him. From Lichas Deianira learned about Iole and, fearing that Heracles loved her more than herself, applied to the tunic the blood of Nessus, believing that it was a love potion. Heracles put on the tunic and began to perform the sacrifice. As soon as the tunic was warmed, the poison of the hydra began to eat into his skin. Heracles picked up Lichas by the feet and flung him down from the promontory. He tried to tear off the tunic but it stuck to his body and he pulled his flesh off with it. In this condition he was brought back by ship to Trachis. Deianira hanged herself when she learned what had happened. Heracles commanded Hyllus, his elder son by Deianira, to marry Iole when he reached manhood, then went to Mount Oeta (in Trachis) and there constructed a pyre, climbed upon it and ordered it to be ignited. When no one would light it, Poeas, who was passing by in search of his flocks, set fire to it. Heracles then bequeathed his bow to him. While the pyre was burning a cloud is said to have enveloped Heracles and to have raised him up to heaven with a crash of thunder. Thenceforth he was immortal. He was reconciled to Hera and married her daughter Hebe,

8   by whom he had sons Alexiares and Anicetus.[42] | The sons born to
Heracles by the daughters of Thespius are as follows: By Procris he
had Antileon and Hippeus (for the oldest daughter had twins); by
Panope, Threpsippas; by Lyse, Eumedes; . . . , Creon; by Epilais, Astyanax; by Certhe, Iobes; by Eurybia, Polylaus; by Patro, Archemachus;
by Meline, Laomedon; by Clytippe, Eurycapys; by Eubote, Eurypylus;
by Aglaia, Antiades; by Chryseis, Onesippus; by Oria, Laomenes; by
Lysidice, Teles; by Menippis, Entelides; by Anthippe, Hippodromus;
by Eury . . . , Teleutagoras; by Hippo, Capylus; by Euboea, Olympus;
by Nice, Nicodromus; by Argele, Cleolaus; by Exole, Erythras; by
Xanthis, Homolippus; by Stratonice, Atromus; by Iphis, Celeustanor;
by Laothoe, Antiphus; by Antiope, Alopius; by Calametis, Astybies; by
Phyleis, Tigasis; by Aeschreis, Leucones; by Anthea, . . . ; by Eurypyle,
Archedicus; by Erato, Dynastes; by Asopis, Mentor; by Eone, Ames-
trius; by Tiphyse, Lyncaeus; by Olympusa, Halocrates; by Heliconis,
Phalias; by Hesychia, Oestrobles; by Terpsicrate, Euryopes; by Elachia,
Buleus; by Nicippe, Antimachus; by Pyrippe, Patroclus; by Praxithea,
Nephus; by Lysippe, Erasippus; by Toxicrate, Lycurgus; by Marse, Bu-
colus; by Eurytele, Leucippus; and by Hippocrate, Hippozygus. These
were Heracles' sons by the daughters of Thespius.

Heracles also had sons by other women. By Deianira, daughter of
Oeneus, he had Hyllus, Ctesippus, Glenus and Onites; by Megara,
daughter of Creon, Therimachus, Deicoon and Creontiades; by Omphale, Agelaus, from whom the family of Croesus was descended; by
Chalciope, daughter of Eurypylus, Thettalus; by Epicaste, daughter of
Augeas, Thestalus; by Parthenope, daughter of Stymphalus, Everes;
by Auge, daughter of Aleus, Telephus; by Astyoche, daughter of Phylas, Tlepolemus; by Astydamia, daughter of Amyntor, Ctesippus; by
Autonoe, daughter of Pireus, Palaemon. |

8   After Heracles joined the gods his sons went to Ceyx to escape
from Eurystheus. But when Eurystheus ordered Ceyx to give them up
and threatened war, they left Trachis in fear and fled through Greece.
They arrived at Athens in their flight, took seats at the altar of Mercy,
and asked for help.[43] The Athenians refused to surrender them and
went to war against Eurystheus, killing his sons, Alexander, Iphimedon,
Eurybius, Mentor, and Perimedes. Eurystheus himself escaped in a
chariot, but was pursued and killed by Hyllus just as he drove past the
Scironian Rocks. Hyllus cut off his head and gave it to Alcmena who
dug out the eyes with weaving pins.[44]

2   After Eurystheus died, the sons of Heracles returned to the Peloponnese and captured all the cities. A year after their return a plague
gripped the entire Peloponnese. An oracle revealed that the sons of
Heracles caused it by returning before the proper time. They then left

1975   BASKIN·   TYPHON

the Peloponnese, went to Marathon, and settled there. Tlepolemus had killed Licymnius accidentally before they left the Peloponnese. (Licymnius had placed himself between Tlepolemus and a servant he was beating with a stick.) Therefore he fled to Rhodes with a group of men and settled there. Hyllus, obeying his father's command, married Iole, and sought to bring about the return of the sons of Heracles. He went to Delphi to inquire how they might come back. The god said for them to wait and return at the third harvest. Hyllus thought that the third harvest meant the third year and so, after waiting that length of time, he returned with his army to the Peloponnese when Tisamenus, son of Orestes, was king there.

In the battle that ensued, the Peloponnesians won and Aristomachus, Hyllus' grandson, died. When Aristomachus' sons reached manhood they consulted the oracle about their return. The god gave the same answer as before and Temenus objected, saying that when they had formerly obeyed it they had suffered misfortune. The god replied that they were to blame for their misfortune because they misunderstood the oracle, for by "the third harvest" was meant not a harvest from the earth but that of a family line, and by "narrows" was meant the broad-bellied sea on the right of the Isthmus. Hearing this Temenus equipped his army and built ships in Locris, now called Naupactus ["Shipbuilding Town"]. While the army was there Aristodemus was struck and killed by a thunderbolt, leaving twin sons, Eurysthenes

3 and Procles, by Argia, daughter of Autesion. It also happened that the army suffered a disaster at Naupactus. For a seer appeared to the soldiers, prophesying in an inspired state. They thought that he was a magician sent by the Peloponnesians to work mischief on the army, so Hippotes, the son of Phylas, the son of Antiochus, the son of Heracles, threw a javelin at him and killed him. Because of this the fleet was destroyed and the army suffered from famine and so was discharged. Temenus consulted an oracle and the god told him that these disasters had happened because of the seer. He was ordered to banish his murderer for ten years and to use the Three-Eyed One as a guide. So they banished Hippotes and sought out the guide.

They came upon Oxylus, the son of Andraemon, sitting on a one-eyed horse. (The other eye had been put out by an arrow.) He had fled to Elis after committing a murder and a year later was returning to Aetolia. On the basis of the oracle they made him their guide. They then met the enemy, defeated both the army and the navy, and killed Tisamenus, the son of Orestes. Their allies, Pamphylus and Dymas, the sons of Aegimius, also died in the battle.

4 When they had gained control of the Peloponnese, they set up three altars to Zeus the Father, sacrificed upon them, and decided to cast

lots for the cities. The first lot was to be for Argos, the second for
Lacedaemon, and the third for Messene. They got a pitcher of water
into which each was to drop a pebble. Temenus and the sons of Aristodemus, Procles and Eurysthenes, dropped in two pebbles, but Cresphontes, wishing to receive Messene, dropped in a clod of earth. Since
this dissolved it was inevitable that only two lots appear. When Temenus' stone was drawn out first, and that of the sons of Aristodemus
5   second, Cresphontes received Messene. They found signs lying on the
altars at which they sacrificed: for those who got Argos there was a
toad, for those who got Lacedaemon, a snake and for those who got
Messene, a fox. The seers interpreted the signs in this way: It was
better for those who found the toad to remain in their city (for this
creature has no strength for walking); those who found the snake
would be fearsome in attack; and those who found the fox would be
crafty.

Now Temenus ignored his sons, Agelaus, Eurypylus, and Callias, in
favor of his daughter Hyrnetho and her husband, Deiphontes. The sons
therefore hired men to kill their father. After he was murdered the
army decided that Hyrnetho and Deiphontes should have the kingdom.

Cresphontes had not ruled for long over Messene when he was
murdered with two of his sons. Polyphontes, a descendant of the sons
of Heracles, then became king and took Merope, the widow of the
murdered king to be his wife against her will. He, too, was killed.
For Merope had a third son, Aepytus, whom she had given to her
father to rear. When he reached manhood he returned secretly, killed
Polyphontes, and regained his ancestral kingdom.[45]

NOTES
(2. 4. 8–2. 8. 5)

1   The modern Greek writer Nikos Kazantzakis inscribed on the
lintel above the door of his house in Crete the words "Everything too
much," thus advertising his view of the meaning of life and the way
to salvation in direct contradiction of the inscription, "Nothing too
much," which Greeks in antiquity saw as they entered Apollo's temple at Delphi (Plato *Charmides* 165a), and which reminded them of
the canonical status in Greek culture of the value of restraint and
moderation.

Kazantzakis' motto aptly fits the mythological figure, Heracles, "who
pushed everything—both good and bad—to superhuman excess..."
(G. Karl Galinsky, *The Herakles Theme* [Oxford, 1972], 82).

It is fitting that the hero of excess was excessively represented:

The "range of his manifestations" in antiquity was "massive," Galinsky says: "The mythological tradition and the ancient literary tradition endowed Herakles more richly than any other ancient hero" (297).

Students of Greek culture should reflect on the gap between Greek preachment—"Nothing too much"—and (mythological) practice: Heracles, the hero of excess, was the most popular Greek hero: "[T]he mythical Herakles was the one true Panhellenic hero. . . . [H]e was the national hero of Greece. . . . [A]ll over Greece Herakles was worshipped as . . . [*alexikakos*], the averter of evil, which was understood in its broadest sense—war, death, ghosts, sickness, and the trials and tribulations of life in general. Against all these the common man called upon him as a trusty and invincible divine helper" (2–3, 4). The gap mentioned above is just a way of saying that ancient Greek culture was more complex (even contradictory) than we realize.

Where did Heracles come from? How is his name, which means "the glory of Hera," to be explained since Hera persecuted him? Martin P. Nilsson, *The Mycenaean Origin of Greek Mythology*, with a New Introduction and Bibliography by Emily Vermeule (Berkeley, Los Angeles, and London, 1972), ch. 3, "Heracles," 187–220, believes that "Heracles" was a common name once widely used. The name precedes the hero; it was not derived from the myth to characterize him. Heracles, moreover, was a fictitious, not a real, person who was localized at various places. Thus he had no burial place (191–93).

Nevertheless, the Heracles who performed the twelve labors lived at Tiryns and was a vassal of Eurystheus, king of Mycenae. His birth at Thebes and localization at Tiryns presented problems for the ancient mythographers. For Nilsson, however, the question Is Heracles originally Theban or Tirynthian? is wrong because the hero is not bound to any locality. That said, though, Nilsson acknowledges that the Greeks tended to localize heroes and so Heracles' placement at Thebes and at Tiryns is old. His story was divided between the two kingdoms: birth at Thebes, labors originating from Tiryns. Tiryns was a town of importance in the Mycenaean age. The localization of Heracles' myths at Tiryns and at Thebes belongs to this period. His first five labors were performed in the neighborhood of Tiryns, and he performed all his labors at the command of Eurystheus, the king of Mycenae. Archaeological and Homeric evidence show that the king of Mycenae was the overlord of the ruler of Tiryns who was his vassal (206–09).

When the Mycenaean kingdom broke down and independent cities arose, the post-Mycenaean age needed a new reason to explain Heracles' subjection to Eurystheus. Enter Hera, the "invidious stepmother" who imposes difficult or impossible tasks on her stepson. Heracles' name, Nilsson states, was the reason that this role was given to Hera.

She was already Tiryns' chief goddess and Heracles' stepmother in fact (210–11).

The existence of a Heracles epic, which created a Heracles cycle of poems, and its time-relation to Homer are problematic (194). The Heracles cycle seems fully developed in Homer where we find the three categories of the myths (Labors, Incidentals, Deeds: see 195), but not the hero's death and apotheosis on Mount Oeta (199). If Homer knew the Heracles cycle, then it seems reasonable to suppose that the Heracles epic, from which it originated, is earlier than Homer, a conclusion Nilsson flatly rejects (194).

In the archaic period (sixth to early fifth centuries b.c.) the Heracles cycle of poems contained at least five works, the latest being the *Heraclea* in fourteen books (9,000 lines) by Panyassis, an early fifth-century poet who was the uncle of Herodotus (Albin Lesky, *A History of Greek Literature*, trans. James Willis and Cornelis de Heer, [New York, 1966], 106 and Galinsky, *The Herakles Theme*, 23–24 and 38, n. 1 to ch. 2).

Heracles' representation in Greek and Latin literatures (and beyond) is enormous, as noted—one need only consult Galinsky's *Herculis labor* to grasp the importance of this mythological figure for Greek and Roman and, indeed, Western culture, from pre-Homeric times to the twentieth century. This very importance, however, with its multiplicity of representations creates a problem. The temptation is to seek something like a Platonic Form of Heracles: the "essential" Heracles, behind all his manifestations. Galinsky well warns that "... the variety of Herakles' roles defies any systematization in the form of thesis or all-embracing exegesis" (294).

Perhaps we lack a terminology (due to deficiency in our modes of thought) by which to relate the "phenomena" grouped under the name "Heracles." In any case, the impossibility of "summing up" Heracles should cause us no more dismay than the impossibility of summing up "the human."

An important book, ignored by Galinsky, Philip E. Slater's *The Glory of Hera* (Boston, 1968), which translates the name Heracles, aims to describe the "social pathology of Greek civilization" through an analysis of Greek mythology, and especially myths of Heracles (xxii; a much shortened version was published as "The Greek Family in History and Myth" in *Arethusa* 7. 1 [1974], 9–44). The position of women in Greece and male attitudes toward them were both cause and symptom of this pathology into which ancient Greek culture was locked in a continuing destructive cycle. The cycle began with derogation of women and sex antagonism (5). Rejection and derogation of women led to rejection and derogation by them of child-rearing: "The Athenian adult male fled the home" and thus "the Athenian male child grew up in a female-dominated environment" (7). Women were all powerful in the home and the Greek male child, experiencing this, grew up with an intense fear of women (8). What caused this fear? According to Slater women's low status and male terror of women "were mutually reinforcing in Hellenic society..." (8). Confined to the home and more or less abandoned by their husbands soon after marriage, Greek women both were sexually deprived and felt humiliated by males (23). The result of these "marital strains" was "maternal scapegoating" (23): The mother vented her feelings on her children, especially her male children (28), hence their fear of women. These feelings, highly charged, were both negative (since she was angry) and positive—too positive (since she was deprived), in other words, highly ambivalent. She wants "to exalt and to belittle her son, to feed on him and to destroy him" (33).

The Greek male child responded to this ambivalence by becoming highly narcissistic—preoccupied with his masculine identity (33 ff.). He also fled the home as soon as possible and preferred to congregate with other (equally narcissistic) males. The cycle is complete: "A society which derogates women produces envious mothers who produce narcissistic males who are prone to derogate women" (45).

Slater adduces two hypotheses to account for this destructive cycle: (1) the transition from matriarchy to patriarchy, whether gradual or sudden (72); and (2) urbanization, which made the husband more absent from the home and confined the wife more, and the attendant breakdown of the extended family, both of which put an unusual burden on the nuclear family which it was very poorly equipped to carry (73).

In the chapter entitled "The Multiple Defenses of Heracles" (337–96), Slater says that "... Heracles exemplifies every mode of response to maternal threat" from Hera's persecution of him (338). In Heracles we find a "compulsive assertion of strength, or, to put it the other way around, a vigorous denial of weakness in the face of maternal hostility" (339). At the same time "the consistent, overt, manifest theme in the Heraclean tales ... is his laboring and suffering" (340).

But the relation between Hera and Heracles was by no means always negative. It was ambivalent and hence "tapped something meaningful in ... [the Greeks'] experience" (340). In essence, the relation was that of mother and son and "it made sense to the Greeks for a maternal figure to use a male both as an extension of herself and as an object of persecution" (343).

Heracles' responses to Hera are a "crude hypermasculinity" (369), particularly in his attack on women, and a "self-abasing strategy," a life of "suffering, servitude and degradation" in which he "consistently performs 'dirty work' for others . . ." (375).

Heracles is "a curious contradiction. On the one hand he is all impulse, with his gross appetites and lack of restraint. . . . On the other, he is a man engaged in chronic labor, with no release from suffering. . . . Heracles is a civilizing force, but not civilized. He is proto-urban, but not urban, chronically industrious without the capacity for sustained effort and self-denial. His is the blind and uncontrolled narcissistic ambition out of which the capacity for civilization may accidentally arise. From his blocked pleasure derives the energy for cultural achievements" (388). As such, for Slater "Heracles, more than any other figure, was a symbol for Greece itself" (387).

While Slater is by no means immune to criticism (see ch. 1, n. 11 for reference to Sarah B. Pomeroy's reservations expressed about his use of evidence), he has managed to make some sense out of contradictory and baffling aspects of Greek culture to which classicists have paid little attention. He has also assimilated the varied manifestations of Heracles into a unity, the difficulty of which was noted above. He does so by fitting these features onto a psychoanalytic, basically Freudian, frame. But the frame itself presumes and imparts unity and so presents us with a "coherent" Heracles. Some, many, or conceivably all of the results may be valid, but it must be remembered that it is the frame which gives unity. Furthermore, whether *any* mythological figure, much less Heracles, can stand as a metaphor for a culture and then be analyzed as though *it*, the figure, were a "person," the analysis then yielding "facts" about the culture—that is problematic indeed.

Heracles in Greek and Latin literature

Homer

Iliad 2. 653–66: Tlepolemos, son of Heracles by Astyocheia, whom he took from Ephyra after he sacked many cities. . . . (Catalog of Ships).

Iliad 2. 678–79: Pheidippos and Antiphos, sons of Thessalos, son of Heracles. . . . (Catalog of Ships).

Iliad 5. 392–404: Aphrodite, wounded by Diomedes in battle, is consoled by her mother, Dione, who tells how Heracles wounded Hera and Hades at Pylos.

Iliad 5. 628–51: Tlepolemos, son of Heracles, taunts Sarpedon as not being Zeus' son and a lesser man than Heracles, who made an expedition against Troy. After their verbal exchange Sarpedon kills Tlepolemos, although the latter's thrown spear wounds him in the thigh (5. 652–62).

Iliad 8. 360–69: Athena complains that Zeus is ungrateful (in helping the Trojans) and does not remember the time she rescued his son Heracles when Eurystheus' labors were too much for him. Time and again Heracles cried to heaven and Zeus sent Athena to help him. If she had acted then like Zeus acts now, she says, Heracles would never have returned from Hades with Cerberus.

Iliad 11. 689–93: Nestor refers to the reduced state of Pylos from the time Heracles conquered it, killing eleven of Neleus' twelve sons. (Only Nestor escaped; see 1. 9. 9 and 2. 7. 3).

Iliad 14. 249–60 (with 15. 18–30): Both passages refer to the storm Hera raised against Heracles, driving him to Cos, when he sailed from Troy after sacking it. In the former passage Sleep reminds Hera that he put Zeus to sleep, allowing her to attack Heracles. In the latter passage Zeus reminds Hera of the time he suspended her from heaven with anvils on her feet because of her attack on Heracles at sea. At that time Zeus rescued Heracles and brought him back to Argos.

Iliad 14. 323–24: Zeus acknowledges his amour with Alcmena, who bore him Heracles, in a passage intended to flatter Hera.

Iliad 15. 638–40: Hector kills the son of Copreus, who took messages to Heracles from Eurystheus (who was afraid of him: 2. 5. 1).

Iliad 18. 114–19: Achilles accepts the death that will come to him after he kills Hector. For not even powerful Heracles, Zeus' dearest son, escaped death: His fate and Hera's relentless anger conquered him.

Iliad 19. 95–133: Agamemnon, apologizing for his part in the quarrel with Achilles, says that he was deluded even as Hera deluded Zeus by contriving for Eurystheus to be born on the day which Zeus intended for Heracles' birth after decreeing that his descendant born that day would rule his neighbors. Zeus was so angry with Delusion that he hurled her from heaven by the hair of her head, and grieved whenever he saw Heracles carrying out some shameful task set for him by Eurystheus.

Iliad 20. 144–48: Poseidon and Hera at Troy return from the battlefield to the stronghold of Heracles which the Trojans and Athena built for him to escape from the sea monster whenever it rushed at him from the shore.

Odyssey 8. 223–25: Odysseus, taunted and angered by two Phaeacian youths for his supposed lack of physical prowess, hurls the discus further than any Phaeacian. He then challenges them all (except his host) to any kind of contest and particularly boasts of his excellence with the bow. "But with men of yore I shall not wish to compete, neither with Heracles nor with Eurytus the Oechalian, who even were wont to compete with the immortals in archery."

Odyssey 11. 266–70: Odysseus in the underworld sees Alcmena, the wife of Amphitryon, "who bore Heracles, courageous, lion-hearted, after she made love in the arms of great Zeus. And Megara [I saw] ... married to Amphitryon's son [Heracles], always inexhaustible in might."

Odyssey 11. 601–27: (11. 565–627 are considered spurious. See W. B. Stanford, ed., *The Odyssey of Homer*, 2 vols. [London and New York, 1959], 1. 381.) "I made out strong Heracles," Odysseus says, "and all around him swirled the dead screaming like frightened birds. He was like black night, bow naked, arrow on string, peering fiercely, poised to shoot. Awesome was the sword belt about his chest, a baldric of gold engraved with incredible deeds: conflicts and battles and murders and man-slayings. May the craftsman who made it never make another such, the man who added that baldric to his art!

"He recognized me at once, when his eyes fastened on me, and grieving for me spoke winged words: 'Zeus-born son of Laertes, inventive Odysseus, poor wretch, so you, too, are suffering some evil fate such as I endured in the light of the sun. I was a son of Zeus, son of Cronus, but endless misery was my lot. I was bound over to a man far inferior and he set upon me hard labors. And once he sent me to bring the dog [from Hades]. For he reckoned no other ordeal to be more difficult for me than this. But I brought it up, led the dog from Hades. Hermes and grey-eyed Athena escorted me.' When he finished speaking he went back inside the house of Hades."

Odyssey 21. 11–38: Penelope goes to the palace store room to fetch Odysseus' bow for the suitors' contest. The passage begins (11), "There lay the supple bow and the arrow-holding quiver," and Homer goes on to relate that Odysseus as a lad had received the bow from Iphitus, son of Eurytus, whom he met in Lacedaemon at the house of Ortilochus where he had been sent by his father and the elders of Ithaca to recover cattle stolen by Messenians. Iphitus was there in search of twelve mares which had strayed with their mule-colts. Later these caused his death, for when he came to the house of Zeus' son, Heracles, "perpetrator of great deeds, he killed him, guest-friend though he was, in his house, foul man, and had no respect for the watch the gods keep, nor the table which he set for him. But after that, he even slew him, and possessed the strong-hooved mares in his hall. While looking for them [earlier], Iphitus had met Odysseus and gave him the bow which great Eurytus used to carry and bequeathed to his boy as he lay dying in the lofty palace. Odysseus gave him in return a sharp sword and trusty spear, the beginning of a close friendship. But they did not get to know each other at table, for before that Zeus' son murdered Iphitus, son of Eurytus. . . ."

Odysseus' encounter in the underworld with the lonely Heracles, pathetically armed and ever on the *qui vive* amid the dead, seems to be picked up by Kazantzakis in books 14 and 16 of his *Odyssey*, although Heracles there is Odysseus' great spiritual ancestor and fellow bowman who lays upon him a thirteenth labor. The probable spuriousness of the passage need not lead us to dismiss the haunting image of Heracles which it presents.

The final passage in the *Odyssey* describing Heracles' slaughter of Iphitus, in flagrant violation of *xenia* ("guest-friendship"), a powerful Homeric code, is, as Galinsky says, "one of the most devastating indictments of Herakles in literature . . ." (*The Herakles Theme*, 12).

The Homeric *Hymn 15, to Heracles*

After the first three lines describing Heracles' birth, the poem (9 lines in all) shows a remarkable similarity to the opening lines of the *Odyssey*, as if the author of the hymn (which T. W. Allen, W. R. Halliday, and E. E. Sikes, eds., *The Homeric Hymns* [Oxford, 1936], 396, date to the sixth century B.C. or later) deliberately linked Heracles and his career to Odysseus and his. The connection between Heracles and Odysseus made by the writer of the Homeric *Hymn* gives a basis in ancient literature to the link Kazantzakis creates between the two heroes in his *Odyssey* (in books 14 and 16).

Hesiod

Theogony: References to Heracles begin and end with mention of his killing of Geryon (289, 982). In a poem of 1022 lines Heracles makes significant appearances at roughly the one-third mark (313–18: Heracles and Iolaus kill the Hydra with Athena's help; 326–32: Heracles kills the Nemean lion); the halfway mark (526–34: Heracles kills the eagle devouring Prometheus' liver and frees him from his troubles); and the end (950–55: After he completed his labors Heracles marries Hebe, daughter of Zeus and Hera on Olympus and is called "blessed" because he accomplished a great work and lives among the immortals, carefree and unaging all his days.) The only other reference to Heracles is at 943: his birth from Alcmena and Zeus.

Shield of Heracles: Authorship by Hesiod is uncertain. The poem, 480 lines long, tells of Heracles' battle against Cycnus, the son of Ares, who killed pilgrims on the way to Delphi. It also describes at length Heracles' shield (139–321), hence its title.

Lyric poetry (except for Pindar)

For infrequent references to Heracles in lyric poetry, see Galinsky, *The Herakles Theme*, 19–21.

The six line fragment of an *epinikion* or victory song by Archilochus (120 in E. Diehl, ed., *Anthologia Lyrica Graeca* [Leipzig, 1958]) may be singled out for mention. It begins, "Hurrah! for the fair victor, lord Heracles, hail!" and continues in the same vein with two more "Hurrahs!" The length of the poem is unknown but it was used as an impromptu (as against commissioned) victory song for winners in athletic contests (see the opening lines of Pindar *Ol.* 9).

An elegiac poem of Tyrtaeus (8 in Diehl, *Anthologia*), an exhortation to valor addressed to Spartan youths, may also be mentioned here. It begins, "Take courage! For you are the race of Heracles unconquerable," as if the utterance of the very name would quicken the hearers into brave action.

Pindar

It is not unnatural that myths of Greece's panhellenic hero should appear with great frequency in the poetry of Greece's panhellenic (and greatest lyric) poet, forty-three of whose forty-five extant poems, about one-fourth of his *oeuvre*, were composed to praise victors at the Olympian, Pythian, Nemean, and Isthmian games, the great panhellenic festivals of Greece. In addition, Heracles appealed to Pindar because of the Dorian background common to myth figure and to poet, and because the hero was considered the founder of the Olympian games, the foremost of the Greek athletic contests (see, e.g., *Ol.* 2. 3–4; *Ol.* 3. 9–38; *Ol.* 6. 67–70; *Ol.* 10. 24–30, 43–59; *Nem.* 10. 32–33; and *Nem.* 11. 27–28).

More importantly, Heracles, a "hero god" for Pindar (*Nem.* 3. 22), was the finest mythical exemplar for what is the "catholic and momentous" subject of Pindar's poetry, "human accomplishment" (David C. Young, *Three Odes of Pindar* [Leiden, 1968], 112). "Thou art able often to give men a bulwark against paralysis of inaction," Pindar prays to Heracles (*Nem.* 7. 96–97), and therefore, "Foolish the man who does not sing Heracles" (*Pyth.* 9. 87). Pindar sang the hero repeatedly, but *Nem.* 1 contains the poet's "most inspired expression of his faith in Herakles" (Galinsky, *The Herakles Theme*, 35–36). The myth, taking up a little more than half of the ode (33–72, end) narrates the life of Heracles from birth to apotheosis with an incredible rapidity emphasizing his earliest feat, the strangling of the two serpents sent by Hera to kill him. The myth (and the poem) concludes, "And in peace for all of endless time, tranquillity in a blest house his chief reward after great exhaustion, he would take blossoming Hebe as his wife in marriage, and feasting by the side of Zeus, the son of Cronus, he would commend holy order" (69–72).

"The final phrase sums up all the philosophic optimism implicit in the entire myth: the poet as well as the hero looks with magnificent inclusiveness over the whole heroic career from birth through seemingly endless and omnipresent trials to blissful attainment, and finds it all good," Peter W. Rose, "The Myth of Pindar's First *Nemean*, ...," *Harv. Stud. in Class. Phil.* 78 (1974), 162 (which see for a balanced analysis of the poem and the part the myth plays in it).

In another poem, of which only a fragment remains (Snell 169), Pindar celebrates order and illustrates its value with a myth of Heracles. The poem begins: "Order [*nomos*], the king of all, men and gods alike, takes the lead, bringing the most violent to judgment with authoritative hand. I judge this from the deeds of Heracles" (1–5). He then briefly mentions Heracles' driving away the cattle of Geryon before turning to a lengthy treatment of his taming the violent man-eating mares of Diomedes. Pindar vividly describes them pulling apart and devouring a groomsman with munching of teeth and crunching of bone as Heracles attacks them (23–32). Such violence is obviously the antithesis of order, the establishment of which through his labors is, to Pindar, Heracles' essential heroic role.

Bacchylides

Although Heracles is mentioned in several of the nineteen poems of Bacchylides which survive, it is *Ode 5* which presents the hero as a developed character. At lines 56–175 of that poem Bacchylides tells of Heracles' encounter with Meleager in the underworld (see ch. 2, n. 9). The meeting of the two heroes was more than likely Bacchylides' invention, according to Adam M. Parry, and "his greatest single stroke of genius" (Robert Fagles, trans., *Bacchylides: Complete Poems*, With ... Introduction and Notes by Adam M. Parry [New Haven and London, 1961], 110). Bacchylides' creation of a complex and compassionate hero and his dramatic treatment of the myth (foreshadowing Euripides' more fully developed characterization of Heracles) makes the poem "a turning point in the literary tradition of Herakles" (Galinsky, *The Herakles Theme*, 27–28). For a recent thoroughgoing discussion of the poem, see Mary R. Lefkowitz, "Bacchylides' *Ode 5*: Imitation and Originality," *Harv. Stud. in Class. Phil.* 73 (1968), 45–96.

In poem 9. 6–9 and the surviving opening lines of 13 (the beginning of the poem is lost), Bacchylides refers to Heracles' first labor, the killing of the Nemean lion.

Poem 16 offers the sequel to the myth told in *Ode 5*: Deianira, consumed by jealousy, sends to Heracles, returning home with his new bride Iole, a robe smeared with what she thinks is a love potion to regain his love. The potion is actually virulent poison given to Deianira by the dying centaur, Nessus, and causes Heracles' death (see 2. 7. 6–7).

Herodotus

In book 2. 42–45 Herodotus, in an excursus on Heracles, says that the Greeks took his name from Egypt. (Amphitryon and Alcmena were of Egyptian origin, he says.) He concludes that Heracles is a very ancient god. At 4. 8–10 Herodotus says that Heracles was the founder of the Scythian race.

Aeschylus

In *Prometheus Bound*, the only surviving play of the trilogy, *Prometheia*, Prometheus predicts to Io that her descendant, Heracles, will free him from Zeus' torture (771–74, 870–72). This Heracles does in the *Prometheus Unbound*, probably the second play of the trilogy, of which sufficient fragments survive to enable us to reconstruct something of its action. In this play "the destinies of the two heroes have become interlocked, and at the close . . . our interest has been transferred in some measure to [Heracles]" (George Thomson, *Aeschylus and Athens* [London, 1966], 314). In fact, Heracles, half-mortal and so closer to mankind than Prometheus, is to continue on earth the benefactions to the human race begun by the Titan (Galinsky, *The Herakles Theme,* 44–45). See also 2. 5. 4 and 2. 5. 11, which describe Heracles' release of Prometheus by substituting for him the centaur Chiron whom Heracles accidentally shot with a poisoned arrow, making a wound which would not heal. But since Chiron was immortal, he could not die, although he wished to. His immortality was transferred to Prometheus (who was immortal, too, but the myth is not entirely logical) who was then freed and Chiron was able to die.

Sophocles

The Women of Trachis: The tragedy uses the myth of Heracles' accidental death caused by his wife, Deianira, jealous of Iole, the new young bride by whom she is being replaced. See 2. 7. 6–7 and n. 42 below.

Philoctetes: One of Sophocles' last plays (usually dated 409 B.C.), the drama presents Heracles as a *deus ex machina* (1409–44 and 1449–51) who commands the intransigent Philoctetes to go to Troy. His bow is indispensable to the Greek chieftains who ten years earlier marooned him on the uninhabited island of Lemnos to rid themselves of his constant cries of pain and the stench from a serpent bite on his foot which would not heal. The appearance at the end of the play of a deified Heracles is Sophocles' invention, but the basis for it, and for Heracles' claim on Philoctetes, is part of the myth tradition: Philoctetes got possession of Heracles' bow which the latter gave either to him (*Philoctetes* 799–803) or to his father, Poeas (2. 7. 7), for lighting his funeral pyre on Mount Oeta, enabling him to die and so to be released from the intolerable pain caused by Nessus' poison, which could not kill him since he was half immortal.

The bow is Philoctetes' only means of staying alive on the deserted island. But the Greeks at Troy must have it, too, for the city's capture is impossible without it, as a seer has told them. The chieftains therefore send Odysseus and the innocent and noble Neoptolemus, son of Achilles, to obtain the bow with or without Philoctetes. Odysseus, intent on gaining the bow by whatever means, tries to manipulate Neoptolemus into taking it by deceit. The young hero ultimately repudiates Odysseus and sides with Philoctetes. Heracles appears in the final scene as the embodiment of the values which have been tested in the play and which have emerged victorious: accomplishment through decency rather than by violent opportunism. "First I shall tell you [Philoctetes] of my experience: the toil, the effort, the pain which I went through until I possessed achievement for all time, as you see me now," Heracles says. "And you as well are bound to undergo this suffering, from these labors to create a life worthy of remembrance" (1418–22). He ends his instruction to Philoctetes and Neoptolemus: "Heed this, when you conquer that land, keep holy before god. For Father Zeus thinks all else of less moment. Yea verily, holiness does not die with the men who die. Whether they live or die it does not perish" (1440–44).

Euripides

Alcestis: See ch. 2, n. 20, 1. 9.15 and 2. 6. 2.

Heracles Mainomenos (= *Hercules Furens*): See 2. 4. 12 and n. 6 below.

Aristophanes

Heracles' appearances in satyr plays, farces, and comedies were far more numerous than his parts in tragedies (Galinsky, *The Herakles Theme*, 81). Most of these works are lost except for fragments, but it is possible at least to view the comic treatment Aristophanes gives him in two plays, *Birds* and *Frogs*. In two plays, *Peace* (752–60) and *Wasps* (1029–43), Aristophanes views himself as a Heracles fighting "beasts" (chiefly the politician, Cleon, but also other scurrilous types) on Athens' behalf.

Apollonius Rhodius

Argonautica (on which see ch. 3., n. 1): Gilbert Lawall, "Apollonius' *Argonautica*: Jason as Anti-Hero," *Yale Class. Stud.* 19 (1966), discusses at length Heracles' role in Apollonius' epic as a "foil" to Jason (124), whose active, violent character is "in direct contradiction to Jason's." Heracles is "awesome but palaeolithic" (128): His chief resource, physical strength, is not sufficient. He does not belong in the (Hellenistic) world but is rather a throwback to a bygone mythical age (131).

Theocritus

Idyll 13 (see ch. 3, n. 4): The poet uses the myth of Heracles and Hylas, his young lover on the Argo who is kidnapped by nymphs when the ship puts in at Mysia for water. Heracles goes berserk in the (pastoral) woods searching for Hylas. Theocritus thus illustrates "the dichotomy between the heroic and the erotic," as Donald J. Mastronarde, "Theocritus' *Idyll* 13," *TAPA* 99 (1968), 279, puts it. The poem (and Theocritus' use of Heracles) touches upon a literary and philosophical predicament of the poet's and subsequent eras: What is the relevance of heroic epic to a postheroic age which still uses the material of, and feels itself culturally a part of, the earlier tradition? (289; On Heracles in Theocritus *Idyll* 13, see also Galinsky, *The Herakles Theme*, 117–19).

Idyll 24 narrates the myth of the infant Heracles' strangling of the two serpents sent by Hera. Theocritus more or less follows Pindar *Nem.* 1 but "he is at pains to reduce ... [the myth] from a heroic to a domestic level" (A. S. F. Gow, ed., *Theocritus*, 2 vols. [Cambridge, Eng., 1952], 2. 415).

Idyll 25 (falsely attributed to Theocritus): The setting is Heracles' journey to and return from Augeas in Elis, whose stables he cleaned, but the labor itself is omitted.

The structure of the poem seems peculiar in omitting what would be thought its most important element: Heracles' cleaning of Augeas' stables. But the poet instead chose for his themes the landscape and Heracles' conversation with Phyleus, the son of Augeas, to whom he describes the killing of the Nemean lion. The Augean labor becomes the context for Heracles' narration. "This conception of an epic in miniature ... is novel and ingenious, and it is very skilfully handled" (paraphrase and quotation from Gow, *Theocritus*, 2. 439).

Plautus

Amphitryo, a comedy (Plautus calls it a "tragicomedy," 59, 63), has as its theme Zeus' seduction of Alcmena during the absence of Amphitryon, in whose guise the god appears (see ch. 4, n. 16).

Lucretius

At *De Rerum Natura* 5. 22–54 Lucretius uses Heracles as a foil for Epicurus, whom the poet extols throughout his work as mankind's greatest benefactor. The monsters which Heracles subdued are at the end of the earth where no one ever goes. Wild beasts continue to live in the forests, but we can avoid them. Rather, our hearts must be purged of the battle and dangers inside them. The true "beasts" are desire and fear, pride, meanness, caprice, luxury, and boredom. Epicurus, who can subdue all these and expel them from the mind by words and not by weapons, is a god. That is, Epicurus is a "truer" Heracles.

Virgil

Aeneid: In book 8 Aeneas, arrived in Italy, seeks help from Evander, a Greek who is king of the Arcadians, against King Latinus. Evander inhabits the site of what will eventually be Rome. Aeneas arrives at his settlement during a festival for Heracles. The king receives him hospitably, promises him aid, invites him and his comrades to join the festival, and explains its origins (184–279): Heracles delivered the land from the predatory, half-human monster Cacus, whom he killed after a battle that shook the earth to its depths, by strangling him. The battle between Heracles and Cacus anticipates the battle-to-come between Aeneas and Turnus: "At one level of interpretation . . . Aeneas acts like Hercules: he kills the man of disorder and thus makes the Rome of the kings and the Republic possible" (paraphrase and quotation from William S. Anderson, *The Art of the Aeneid* [Englewood Cliffs, N.J., 1969], 71).

Later in the evening Aeneas listens to a hymn of Heracles' feats (285–305). The details further link the two: "Like Aeneas, Hercules has wandered far and wide, suffering a thousand toils because of the savage hatred of unjust Juno" (Anderson, *Art of the Aeneid,* 72). Evander then walks with Aeneas to his dwelling, pointing out sights on the way as Virgil reminds "his Roman audience of the difference between this diminutive Rome and what will come to be—all, of course, because Aeneas advances the cause begun by Hercules" (72).

Evander invites Aeneas into his humble home saying, "Heracles did not disdain my hospitality . . ." (362–65). "The identity between heroes is almost complete" (Anderson, *Art of the Aeneid*, 72). See also Galinsky, *The Herakles Theme*, 131–49.

Propertius

Heracles as a prototype for Aeneas thus became a symbol for Augustus, but on that very account he is not taken so seriously by Propertius (Galinsky, *The Herakles Theme*, 153)—if he is not even mocked. In 1. 13. 23–24 Heracles, burning on his pyre on Mount Oeta, is really (and merely) "on fire" for Hebe in heaven.

Propertius 4. 9 begins with a rendition of Heracles' fight with Cacus probably intended to parody Virgil's treatment (lines 1–20). Propertius then invents: Overcome by thirst after dispatching Cacus and unable to find water, Heracles forces his way past the high priestess and into the shrine of the Bona Dea, from which men were absolutely excluded, and laps up water from the spring at the site, drying it up.

Ovid

Heroides 9: Deianira in a complaining letter to Heracles plays to perfection the role of martyr: "I am glad that Oechalia is added to our successes, but that the victor has succumbed to the vanquished—that makes me weep," she begins (1–2). Everyone knows that Iole has the great Heracles under her thumb. What would your heavenly father, Zeus, think? It is Aphrodite, not Hera, who afflicts you (3–12). And so she continues to the end of the poem.

Metamorphoses 9. 1–323: Ovid divides his narration into four parts: (1) Heracles' successful fight with Achelous for the hand of Deianira, amusingly recounted by the loser (1–92); (2) Heracles, Deianira, and Nessus, with Ovid as narrator: Nessus, dying from a poisoned arrow of Heracles who shot him as he tried to rape Deianira, dips his robe in the poisonous blood from the wound, and gives it to the naive Deianira as a love charm (93–133); (3) the death of Heracles: Deianira hears a rumor that Heracles has fallen in love with Iole. Although the focus in this section is almost exclusively on Heracles, at 141–51 Ovid portrays Deianira quite differently from the self-centered martyr of *Heroides* 9. Terrified by the news that Iole is coming to live at the palace, Deianira first weeps uncontrollably. Then she says, "What am I crying for? That will only make Iole happy." Aware that Iole will arrive at any moment, she tries to think what is best to do. Finally she decides to send to Heracles the shirt of Nessus which, she believes, returns strength to faded love. Heracles dons the shirt, is consumed by pain from the poison, and prepares to die on a pyre on Mount Oeta. Zeus takes the hero's divine half and makes it immortal (134–275). (4) Alcmena and the birth of Heracles, told by Alcmena (275–323; see ch. 4, n. 14). As Anderson, *Ovid*, 436–37, notes, the poet deliberately undercuts the solemnity of Heracles' death and apotheosis by placing after it an amusing and almost folksy account of his birth by his mother. Moreover, Ovid makes a parallel between Heracles' experience of death and Alcmena's childbirth: Both suffer incredible pain and cry out to heaven in vain; both are Juno's victims; Alcmena undergoes *labores* (289) and so does Heracles; pregnant, Alcmena literally possesses *gravitas* (287) and on the pyre Heracles is refined to *augusta gravitas* (270).

Galinsky goes even further: Heracles' apotheosis, reduced as it is, anticipates in the later books and so is a comment on the deifications of Romulus, Aeneas, and Julius Caesar, an Augustan theme. In the phrase *augusta gravitas* (followed by Alcmena's *gravitas*, as noted above), there may even be a mocking allusion to Augustus himself (*The Herakles Theme*, 157, 160).

For brief references to Heracles in Ovid, see *Met.* 12. 542–76, Heracles' attack on Pylus; *Amores* 3. 6. 35–38, Heracles versus Achelous; *Ars Amatoria* 2. 217–22, Heracles spinning wool for Omphale; 3. 153–56, Heracles fell in love with Iole at Oechalia because of her tousled hair, natural under the circumstances (the destruction of her city), but cultivated disarray *is* attractive.

Seneca

The playwright-philosopher used the figure of Heracles for "his Stoic conception of the hero" (Galinsky, *The Herakles Theme*, 167), creating two dramas from myths of Heracles, the *Hercules Furens* and the *Hercules Oetaeus*. In the former play Heracles builds his funeral pyre so that he can return to the underworld, but in the latter play the pyre symbolizes the *virtus* that make him worthy of heaven. Taken together, the two plays manifest the evolution of Heracles for Seneca, from a hero of physical strength to one of spiritual strength (173). Heracles illustrates the heart of Seneca's Stoic philosophy: endurance, and the belief that life is a preparation for death (178, 180).

2   See the references to Pindar *Nem.* 1 and Theocritus *Idyll* 24 in n. 1.

Ancient mythographers, as Nilsson (*Mycenean Origin of Greek Mythology*, 195) notes, divided the myths of Heracles into three cycles:

(1) The Twelve Labors, performed at the command of Eurystheus;

(2) Incidentals, actions performed while he executed his labors;

(3) Deeds, warlike expeditions undertaken on his own or with

others (e.g., the expedition of the Argonauts). These are framed by myths of his birth and of his death and apotheosis. Apollodorus, we can see, follows this order.

3   See 1. 3. 2 and ch. 1, n. 5. According to Theocritus *Idyll* 24. 111–16, Heracles learned wrestling from Harpalycus, son of Hermes (as well as boxing and the free-for-all known as the pankration). Linus as an old man taught Heracles to read (24. 105), while "Eumolpus made him a poet and moulded his hands around the boxwood lyre" (24. 109–10).

4   The lion skin, together with the club (cut at Nemea: 2. 4. 11) were the identifying attributes of Heracles, as Greek art well testifies. Dionysus in Aristophanes *Frogs* 45–47 thinks that he can impersonate the hero by donning a lion's skin and carrying a club. The more general belief was that Heracles wore the skin of the Nemean lion. According to Pausanias 1. 41. 3–4 Alcathous, son of Pelops, killed the lion of Cithaeron. Pindar *Isth.* 6. 47–48 and Euripides *Heracles* 361–63 agree that Heracles wore the skin of the Nemean lion. The writer of pseudo-Theocritus *Idyll* 25 says that after Heracles killed the Nemean lion, he skinned it with its own claws and wore its hide as protection in battle (276–79).

5   Frazer, *Apollodorus* 1. 182 relates Pherecydes' version of the marriage of Alcmena and Rhadamanthys: As Heracles' sons were carrying the body of their aged grandmother in its coffin to the grave, Hermes, ordered by Zeus, stole the corpse, substituting a stone in its place. He carried off Alcmena to the Islands of the Blest where she married Rhadamanthys. The sons of Heracles, realizing that the coffin had suddenly become quite heavy, set it down, opened it up, and discovered the stone. They took it out and placed it in a grove near Thebes which became a shrine of Alcmena.

6   Heracles was called Alcides after his grandfather, Alcaeus, son of Perseus (2. 4. 5).

Euripides' *Heracles* draws upon the story of Heracles' madness and murder of his children. The playwright freely alters the myth in the play. First, Heracles not only kills his three children (but not Iphicles'), but also their mother, his wife, Megara. Second, whereas Heracles traditionally undergoes the twelve labors for Eurystheus in expiation for the murder of his children, in the *Heracles* he undertakes the labors in order to restore his father, Amphitryon, to Argos from which he was exiled to Thebes for the murder of his uncle, Electryon (13–21). He returns in triumph to Thebes from the successful performance of the labors, rescues his family from the tyrant Lycus, who usurped the throne there, then is suddenly stricken with insanity sent by Hera and kills his wife and sons. Third, rather than dying on the funeral pyre on Mount Oeta with his immortal half taken to heaven (the myth used by Sophocles in the *Women of Trachis*), Heracles accepts Theseus' offer to cleanse him from the pollution caused by the murder of his family and to live at Athens sharing Theseus' wealth. When he dies Athens will bury him and establish a cult at his gravesite. Fourth, Euripides invents Lycus as a persecutor of Heracles' family to set into greater relief Heracles' role as savior of his family, which role serves in turn to increase the dramatic shock of Heracles' insane murder of wife and children. See D. J. Conacher, *Euripidean Drama: Myth, Theme and Structure* (Toronto, 1967), 82, and Galinsky, *The Herakles Theme*, 58.

What is the point of Euripides' alterations of the myth? What, indeed, is the meaning of the play? To Anne Pippin Burnett, Heracles suffers Hera's Jehovah-like wrath because of his "peculiar superiority, that invincible success . . . that had made him the most blessed of men. . . . His deeds, his aspect, and his singular good fortune constitute a threat in themselves. . . . And so Heracles had to pay a penalty. . . . He had to undergo suffering as great as his good fortune had been. . . ." He had to lose his divinity and appear "wholly man" (see her *Catastrophe Survived* [London, 1971], 178, 179).

As "wholly man," Heracles must learn to live with, must learn to endure, immense guilt. It cannot be wished away, rationalized away, or psychoanalyzed away. It must be borne. Euripides makes the point superbly in Heracles' debate with himself whether to take his arms to Athens: "Bitter the fellowship of these weapons. I cannot decide whether to take them or cast them away. Knocking against my side they will seem to say, 'With us you killed children and wife. You wear the murderers of your sons.' Can I carry them in my arms? What am I saying? Stripped of the weapons with which I performed the finest works in Greece must I put myself in jeopardy to my enemies and die in shame? I must not abandon them. Painful as it is, I must keep them" (1377–85). Carrying his weapons he carries both his greatness and his sin.

What enables Heracles to live and bear his guilt is human love, specifically the love of his great friend Theseus (1223–25, 1234, cf. 1252, 1337). As they leave for Athens Theseus says, "Put your hand around my neck and I shall lead the way." Heracles replies, "A yoke of love . . ." (1402–03; see also 1404, 1425–26 and cf. 1427–28).

7   For general references to the labors of Heracles, see Sophocles *Women of Trachis* 1091–1101, Euripides *Heracles* 359–424 and 1270–78, Virgil *Aeneid* 8. 287–300, and Ovid *Met.* 9. 182–98. References to individual labors can be found in n. 1.

8   In return for helping the hydra, Hera made the crab a constella-

tion in the sky: Cancer (Latin for "crab"). See Frazer, *Apollodorus* 1. 189.

9   According to Pindar *Ol.* 3. 13–34 Heracles, in pursuit of the Cerynitian doe which Taygete, daughter of Atlas, consecrated to Artemis, entered the land of the Hyperboreans (literally, "beyond the north wind") where for the first time he saw olive trees growing. He immediately wanted them to plant at Olympia, where he had founded the Olympian games, for the site at that time was bare of trees and so exposed to the sun. He persuaded the Hyperboreans to give him some olive trees both for shade and to provide leaves for crowns for Olympian victors.

10   Diodorus Siculus 4. 12. 3–8 says that Dionysus had left the wine with centaurs four generations earlier, ordering them to open it only for Heracles. Pholus recalled Dionysus' instructions when Heracles came and opened the wine. Because of its age and strength it had acquired a strong, sweet smell which was carried to the centaurs nearby and made them crave it to the point of madness. They rushed to Pholus' house to get at the wine, and there occurred the battle between them and Heracles which Apollodorus describes, including the death of Pholus. Diodorus' account agrees in the main with that of Apollodorus, although with regard to Chiron, he simply says that Heracles shot and killed him without intending to. See 2. 5. 11 for a later reference to Chiron's death as a substitute for Prometheus.

11   Pausanias 8. 22. 4–5 says that these birds attacked and killed men, having beaks capable of piercing armor of bronze and iron; and Hyginus *Fabulae* 20 (see also 30) says that they could shoot feathers from their wings like arrows. One thus wonders why they would fear wolves.

12   For the Cretan bull, see 3. 1. 3–4. This is the bull by which Pasiphae, wife of Minos, conceived the Minotaur. It became the bull of Marathon which Theseus killed (Epitome 1. 5 and ch. 9, n. 3).

Pindar tells the story of Heracles' capture of the violent, man-eating mares of Diomedes in a poem celebrating order (*nomos*), "king of all, men and gods alike" (frag. 169 Snell, 1–2). See the reference to the fragment in n. 1. According to Diodorus Siculus 4. 15. 3–4 Heracles subdued the mares by feeding them Diomedes, who had taught them to eat human flesh in the first place.

13   Apollonius Rhodius *Argonautica* 2. 966–69 says that Heracles once ambushed Melanippe, Hippolyte's sister, in the land of the Amazons, but let her go unharmed in return for Hippolyte's gleaming belt.

14   Thus the origin of the famous Trojan treachery which was

continued in Paris' seduction of Helen away from the house in which he was her husband's guest. Homer *Iliad* 21. 441–57 tells the story of Laomedon's cheating Poseidon and Apollo, the former of whom built Troy's walls while the latter herded the king's cattle. Rather than pay them for their labors, Homer says, Laomedon threatened to tie them up, cut off their ears, and sell them into slavery.

Pindar *Ol.* 8. 31–46 gives a version of this story in which Apollo prophesies the first and second expeditions against Troy (that of Heracles and the one led by Agamemnon). Virgil *Georgics* 1. 501-02 and Horace *Odes* 3. 3. 17–24 also mention Laomedon's fraud. Horace's poem (in lines 17–68) makes Troy the symbol of Rome's horrible past from which it must remain free.

At *Iliad* 5. 628–51 Homer refers to Heracles' sack of Troy and killing of Laomedon for cheating him of the promised mares. At *Iliad* 5. 265–72 Homer says that Zeus gave them (stallions, not mares) to Tros, in recompense for Ganymedes (who was Laomedon's uncle, Tros thus being Laomedon's grandfather). The Homeric *Hymn 5, to Aphrodite* 207–12 explains that after Zeus abducted Ganymedes, Tros was inconsolable, for he did not know where the divine whirlwind had carried away his son. He grieved for him so much that Zeus pitied him and gave him as compensation high stepping horses, such as the gods ride. (For the rape of Ganymedes, see 3. 12. 2 and ch. 7, n. 19.)

Pindar *Isth.* 6. 26–31 mentions Heracles' sack of Troy with Telamon's help and Ovid *Met.* 11. 194–217 quickly sketches the story of Troy's "twice perjured walls" up through the destruction of the city by Heracles and Telamon. Telamon receives Hesione as his prize. (For the expedition, see 2. 6. 4.) As Frazer, *Apollodorus* 1. 208 notes, Heracles' rescue of Hesione is similar to Perseus' rescue of Andromeda (2. 4. 3).

15   Hesiod, Pindar, and Herodotus all refer to Heracles' mission to get the cattle of Geryon (n. 1). According to Herodotus 4. 8, the island, Erythia, was outside the Mediterranean Sea—west of the Pillars of Heracles which mark the Straits of Gibraltar—and so in the Atlantic Ocean. See n. 16.

16   The pillars Heracles set up on either side of the Straits of Gibraltar marked the western limit of the known world, beyond which was the vast, unknown, and terrifying Atlantic Ocean, filled with monsters. For Pindar the Pillars of Heracles were a metaphor for the outermost limit of human achievement beyond which it was unwise— if not impossible—to attempt to go (*Ol.* 3. 43–45, *Nem.* 3. 19–23, *Isth.* 4. 11–13). The significance of the Pillars of Heracles may have had visual representation, too. Herodotus 2. 44 made a visit to Tyre in Phoenicia collecting information about Heracles. There he visited a

temple of the hero richly decorated and containing many offerings, among which were two pillars, one of solid gold, the other of emerald which shone with great brilliancy at night.

17   If Heracles had not returned the golden cup to the Sun he could not have crossed the ocean from west to east during the night and mounted the chariot and team which carried him up into the sky at dawn to make the sunlight of a new day. There was a natural sympathy between Heracles and the Sun because they labored continually. For as the elegiac poet Mimnermus tells us, all his days the Sun's lot is toil, with no rest ever for him and his horses, except the time he spends at night crossing the ocean in the golden cup, during which he sleeps (poem 10 in Diehl).

18   For an adventure of Heracles omitted by Apollodorus, see Frazer, *Apollodorus* 1. 214–15. Apollodorus had no interest in Roman mythology and so passes quickly over Heracles' Italian adventures. The hero had special importance for the Romans, however. See n. 1, Heracles in Virgil; and Frazer, *Apollodorus* 1. 216–17, for ancient works which tell of his adventures, his popularity, and his widespread worship in Italy.

19   Frazer, *Apollodorus* 1. 218–19 notes that Heracles, Cadmus, and Apollo all served others for eight years in expiation for killings of various kinds (see 2. 4. 12, 3. 4. 2, and 3. 10. 4) and concludes that ancient Greek homicides were exiled for eight years during which time they did penance by laboring for others.

20   Hera was so delighted with her present that she had the apples planted in the garden of the gods beside Mount Atlas, also called the garden of the Hesperides. It was not in the land of the Hyperboreans (the Far North) as Apollodorus twice says, but in the Far West. On the golden tree that sprang up, gleaming golden leaves covered shining branches hung with bright golden apples (Ovid *Met.* 4. 637–38). Hera set a serpent to guard the tree because Atlas' daughters were in the habit of pilfering the apples (Frazer, *Apollodorus* 1. 220–21).

21   This Cycnus is to be distinguished from the Cycnus (also a son of Ares) whom Heracles kills in Itonus (2. 7. 7).

22   Nereus' transformations recall those of Proteus for the same purpose in Homer *Odyssey* 4. 384–570, the changes Thetis undergoes to avoid marriage with or the embrace of Peleus (3. 13. 5 and ch. 7, n. 37), and the forms Achelous assumes when he wrestles with Heracles for marriage with Deianira (2. 7. 5 and Sophocles *Women of Trachis* 1–17).

23   Antaeus had built a temple to Poseidon which he roofed with the skulls of strangers whom he had killed (Pindar *Isth.* 4. 52–56, who briefly relates Heracles' wrestling with Antaeus, giving the incidental information that Heracles was short in stature [53]).

24   For a discussion of the probability of human sacrifice in Egypt (with reference to ancient sources), see Frazer, *Apollodorus* 1. 224–25. For human sacrifice in Greece see Frazer, *Apollodorus* 1. 201–03.

25   Apollodorus appears to tell the same story (but with a different locale) at 2. 7. 7 where he calls the driver Thiodamas. Frazer, *Apollodorus* 1. 226–27 quotes ancient sources which say that Heracles' victim was not a cattle driver, as Apollodorus says here, but a farmer named Thiodamus who was plowing a field.

Not only were curses a part of the ritual of the sacrifice of a plowing ox to Heracles, but, Frazer notes, at Eleusis cursing accompanied the act of sacred plowing by priests, and Greeks generally thought curses effective in promoting the fertility of the ground.

26   On Heracles' freeing of Prometheus, see the references in n. 1 above to Hesiod *Theogony* 526–34; to Aeschylus *Prometheus Bound* 771–74 and 870–72; and to the lost *Prometheus Unbound* (in none of which is Chiron mentioned). See also 2. 5. 4 which narrates Heracles' accidental shooting of Chiron with a poisoned arrow. The wound could not heal, but Chiron could not die, although he wished to. The solution was to give Chiron's immortality to Prometheus, allowing the one to die, the other to be set free.

27   Homer *Iliad* 5. 395–97 says that Heracles shot Hades "in Pylos among the dead" (397) and the passage is taken to refer to Heracles' attack on Pylos in the Peloponnese where he wounded not only Hades but also Hera (see *Iliad* 5. 392–404, referred to in n. 1). Nilsson, *Mycenean Origin of Greek Mythology*, 203–04 would translate the Greek *en Pylôi* (5. 397) not "in Pylos" but "in the Gate," and adding the rest of the passage, "among the dead," would interpret this Pylos as the gate of the underworld and Heracles' fight as combat with Death, "the supreme deed of the strong hero. . . . The victory over the God of Death is the end of Heracles' career. . . ." Since Homer failed to understand the significance of this myth, its sense was lost and *Pylos* became the Peloponnesian city where Neleus ruled. Thereupon the hero's "combat with the God of Death was superseded by Heracles' overcoming of the guardian of the Underworld; that is, by the bringing back of Cerberus. This myth contains the same idea, the victory over Death, in another setting." Thus the bringing up of Cerberus, Heracles' victory over death, is his final and crowning labor.

It was natural for Heracles to wish to be initiated into the Eleusinian mysteries before entering the underworld since they honored Demeter and her daughter Persephone, carried off by Hades to be queen of the dead.

For Heracles' encounter with Meleager in the underworld, see ch. 2, n. 9 and the reference to Bacchylides *Ode 5* in n. 1.

Theseus, whom Heracles rescues, went to Hades to accompany his friend and companion Pirithous who wanted to carry off Persephone to be his wife. When they arrived the god of the underworld invited them to sit on the chair of forgetfulness, from which they were unable to rise (Epitome 1. 23–24). The freeing of Theseus considerably delayed Heracles' return (Euripides Heracles 619) but earned him Theseus' gratitude and love for the rest of his life (Heracles 1169–71, and especially 1214–28). In the play Theseus literally takes the hand of the paralyzed Heracles and lifts him up to go to Athens (1394–1400) as Heracles once took him by the hand and raised him up in Hades to return to the upper world.

On Ascalaphus, see 1. 5. 3 and ch. 1, n. 18.

Frazer, Apollodorus 1. 237 notes locations other than Troezen where Heracles ascended from the underworld with Cerberus. Heracles dragged the dog along the upward path bound to a steel-link chain, resisting, turning his eyes away from the daylight and bright sunshine, and snarling and barking in rage from his three mouths. He spattered the green fields with white foam which, taking root in the fertile soil, produced the noxious plant from which is made the deadly poison, aconite (Ovid Met. 7. 408–19).

28   There are at least three versions (including Apollodorus') of Heracles' murder of Iphitus, and two motives for his sacking Oechalia and killing Eurytus. Homer Odyssey 21. 11–38 gives the most violent version of the former: Heracles coveted mares of Iphitus which the boy had recently recovered, and killed him to get them while Iphitus was a guest in Heracles' house, the grossest imaginable violation of xenia, the Greek code of guest-friendship.

In Sophocles' Women of Trachis Lichas lies to Deianira, telling her that Heracles came to Eurytus' palace as an old friend, but Eurytus maligned and insulted him, got him drunk, and threw him out of his house (262–69; in this "version" it is Eurytus who greatly abuses xenia). Later, when Iphitus came to Heracles at Tiryns looking for strayed horses, Lichas says, in revenge Heracles threw the unsuspecting boy off a high cliff (269–73). Apollodorus rationalizes Heracles' murder of Iphitus by attributing it to madness.

Lichas tells Deianira that Heracles' treachery angered Zeus who sent him from the country to be sold (274–78). Omphale, queen of Lydia, bought him and he worked for her as a slave for a year and was so consumed by humiliation that he vowed to enslave Eurytus, his wife, and child. When the year was up he returned to Oechalia with an army and attacked the city (252–60). The messenger in the play later gives Deianira the truth: When Heracles could not persuade Eurytus to give him his daughter, Iole, as his concubine, he found an excuse to attack

Oechalia and destroyed it (351–65). Lichas is forced to admit that Heracles sacked Oechalia for love of Iole (476–78). His story to Deianira is a compound of the true and the false: Heracles did murder Iphitus and for penance worked as a slave for Omphale (38–40, 69–70). His falsification recalls the lying tales of Odysseus in Homer's *Odyssey* as well as Pindar's strictures against false myths (*Ol.* 1. 28–32 and *Nem.* 7. 20–23). Its improvised quality should make us wary of claims to the "authenticity" of myths, especially in a literature which is so fragmentary.

29   The Cercopes were the ape-men of antiquity. See Ovid *Met.* 14. 91–100 and Frazer, *Apollodorus* 1. 241–43.

30   Apollodorus narrates the voyage of the Argo to Colchis at 1. 19. 26, the hunt of the Calydonian boar at 1. 8. 2–3, and Theseus' clearance of the Isthmus at 3. 16. 1–Epitome 1. 4.

31   For references to this first sack of Troy and events causing it, see 2. 5. 9 and n. 14.

32   For Hera's persecution of Heracles after he captured Troy, see Homer *Iliad* 14. 249–60 and 15. 18–30, in the latter of which Zeus reminds Hera of his hanging her from heaven. See the references to these passages in n. 1 and also 1. 3. 5.

For Heracles' help given to the gods in their battle against the Giants, see 1. 6. 1–2.

33   Heracles sought to avenge himself on Augeas who cheated him of the cattle he promised him for cleaning Augeas' stables in one day (2. 5. 5). Apollodorus' account of Heracles' ambush of Eurytus and Cteatus and destruction of Elis agrees more or less with that of Pindar *Ol.* 10. 26–38. Pindar refers frequently to Heracles' establishment of the Olympian games (see n. 1).

34   For Heracles' attack on Pylos, defended by Hera and Hades (as well as by Pylians), see the references in n. 1 to Homer *Iliad* 5. 392–404 and Nilsson's analysis (*Mycenean Origin of Greek Mythology*) of 5. 395–97 in n. 27. See also *Iliad* 11. 689–94 and Pindar *Ol.* 9. 30–41, who omits Hera and adds Poseidon and Apollo to the divine defenders against Heracles at Pylos, but repudiates the tale as impious. Hesiod *Shield of Heracles* 357–67 says that Heracles knocked Ares to the ground with spear thrusts at his shield and wounded him in the thigh. At lines 424–66 of the work Ares, maddened by grief at the death of his son, Cycnus, attacks Heracles, who (again) wounds him in the thigh and the god retreats.

On Periclymenus, see 1. 9. 9 (and Frazer, *Apollodorus* 1. 84–85). Ovid *Met.* 12. 556–72 says that during the battle Periclymenus changed himself into an eagle and swooped down on Heracles, lacerating his face with beak and talons. But Heracles shot him with an arrow, wounding him slightly where wing joins body, but disabling him. Unable to fly he fell to the ground and the impact drove the arrow through his side and throat and killed him.

35   Apollodorus at 3. 9. 1 retells the story of Auge but with different details, and the two versions should be read with that of Diodorus Siculus 4. 33. 7–12 (with yet different details). This particular myth in its varying versions was quite popular in antiquity, and both Sophocles and Euripides wrote tragedies based on it (Frazer, *Apollodorus* 1. 252–55). The myth, furthermore, belongs to a pattern of which there are many particular instances in Greek mythology, e.g., Zeus-Danae-Perseus (in one version of the Auge myth Aleus puts her and Telephus into a chest and throws them into the sea: Pausanias 8. 4. 9); Zeus-Semele-Dionysus (Pausanias 3. 24. 3–4 relates that Semele gave birth to Dionysus, contrary to the usual story [see 1. 4. 3], and that Cadmus, when he found out, set mother and infant adrift in a chest which washed ashore at Brasiae [in the Peloponnese] with Semele dead but the baby still alive.); Zeus-Io-Epaphus; Helius-Clymene-Phaethon; Apollo-Coronis-Asclepius and Apollo-Creusa-Ion (the basis for Euripides' *Ion*, which survives). For a discussion of this type of myth, see Anne Pippin Burnett, trans., *Ion by Euripides* (Englewood Cliffs, N.J., 1970), Introduction, especially 1–7. Apollodorus, incidentally, ignores the Ion myth: See 1. 7. 3 at which he merely reports that Xuthus had Ion by Creusa. Euripides' *Ion*, however, should be read by students of Greek drama since it "is at once the most personal and the most universal of his plays, the one that makes the broadest claims, both for gods and men . . ." (14). For a longer and more detailed analysis of the play, see Burnett's *Catastrophe Survived*, ch. 5, "*Ion*," 101–29. See also Cedric Whitman, *Euripides and the Full Circle of Myth* (Cambridge, Mass., 1974), ch. 3, "*Ion*," 69–103.

36   Heracles first hears of Deianira in the underworld where, weeping at the story Meleager tells him of his death and moved by love, he asks the hero if he has a sister at home in the upper world with a nature like his, for he would willingly marry her. Meleager replies, Yes, Deianira . . . (Bacchylides *Ode* 5. 155–75; for reference to the poem see ch. 2, n. 9 and n. 1).

For an amusing account of Heracles' battle with Achelous for Deianira (told by the loser), see Ovid *Met.* 9. 1–92; for a touching one (told by Deianira), see Sophocles *Women of Trachis* 1–25; and for an extremely affecting one (told by the Chorus in the same play), see 503–30.

Amalthea, whose milk the infant Zeus drank (1. 1. 7), was a goat according to Callimachus *Hymn* 1. 47–48 and Diodorus Siculus 5. 70. 3.

Her horn was the original Cornucopia or Horn of Plenty. See also Frazer, *Apollodorus* 1. 257.

37   Heracles had begotten fifty sons by Thespius' fifty daughters (2. 4. 10).

38   Diodorus Siculus 4. 36. 2–3 says that the boy made some mistake while serving Heracles and he struck him hard, but had not intended to kill him.

39   The "love potion" the dying Nessus gives to Deianira is the means by which the tragedy of Sophocles' *Women of Trachis* is executed. For the story of Nessus' attempted rape of Deianira and the poisonous "gift" he gives her before he dies, see Ovid *Met.* 9. 93–133 and the *Women of Trachis* 555–81.

40   Heracles' encounter with Thiodamas seems to repeat a story told at 2. 5. 11 (see n. 25).

41   Heracles' battle with this Cycnus is the subject of Hesiod's *Shield of Heracles* (see 57–138 and 325–423). He fights, but does not kill, another Cycnus, also a son of Ares, at 2. 5. 11. The Cycnus referred to here, "killer of strangers" (Euripides *Heracles* 391; see 389–93), cut off their heads to use in building a temple to Ares (see Frazer, *Apollodorus* 1. 264), a variation of Antaeus' roofing with skulls the temple he built to his father Poseidon (Pindar *Isth.* 4. 52–56).

42   Heracles bore a long standing grudge against Eurytus for denying him marriage with his daughter, Iole, whom Heracles had won fairly in an archery contest (2. 6. 1–3) before he married Deianira (as Apollodorus arranges his material; see n. 28 for the two motives for conquering Oechalia given in Sophocles' *Women of Trachis*). The capture of Oechalia begins the myth of the end of Heracles' life on earth, his apotheosis on the funeral pyre on Mount Oeta, and his marriage with Hebe. Elements of or references to the myth are found in the following works: Seneca *Hercules Oetaeus:* The myth entire including remarks by the deified Heracles from heaven, 1940–43, 1963–76; Ovid *Met.* 9. 33–133: Nessus' foiled attempt to rape Deianira and the gift to her of the potion (see also 2. 7. 6); Bacchylides 16 and Ovid *Heroides* 9: Deianira sends to Heracles the fatal potion; Sophocles *Philoctetes* 799–803: Philoctetes' (not Poeas') lighting the pyre on Mount Oeta; *Met.* 9. 134–275: the death and apotheosis of Heracles; Homer *Odyssey* 11. 602–04 (if genuine), Hesiod *Theogony* 950–55, Pindar *Nem.* 1. 71–72, *Nem.* 10. 16–17, *Isth.* 4. 55–60, Euripides *Heraclidae* 915–16, and *Met.* 9. 400–01: Heracles' marriage with Hebe in heaven.

From this myth (but omitting Heracles' apotheosis and marriage with Hebe) and from the myth of Heracles' winning of Deianira,

Sophocles created the *Women of Trachis*, a bitter play which is a monument of Sophoclean irony: The mighty Heracles is brought down by the action of a quiet woman who aimed only at retaining his love because she loved him deeply, a woman who is as intelligent, sensitive, and faithful as he is violent, unfeeling, and faithless. In understanding she is the equal of Euripides' *Phaedra* (in the *Hippolytus*). Hearing of Iole she says, People cannot help falling in love; it happens: It happened to me, so why not to another like me? It is madness to blame my husband—with him it's a disease—or this woman who intended me no harm (438–48). But although she has learned to accept Heracles' infidelity, his "disease" (the same word again at 544), she is shaken by the idea of living in the same house with Iole, sharing her marriage with her. What woman could, she asks? "For I see her youth is coming to full bloom while mine is fading. The eyes of men love to pluck the blossoms; from the faded flowers they turn away" (545–49 with Michael Jameson's trans. of 547–49 [Chicago series]).

As for the meaning of the play, Gilbert Murray has said, "If we watch seriously the doings and farings of the world we do see the tender things of life trampled down by the brutal; we see infinite mistakes and we cannot but feel a large pity for mankind in all the evil that man suffers and inflicts and regrets. And further—if we regard the non-human part of the universe as definitely the work of conscious, reasoning, anthropomorphic beings, such as the Greek gods—we must, if we give them human qualities at all, attribute to them an appalling cruelty" (*Greek Studies*, [Oxford, 1946], ch. 6, "Heracles, 'The Best of Men,' " 122).

The myths of Heracles have continued to appeal to the literary imagination. Of particular interest are Ezra Pound's *Sophokles: Women of Trachis* and Archibald MacLeish's *Herakles*, for which see Galinsky, *The Herakles Theme*, 240–48.

The most haunting evocation of Heracles in modern literature (ignored by Galinsky) is that of Nikos Kazantzakis in *The Odyssey, A Modern Sequel* (translated with Introduction, Synopsis and Notes by Kimon Friar [New York, 1965]). Heracles, "the great ancestor and racial chieftain" as Kazantzakis calls him in *Report to Greco* (trans. P. A. Bien [New York, 1965], 164) is one of Odysseus' three Fates in book 14 of *The Odyssey*, to whom he gives his heart's blood in a dream so that the old hero may be animated and speak.

There was a natural affinity between Heracles and Odysseus in Greek mythology which Kazantzakis develops and articulates. Both were great archers. Heracles learned archery from Eurytus (2. 4. 9) and Odysseus got his powerful bow—which he alone could string—from Eurytus (Homer *Odyssey* 21. 11–38). In n. 1 I called attention to the

similarity between the Homeric *Hymn 15, to Heracles* and the opening
lines of the *Odyssey*, as if the writer of the Homeric *Hymn* sought to
identify the two great archer heroes. In the *Odyssey* at 8. 202–25 Odysseus boasts to the Phaeacians of his prowess with the bow (among
other things) and challenges one and all to a contest, but yields to
such men of old, he says, as the bowmen Heracles and Eurytus.

Odysseus encounters Heracles in the underworld in an eerie passage
Kazantzakis might have imagined (*Odyssey* 11. 601–27): "I made
out strong Heracles," Odysseus says, " and all around him swirled the
dead, screaming like frightened birds. He was like black night, bow
naked, arrow on string, peering fiercely, poised to shoot. . . . He recognized me at once, when his eyes fastened on me, and grieving for
me spoke winged words: 'Zeus-born son of Laertes, inventive Odysseus,
poor wretch, so you, too, are suffering some evil fate such as I endured
in the light of the sun. . . .' "

For Kazantzakis it is the bow, with its special symbolic value, which
above all creates the bond between the two heroes. The epigraph of
Report to Greco runs: THREE KINDS OF SOULS, THREE PRAYERS: (1) I AM A
BOW IN YOUR HANDS, LORD. DRAW ME, LEST I ROT. (2) DO NOT OVERDRAW
ME, LORD. I SHALL BREAK. (3) OVERDRAW ME, LORD, AND WHO CARES IF I
BREAK!

In book 14 of Kazantzakis' *The Odyssey*, Odysseus in a dream-vision
sees Heracles, one of his three Fates, appearing like a mo013uldering corpse
from the grave, crawling with white worms:

> The archer brimmed with tears to see his great forebear: "Heracles,
> sacred spite, man's great daemonic soul, . . . I thought to see you
> spring from earth on your black steed with Death's own bloody
> head swinging from your saddle horns, but see, your teeth are
> chattering and your knees show rot. . . ."

Heracles gains strength from the blood of Odysseus' heart and urges
Odysseus on. He himself failed to become "a deathless god on earth"
but he raised two pillars as signs, " 'that you may see how far I've
gone, and go still further. / The final labor remains—kneel, aim, and
shoot!' " Odysseus shudders, agitated, and asks, " 'Lord of our race,
give me your blessing! What is my task?' / But the much-wounded
form with hopeless grief replied: / 'Ah, I can't quite make out what
the last labor is . . .' " (394–433). In book 16 Odysseus hears a voice
within him calling his name. He recognizes it as the voice of Heracles.
He calls in return: " 'O Flame, distilled to pure light from your constant
strife, / body that bent like a stout bow and shot your shaft, / the
sharpened soul, and with it slashed the world's frontiers, / Father, it's
you I call both in despair and joy!' " Odysseus asks him to give the

final task. Heracles is now able to name the thirteenth labor, the last
foe to be vanquished:

"When you have purified your heart of gods and demons,
of virtues great and small, of sorrows and of joys,
and only Death's great lighthouse stays, the glowing mind,
then rise, my heir, and sternly cleave your mind in two:
below will lie your last great foe, rotten-thighed Hope,
above, the savage Flame, no light, no air, no fire,
scornful and superhuman in man's hopeless skull."

Heracles recedes, Odysseus shuts his eyes to taste

the silence in his loins that thrust his soul so high
that it leapt motionless in a great flaming kiln,
a fire no thorns could feed, where no wind ever blew;
upright, it stood on strife's high peak, stripped of desire.
The lone man gently smiled and hailed his haughty heart:
"Dear heart, you've flown beyond the final labor, Hope.
You've grown serene, all storms have merged within your depths,
sorrows have piled so high that now they form your joys.
Where shall you turn, dear heart? Whom shall you speak to now?
Slowly, in a great hush, you glide in dark like a wild hawk."

(1108–21, 1175–94)

43   Only the Athenians had an altar of Mercy, located in the Agora,
according to Pausanias 1. 17. 1, and a sign, he says, of their humanity.
Diodorus Siculus 13. 22. 7 says that the Athenians were the first to
have such an altar, implying that other cities had such altars, too. A
small altar of Mercy was discovered at Epidaurus in the late nineteenth
century, proving Diodorus correct. See J. G. Frazer, *Pausanias's Description of Greece*, 6 vols. (London, 1898), 2. 144. After the defeat of
the Seven against Thebes, Adrastus, leader of the expedition, escaped
to Athens and took refuge at the Altar of Mercy (3. 7. 1).
44   Euripides' *Heraclidae* varies substantially from Apollodorus'
brief account of the war the Athenians waged against Eurystheus and
the Argives on behalf of Heracles' children, seeking refuge at Athens.
Iolaus, presented as an old man, leads the band of refugees, rather
than Hyllus. The Athenians prepare to defend them against Eurystheus
but their king, Demophon, reports that all the oracles agree that a
young woman of noble birth must be sacrificed to Persephone to ensure
Athenian victory (403–09). Demophon refuses to choose an Athenian
woman and leaves the matter to Iolaus and the children of Heracles.
They are at an absolute loss until Heracles' daughter, Macaria, offers
herself for sacrifice (500–34) with a strangely courteous, quiet courage.

Nor does she think of her death as pious martyrdom: If she does not die now (and she refused the idea of drawing lots with her sisters: 547–51), she may be killed later when Athens is taken, or else if they all leave Athens, are turned away from other places, if her brothers are killed and she survives, who would want her?

Macaria is balanced by a savage and vengeful Alcmena at the end of the play. Eurystheus is not killed in battle but brought back to Athens as a prisoner-of-war. Alcmena, filled with bitter (and justifiable) hatred (941–60), wants him killed, contrary to Athenian law. She forces her will on the reluctant Athenians (she will kill him herself, if necessary: 980) and orders soldiers to take him away, kill him, and throw his body to the dogs (1045–52). So be it, the Chorus says, we are not guilty (1053–55). According to Pindar *Pyth.* 9. 79–81 Iolaus killed Eurystheus, and this was probably the common tradition (Frazer, *Appollodorus* 1. 279).

45   Tlepolemus' killing of Licymnius, an aged uncle of Heracles, and his exile to Rhodes (2. 8. 2) are mentioned by Homer *Iliad* 2. 653–70 and Pindar *Ol.* 7. 27–37, the latter of whom says Tlepolemus killed Licymnius in anger.

Heracles' son Hyllus was killed in the second attempt of the sons of Heracles to return to the Peloponnese (2. 8. 2). His death may have been mentioned in the lacuna in the text at 2. 8. 2 between "with his army" and "to the Peloponnese" as Frazer, *Apollodorus* 1. 283 suggests.

The descendants of Heracles under the leadership of Temenus, successfully returned to the Peloponnese and took control of it, along with the Dorians, in the eightieth year after the capture of Troy, according to Thucydides 1. 12. Temenus and his brothers, Cresphontes and Aristodemus (whose two sons cast one lot together with their uncles for one-third of the Peloponnese), were great-great grandsons of Heracles.

CHAPTER SIX

The Family of Agenor: Europa, Cadmus, and Minos;
Cadmus' Founding of Thebes; Oedipus;
the Seven Against Thebes; the Epigoni
(3. 1. 1–3. 7. 7)

BOOK 3 1 Now that I have narrated the story of the line of Inachus from Belus down to the descendants of Heracles, I shall tell of Agenor. For as I said above [2. 1. 4], Libya had two sons by Poseidon, Belus and Agenor. Now Belus ruled over the Egyptians and had the sons I mentioned earlier, while Agenor went to Phoenicia, married Telephassa, and had a daughter, Europa, and three sons, Cadmus, Phoenix, and Cilix. | Some claim that Europa was the daughter of Phoenix and not of Agenor. | ¹ Zeus fell in love with her and changing himself into a tame bull, carried her on his back across the sea to Crete. There Zeus slept with her and she later gave birth to Minos, Sarpedon, and Rhadamanthys | although according to Homer [*Iliad* 6. 198–99], Sarpedon was the son of Zeus and Laodamia, daughter of Bellerophon | . When Europa disappeared, her father Agenor sent his sons to look for her, ordering them not to return until they found her. Their mother, Telephassa, and Thasus, son of Poseidon | or of Cilix, as Pherecydes says | , joined them in the search. When they were unable to find Europa after looking everywhere, they gave up the idea of returning home and settled in various places: Phoenix in Phoenicia; Cilix near Phoenicia (and he called all the land subject to him near the Pyramus River Cilicia); and Cadmus and Telephassa in Thrace. Thasus founded a city Thasus on an island near Thrace and settled there.

2   Asterius, the ruler of the Cretans, married Europa and reared her children. When they were grown up they quarrelled with each other for they all were in love with a boy named Miletus, a son of Apollo and Aria, daughter of Cleochus. Because the boy preferred Sarpedon, Minos fought his brother and won. Miletus fled to Caria where he founded a city which he called Miletus, after himself.² Sarpedon fled to Cilix, with whom he allied himself in a war against the Lycians in return for a portion of land. He became king of Lycia and was allowed

by Zeus to live for three generations.³ | Some say that the brothers were in love with Atymnius, the son of Zeus and Cassiepea, and quarrelled over him. | Rhadamanthys, after making laws for the islanders, fled to Boeotia and married Alcmena. In Hades he acts as a judge with Minos.⁴

Settling in Crete, Minos made laws, and after marrying Pasiphae, the daughter of the Sun and Perseis | although Asclepiades says that his wife was Crete, the daughter of Asterius |, had sons named Catreus, Deucalion, Glaucus, and Androgeus, and daughters named Acalle, Xenodice, Ariadne, and Phaedra.⁵ | By a nymph Paria he had Eurymedon, Nephalion, Chryses, and Philolaus, and by Dexithea, Euxanthius. |

3   When Asterius died childless, Minos sought to rule over Crete but was opposed. He then claimed that he received the kingship from the gods and, in order to prove it, said that whatever he prayed for would occur. While sacrificing to Poseidon he prayed for a bull to appear from the sea and promised to sacrifice it. When Poseidon sent to him a handsome bull he received the kingship, but sent the bull to his herds and sacrificed another. He was the first to control the sea and ruled
4   over almost all the islands.⁶ Because he had not sacrificed the bull Poseidon in anger made it wild and aroused desire for it in Pasiphae. In love with the bull, Pasiphae asked help from Daedalus, a master craftsman banished from Athens for murder. He built a wooden cow on wheels, hollow on the inside and covered with the hide of a cow. He placed it in the meadow where the bull usually grazed and instructed Pasiphae to get inside it. The bull came and mounted it as though it were a real cow. She gave birth to Asterius who was called the Minotaur. He had the face of a bull but a human body. Minos, in accordance with certain oracles, kept him shut up in the labyrinth. Constructed by Daedalus, the labyrinth was a large chamber with "a complex set of turns concealing the exit." | The story of the Minotaur, Androgeus, Phaedra and Ariadne I shall tell later in the account of Theseus [3. 15. 1, 3. 15. 7–8, and Epitome 1. 7–15]. | ⁷

2   Catreus, the son of Minos, had three daughters, Aerope, Clymene, and Apemosyne, and a son Althaemenes. When Catreus asked the oracle how his life was to end the god told him he would die by the hand of one of his children. Catreus kept the prophecy secret but Althaemenes heard of it and, fearful of murdering his father, set sail from Crete with his sister Apemosyne. He put in at Rhodes and settled in a place which he called Cretinia. He ascended Mount Atabyrium and gazed out over the neighboring islands. Seeing Crete and remembering his father's gods, he set up an altar to Zeus Atabyrius.

Not long afterwards Althaemenes murdered his sister. Hermes was in love with her but she fled from him and he was unable to catch her (for she could run faster than he). He then spread newly skinned cowhides on the path so that, returning from the spring, she slipped and fell and was raped. She revealed to her brother what had happened.

2 He believed that she was using the god as a pretense and so kicked her to death.

Catreus gave Aerope and Clymene to Nauplius to sell in foreign lands. Aerope was married to Plisthenes to whom she bore Agamemnon and Menelaus, and Clymene was married to Nauplius who had by her Oeax and Palamedes.[8] Catreus, grown very old, was anxious to deliver the kingdom to his son Althaemenes and for this reason went to Rhodes. When he disembarked from the ship with the heroes at a deserted spot on the island he was driven back by cowherds. They thought pirates had invaded them and were unable to hear him telling them who he really was because of the barking of the dogs. While they were throwing rocks at him Althaemenes arrived, threw his javelin, and killed him, not knowing that he was his father. When he later learned what he had done he was swallowed up by a chasm in answer to a prayer.

3 To Deucalion were born Idomeneus, Crete, and an illegitimate son, Molus. But Glaucus, while still a child, fell into a jar of honey as he chased a mouse and drowned [Deucalion and Glaucus were sons of Minos: 3. 1. 2]. When he disappeared, Minos searched for him everywhere and asked seers where to find him. The Curetes told him that he had a tri-colored cow among his herds and that the man best able to describe its color would also restore his son alive. So when the seers were gathered together Polyidus, the son of Coeranus, compared the color of the cow's hide to a mulberry.[9] He was compelled to seek the child and found him through the art of divination. But Minos told him that he also had to bring him back to life and shut him up with the corpse of the boy. While wondering what to do he observed a snake moving toward the body. He killed it with a stone, fearing that he, too, would die if the body suffered any harm. Another snake appeared, saw the first one dead, and went away. It returned with an herb which it spread over the entire body of the dead snake. When the herb was applied to it, it revived. Polyidus, amazed to see this, applied the same herb to the

2 body of Glaucus and brought him back to life.[10] Minos received back his son but even so did not permit Polyidus to return to Argos until he taught Glaucus the art of divination, which he did since he had no choice. But when he sailed away he ordered Glaucus to spit in his mouth. After doing this Glaucus forgot the art of divination. This will suffice for the descendants of Europa.

4 Cadmus buried Telephassa at her death. After enjoying the hos-

pitality of the Thracians he went to Delphi to inquire about Europa. The god told him not to concern himself with Europa but to take a cow as a guide and to found a city wherever it fell out of weariness. After receiving the oracle he traveled through Phocis. He encountered a cow among the cattle of Pelagon and followed along behind it. It passed through Boeotia and sank down at a place which is now the city of Thebes. Wishing to sacrifice the cow to Athena he sent some of his companions to bring water from the spring of Ares. A serpent, said by some to be the offspring of Ares, was guarding the spring and killed most of those sent for water. Cadmus killed the serpent in anger and at Athena's suggestion planted its teeth.[11] Armed men sprang up from them whom they called Sparti ["Sown Men"]. These killed each other, some fighting by accident, others out of ignorance. | Pherecydes says that Cadmus, when he saw men in armor springing up from the ground, threw stones at them. They thought that they were being struck by each other and started fighting among themselves. | Five survived: Echion, Udaeus, Chthonius, Hyperenor, and Pelorus. Cadmus worked for Ares for an eternal year to atone for those whom he had killed. The eternal year was at that time equivalent to eight of our years.[12]

2

After he served Ares, Athena secured the kingdom for him and Zeus gave him a wife, Harmonia, the daughter of Aphrodite and Ares. All the gods left heaven and came to the land of Cadmus to celebrate the marriage with feasting and songs. Cadmus gave Harmonia a robe and the necklace made by Hephaestus.[13] | Some say that Hephaestus gave it to him, but Pherecydes says that Europa did, having received it from Zeus. | Cadmus had daughters named Autonoe, Ino, Semele, and Agave, and a son Polydorus. Athamas married Ino; Aristaeus, Autonoe; and Echion, Agave.

3

Zeus fell in love with Semele and slept with her without Hera's knowledge. He had agreed to do anything she asked and she was persuaded by Hera to ask Zeus to come to her in the same way he came to Hera when he was courting her. Unable to refuse, Zeus came to her bedroom in a chariot with lightning and thunder and hurled a thunderbolt. Semele thereupon died from fright but Zeus snatched from the fire the baby with which she was six months pregnant and sewed it up in his thigh. At Semele's death Cadmus' other daughters spread the story that she had slept with a mortal, lied that he was Zeus, and for this reason was struck with a thunderbolt.[14]

When the baby was due Zeus removed the stitches, gave birth to Dionysus, and gave him to Hermes who brought him to Ino and Athamas and persuaded them to rear him as a girl. In anger Hera drove them insane. Athamas hunted down and killed his older son, Learchus, thinking that he was a deer. Ino threw her son Melicertes into a boiling cauldron and, carrying the dead child in it, leaped into the sea. Sailors, to whom they give aid in storms at sea, named her Leucothea and the boy Palaemon.[15] Sisyphus established the Isthmian games in honor of Melicertes. Zeus escaped Hera's wrath by changing Dionysus into a kid,[16] and Hermes brought him to the nymphs who lived at Nysa in Asia. Zeus later changed them into stars and named them Hyades.

4   Autonoe and Aristaeus had a son, Actaeon, whom Chiron brought up to be a hunter and who was later devoured on Mount Cithaeron by his own dogs. | Acusilaus says that he died in this way because Zeus was angry at him for seeking to marry Semele, but it is more commonly believed that it was because he saw Artemis bathing. For they say that the goddess immediately changed him into a deer and drove mad the fifty dogs hunting with him, who then in ignorance devoured him. | After Actaeon died, his dogs searched for their master and came howling to the cave of Chiron. He made an image of Actaeon which stopped their grieving.[17]

5   Dionysus invented the making of wine from grapes and, after he was driven mad by Hera, wandered about in Egypt and Syria. Proteus, king of Egypt, received him first but later he came to Cybela in Phrygia. There he was purified by Rhea, learned the rites of initiation and, after receiving from her the robe of the initiate, hastened through Thrace. Lycurgus, son of Dryas and king of the Edonians, who live beside the river Strymon, was the first to treat him with contempt and expel him. Dionysus took refuge in the sea with Thetis, the daughter of Nereus, but his devotees, the Bacchae, and the group of Satyrs who attended him, were taken prisoner. The Bacchae were later suddenly released. Dionysus drove Lycurgus insane, who in madness struck and killed his son Dryas with an axe, thinking that he was chopping a branch from a grapevine. After he had cut off his son's extremities, he regained his sanity. When the land remained barren the god declared in an oracle that it would bear fruit if Lycurgus were put to death. On hearing this the Edonians led him to Mount Pangaeum and bound him. There he was destroyed by horses through the will of Dionysus.[18]

2   Dionysus traveled through Thrace and came to Thebes. He forced the women there to abandon their houses and participate in wild and frenzied rites on Mount Cithaeron. Now Pentheus, the son of Agave and Echion, who had inherited the kingship from Cadmus, tried to prevent these rites. He went to Mount Cithaeron to spy on the Bacchae and there had his limbs torn off by his mother, Agave. She had gone mad and thought that he was a wild animal.[19] Having proven to the Thebans that he was a god, Dionysus went to Argos where he again drove women mad because the inhabitants would not honor him. In

the mountains they ate the flesh of their nursing children [see 2. 2. 2].

3   Wishing to cross from Icaria to Naxos, Dionysus rented a Tyrrhenian pirate ship. After the pirates put him on board, they sailed past Naxos and hurried to Asia in order to sell him. But he turned the mast and the oars into snakes and filled the ship with ivy and the sound of flutes. The pirates went mad and, jumping into the sea to escape, were changed into dolphins. So men became aware that he was a god and honored him. He brought up his mother from Hades, named her Thyone, and ascended into heaven with her.[20]

4   Cadmus and Harmonia left Thebes and went to the Encheleans. When the Illyrians made war on the Encheleans, the god said in an oracle that they would defeat the Illyrians if they had Cadmus and Harmonia as their leaders. Believing the god, they made them their commanders in the war against the Illyrians and defeated them. Cadmus was then king of the Illyrians and a son, Illyrius, was born to him. He was later changed into a serpent along with Harmonia and sent by Zeus into the Elysian Fields.[21]

5   After becoming king of Thebes, Polydorus married Nycteis, daughter of Nycteus, the son of Chthonius, and by her had Labdacus. He had a turn of mind similar to that of Pentheus and died after him. Labdacus left a year-old son, Laius, but Lycus, a brother of Nycteus, took over the rule while he was a child. Both Lycus and Nycteus had fled from Euboea in Boeotia after killing Phlegyas, the son of Ares and Dotis, and settled at Hyria. From there they came to Thebes and became citizens through their friendship with Pentheus. Lycus was chosen commander-in-chief by the Thebans, assumed the kingship, and ruled for twenty years. He was murdered by Zethus and Amphion for the following reason. Zeus made love with Antiope, a daughter of Nycteus. When her father threatened her after she became pregnant, she ran away to Epopeus at Sicyon and married him. Nycteus, in a fit of depression, commanded Lycus to punish Epopeus and Antiope and then killed himself.[22] Lycus led an army against Sicyon, defeated it, killed Epopeus, and took Antiope prisoner. On the return march she gave birth to two sons at Eleutherae in Boeotia and they were put out to die. A cattle herder found them and reared them, calling one Zethus and the other Amphion. Zethus devoted himself to tending cattle and Amphion practised playing a lyre which Hermes gave to him. Lycus and his wife Dirce imprisoned Antiope and tortured her. But one day her bonds came loose by themselves and she went unobserved to the hut of her sons seeking refuge. They recognized their mother, killed Lycus, and tied Dirce to a bull. After her death they threw her body into a spring which is called Dirce after her. They then took over the rule, built a wall around the city, the stones following the sound of Amphion's lyre,

and banished Laius.[23] He lived in the Peloponnese as a guest of Pelops. While teaching Pelops' son Chrysippus to drive a chariot, he fell in love with him and carried him off.[24]

6 Zethus married Thebe, after whom the city of Thebes is named. Amphion married Niobe, the daughter of Tantalus. | She had seven sons: Sipylus, Eupinytus, Ismenus, Damasichthon, Agenor, Phaedimus, and Tantalus; and seven daughters: Ethodaia (or as some say, Neaera), Cleodoxa, Astyoche, Phthia, Pelopia, Astycratia, and Ogygia. Hesiod says that she had ten sons and ten daughters; Herodorus, two male and three female children; and Homer, six sons and six daughters. | Niobe said that her children were more beautiful than Leto's. Leto in anger incited Artemis and Apollo to kill them and Artemis shot down all the females in the house while Apollo killed all the males on a hunt on Mount Cithaeron. Of the sons Amphion alone was saved, and of the daughters the elder, Chloris, whom Neleus married. | According to Telesilla, Amyclas and Meliboea were saved while Amphion [the father] was also shot by Artemis and Apollo. | Niobe herself left Thebes and went to her father, Tantalus, in Sipylus where she prayed to Zeus and was turned to stone. Now tears flow night and day from the stone.[25]

7 After the death of Amphion, Laius became king. He married a daughter of Menoeceus whom some call Jocasta, others Epicasta. Although the oracle of Apollo had warned him not to have children (for the son born to him was fated to kill his father), once when he was drunk he made love with his wife. When she later gave birth to a boy, he pierced his ankles with pins and gave him to a herdsman to expose. The herdsman put him out on Mount Cithaeron, but cattle herders of Polybus, the king of Corinth, found the baby and brought him to the king's wife Periboea. She claimed the baby as her own, treated his ankles, and named him Oedipus because of his swollen feet.

When the boy grew to manhood, his fellows were envious of his strength and taunted him for being adopted. He questioned Periboea but could learn nothing from her so he went to Delphi and asked the oracle who his true parents were. The god replied that he must not go to his native land for if he did he would murder his father and have intercourse with his mother. Hearing this and supposing that the god meant Polybus and Periboea, whom he thought of as his parents, he did not return to Corinth. As he was driving a chariot through Phocis, he encountered Laius, also traveling in a chariot, at a narrow point in the road. Polyphontes, Laius' herald, ordered him to get out of the way and when Oedipus refused, killed one of his horses. Enraged, Oedipus killed both Polyphontes and Laius, and then drove on to

8 Thebes.

Damasistratus, king of Plataea, buried Laius, and Creon, son of Menoeceus, became king [of Thebes]. While he was king the city suffered a horrible misfortune. Hera sent upon it the Sphinx, the offspring of Echidna and Typhon, having the face of a woman, chest, feet, and tail of a lion and the wings of a bird. The Sphinx sat on Mount Phicium and asked the Thebans the following riddle which she had learned from the Muses: What has one voice and is four-footed, two-footed and three-footed?

When the Thebans learned from an oracle that they would be free from the Sphinx when they solved the riddle, they met often to try to discover the answer. Each time they gave a wrong answer, however, the Sphinx seized and devoured one of them. After many had died, including Haemon, the son of Creon, the king proclaimed that he would give the kingship and the widow of Laius as wife to whoever solved the riddle. Hearing of this, Oedipus gave the answer: Man. For he is four-footed as a baby, crawling on his four limbs; when grown he is two-footed; and as an old man he uses a cane as his third foot. The Sphinx thereupon threw herself down from the acropolis.

Oedipus became king, married his mother unawares, and by her had two sons, Polynices and Eteocles, and two daughters, Ismene and Antigone. | Some say that the children were born to him by Eurygania the daughter of Hyperphas. | When they learned what they had done in ignorance, Jocasta hanged herself and Oedipus blinded himself and was banished from Thebes. He laid a curse on his sons, who made no effort to prevent his exile. Oedipus arrived with Antigone at Colonus in Attica (where the grove of the Eumenides is) and became a suppliant. There he was received by Theseus and died soon afterwards.[26]

6 Eteocles and Polynices agreed to rule in alternate years. Some say that Polynices ruled first and after a year handed over the kingdom to Eteocles, but others say that Eteocles ruled first and after a year was unwilling to give up the kingship. Polynices, exiled from Thebes, went to Argos, taking with him the necklace and the robe which Cadmus had given to Harmonia as wedding gifts. At that time Adrastus, the son of Talaus, was king of Argos. Polynices came near the palace at night and fought with Tydeus, the son of Oeneus, who had fled from Calydon. At the sound of their shouting, Adrastus appeared and separated them. A seer had once told him to yoke his daughters to a boar and a lion. Remembering this, he chose them as their husbands, for one had the forepart of a boar on his shield, the other that of a lion. Tydeus then married Deipyle and Polynices, Argia.[27] Adrastus promised to restore them both to their respective countries. First he wanted to make an expedition against Thebes and he gathered together his chieftains.

2   Amphiaraus, the son of Oicles, was a seer. He knew in advance that all who went on the expedition, except Adrastus, were destined to die, so he drew back from it himself and tried to discourage the rest. Polynices went to Iphis, the son of Alector, and asked how Amphiaraus could be made to go on the expedition. He replied that he could be induced to go if his wife, Eriphyle, received Harmonia's necklace. Amphiaraus had forbidden Eriphyle to accept gifts from Polynices, but Polynices gave her the necklace anyway and asked her to persuade her husband to go on the expedition. She had the power to do this because once when he and Adrastus had a disagreement, Amphiaraus swore after it was settled to allow Eriphyle to decide any future conflict he might have with Adrastus. So when Amphiaraus was opposed to the war against Thebes which Adrastus advocated, Eriphyle accepted the necklace and insisted that her husband go with Adrastus and the army.[28] Amphiaraus, compelled to go to war, commanded his sons to kill their mother when they were grown and to march against Thebes themselves.

3   Adrastus mobilized an army with seven commanders and hastened to make war on Thebes. | The commanders were the following: Adrastus son of Talaus, Amphiaraus son of Oicles, Capaneus son of Hipponous, and Hippomedon son of Aristomachus (some say of Talaus). These were from Argos. There were also Polynices the son of Oedipus from Thebes, Tydeus the son of Oeneus from Aetolia, and Parthenopaeus the son of Melanion from Arcadia. Some do not count Tydeus and Polynices among them, including, rather, Eteoclus son of

4 Iphis and Mecisteus. | [29] They came to Nemea which was ruled by Lycurgus. As they were looking for water Hypsipyle offered to lead them to a spring. (Hypsipyle was a slave in Lycurgus' house, for the Lemnian women, after learning that Thoas had been saved [1. 9. 17], killed him and sold her to Lycurgus.) She abandoned Opheltes, the infant son of Eurydice and Lycurgus, whom she was nursing, in order to show them the way to the spring, and the boy was killed by a snake. Adrastus and those with him returned with her, killed the snake and buried the child. Amphiaraus said that this was a sign prophetic of the future, and they then called the boy Archemorus ["Beginning of Doom"]. They instituted in his honor the Nemean games.[30] Adrastus won the horse race; Eteoclus, the foot race; Tydeus, the boxing match; and Amphiaraus, the broad jump and the discus throw. Laodocus won the javelin throw; Polynices, the wrestling match; and Parthenopaeus won the archery contest.

5   When they came to Mount Cithaeron they sent Tydeus to order Eteocles to abide by the original agreement and to relinquish the kingdom to Polynices. When Eteocles ignored their order, Tydeus chal-

lenged the Thebans individually to fight him and defeated as many as accepted the challenge. The Thebans then armed fifty men to ambush him as he departed, but he killed them all except for Maeon and returned to the camp.[31]

6   The Argives put on their armor and approached the walls. There were seven gates and each commander took up a position at one of them: Adrastus, at the Homoloidian gate; Capaneus, at the Ogygian; Amphiaraus, at the Proetidian; Hippomedon, at the Oncaidian; Poly- nices, at the Hypsistan; Parthenopaeus, at the Electran; and Tydeus, at the Crenidian.[32] Eteocles also armed the Thebans, chose an equal number of commanders and formed the army for battle.

7   He consulted a seer to learn how they might defeat the enemy. There lived among the Thebans a blind seer, Tiresias, from the line of Udaeus, a *Spartus* ["Sown man": 3. 4. 1–2]. Tiresias was the son of Everes and a nymph, Chariclo. Different accounts are given about his blindness and his power of divination. | Some say that he was blinded by the gods for revealing to men what they want to keep hidden.

Pherecydes says that he was blinded by Athena, for she was a friend of his mother, Chariclo, and Tiresias once accidentally saw her naked. The goddess covered his eyes with her hands and made him blind. When Chariclo asked her to restore his sight she was unable to do so, but instead opened his ears, enabling him to understand all the sounds that birds make, and gave him a staff of cornel wood, with which he could walk as well as those who can see.

Hesiod says that Tiresias saw snakes copulating on Mount Cyllene and, after wounding them, was changed from a man to a woman. Having observed the same snakes copulating again, he was changed back to a man. For this reason Hera and Zeus who were arguing whether women or men get more pleasure from making love, asked his opinion. He said that a woman gets nine times as much pleasure from love-making as a man does. For this Hera blinded him, but Zeus gave him the power of divination and he lived for a long time. | [33]

When the Thebans consulted Tiresias, he said that they would win if Menoeceus, the son of Creon, freely offered himself as a sacrifice to Ares. When Menoeceus heard this he killed himself in front of the gates. After the battle began, the Thebans were driven back to the walls. Capaneus seized a ladder and scaled the walls, but Zeus hurled

8   a thunderbolt at him. The battle then turned into a rout of the Argives. Since many had died, Eteocles and Polynices, obeying a de- cision of both armies, fought in hand-to-hand combat for the king- dom and killed each other. In a later fierce battle the sons of Astacus distinguished themselves, for Ismarus killed Hippomedon, Leades killed Eteoclus, and Amphidicus killed Parthenopaeus. | According to Eurip-

ides, Periclymenus, the son of Poseidon, killed Parthenopaeus. | Melanippus, the remaining son of Astacus, wounded Tydeus in the belly. As he lay dying, Athena brought a medicine which she had begged from Zeus, by means of which she planned to make him immortal. Amphiaraus, however, was aware of her intention. Because he hated Tydeus for persuading the Argives to go on the expedition to Thebes contrary to his judgment, he cut off the head of Melanippus and gave it to him. Tydeus split it open and gulped down the brains. When Athena saw this she withheld the medicine in disgust. Amphiaraus fled to the river Ismenus. Before Periclymenus could strike him from behind Zeus split open the earth with a thunderbolt. Amphiaraus disappeared into the chasm with his chariot and charioteer, Baton, | or as some say, Elato | , and was made immortal by Zeus. Adrastus alone survived, saved by his horse Arion. Demeter gave birth to it after she had intercourse with Poseidon in the form of a Fury.[34]

7   Creon inherited the kingdom of Thebes and threw out the corpses of the Argives unburied. After forbidding their burial by a proclamation, he set guards over them. But Antigone, the daughter of Oedipus, secretly carried off Polynices' body and buried it. She was caught by Creon himself and buried alive in a tomb.[35]

Adrastus escaped to Athens, where he took refuge at the altar of Mercy. Laying upon it the suppliant's olive branch, he prayed for the burial of the dead. The Athenians made an expedition with Theseus to Thebes, captured it, and gave the dead to their relatives to bury. While Capaneus' pyre was burning, his wife, Evadne, the daughter of Iphis, threw herself upon it and was burned up with him.[36] Ten years later the sons of those who had died, who were called Epigoni, undertook an expedition against Thebes to avenge their fathers' deaths. When they consulted the oracle, the god prophesied victory if Alcmaeon commanded the army. He joined the expedition, although he was unwilling to lead the army until he punished his mother. (Eriphyle, after receiving Harmonia's robe from Thersander the son of Polynices, persuaded her sons also to join the army.) They chose Alcmaeon to lead them and made war on Thebes.[37] | The members of the expedition were: Alcmaeon and Amphilochus, sons of Amphiaraus [and Eriphyle]; Aegialeus, son of Adrastus; Diomedes, son of Tydeus; Promachus, son of Parthenopaeus; Sthenelus, son of Capaneus; Thersander, son of Polynices; and Euryalus, son of Mecisteus. |

3   First they destroyed the neighboring villages. They were then attacked by the Thebans under the command of Laodamas, the son of Eteocles, and fought bravely. Laodamas killed Aegialeus and Alcmaeon, Laodamas. After his death the Thebans withdrew inside the walls. On the advice of Tiresias they sent a herald to the Argives to

negotiate a truce and then, putting their wives and children into wagons, fled from the city. They arrived by night at the spring called Tilphussa. After drinking from it Tiresias died. After a long journey the Thebans built a city, Hestiaea, to settle in.

The Argives, learning later of the flight of the Thebans, entered the city, looted it, and pulled down the walls. They sent part of the booty, along with Tiresias' daughter Manto, to Apollo at Delphi, for they had vowed that if they captured Thebes they would dedicate to him the finest of the spoils.

After the capture of Thebes, Alcmaeon learned that his mother, Eriphyle, had accepted a bribe to kill him also and was the more outraged.[38] In obedience to an oracle from Apollo, he killed her. | Some say that he killed Eriphyle with the help of his brother Amphilochus, others that he did it alone. |

An avenging Fury persecuted Alcmaeon for murdering his mother. Driven insane, he went first to Oicles [his grandfather] in Arcadia and from there to Phegeus in Psophis. He was purified of the murder by Phegeus and married his daughter Arsinoe, to whom he gave both the necklace and the robe. The land later became barren because of him and when the god told him in an oracle to go to the river Achelous and to receive purification from it, he went first to Oeneus in Calydon who extended him hospitality, then to the Thesprotians. He was driven from their country but finally arrived at the springs of the Achelous, was purified by the river, and married Callirrhoe, the daughter of Achelous. On land formed by deposits from the river he founded a settlement. After the marriage Callirrhoe wanted the necklace and the robe and said that she would not live with him until she got them. Alcmaeon then went to Psophis and told Phegeus that it was prophesied that he would be released from his madness when he brought the necklace and the robe to Delphi and dedicated them. Phegeus believed him and gave them to him. When a servant revealed that Alcmaeon was taking them to Callirrhoe, Phegeus ordered his sons to ambush and kill him. Arsinoe rebuked Phegeus' sons and they put her into a chest, carried her to Tegea, and gave her to Agapenor to be a slave, spreading the lie that she was guilty of Alcmaeon's murder.

When Callirrhoe learned of Alcmaeon's death, she asked Zeus, when he made love to her, to allow her sons by Alcmaeon to avenge their father's murder when they were full grown. Suddenly full grown, they set out to get revenge for his death. The sons of Phegeus, Pronous and Agenor, brought the necklace and the robe to Delphi to be dedicated. They lodged with Agapenor, with whom Alcmaeon's sons, Amphoterus and Acarnan, were also staying at that time. These killed their father's murderers and went to Psophis where they entered the palace and killed Phegeus and his wife. Pursued by citizens of Psophis as far as Tegea, they were saved by the aid of the Tegeans and some Argives, and their pursuers were routed and fled. They told their mother what had happened and then went to Delphi and consecrated the necklace and the robe in accordance with the command of Achelous. They then traveled to Epirus, collected settlers and founded Acarnania.[39]

| Euripides says that at the time of his madness Alcmaeon had two children by Tiresias' daughter Manto, a son Amphilochus and a daughter Tisiphone, and that he brought them as infants to Corinth and gave them to Creon, king of Corinth, to rear. Creon's wife sold Tisiphone, because she was so beautiful that she was afraid Creon would marry her. Alcmaeon himself bought her and kept her as a maid servant, unaware that she was his daughter. He went to Corinth to recover his children and brought back his son Amphilochus, who settled Amphilochian Argos in accordance with the oracles of Apollo. | [40]

NOTES
(3. 1. 1–3. 7. 7)

1   According to Hyginus *Fabulae* 6 and 178, the mother of Europa and Cadmus was Argiope. Other sons attributed to Agenor are Thasos (by the Scholiast on Euripides *Phoenissae* 6, and Pausanias 5. 25. 12) and Phineus (1. 9. 21). Homer *Iliad* 14. 321–22 and Bacchylides 16. 29–33 say that Phoenix was the father of Europa.

Ovid *Met.* 2. 836–75 describes Zeus' seduction of Europa: Although, as Ovid says, *Non bene conveniunt . . . maiestas et amor,* Jupiter deliberately takes the form of a bull as white and smooth as snow no foot has trod nor south wind has stirred and proceeds to win Europa little by little through his beauty and gentleness. She feeds him flowers; he kisses her hands, dances, and rolls in the sand for joy. She pats his breast and winds garlands around his horns. Boldly (and unknowing, of course), she leaps upon his back. He edges slowly toward the sea, steps into the water, and then is off at full speed. Europa, trembling, looks with longing at the receding shore. As she holds on to a horn with one hand, she grips his back with the other. Her garments fluttering in the wind seem to hint at an inner *frisson* at future delight.

Herodotus 1. 2 includes the myth in his account of the woman-stealing between Greeks and Asians which led to the Persian Wars in the early fifth century B.C.

2   Ovid makes no mention of the rivalry of Europa's sons for the

love of Miletus. Instead, he says that Miletus (whose mother, according to him, is Deione) tried to usurp the rule of the aged Minos. The king was afraid to banish him, but Miletus fled of his own accord to Asia where he founded the city bearing his name. There he married Cyane and by her had a daughter, Byblis, and a son, Caunus (*Met.* 9. 441–53).

3   By means of attributing such long life to Sarpedon, Apollodorus avoids the chronological difficulty of identifying Sarpedon, the son of Zeus and Europa, with the Lycian ally of Troy in the *Iliad* whom Homer makes the son of Zeus and Laodamia (6. 198–99). Another way of treating the same problem was to make the Homeric Sarpedon the grandson of the original Sarpedon (Diodorus Siculus 5. 79. 3). A notable hero in the *Iliad*, he urges his cousin, Glaucus, on to battle in words which express directly the heroic code in the poem (12. 310–28). In a lengthy passage Homer describes Zeus' grief at the impending death of his son, which the lord of Olympus is powerless to prevent, the fight over his body, and its removal by Sleep and Death to Lycia for burial (*Iliad* 16. 419–683).

In Lycia, of which Sarpedon was king, descent was traced through the female line, a custom remarkable to Herodotus (1. 173) and so, one supposes, to the Greeks of his time.

4   Rhadamanthys is a judge in Hades, separating the good from the wicked, because he was the most just of men on earth (Diodorus Siculus 5. 79. 1–2).

5   The union of Minos and Pasiphae is an example, according to Frazer, *Apollodorus* 1. 302–03, of a ritual marriage between sun and moon.

6   Apollodorus' assessment of Minos' power agrees with that made by Herodotus (1. 171) and Thucydides (1. 4 and 8).

7   The words in quotation marks may come from Sophocles' tragedy, the *Daedalus*. Euripides, too, was drawn to this myth, writing a play entitled *The Cretans*. Neither survives. (See Frazer, *Apollodorus* 1. 305, 306.) Michael Ayrton, a modern author, has written a novel entitled *The Maze Maker* (New York, 1967), which he calls "an autobiography of Daedalus" (in D. R. Dudley, ed., *Virgil* [London, 1969], 185–86; see also ch. 9, n. 4).

8   Atreus is usually considered the father of Agamemnon and Menelaus.

9   According to Hyginus *Fabulae* 136, three times a day (or once every four hours) the cow changed from white to red to black. A ripening mulberry is first white, then changes to red, and finally to black.

10   At 3. 10. 3–4 Apollodorus lists Glaucus among those raised from the dead by Asclepius. (The list of persons Asclepius raised from the dead may be spurious. See Frazer, *Apollodorus* 2. 16, n. 3 to the Greek

text.) For resurrections in myths around the world (frequently by means of snakes), see Frazer, *Apollodorus* 2. 363–70, appendix 7, "The Resurrection of Glaucus."

11   Cadmus planted only half of the teeth. Apollodorus tells us that Athena kept the other half and gave them to Aeetes, king of Colchis, who forced Jason, when he arrived at Colchis in quest of the golden fleece, to sow them and then to fight the armed men who sprang up from the ground (1. 9. 23).

12   Ovid *Met.* 3. 3–137 tells the story of Cadmus' exile from Phoenicia and eventual founding of Thebes.

The Greeks believed that Cadmus introduced writing into Greece when he arrived from Phoenicia, for the Greek alphabet is based on the Phoenician alphabet (Herodotus 5. 58–59). The discovery in 1964 of inscribed Mesopotamian cylinder seals from a Mycenean site on the Cadmea, as the citadel of Thebes was called, offers the possibility of an historic basis for the myth. Writing had existed earlier in Greece in the last part of the Mycenean Age (ca. 1400–1120 B.C.) in the form of a script called Linear B, probably Greek, which was used by palace scribes. It disappeared with the break-up of the Mycenean kingdoms in the twelfth and eleventh centuries B.C.

The aged Cadmus plays a prominent part in Euripides' *Bacchae* and represents, if any character does, the poet's point of view. He is willing to accept the strange new rites of Dionysus for what they are worth, unlike his rigid grandson, Pentheus. At the end of the play Cadmus' insane daughter, Agave, comes onstage carrying the head of her son, Pentheus, whom she helped to pull apart. Cadmus carefully leads her back to reason, employing a "flawless therapeutic strategy" according to George Devereux, "The Psychotherapy Scene in Euripides' *Bacchae*," *Journal of Hellenic Studies* 90 (1970), 35–48.

As for Cadmus' atonement for the Sparti whom he killed, see ch. 5, n. 19 and Frazer, *Apollodorus* 1. 218–19.

13   It was a happy occasion: The gods brought gifts and sat in golden chairs, and the Muses sang a song. Peleus was the only other mortal honored by the gods' presence at his marriage to Thetis. See Pindar *Pyth.* 3. 86–95. Despite such auspicious beginnings, the later lives of the children of these couples were disastrous. The necklace and robe given to Harmonia (by various givers other than Cadmus, according to Apollodorus and Diodorus Siculus 4. 65. 5 and 5. 49. 1) seem cursed after they passed out of her hands, and brought destruction to their later owners. See 3. 6. 2, 3. 7. 2, and 3. 7. 5–7.

14   In Ovid's version of the myth of Zeus and Semele (*Met.* 3. 259–315), Hera appears to Semele in the guise of her old nurse and urges her to make her request of Zeus in order to test her lover, since many

mortal lovers, she says, have entered women's beds pretending to be gods. Zeus could not refuse Semele's wish, which she does not specify until he grants it, because he swears by the River Styx to give her what she asks. A god's oath by the Styx could not be broken. Nevertheless, he brings less powerful thunderbolts, but even these Semele could not endure and her body was burned up.

In Euripides' *Bacchae* Dionysus returns to Thebes, where Semele's grave still smolders, and drives his mother's sisters insane to punish them for their slander against her and to make the city recognize his divinity (*Bacchae* 1–63; see also 242–45 and 286–97).

Pausanias 3. 24. 3–4 relates that Semele gave birth to Dionysus, and Cadmus, thus discovering her sin, set her adrift at sea in a chest with her infant son. The chest washed ashore at Brasiae (in the eastern-most finger of the Peloponnese) with Semele dead but her baby still alive. The people of the town buried Semele and reared Dionysus. His aunt, Ino, eventually wandered there and became his nurse. This variant has an obvious parallel with the myth of Danae and Perseus, similarly set adrift, although both survive the ordeal (2. 4. 1–2; see also 2. 7. 4 and ch. 5, n. 35).

15   Ovid *Met.* 4. 416–542, gives a full version of the story of Athamas and Ino: Juno, still enraged over Semele, sees Athamas and Ino prospering and is determined to destroy them. She descends to Hell to enlist the aid of the Furies. One of them, Tisiphone, ascends and maddens Ino and Athamas. Athamas thinks his baby son, Learchus, is a lion cub, swings him round and round over his head, and releases him to sail through the air and crash head first into a rock wall. From grief or madness Ino leaps into the sea with Melicertes. Venus, pitying them, intercedes with Neptune who grants mother and child divinity and gives them their new names.

16   Dionysus changed himself into a goat when the gods fled to Egypt and turned themselves into animals to escape the Giant Typhoeus (Ovid *Met.* 5. 325–31; see also ch. 1, n. 23). The ancient Greeks, it is clear, firmly associated Dionysus with the goat. Virgil, no doubt, reflects the Roman view (and perhaps the general ancient view) when he says (*Georgics* 2. 380–84) that goats were sacrificed to Dionysus because in grazing they destroyed grape vines, and from these sacrifices tragedy and comedy originated.

To modern scholars the origin of tragedy (from Greek *tragoidia,* perhaps "song for a goat prize") and the nature of the relation among Dionysus, goat, and tragedy are less clear and more complex. The fact of the relation, though, is not in doubt. An excellent short essay on tragedy, including, of course, its connection with Dionysus and goats, is Edwin Dolin's Introduction to Albert Cook and Edwin Dolin, eds.,

An Anthology of Greek Tragedy (Indianapolis and New York, 1972).
17   Ovid *Met.* 3. 138–252 narrates the more common version that
Artemis changed Actaeon into a stag because he accidentally saw her
bathing. In the ironic account of the hunter who is hunted and killed
by his own dogs, Ovid emphasizes, as he does with so many of his
heroes and heroines, Actaeon's struggle as a stag to speak, to make
human communicative utterance, as his dogs tear his flesh and his
companions search for him, calling his name.
18   E. R. Dodds, ed., *Euripides: Bacchae* (Oxford, 1960), xi–xii,
notes that in the classical age "Dionysus was not solely, or even mainly,
the god of wine," but was rather, the god of the whole of liquid
nature—"the liquid fire in the grape, the sap thrusting in a young tree,
the blood pounding in the veins of a young animal, all the mysterious
and uncontrollable tides that ebb and flow in the life of nature." Dodds'
Introduction to his edition of the *Bacchae* is probably the best short
essay on Dionysus in English. See also his *The Greeks and the Irrational* (Berkeley and Los Angeles, 1963), appendix 1, "Maenadism,"
270–82. For longer treatment, see R. P. Winnington-Ingram, *Euripides
and Dionysus* (Cambridge, Eng., 1948).

Homer, in the oldest literary reference to the god, calls him "mad
Dionysus" (*Iliad* 6. 132), and Walter F. Otto, *Dionysus: Myth and Cult*
(Bloomington and London, 1965), 135, sees madness as the central
meaning of the god: Dionysus is "the wild spirit of antithesis and
paradox," representing "the mystery of life which is self-generating,
self-creating. The love which races toward the miracle of procreation
is touched by madness. So is the mind, when it is staggered by the
impulse to create" (136).

Tiresias describes the meaning of Dionysus in a particularly fine
speech at *Bacchae* 266–327.

See additionally W. K. C. Guthrie, *The Greeks and Their Gods*
(London, 1950), ch. 6, "Dionysos," 145–82, and the famous essay by
Friedrich Nietzsche on the symbiotic opposition of the Dionysian and
the Apollonian in Greek art, *The Birth of Tragedy*, trans. Francis
Golffing (Garden City, N.Y., 1956).

Herodotus 2. 48–49 traces the entry of Dionysian rites into Greece
to the seer Melampus, who learned about them from the Egyptians
and from Cadmus of Tyre, who founded Thebes.

Homer *Iliad* 6. 132–40 briefly relates Lycurgus' opposition to Dionysus which angered all the gods. They blinded him and he died soon
afterwards, a victim of their hatred.

Lycurgus' death may be related to stories of human sacrifice by
means of horses to ensure fertility. See ch. 5., n. 12.
19   Apollodorus thus gives in brief outline the plot of Euripides'

strangest play, the *Bacchae*. For introduction to and commentary on the play, see Dodds, *Bacchae* and *Greeks and the Irrational*, and R. P. Winnington-Ingram, *Euripides and Dionysus*.

For Ovid's version of the myth of Pentheus' opposition to Dionysus at Thebes see *Met.* 3. 511–733.

20   Dionysus and the pirates are the subject of the Homeric *Hymn 7, to Dionysus*. In this version, sweet wine streams through the ship and a heavenly fragrance fills it. Sail, mast, and oar locks are covered with vines, ivy, flowers, and garlands. Dionysus changes himself into a lion and springs upon the captain, so frightening the sailors that they jump into the sea from fear and are changed into dolphins.

The myth explains the humane and human qualities of dolphins, widely noticed in antiquity. Such qualities were seen to "prove" that dolphins were once human beings.

The story of Arion, told by Herodotus 1. 23–24, has curious affinities with this myth. Sailors conveying Arion from Tarentum to Corinth order him to leap overboard so they can seize his money. He asks to be allowed first to play the lyre and to sing. The sailors grant his request. When Arion finishes his song he leaps overboard but is taken up by a dolphin and carried on its back to Corinth. (Was the purpose of his singing to draw the dolphin to the ship?) There he confronts the sailors in the presence of Periander, king of Corinth.

Arion, as Herodotus says (1. 23), gave literary form to the dithyramb, a type of choral poetry associated with Dionysus and sung by his followers. It is believed to be the precursor of tragedy. Arion was also credited in antiquity by some with the invention of tragedy. (See D. W. Lucas, *Aristotle: Poetics* [Oxford, 1968], 81 f., comment on 1449a 14.) Tragedy in its origin and maturity is firmly connected with rites of Dionysus (n. 16). One senses that Dionysus and Arion are themselves connected, or perhaps share aspects of some single earlier figure.

Ovid in his version of Dionysus and the pirates (which Bacchus tells Pentheus: *Met.* 3. 582–691) enjoys describing the surprised horror of the pirate crew as they change into dolphins in the act of sailing the ship. Ezra Pound's version of Ovid's lines (Canto II) gives a realism to the supernatural occurrence which even surpasses the Roman poet's narrative.

For further discussion of Dionysus, see Frazer, *Apollodorus* 1. 318–33. For additional references in classical works to Dionysus, see Edward Tripp, *The Meridian Handbook of Classical Mythology* (New York, 1974), 211.

21   Dionysus in Euripides *Bacchae* 1330–43 predicts the wanderings, war, change into serpents, and final coming to rest of Cadmus and Harmonia.

Ovid *Met.* 4. 563–603 tells of Cadmus and Harmonia leaving Thebes in despair after the deaths of Ino and Melicertes (unaware that they were changed into gods). They eventually come to Illyria in their wandering. Weighed down by old age and sorrow, they retrace together the fate of their family line and their own troubles, searching for a clue to explain so much suffering. Cadmus thinks that the killing of the serpent and the sowing of its teeth must have angered the gods, so he prays to be changed into a serpent. His prayer is answered immediately, although the metamorphosis occurs in a kind of slow motion before the eyes of a horrified Harmonia. As his form and skin become snake-like, he begs her to take his hand before it disappears. His tongue is suddenly forked; he can speak no more, only hiss (as often with Ovid's characters who are sealed off in ultimate identities and denied language). Harmonia prays desperately to be changed to a serpent also. Her prayer is answered and they live peacefully as gentle snakes in the woods, neither fearing men nor harming them.

22   In the sentence in 3. 5. 5, "Both Lycus . . . Hyria," the adjective translated "in Boeotia" has been applied to "Euboea" rather than to "Dotis," (Frazer's conjecture). There is a lacuna in the text following this sentence. "From . . . Thebes" was supplied by Frazer. (See *Apollodorus* 1. 336 and 337.)

Pausanias' account of the time from the death of Polydorus to the kingship of Laius (2. 6. 1–2 and 9. 5. 4–5) is clearer than that of Apollodorus, although he differs from him in the story of Epopeus, Antiope, and the death of Nycteus. Apollodorus seems to follow Euripides' lost play, *Antiope.* According to Pausanias, Polydorus, son of Cadmus, on his death bed entrusted the kingship of Thebes to his wife's father, Nycteus, because his son, Labdacus, was still a child. Nycteus, however, was fatally wounded in a war with Epopeus, king of Sicyon, who had abducted Antiope, another daughter of Nycteus. Before he died Nycteus turned over the rulership of Thebes to his brother, Lycus. When Labdacus came of age, Lycus gave him the sovereignty. But Labdacus then died an untimely death while his son, Laius, was a child, and so Lycus once again served as regent until Laius was old enough to assume the rule. Apollodorus implies that Labdacus was murdered by followers of Dionysus for opposing the god's rites.

23   Amphion and Zethus, Greek brothers resembling somewhat the biblical Jacob and Esau, quarrelled about the value of their respective pursuits, Zethus urging Amphion to abandon music and poetry for cattle breeding and war (see Frazer, *Apollodorus* 1. 338–39). The artistic Amphion and the practical Zethus embody an opposition strongly felt by the Greek mind between thought (including speech) and action.

Ajax and Odysseus are two better known myth figures who personify this opposition, the former characterized as a doer of deeds, the latter as a speaker of words in the Homeric poems (see Epitome 5. 6–7 and ch. 11, n. 22). The antithesis between word and deed, thought and action, is central in the thinking of the Greek historian, Thucydides. See Adam Parry, "Thucydides' Use of Abstract Language," *Yale French Studies* 45 (1970), 3–20.

As for the building of the wall of Thebes, Apollonius Rhodius *Argonautica* 1. 735–41 gives a brief but vivid description: Zethus heaves on his shoulder massive mountain peaks and staggers off under their weight. Amphion walks lightly along, plucking his golden lyre, while bewitched boulders twice the size of his brother's bump along behind him.

The opposition in its specific form in the myth of Amphion and Zethus later sharpens into controversy: The poet and pre-Socratic philosopher, Xenophanes, deplores the preference in city affairs given to the athlete over the intellectual and asserts, "My poetic intellect is superior to the brawn of men and horses" (2. 11–12). The culmination of the debate is found in Plato's declaration that political states will never reach their goal of perfection until they are ruled by philosopher-kings (*Republic*, Book 6, 449a 11–c 5).

Pausanias 9. 5. 7–8 says that Amphion was the first to play the lyre, having been taught by Hermes, and that he added three strings to its original four.

24   Laius, by this act, was credited in antiquity with the invention of homosexuality (by the Scholiast on Euripides *Phoenissae* 1760). Chrysippus killed himself for shame. By one account Pelops made war on Thebes (where Laius took the boy) in order to recover his son (Hyginus *Fabulae* 85). The argument of the *Phoenissae* says that Pelops put a curse on Laius for the rape: The son he bore would kill him. As Apollodorus tells us a little further on (3. 5. 7), Laius got drunk once, slept with his wife, and she had a child, Oedipus. Thus he fulfilled Pelops' curse. Hera sent the Sphinx, the Scholiast says, to plague the Thebans for failing to punish Laius. For an interesting psychoanalytic perspective on Laius' crime, as against that of Oedipus, who killed his father, see George Devereux, "Why Oedipus Killed Laius," in Hendrik M. Ruitenbeek, ed., *Psychoanalysis and Literature* (New York, 1964), 168–86.

25   The many opinions in antiquity as to the number of Niobe's children and the popularity of the story among sculptors indicate that the myth was important and widely known. (See Frazer, *Apollodorus* 1. 340–41.) Aeschylus and Sophocles each wrote a tragedy, *Niobe*, but only fragments of them remain. At *Iliad* 24. 602–17, Achilles urges Priam, grieving near the corpse of his son, Hector, to take food: "Even

Niobe remembered to eat." He then tells the story of the killing of her children. Although all twelve died, he says, "she remembered to eat when she was exhausted from weeping," a bit of that Mediterranean wisdom responsible, no doubt, for the Greeks' durability.

The only complete literary narration of the myth to survive is Ovid *Met.* 6. 146–312. In his version, and apparently this was his innovation, Niobe claims divinity greater than Leto's and rebukes her subjects for worshipping such a paltry goddess whom they cannot even see. The death of her six sons does nothing to diminish her arrogance. On the contrary, she grows defiant. But when five of her six daughters have been killed, she prays that the remaining child be spared. It is too late: The last girl dies even as Niobe begs for her life. Niobe suddenly pales and becomes rigid. Her eyes are fixed and staring, her tongue congeals. Like stone she sits, tears endlessly flowing from her eyes.

According to Ovid *Met.* 6. 271–72, Amphion committed suicide from grief. Hyginus *Fabulae* 9 says that Amphion attacked the temple of Apollo, in rage or madness, and the god shot and killed him. For an excellent commentary on the myth, see William S. Anderson, ed., *Ovid's Metamorphoses: Books 6–10* (Norman, Okla., 1972), 171–94.

26   The story of Oedipus is perhaps the Greek myth best known to modern minds. Edmund Leach says that almost all of the stories in Greek mythology are variations of the pattern of which it is the most perfect expression. See his *Claude Lévi-Strauss*, (New York, 1970), 82. Its reach and influence have been the greatest of any myth except, perhaps, for the Christian (which can be considered a version of the Oedipus myth), thanks to the creative imaginations of Sophocles and Freud, for whom it offered the ultimate definition of the human in their own times. Freud saw the action of Sophocles' *Oedipus Tyrannus*, produced in Athens perhaps in 429 B.C., as a "process that can be likened to the work of a psychoanalysis" (Sigmund Freud, *The Interpretation of Dreams* [New York, 1965], 295). The play, of course, is much richer than Freud implies.

It is worth noting that Claude Lévi-Strauss and Ludwig Wittgenstein, two of the most creative thinkers of the twentieth century, have similar things to say about Freud's use of the Oedipus myth. Lévi-Strauss suggests that "not only Sophocles, but Freud himself, should be included among the recorded versions of the Oedipus myth on a par with earlier or seemingly 'authentic' versions." (See his *Structural Anthropology*, trans. C. Jacobson and B. G. Schoepf [Garden City, N.Y., 1967], ch. 11, "The Structural Study of Myth," 213.)

Wittgenstein says that "Freud refers to various ancient myths in these connexions, and claims that his researches have now explained how it came about that anybody should think or propound a myth of that sort.

"Whereas in fact Freud has done something different. He has not given a scientific explanation of an ancient myth. What he has done is to propound a new myth. The attractiveness of the suggestion, for instance, that all anxiety is a repetition of the anxiety of the birth trauma, is just the attractiveness of a mythology. 'It is all the outcome of something that happened long ago.' Almost like referring to a totem" (*Lectures and Conversations, . . .* [Berkeley and Los Angeles, 1972], "Conversations on Freud," 51).

The Oedipus myth means many things to many people. To Lévi-Strauss (as he is interpreted by Leach, *Lévi-Strauss*, 83), it implies that "Hell is ourselves," that is, " 'self-interest is the source of all evil.' "

The earliest recorded version of the myth comes, curiously enough, as news from the underworld reported by Odysseus (Homer *Odyssey* 11. 271–80; he calls Jocasta Epicastê): "I saw the mother of Oedipus, lovely Epicastê, who did an awful deed in the ignorance of her mind: She married her own son. And he killed his father and married her. Afterwards the gods made the thing notorious among men. But he ruled the Cadmeans in fair Thebes and suffered woe because of the gods' destructive wills. She descended into the house of Hades with his strong-shut gate after she fastened a noose high from an upper rafter, gripped by dread. To him she left behind great pain of which she was the mother, and the Furies finished it."

Sophocles' two plays, *Oedipus Tyrannus* and *Oedipus at Colonus* (the second written probably in 406 B.C. and produced posthumously in 401 [Sophocles died in 405]) are the finest literary representations of the myth and have given it the shape in which it is best known to us. Euripides narrates the tale in his *Phoenissae* 1–62, and Seneca wrote an *Oedipus Rex* which owes a considerable debt to Sophocles' first play on the subject.

The writing on Oedipus in myth and literature is sizable. For parallel stories in the folklore of various cultures, see Frazer, *Apollodorus* 2. 370–76, appendix 8, "The Legend of Oedipus." Thomas Gould, trans., *Oedipus the King by Sophocles* (Englewood Cliffs, N.J., 1970), offers a good translation and commentary and an excellent short bibliography. Robert Fitzgerald's translation of *Oedipus at Colonus* in the Chicago series is unsurpassed. Philip Mayerson, *Classical Mythology in Literature, Art, and Music* (Waltham, Mass. and Toronto, 1971), 333–35, lists literary adaptations of the Oedipus myth from Julius Caesar (lost) to Jean Cocteau.

For psychoanalytic treatment of the myth, see Patrick Mullahy,

Oedipus: Myth and Complex (New York, 1948), for his presentation of the theories of Freud, Jung, Adler, Rank, Sullivan, Horney, and Fromm, from which one may turn to works of these authors themselves. Géza Róheim, *The Riddle of the Sphinx* (London, 1934), offers a psychoanalytic treatment of the Greek Sphinx (and such monsters in other cultures), all of which, according to the author, represent the primal scene.

Martin Kallich, Andrew MacLeish, and Gertrude Schoenbohm, eds., *Oedipus: Myth and Drama* (New York, 1968), present texts of Sophocles', Dryden's and Lee's King Oedipus plays and von Hofmannsthal's *Oedipus and the Sphinx,* along with a selection of literary, anthropological, and psychological essays on the myth.

One of the finest modern evocations of the Oedipus myth is that of Archibald MacLeish in remarks at the ground-breaking for the Robert Frost Library at Amherst College on October 26, 1963, in which he compared Robert Frost to the old, worn Oedipus: ". . . like the citizens of Colonus at the death of Oedipus in Sophocles' great play, the passive part is ours. *He* [Frost] gives: we take.

"Not that Frost was Oedipus precisely—except, perhaps, in his constant readiness to talk back to sphinxes. But there is something in the ending of that myth that gives this myth of ours its meaning. You remember how it goes—the wretched, unhappy, humbled, hurt old king, badgered and abused by fate, gulled by every trick the gods can play him, tangled in patricide and incest and in every guilt, snarled in a web of faithful falsehoods and affectionate deceptions and kind lies, exiled by his own proscription, blinded by his own hands, who, dying, has so great a gift to give that Thebes and Athens quarrel over which shall have him. You remember what the gift is too. 'I am here,' says Oedipus to Theseus, King of Athens, 'to give you something, my own beaten self, no feast for the eyes . . .' And why is such a gift worth having? Because Oedipus is about to die. But why should death give value to a gift like that? Because of the place where death will meet him. . . . And what is that place? The Furies' wood which no man dares to enter: the frightening grove sacred to those implacable pursuers, ministers of guilt, who have hounded him across the world. . . . The gift that Oedipus has to give is a great gift because that beaten suffering self, no feast for the eyes, faces the dark pursuers at the end.

"Frost, I said, was not Oedipus, and so he wasn't. But he too has that gift to give. And I can imagine some late student reading his poems in the library that bears his name and feeling, like Theseus, that the beaten and triumphant self has somehow, and mysteriously, been given *him*—a self not unlike the old Theban King's.

"Quarrelsome? Certainly—and not with men alone but gods. Tangled in misery? More than most men. But despairing? No. Defeated by the certainty of death? Never defeated. Frightened of the dreadful wood? Not frightened either. A rebellious, brave, magnificent, far-wandering, unbowed old man who made his finest music out of manhood and met the Furies on their own dark ground."

27   Apollodorus tells us at 1. 8. 5–6 that Tydeus was exiled from Calydon for murder and came to Thebes, married Adrastus' daughter, Deipyle, and perished in the expedition led by Adrastus against Thebes.

The story of the night brawl between Polynices and Tydeus, the prophecy to Adrastus to marry his daughters to a boar and a lion, and Adrastus' acceptance of the two heroes as sons-in-law is told in two of Euripides' plays. Adrastus narrates the story in the *Suppliant Women* (132–46) and Polynices in the *Phoenician Women* (408–25). In both plays it is the animal-like ferocity with which the two heroes fight, not their shield devices, which leads Adrastus to connect them to the prophecy (identified as Apollo's).

In Aeschylus' *Seven Against Thebes* neither Tydeus nor Polynices carry shields with the devices Apollodorus describes (Tydeus: 387–90; Polynices: 642–49).

28   At 3. 4. 2 Apollodorus says that Cadmus gave Harmonia the necklace, along with a robe, as a wedding present (see n. 13 for other possible givers of the gift). These heirlooms created mischief and destruction wherever they went (as here; see also 3. 7. 2 and 3. 7. 5–7), until they were finally dedicated to Apollo at Delphi and deposited there (3. 7. 7).

Eriphyle was Adrastus' sister (1. 9. 13) and this relation probably gave her additional sway over Amphiaraus.

29   Apollodorus may have drawn his list of the seven chieftains from Euripides *Phoenician Women* 119–81, with whom he is in agreement. Aeschylus *Seven Against Thebes* 375–649, Sophocles *Oedipus at Colonus* 1309–20, and Euripides *Suppliants* 860–929, however, list Eteoclus as one of the Seven (all of whom fought and were killed) but not Adrastus, their leader and the only chieftain to survive the expedition. Mecisteus was Adrastus' brother (1. 9. 13).

30   Euripides wrote a tragedy, *Hypsipyle*, many fragments of which were discovered at Oxyrhynchus in Egypt in the late nineteenth century. For the most recent reconstruction of the play, see G. W. Bond, ed., *Euripides: Hypsipyle* (Oxford, 1963).

Bacchylides 9. 10–20 briefly narrates the myth of the founding by the Seven of the Nemean games in honor of Archemorus, whom the serpent killed as a sign of the coming slaughter, he says. But it did not persuade them to march back home.

31   Apollodorus' version of Tydeus' embassy to Thebes follows

Homer *Iliad* 4. 382–98 at which Agamemnon tells the story to Tydeus' son, Diomedes, as a conventional shame-inducing tactic designed to urge him on to battle. Athena gives a briefer version of Tydeus' embassy at *Iliad* 5. 801–08.

32   Aeschylus *Seven Against Thebes* 375–649 stations different heroes at different gates, omitting Adrastus, adding Eteoclus, and naming two gates which Apollodorus omits. (He supplies the names of two gates which Aeschylus does not mention.) See also Frazer, *Apollodorus* 1. 360–61.

33   There is a lacuna in the text between "for she was a friend of his mother, Chariclo" and "saw her naked." Frazer (*Apollodorus*, 1. 363) supplies "and Tiresias once accidentally."

The story here attributed to Pherecydes of the blinding of the Theban seer Tiresias (who is first mentioned by Apollodorus at 2. 4. 8) is told more fully by the Hellenistic Greek poet Callimachus (ca. 305–ca. 240 B.C.) in *Hymn 5, On the Bath of Pallas* 57–130: Athena and Chariclo were bathing during the noontime quiet in a spring on Mount Helicon when Tiresias, hot and thirsty from hunting, came with his dogs to the spring to get a drink and saw Athena naked. Angered, the goddess blinded him, but then in pity for his grieving mother explained to her that a law of the gods required that no human see a god naked against his or her will.

The second story of Tiresias' blinding, told by Hesiod, Apollodorus says (where is not known), is found in Ovid *Met.* 3. 316–38. The Roman poet says that Tiresias remained a woman for seven years. While Tiresias in Ovid's version takes the side of Zeus, he does not venture to calculate the precise degree by which a woman's sexual pleasure exceeds that of a man.

Tiresias appears several times in surviving Greek literature. In the *Odyssey*, Odysseus goes to the underworld on Circe's instructions to hear prophecy of his future from the shade of the seer. At 11. 90–137 he predicts Odysseus' return to Ithaca under certain conditions and the slaughter of the suitors. He instructs him to sacrifice to Poseidon and to the other gods and prophesies his death.

Tiresias is a character in four Greek dramas. In Sophocles *Oedipus Tyrannus* 300–462 and *Antigone* 988–1090, he is not only seer but adversary to Oedipus (in the former play) and to Creon (in the latter play). In Euripides *Bacchae* 170–369 the aged, blind Tiresias comes onstage incongruously bedecked with fawn skins and ivy and carrying a wand as a convert to Dionysus, the new god who has come to Thebes. He is followed by old Cadmus, similarly dressed. Tiresias is again cast in a role of opposition, this time to the rigid, ignorant young Pentheus who violently opposes Dionysus. At lines 266–327 Tiresias out of his wisdom describes the meaning of Dionysus: Mankind has two great blessings from the gods, he says, bread and wine, which nourish and sustain him. In wine men find release from suffering and grief, and release also in the rites and dance to Dionysus who gives his worshippers power of prophecy. "I, then, and Cadmus, whom you [Pentheus] ridicule, shall crown our heads with ivy and we shall dance, to you a foolish pair of old grey beards, but we must dance."

Finally, Tiresias appears in Euripides' *Phoenician Women* 834–959, sent for by Creon, king of Thebes, who asks him how to save the city threatened by the expedition led by Adrastus and Polynices. The king must sacrifice his son, Tiresias says. For once the seer is not reviled nor threatened for his bad news: Creon falls on his knees before him, begging him not to reveal the prophecy to the city (923–25). Tiresias refuses to keep silent (926).

34   The myth of the expedition against Thebes undertaken by Adrastus and Polynices is the subject of two surviving plays, Aeschylus' *Seven Against Thebes* and Euripides' *Phoenician Women*. (The myth, though "outside the drama," nevertheless bears upon the action of two others: Euripides' *Suppliant Women* and Sophocles' *Oedipus at Colonus*.) The *Phoenician Women* retells the myth of the house of Cadmus up to the present campaign of the Seven (1–87, 865–83, 1019–66). The trouble began with the lust of Laius, who made Jocasta pregnant contrary to the will of the gods (21–27, 867–69).

Aeschylus' *Seven Against Thebes* is the third and only surviving play of a trilogy on the Oedipus myth, the first two of which were named *Laius* and *Oedipus*. The true subject of the *Seven*, according to Anne Burnett, "Curse and Dream in Aeschylus' *Septem*," *Greek, Roman, and Byzantine Studies* 14. 4 (1973), 343–68, is the death of Eteocles, or rather, "the death, and the Curse that caused it," which, she says, "shape the gesture, the poetry and the spectacle of this tragedy" (346). The chieftains on both sides independently draw lots to oppose each other at each of the seven gates of the city. The lot decrees the same gate for the warring brothers, Polynices and Eteocles. When Eteocles learns where the lot has placed him he is filled with terror, for he recognizes the fulfillment of his father's curse (*Seven*, 653–55) which he thought earlier might not portend destruction, might even save Thebes (69–76). His recognition, says Burnett, "is not one of crude identity; it is instead of the sort that Aristotle thought the best, one of situation. Like Oedipus in *Oedipus Rex*, Eteocles finds himself in a new rôle, but unlike Oedipus, he finds that his performance is still ahead of him" (352).

By means of the lot, which is central to the play, Aeschylus shows that man's destiny has "the appearance of pure chance and the reality of divine direction. . . . The trilogy of which *Septem* [i.e., the *Seven*] was the conclusion told of three such imperative portions which fell at different times to different members of a single family, and it described with three generations, the full human range of human response to its allotted destiny. . . ." Apollo commanded Laius to save Thebes by not continuing his family line with a son. Laius arrogantly disobeyed and Oedipus' birth was "a temporary defiance of Apollo's fixed intent." The next lot was more active: to Oedipus was assigned the death of Laius and the creation of new members of the race whom he was then to curse. Oedipus did not accept his lot willingly, rather, he complied with it unknowingly. "And so to the monstrous offspring of Oedipus a third and final version of the racial portion was assigned: they were to destroy each other."

The response of Oedipus' sons to the third command is the subject of the *Seven*, a play "that had to ease the tension Aeschylus had made between heaven's absolute demands and the flawed obedience of the house of Laius." Unlike the two previous generations the third "in the person of Eteocles, at last offers a disciplined, knowing submission to a thrice-dreadful destiny and so puts the true stamp of heroism on the fate of the Theban royal family" (366–67).

For a more general analysis of the play (with many original observations), see Anthony Hecht and Helen H. Bacon, trans., *Aeschylus: Seven Against Thebes* (New York and London, 1973), Introduction, 3–17. For Hecht and Bacon the play is "not merely the culmination but the terrible re-enactment of the tragedies of Laius and Oedipus, of disobedience, parricide and incest. . . . The violent desire for exclusive possession of the mother is a tragedy Oedipus unconsciously acted out, becoming blind that he might see what he could not see with his eyes. The violent desire for the exclusive possession of the mother land, the unwillingness of either to be content with a lesser or equal share, drives Oedipus' two sons, who are also his brothers, to murder each other, each one blindly believing justice to be on his side" (8–9).

Pindar *Nem.* 9. 16–27 briefly sketches the doomed expedition to Thebes, ending his narration with the disappearance of Amphiaraus with his chariot and horses into a chasm in the earth. He was said to reign in the underworld, fully alive, since he did not actually die (Sophocles *Electra* 837–41).

As to Demeter and the birth of Arion, Pausanias 8. 25 4–9 says that Demeter, searching for Persephone, was followed by Poseidon who wanted to make love with her. To escape from him she turned herself into a mare, but he discovered her, changed himself into a horse, and so had intercourse with her. She was enraged and was thence surnamed Fury. By Poseidon she had a human daughter whose name was a secret, and the horse Arion, famous, Homer tells us, for his swiftness (*Iliad* 23. 346–47).

35   Apollodorus here gives the barest outline of the myth from which Sophocles created *Antigone*, perhaps the best known of his plays after the *Oedipus Tyrannus*. Apollodorus omits the suicides of Antigone, Haemon (Creon's son to whom she is betrothed), and Eurydice (Haemon's mother and Creon's wife).

Antigone has often been read and taught as a manifesto for civil disobedience, deriving its authority from its canonical status as Greek literature. This status is well deserved, but as one critic of the play has said, "It is a very superficial criticism which interprets the character of Creon as that of a hypocritical tyrant, and regards Antigone as a blameless victim." Sophocles makes us feel, the writer continues, "that Creon, as well as Antigone, is contending for what he believes to be right, while both are conscious that, in following out one principle, they are laying themselves open to just blame for transgressing another...." There is then, a "balance of principles," an "antagonism between valid claims." Moreover, "the struggle between Antigone and Creon represents the struggle between elemental tendencies and established laws by which the outer life of man is ... brought into harmony with his inward needs. Until this harmony is perfected, we shall never be able to attain a great right without also doing a wrong. Reformers, ... revolutionists, are never fighting against evil only; they are also placing themselves in opposition to ... a valid principle which cannot be infringed without harm."

A person's intellect, moral sense or affection may place him in opposition to the rules of society. Such a person "must not only dare to be right, he must also dare to be wrong.... Like Antigone, he may fall a victim to the struggle and yet he can never earn the name of a blameless martyr anymore than the society—the Creon he has defied, can be branded as a hypocritical tyrant" (George Eliot, "The Antigone and its Moral" [1856], in Thomas Pinney, ed., *Essays of George Eliot* [New York and London, 1963], 261–65, quotations from 264–65).

For a different version of the myth, on which Euripides possibly based his *Antigone* (now lost), see Frazer, *Apollodorus* 1. 373.

36   The story of Adrastus' flight to Athens, where he seeks refuge and burial for the Argives who died in the expedition of the Seven, is the basis for Euripides' *Suppliant Women*. At Athens' insistence, backed by force of arms, Thebes allows the defeated Argives to bury their dead. In the play Adrastus and the suppliants actually take refuge at Eleusis (near Athens) before the altars of Demeter and Persephone, rather than at the Altar of Mercy at Athens as Apollodorus says (2. 8. 1 and ch. 5, n. 43).

The play has puzzled critics of Euripides primarily because the playwright seems to express an uncharacteristic piety toward the gods. D. J. Conacher, *Euripidean Drama: Myth, Theme and Structure* (Toronto, 1967), 95, reminds us that while Euripides sought to express the truths he saw through myths, he "treated myth in more than one way and with more than one purpose."

37   In Homer *Iliad* 4. 404–10 Sthenelus, one of the Epigoni (son of Capaneus), briefly describes the second expedition against Thebes, apparently a popular subject in antiquity. Herodotus 4. 32 refers to an epic, *Epigoni*, expressing doubt that it was composed by Homer as some thought, and Aeschylus and Euripides both wrote tragedies entitled *Epigoni*.

Eriphyle accepts Harmonia's robe from Polynices' son as a bribe to persuade her sons to join the Epigoni, even as earlier she accepted Harmonia's necklace from Polynices himself as a bribe to persuade her husband, Amphiaraus, to join the Seven in the expedition against Thebes. He was a seer and knew in advance that he would die on it (3. 6. 2). These heirlooms from the house of Cadmus were originally wedding gifts to Harmonia (3. 4. 2), which somehow came into Polynices' hands (3. 6. 1).

38   See 3. 6. 2 and n. 28.

39   Like Orestes, who murdered his mother, Clytemnestra (Epitome 6. 24–25 and ch. 12, n. 11), Alcmaeon is pursued by a Fury after killing Eriphyle, *exul mentisque domusque* as Ovid *Met.* 9. 409 says, "an exile from mind and home." (Ovid tells the story of Alcmaeon briefly and somewhat obscurely at *Met.* 9. 407–17.)

The land of Psophis becomes barren because of Alcmaeon's murder of his mother just as Greece becomes barren because of Pelops' murder of Stymphalus, king of Arcadia (3. 12. 6). The land, cattle, and women of Thebes are blighted because of the unpurged slaying of Laius by Oedipus (Sophocles *Oedipus Tyrannus* 22–27, 96–98).

Thucydides 2. 102 says that Apollo told Alcmaeon in an oracle that his madness would not end until he should find a place to live which did not exist at the time he killed his mother. He went to the Achelous and discovered a newly formed alluvial deposit at the river's mouth. He settled there, naming the area Acarnania, after his son, Acarnan.

Pausanias twice says that Phegeus' sons (rather than Alcmaeon's) dedicated Harmonia's necklace at Delphi (8. 24. 10 and 9. 41. 2).

40   Apollodorus may here refer to one of the two tragedies by Euripides (now lost), both named *Alcmaeon*.

CHAPTER SEVEN

The Family of Pelasgus, Including Lycaon, Callisto,
and Arcas; Atalanta; the Family of Atlas,
Including Hermes; Asclepius; the Birth of Helen;
Castor and Pollux; Helen's Marriage with Menelaus;
Dardanus and the Trojan Line; the Founding of Troy;
Priam and His Children; the Family of Asopus,
Including Aeacus, Peleus, and Telamon, and
Achilles and Ajax
(3. 8. 1–3. 13. 8)

BOOK 3 8 Let us return now to Pelasgus. | Acusilaus says that he was a son of Zeus and Niobe, as I have thought [2. 1. 1], but Hesiod says that he was born from the earth. | To him and to Meliboea, the daughter of Ocean, | or as some say, to a nymph, Cyllene | a son Lycaon was born, who was king of Arcadia and by many women had fifty sons. | They were Melaeneus, Thesprotus, Helix, Nyctimus, Peucetius, Caucon, Mecisteus, Hopleus, Macareus, Macednus, Horus, Polichus, Acontes, Evaemon, Ancyor, Archebates, Carteron, Aegaeon, Pallas, Eumon, Canethus, Prothous, Linus, Coretho, Maenalus, Teleboas, Physius, Phassus, Phthius, Lycius, Halipherus, Genetor, Bucolion, Socleus, Phineus, Eumetes, Harpaleus, Portheus, Plato, Haemo, Cynaethus, Leo, Harpalycus, Heraeeus, Titanas, Mantineus, Clitor, Stymphalus and Orchomenus. [Apollodorus only names forty-nine.] | These were the most arrogant and impious of all men. Zeus, wishing to determine how impious they were, came to them in the guise of a laborer. They offered him hospitality, and at the suggestion of the elder brother, Maenalus, slaughtered one of the native children, mixed his viscera with the sacrifices, and placed them before him. Zeus in disgust overturned the table at the place which is even now called Trapezus ["Table"], and with thunderbolts killed Lycaon and his sons, except for Nyctimus, the youngest. Before he could strike him, Earth seized his hand and checked his wrath. After Nyctimus inherited the kingdom, the flood in the time of Deucalion occurred. | Some say that it was caused by the impiety of Lycaon's sons.[1] |

| Eumelus and some others say that Lycaon also had a daughter, Callisto. Hesiod, however, claims that she was one of the nymphs; Asius says that she was the daughter of Nycteus; and Pherecydes says that she was the daughter of Ceteus. | She hunted with Artemis, wore the same type of clothing as the goddess, and swore to her to remain

a virgin. But Zeus fell in love with her and went to bed with her against her will | in the form, some say, of Artemis, but as others say, of Apollo | . Wishing to prevent Hera from finding out, he changed Callisto into a bear, but Hera persuaded Artemis to shoot her down like a wild animal. | Some say that Artemis shot her because she did not preserve her virginity. | When Callisto died, Zeus snatched up the child with which she had been pregnant, named it Arcas, and gave it to Maia in Arcadia to bring up. He then changed Callisto into a star which he called the Bear.[2]

9   Arcas had two sons, Elatus and Aphidas, by Leanira, the daughter of Amyclus, | or by Meganira, the daughter of Croco, or, as Eumelus says, by the nymph Chrysopelia | . They divided the land between them, but Elatus had all the power. By Laodice, the daughter of Cinyras, he had two sons, Stymphalus and Pereus. Aphidas had a son, Aleus, and a daughter, Stheneboea, whom Proetus married. To Aleus and Neaera, the daughter of Pereus, were born a daughter, Auge, and sons, Cepheus and Lycurgus.

Auge was seduced by Heracles, but concealed the baby she had by him in a sacred grove of Athena whose priestess she was. When the land failed to yield crops and oracles revealed that there was something sacrilegious in the grove of Athena, Auge was discovered by her father and handed over to Nauplius to be put to death. But Teuthras, the ruler of the Mysians, took her from him and married her. The baby later born to her was exposed on Mount Parthenius. It was suckled by a doe and called Telephus. He was reared by herdsmen of Corythus and went to Delphi in search of his parents. On learning from the god where they were, he went to Mysia and became the adopted son of Teuthras. When Teuthras died he succeeded to the kingship.[3]

2   To Lycurgus and Cleophyle (or Eurynome) were born Ancaeus, Epochus, Amphidamas, and Iasus. Amphidamas had a son, Melanion, and a daughter, Antimache, whom Eurystheus married.

To Iasus and Clymene, the daughter of Minyas, Atalanta was born. Her father, desiring a male child, exposed her. A she-bear came to her and suckled her, however, until hunters found her and reared her among themselves. When Atalanta grew up she remained a virgin. Always carrying her weapons with her, she lived in the wilderness as a huntress. When the centaurs Rhoecus and Hylaeus tried to rape her, she shot and killed them. She went with the chieftains on the hunt for the Calydonian boar, and in the games held in Pelias' honor wrestled with Peleus and won.

She later found out who her parents were. When her father tried to persuade her to marry, she chose a place for a foot race, drove a stake four and a half feet long into the ground in the middle of it, and giving her suitors a head start from that point, ran after them in armor. The ones she caught died on the spot, but if ever she should fail to catch one, he was to have marriage with her as his reward. After many had died, Melanion, in love with her, came to the race bringing golden apples which he had obtained from Aphrodite. As she chased him he threw down the apples and Atalanta, stopping to pick them up, lost the race. Melanion then married her. It is said that once while hunting they entered a grove sacred to Zeus and there, after making love, were changed into lions. | Hesiod and some others say that Atalanta was a daughter of Schoeneus, not of Iasus, but Euripides says that she was a daughter of Maenalus and that her husband was Hippomenes, not Melanion. | By Melanion (or by Ares) she had a son, Parthenopaeus, who was a member of the expedition against Thebes.[4]

10   To Atlas and Pleione, the daughter of Ocean, there were born seven daughters at Cyllene in Arcadia, who were called Pleiades.[5] | They were Alcyone, Merope, Celaeno, Electra, Sterope, Taygete, and Maia. | Of these, Sterope was married to Oenomaus and Merope to Sisyphus. Poseidon had intercourse with Celaeno and Alcyone. Celaeno bore him Lycus, whom Poseidon allowed to live in the Islands of the Blest, and Alcyone had a daughter, Aethusa, the mother of Eleuther by Apollo, and of two sons, Hyrieus and Hyperenor. To Hyrieus and a nymph, Clonia, were born Nycteus and Lycus; to Nycteus and Polyxo, Antiope; and to Antiope and Zeus, Zethus and Amphion [3. 5. 5]. Zeus made love with the other daughters of Atlas.

2   Maia, the oldest, made love with Zeus in a cave on Mount Cyllene and gave birth to Hermes. He was wrapped in swaddling clothes and laid on the winnowing fan, but got up and went to Pieria where he stole the cattle which Apollo was tending. In order not to be given away by the tracks, he put shoes on their hooves and brought them to Pylus. He hid the cattle in a cave, except for two which he sacrificed. He fastened the skins of these to rocks, boiled and ate some of the flesh, and burned up the rest. He then quickly left for Cyllene. In front of the cave he found a tortoise looking for food. He removed it from its shell over which he stretched strings made from the hide of the cows which he had sacrificed. He thus invented the lyre and made a pick for it as well.

Apollo came to Pylus in search of his cattle and questioned the inhabitants, who claimed to have seen a boy driving them, but were unable to say where he had taken them because they could not discover any tracks. When he learned the identity of the thief through divination, he went to Maia on Cyllene and accused Hermes of the theft. She, however, pointed to Hermes wrapped in swaddling clothes. Apollo nonetheless carried him to Zeus and demanded his cattle back. When Zeus ordered Hermes to return them he denied taking them. Failing to persuade them, he then led Apollo to Pylus and gave the cattle back to him. Apollo heard the lyre and gave the cattle to Hermes in exchange for it. While grazing them Hermes made for himself a shepherd's pipe and played it. Apollo wanted this, too, and offered to give him the golden staff which he carried while tending cattle. Hermes wished in addition to learn divination. He gave the pipe to Apollo and the god taught him the art of divining by means of pebbles. Zeus made him his own herald and that of the underworld gods.[6]

3   Taygete [one of the Pleiades] bore to Zeus a son, Lacedaemon, after whom the country of Lacedaemon is named. To him and to Sparta, the daughter of Eurotas (who was a son of Lelex, born from the earth, and of the river nymph Cleocharia), were born a son, Amyclas, and a daughter, Eurydice, whom Acrisius married. Amyclas and Diomede, the daughter of Lapithes, had sons named Cynortes and Hyacinthus. | They say that Apollo was in love with Hyacinthus and accidentally struck him with a discus and killed him [see 1. 3. 3]. | Cynortes had a son Perieres, who married Gorgophone, the daughter of Perseus, | according to Stesichorus, | and gave birth to Tyndareus, Icarius, Aphareus, and Leucippus.[7] To Aphareus and Arene, the daughter of Oebalus, were born sons named Lynceus, Idas, and Pisus. | According to many, Idas was a son of Poseidon. | Lynceus had vision so penetrating that he was able to see things underground. Leucippus had daughters named Hilaira and Phoebe. The Dioscuri [Castor and Pollux] carried these off and married them [see 3. 11. 2].

In addition to these, Leucippus had another daughter, Arsinoe. Apollo had intercourse with her and she gave birth to Asclepius. | Some maintain that Asclepius was born not to Arsinoe, but to Coronis, the daughter of Phlegyas in Thessaly.[8] And they say that Apollo, falling in love with her, immediately made love with her, but that she, against her father's better judgment, lived with Ischys, the brother of Caeneus. Apollo cursed the crow that brought him this information, changing it from white to black, then killed Coronis. He snatched her baby [Asclepius] from the pyre where her body was being burned and brought him to Chiron the centaur, who reared him, taught him the art of healing and how to hunt. | Asclepius became a surgeon and raised the art of medicine to new levels: He prevented some from dying and restored to life others who had already died. For he had received from Athena the blood from the veins of the Gorgon and used that from the left side for killing men, that from the right for saving them. By this means he brought the dead back to life. | Some who are said to have been raised by him are: Capaneus and Lycurgus, according to

Stesichorus in the *Eriphyle*; Hippolytus, according to the author of the *Naupactica*; Tyndareus, according to Panyasis; Hymenaeus, according to the Orphics; and Glaucus, son of Minos, according to Melesagoras [but see 3. 3. 1]. |

Zeus was afraid that after men were healed by Asclepius they would help each other and so he killed him with a thunderbolt.[9] Angered by this, Apollo killed the Cyclopes who had forged the thunderbolt for Zeus. Zeus was about to cast Apollo into Tartarus, but Leto begged him not to and so he ordered him to work for a man as a hired hand for a year. Apollo went to Admetus, the son of Pheres, at Pherae and worked for him as a herdsman, making all the cows bear twin calves.[10]

| Some say that Aphareus and Leucippus were sons of Perieres, the son of Aeolus, while others say that Perieres was the son of Cynortes and had a son Oebalus to whom the river nymph Batia bore Tyndareus, Hippocoon, and Icarius. Hippocoon had sons named Dorycleus, Scaeus, Enarophorus, Eutiches, Bucolus, Lycaethus, Tebrus, Hippothous, Eurytus, Hippocorystes, Alcinus, and Alcon. |

With the help of his sons, Hippocoon expelled Icarius and Tyndareus from Lacedaemon. They fled to Thestius and allied themselves with him in a war against his neighbors. Tyndareus married Leda, the daughter of Thestius. After Heracles killed Hippocoon and his sons, they returned to Lacedaemon and Tyndareus became king [2. 7. 3].

Icarius and Periboea, a river nymph, had sons named Thoas, Damasippus, Imeusimus, Aletes, and Perileus, and a daughter, Penelope, whom Odysseus married.[11] To Tyndareus and Leda were born Timandra, whom Echemus married, Clytemnestra, whom Agamemnon married, and Phylonoe, whom Artemis made immortal. Zeus came to Leda in the form of a swan and both he and Tyndareus made love with her on the same night. By Zeus she had Pollux and Helen; by Tyndareus, Castor and Clytemnestra.[12] | Some say that Helen was the daughter of Nemesis and Zeus. For fleeing Zeus' advances, Nemesis changed herself into a goose, but Zeus turned himself into a swan and made love with her. As a result of their love-making she laid an egg which a shepherd found in a grove and brought to Leda. She placed it in a chest and watched over it. In due course Helen was hatched from it, and Leda reared her as her own daughter. | When Helen had grown into a beautiful woman, Theseus seized her and brought her to Aphidnae. While he was in Hades, Castor and Pollux marched against the city and captured it, recovered Helen and took away Aethra, the mother of Theseus, as a prisoner.[13]

The kings of Greece went to Sparta seeking to marry Helen. | They were: Odysseus, son of Laertes; Diomedes, son of Tydeus; Antilochus, son of Nestor; Agapenor, son of Ancaeus; Sthenelus, son of Capaneus; Amphimachus, son of Cteatus; Thalpius, son of Eurytus; Meges, son of Phyleus; Amphilochus, son of Amphiaraus; Menestheus, son of Peteos; Schedius and Epistrophus, sons of Iphitus; Polyxenus, son of Agasthenes; Peneleos, son of Hippalcimus; Leitus, son of Alector; Ajax, son of Oileus; Ascalaphus and Ialmenus, sons of Ares; Elephenor, son of Chalcodon; Eumelus, son of Admetus; Polypoetes, son of Pirithous; Leonteus, son of Coronus; Podalirius and Machaon, sons of Asclepius; Philoctetes, son of Poeas; Eurypylus, son of Evaemon; Protesilaus, son of Iphiclus; Menelaus, son of Atreus;

9   Ajax and Teucer, sons of Telamon; and Patroclus, son of Menoetius.[14] | When Tyndareus saw their number he was afraid that when he chose one of them for his daughter the rest would resort to violence. Odysseus promised, however, that if Tyndareus would help him win Penelope he would advise him of a way to avoid violence. When Tyndareus promised to help him, Odysseus told him to make all the suitors swear an oath to aid the man chosen as Helen's husband if anyone did anything to harm the marriage. On hearing this Tyndareus made the suitors swear the oath, chose Menelaus to be Helen's husband, and asked Icarius to allow Penelope to marry Odysseus.[15]

11   Menelaus had Hermione by Helen | and, according to some, a son, Nicostratus. | By an Aetolian slave, Pieris | or as Acusilaus says, by Tereis | , he had a son, Megapenthes | ; and by a nymph, Cnossia, according to Eumelus, he had a son, Xenodamus. | [16]

2   Of Leda's sons, Castor was skilled in the art of war, Pollux in boxing. Because of their strength they were called Dioscuri | "sons of Zeus" | . Wishing to marry they carried off from Messene the daughters of Leucippus and married them. Pollux and Phoebe had a son, Mnesileus, and Castor and Hilaira also had a son, Anogon.

They drove off cattle from Arcadia with Idas and Lynceus, the sons of Aphareus, and permitted Idas to divide them. He cut up a cow into four parts and said that half of the booty would belong to the one who ate his share first and the rest to the one who ate his share second. Idas thereupon devoured his own share ahead of the others, ate that of his brother, and with him drove the cattle into Messene. But the Dioscuri made an expedition against Messene and drove away those cattle and many others. They then waylaid Idas and Lynceus. When Lynceus saw Castor, he pointed him out to Idas who killed him. Pollux pursued them and killed Lynceus with a throw of his spear, but while chasing Lynceus he was hit on the head by a rock hurled by Idas and fell unconscious. Zeus struck Idas down with a thunderbolt and carried Pollux to heaven. Since Castor was dead, Pollux refused immortality and so Zeus granted that they live on alternate days with the gods and with the dead. When the Dioscuri joined the gods, Tyndareus summoned Menelaus to Sparta and gave him the kingdom.[17]

12   Electra, the daughter of Atlas, had two sons by Zeus named Iasion and Dardanus. Iasion was in love with Demeter and while attempting to rape her was struck and killed by a thunderbolt.[18] Grieving over the death of his brother, Dardanus left Samothrace and went to the mainland opposite. There Teucer, son of the river Scamander and the nymph Idaea, was king. The inhabitants of the land were called Teucrians after him. Dardanus was welcomed by the king, accepted his daughter Batia and a portion of his land, and founded a

2   city, Dardanus. When Teucer died he called the entire land Dardania. He had two sons Ilus and Erichthonius. Ilus died childless and Erichthonius inherited the kingdom, married Astyoche, the daughter of Simoeis, and had a son, Tros. When he succeeded to the kingdom, Tros called the land Troy after himself. He married Callirrhoe, the daughter of Scamander, and had a daughter, Cleopatra and sons, Ilus, Assaracus, and Ganymede, the last of whom, because of his beauty, Zeus carried off upon an eagle and made the cupbearer of the gods. Assaracus and Hieromneme, the daughter of Simoeis, had a son, Capys, who had a son, Anchises, by Themiste, the daughter of Ilus. Aphrodite desired Anchises, made love with him, and bore Aeneas, and Lyrus, who died childless.[19]

3   Ilus went to Phrygia where games were being held by the king and won at wrestling. As a prize he received fifty boys and fifty girls. The king, in obedience to an oracle, gave him a spotted cow and told him to found a city at the place where it lay down. He followed the cow and it lay down when it came to the hill called Phrygian Ate. There Ilus founded a city and called it Ilium.[20] He prayed to Zeus to give him a sign and then in the morning light caught sight of the Palladium [a statue of Pallas] which had fallen from heaven and was lying in front of his tent. It was four and a half feet high, with its feet close together, and held raised in its right hand a spear and in its left a distaff and spindle.

The following story is told about the Palladium. They say that when Athena was born she was reared by Triton, who had a daughter Pallas. Both were skilled in the art of war and once fought each other. When Pallas was about to strike Athena, Zeus, in fear, held the aegis in front of her. Pallas, startled, looked up, was wounded by Athena, and fell. In her grief Athena fashioned a wooden image of her and around its breast put the aegis which had frightened her. She set the image beside a statue of Zeus and paid honor to it. Later Electra took refuge at the Palladium after she was seduced, and Zeus threw it, along with Ate, into the Ilian country. Ilus then built a temple for it and paid honor to it. This is the story told about the Palladium.[21]

Ilus married Eurydice, the daughter of Adrastus, and by her had Laomedon, who married Strymo, the daughter of Scamander | or, according to some, Placia, the daughter of Otreus, but according to others, Leucippe |, and had sons named Tithonus, Lampus, Clytius, Hicetaon, and Podarces, and daughters named Hesione, Cilla, and Astyoche.[22] By a nymph Calybe, he had a son Bucolion.

4   Dawn was in love with Tithonus and carried him off and brought him to Ethiopia. There she made love with him and bore sons named
5   Emathion and Memnon.[23]

After Ilium was captured by Heracles, as I mentioned a little before [2. 6. 4], Podarces, who was called Priam, became king. He married first Arisbe, the daughter of Merops, by whom he had a son, Aesacus, who married Asterope, the daughter of Cebren. When Asterope died, Aesacus mourned for her so much that he was changed into a bird.[24] Priam gave Arisbe to Hyrtacus and married Hecuba, the daughter of Dymas, | or as some say, of Cisseus, or as others say, of the river Sangarius, and Metope |.[25] Hector was her first born son. When her second child was due, Hecuba dreamed that she gave birth to a burning torch which spread fire over the entire city and burned it. When Priam learned of the dream from Hecuba, he sent for his son Aesacus, for he was an interpreter of dreams who had been taught by his maternal grandfather Merops. He declared that the baby was born to be the destroyer of his country and ordered it to be exposed. When it was born Priam gave it to a servant named Agelaus to take to Mount Ida and expose. There a bear suckled it for five days. When Agelaus found it safe he took it up, brought it to his home, and reared it as his own son, naming it Paris. When he became a young man he was superior to most young men in beauty and strength. He took the name Alexander ["Warder-off-of-men"] because he fought off robbers and protected the flocks. Later on he learned who his true parents were.[26]

After him, Hecuba gave birth to daughters named Creusa, Laodice, Polyxena, and Cassandra. Apollo, wishing to make love with Cassandra, promised to teach her the art of divination. After learning it she refused to make love with him, whereupon the god denied her the ability to convince anyone whenever she prophesied.[27] | Afterwards Hecuba had sons named Deiphobus, Helenus, Pammon, Polites, Antiphus, Hipponous, Polydorus, and Troilus, the last of whom she is said to have had by Apollo.

By other women Priam had sons named Melanippus, Gorgythion, Philaemon, Hippothous, Glaucus, Agathon, Chersidamas, Evagoras,

Hippodamas, Mestor, Atas, Doryclus, Lycaon, Dryops, Bias, Chromius, Astygonus, Telestas, Evander, Cebriones, Mylius, Archemachus, Laodocus, Echephron, Idomeneus, Hyperion, Ascanius, Democoon, Aretus, Deiopites, Clonius, Echemmon, Hypirochus, Aegeoneus, Lysithous, Polymedon, and daughters named Medusa, Medesicaste, Lysimache, and Aristodeme. |

6   Hector married Andromache, the daughter of Eetion, and Alexander married Oenone, the daughter of the river Cebren. Oenone had learned the art of divination from Rhea and warned Alexander not to sail after Helen. Failing to persuade him, she told him to come to her if ever he were wounded, for she alone could heal him. He carried off Helen from Sparta and during the war at Troy was shot by Philoctetes with the bow of Heracles. He returned to Oenone on Ida, but she was angry because he had deserted her and refused to heal him. Alexander was carried back to Troy where he died. Oenone changed her mind and brought medicine with which to heal him. When she found him dead she hanged herself.[28]

The Asopus River was a son of Ocean and Tethys, | or as Acusilaus says, of Pero and Poseidon, or as some others say, of Zeus and Eurynome | . He married Metope, the daughter of the river Ladon, who bore him two sons, Ismenus and Pelagon, and twenty daughters, one of whom, Aegina, Zeus carried off. Looking for her, Asopus came to Corinth and learned from Sisyphus that Zeus had taken her away.[29] While Asopus was pursuing him the god hurled thunderbolts at him and sent him back to his own river. (Because of this even to the present time live coals are found in that river.) [30] Then he brought Aegina to the island named at that time Oenone, but now called Aegina after her, had intercourse with her, and by her had a son, Aeacus. Since Aeacus was alone on the island, Zeus turned the ants into men for him.[31] Aeacus married Endeis, the daughter of Sciron, who bore two sons to him, Peleus and Telamon. | Pherecydes says that Telamon was a friend, not a brother of Peleus, and was the son of Actaeus and Glauce, the daughter of Cychreus. | Aeacus later had intercourse with Psamathe, the daughter of Nereus, who changed herself into a seal to avoid making love with him, and who bore him a son, Phocus.[32]

Aeacus was the most religious of all men. Greece at this time was afflicted with barrenness because of Pelops. For when he was at war with Stymphalus, the king of the Arcadians, and was unable to capture Arcadia, Pelops pretended friendship with the king, then killed him, dismembered him, and scattered the parts. Oracles of the gods declared that Greece would be freed from its present trouble if Aeacus would pray for it. He did so and Greece was delivered from its barrenness. After he died he was honored even in Pluto's house and he keeps the keys of Hades.[33]

Since Phocus was superior to his brothers, Peleus and Telamon, in athletic contests, they plotted against him. It was decided by lot that Telamon would kill him and he struck him on the head with a discus when he was exercising. With the help of Peleus he carried off the body and hid it in some woods. When the murder was discovered

7   Aeacus drove the brothers from Aegina into exile. Telamon went to Salamis, to Cychreus, the son of Poseidon and Salamis, the daughter of Asopus. Cychreus had become king of the island after killing a snake which was ravaging it, and dying childless, left the kingdom to Telamon. He married Periboea, the daughter of Alcathus, the son of Pelops. When Heracles prayed for a male son for Telamon and when, following his prayer, an eagle appeared, Telamon called the son born to him Ajax. With Heracles he led an army against Troy and received as a war prize Hesione, the daughter of Laomedon, who bore him a son, Teucer [see 2. 6. 4].

13   Peleus fled to Phthia to the house of Eurytion, the son of Actor, and was purified by him of the murder. He accepted his daughter Antigone and one-third of the country.[34]

Peleus had a daughter Polydora, whom Borus, the son of Perieres,
2   married. He went with Eurytion to hunt the Calydonian boar. Throwing a javelin at it he struck and killed Eurytion by mistake [see 1. 8. 2]. Again in exile, he went from Phthia to Acastus at Iolcus and was puri-
3   fied by him of the killing of Eurytion. Peleus took part in the games in honor of Pelias by wrestling with Atalanta [3. 9. 2].

Astydamia, the wife of Acastus, desired Peleus and sent him a message proposing sexual intercourse. Unable to persuade him, she informed Peleus' wife [Antigone] that he was going to marry Sterope, the daughter of Acastus. Hearing this, she hanged herself. Astydamia falsely accused Peleus to Acastus, saying that he had tried to make love with her.[35] Acastus was unwilling to kill a man whom he had purified, so he took him hunting on Mount Pelion. During a contest in hunting Peleus caught animals, cut out their tongues and put them in a leather pouch, and let the animals go. The men with Acastus caught these same animals and ridiculed Peleus for catching nothing. But he showed them the tongues and said that he had caught the animals whose tongues he had.

While Peleus was sleeping on Mount Pelion, Acastus deserted him, buried his sword in cow manure, and returned home. When Peleus awakened and was looking for his sword, he was captured and nearly killed by centaurs. Chiron, however, saved him, found his sword and returned it to him.

4 Peleus married Polydora, the daughter of Perieres, who bore a son,
5 Menesthius, who was his in name only, for the actual father was the Sperchius River.[36] He later married Thetis, the daughter of Nereus, for whom Zeus and Poseidon competed to marry. When Themis prophesied that the son born to her would be stronger than his father, they withdrew. | Some say that when Zeus was intent on making love with her, Prometheus told him that the son born to her would rule heaven. Still others say that Thetis did not want to make love with Zeus because she had been reared by Hera, and that Zeus in anger wanted to make her live with a mortal. | When Chiron, then, advised Peleus to seize her and to hold on to her, even though she changed her shape, he watched for his opportunity and carried her off. And although she changed first into fire, then into water, and then into a wild animal, he did not let her go until she resumed her original shape. He married her on Mount Pelion and there the gods ate, drank, and sang wedding hymns. Chiron gave to Peleus an ash spear, and Poseidon gave him two immortal horses named Balius and Xanthus.[37]

6 Thetis bore a son to Peleus which she wanted to make immortal. She therefore placed him in the fire during the night without Peleus' knowledge, in order to burn away the mortal part of him inherited from his father, and by day anointed him with ambrosia. But Peleus observed this and seeing the child struggling in the fire let out a shout. Thetis, hindered from carrying out her plan, abandoned her infant son and went to the Nereids. Peleus brought the child to Chiron who took him in and fed him on the viscera of lions and wild pigs and on the marrow of bears. He named him Achilles because he had *not* [a] put his *lips* [*cheilê*] to the breast. (He was originally named Ligyron.)[38]

7 After this Peleus sacked Iolcus with Jason and the Dioscuri and killed Astydamia, the wife of Acastus. He dismembered her and led the army between the parts of her body into the city.[39]

8 When Achilles was nine years old Calchas said that Troy could not be taken without him. Having foreknowledge that he would die if he went on the expedition Thetis disguised him as a young girl and put him in the keeping of Lycomedes. While growing up at Lycomedes' court, Achilles had an affair with his daughter Deidamia. The son Pyrrhus which she bore to him was later called Neoptolemus. When Odysseus came to the court of Lycomedes in search of Achilles he found him by sounding a trumpet. In this way Achilles went to Troy.

Phoenix, the son of Amyntor, accompanied him. He had been blinded by his father when his father's concubine Phthia falsely accused him of seducing her. Peleus brought him to Chiron who restored his sight and then Peleus made him king of the Dolopes. Patroclus, the son of Menoetius and Sthenele, the daughter of Acastus, also accompanied Achilles. | Or the mother of Patroclus was Periopis the daughter of Pheres; or as Philocrates says, Polymele, the daughter of Peleus. | In Opus he had quarreled over a game of dice with a boy, Clitonymus, the son of Amphidamas, and killed him. He then fled with his father and lived with Peleus, where he became the lover of Achilles.[40]

NOTES
(3. 8. 1–3. 13. 8)

1   In another version of the myth found in Suidas (or the Suda), a tenth-century A.D. historical and literary encyclopedia (s. v. *Lykaôn*), Lycaon, wishing to make his subjects righteous, told them that Zeus constantly was among them in disguise to discover who was righteous and who was not. Once when he was offering a sacrifice to Zeus, some of his sons killed a child and mixed its flesh with that of the sacrificial animal, wishing to find out if the god were truly present, for they believed that he would react if he were. He did: He caused storms and lightning in which all the murderers of the child died.

In Ovid's version (*Met.* 1. 163–243) Jove, visiting earth, found himself at nightfall in Arcadia and revealed his presence (apparently seeking hospitality). The common people received him prayerfully, but Lycaon mocked their piety and to test Jove's identity as a god, planned to murder him in his bed. Not content with that, he offered him human flesh for dinner. When the meal was placed before him, Jove destroyed the house with a bolt of lightning. Lycaon fled to the fields, howling as he tried to speak, for because of his bloodthirstiness he was transformed into a wolf.

Lycaon was only one example of the many wicked households on earth which deserved destruction, and so Jove resolved to destroy mankind by a flood which only Deucalion and Pyrrha survived (see *Met.* 1. 260–437, 1. 7. 2 and ch. 2, n. 2).

For a discussion of this myth as evidence of the practice of human sacrifice and cannibalism in Arcadia even into the second century A.D., see Frazer, *Apollodorus* 1. 390–93.

2   Ovid's treatment of the Callisto myth (*Met.* 2. 401–531) is more coherent than Apollodorus' and contains a favorite Ovidian theme. The story: Jove sees the huntress in the woods and the combination of her

beauty and the casual disarray of her hair and dress as she wanders carrying spear and bow arouses him to make love with her. But she is a soldier of Diana (*miles erat Phoebes*, 415) and the goddess' most loved devotee. When Jove sees her lie down to rest alone in the deepest part of the forest he thinks, "My wife will never know, but if she does find out, O, it's worth it, it's worth it!"

Taking the form of Diana he appears to Callisto, who jumps up from the grass and welcomes her (or him) happily. Jove kisses her eagerly—in a manner most unmaidenlike. As Callisto begins to describe her morning's hunt, Jove embraces her and thus reveals his true identity. Callisto struggles, but is overcome by force. Desire satisfied, Jove returns to heaven.

Diana now comes upon Callisto, followed by her band of virgin huntresses, Callisto's companions. The goddess calls to her, but she hangs back: it might be Jove again. The presence of the other maidens reassures her and she joins them. She struggles to conceal her expression of guilt, keeps her eyes on the ground, and does not go to Diana's side as she usually did. Rather, she is silent and blushes, and if Diana were not herself a virgin, she would have perceived Callisto's guilt by a thousand signs. The other maidens do (?).

Nine months later, after a hot morning spent hunting, Diana and her band come upon cool woods with a flowing stream and decide to take off their clothes and swim. The others strip, but Callisto delays, removing her clothes slowly. Finally naked, she exposes her crime, her swollen belly, which she tries to cover with her hands. Diana at once cries, "Get out of here, do not pollute this sacred spring," and drives her from her company.

Juno had been keeping tabs on Callisto, waiting for a suitable time for vengeance. The birth of a boy whom the girl names Arcas feeds Juno's rage (he will be proof to all of Jove's philandering) and she grabs the girl by the hair, flings her to the ground, and while Callisto pleads with outstretched arms, turns her into a bear. Callisto, praying, hears her prayer turn into the guttural sounds of a bear (another example of blocked human utterance, a favorite Ovidian theme). Her mind remains the same as she continues to raise her hands, or rather paws, in prayer to Jove, who ignores her. Frightened now by everything in the woods, she can never rest: The huntress has now become a hunted object. She even hides from bears, forgetting that she is one.

Years pass. One day Arcas, now fifteen, is hunting in the Arcadian woods and comes upon his mother. She recognizes him; he obviously does not recognize her and fears the creature which has fixed its eyes upon him. As she shuffles closer to her son he prepares to hurl his javelin through her heart. Jove at once intervenes, catches them up to heaven, and makes them constellations. She becomes Arctus, the Great Bear, he Arctophylax, Guardian of the Great Bear.

Juno, furious at this turn of events, descends to Tethys and Ocean, complaining that her power is nothing if potential wrongdoers see Callisto made a constellation in heaven after injuring her. She begs Ocean not to allow the new constellation ever to touch his pure waters. And so the Great Bear ceaselessly revolves around the North Star, never setting in the Ocean, as other constellations do.

The reader sensitized to concerns of twentieth-century women will have noticed that in Ovid's version Callisto is raped and then considered guilty of a crime by two types of women: Diana and the virgin huntresses (her "sisters"), who cast her from their midst, and Juno, the married woman who is insanely jealous of the younger objects of her husband's satyriasis. The result is that Callisto has nowhere, nowhere at all, to turn, and so "turns" wild, in the end saved only most casually by Jove from a bitter death.

3   For Heracles' seduction of Auge, see 2. 7. 4 and ch. 5, n. 35.

4   Artemis taught Atalanta archery and how to hunt with dogs (Callimachus *Hymn 3, to Artemis*, 215–17). Apollodorus at 1. 9. 17 names her as one of the Argonauts sailing with Jason after the Golden Fleece. Apollonious Rhodius *Argonautica* 1. 769–73, however, says that although she was eager to sail on the Argo, Jason dissuaded her, fearing the effect a beautiful woman aboard ship would have upon an all male crew.

For her presence at the hunt for the Calydonian boar, see 1. 8. 2–3 and ch. 2, n. 9. Apollodorus mentions briefly Atalanta's wrestling match with Peleus at 3. 13. 3.

Theocritus *Idyll* 3. 40–42 and Ovid *Met.* 10. 560–704 name Atalanta's successful suitor Hippomenes, apparently following Euripides (who, Apollodorus tells us, named him thus). Ovid's version of the myth of Atalanta differs considerably from Apollodorus': The girl was both swift of foot and beautiful. She asked an oracle about marrying and the oracle replied, "You do not need a husband, Atalanta; avoid marriage. You will not avoid it, though, and you will lose your very self but still live" (10. 564–66). Terrified, she lives in the woods, unmarried, harshly rejecting the crowds of suitors who press her, avoiding marriage by setting a condition that she can only be possessed if first conquered on the race course: "Compete with me in a foot race. To the swift a wife and bridal chamber will be the reward, death the price to be paid by the slow" (10. 570–72). Harsh terms, but she was so beautiful that scores of suitors were willing to race her for marriage or for death.

Hippomenes among the spectators condemns the fools willing to risk their lives for a wife—until he sees her nude, ready for a race. "My God!" he exclaims: "Forgive me, you men whom I blamed. I did not realize for whom you ran" (10. 580–82). He has fallen in love, hopes no one wins, is fearful, decides to run himself, enters the race. "I am Neptune's great-grandson. If I win, no disgrace to you. If I lose, you will have great renown for defeating Hippomenes" (10. 605–08).

Atalanta regards him softly while he speaks, and in a beautiful soliloquy (10. 611–35) wonders at his beauty, his willingness to risk his life for her, and is fearful lest she defeat him and he die. Either he should withdraw—or run faster. Such a sensitive face. She wishes she had never seen him. "You are the only one," she says, "with whom I would willingly share my bed" (635).

She has fallen in love and does not know what it is (637). Venus gives Hippomenes three golden apples from Cyprus. The race begins; Hippomenes throws down the apples one at a time and Atalanta, stopping to pick them up, loses the race. Hippomenes neglects to thank Venus. In anger, she filled him with desire for Atalanta one day just as they passed a chapel of Cybele in the woods, and they entered it and made love. As a result of that sacrilege, Cybele turned them into lions. The oracle came true: Atalanta lost her self but still lives on.

For variants in the myth, see Frazer, *Apollodorus* 1. 398–401. For Atalanta's son, Parthenopaeus, one of the Seven against Thebes, see 3. 6. 3, 4, 6 and 8.

5   The name of the Pleiades is most likely derived from *peleia*, "dove" (cf. the longer form *Peleiades*), the group of stars thought of as doves fleeing from the hunter, Orion. The word has also been influenced by the verb *pleô*, "I sail," because the rising and falling of the Pleiades have significance for sailors. So Pierre Chantraine, *Dictionnaire Étymologique de la Langue Grecque*, Tome 3 (Paris, 1974), s. v. *Pleiades*, 913. Frazer, *Apollodorus* 2. 3 explains the connection with *pleô* more precisely: "[I]n the Mediterranean area these stars were visible at night during the summer, from the middle of May till the beginning of November, which coincided with the sailing season in antiquity."

6   The myth of the birth and early exploits of Hermes is based on the Homeric *Hymn 4, to Hermes* and may have been influenced by Sophocles' *Ichneutae*, a satyr play, the subject of which is the infant Hermes' theft of Apollo's cattle (lengthy fragments survive). See Frazer, *Apollodorus* 2. 5–11 for a detailed account of the minor divergences between the Homeric *Hymn* and Apollodorus' version of the myth, for a synopsis of the *Ichneutae*, and for other comments on the myth.

In Ovid *Met.* 2. 680–707 a herdsman named Battus observes a full-grown Mercury stealing cattle left unattended by Apollo, who is absorbed in playing his pipes and thinking of love. Mercury buys the old rustic's silence by giving him a beautiful heifer. Battus reassures Mercury by pointing to a rock and saying that it will talk before he does. Mercury pretends to go on, but shortly returns in changed form and, as if looking for stolen cattle, asks Battus if he has seen any go by, promising a cow and a bull as reward for information about the theft. The herdsman, delighted at the prospect of increasing his reward, shows where the cattle are. Mercury, laughing, says, "You rascal, would you betray me to myself in person?" (Humphries' trans.) and turns him into stone, the touchstone used to detect liars. (Ovid derives his version from the *Great Eoiae*, frag. 16, attributed to Hesiod and preserved by Antoninus Liberalis 23, which relates Hermes' theft of cattle from Apollo but is otherwise entirely different from the Homeric *Hymn.* See Hugh G. Evelyn-White, ed., *Hesiod, the Homeric Hymns and Homerica* [Cambridge, Mass. and London, 1936], 262–67 and the Homeric *Hymn 4, to Hermes* 87–93, 187–212.)

Ovid's myth illustrates nicely Hermes' original role in Greek mythology, not so much as thief and patron of thieves but rather as trickster. As such he is "a patron of stealthy action in general." This concept of him is found at the beginnings of Greek mythology according to Norman O. Brown, *Hermes the Thief* (New York, 1969), 8, (from which the quotation is taken). His trickery is ultimately manifested as magical power, particularly the magic power of words (9–15).

Viewing Hermes primarily as magician we can account for his role as craftsman-god, e.g., inventor of the lyre and the rustic pipes in the Homeric *Hymn.* The craftsman-god who has skill in making things (a kind of trickiness) is also the deity of gain (the craftsman's profit) and promotes human welfare (21–25).

Hermes is above all the patron of heralds, himself a herald in the Homeric poems. Heralds in Homeric society were more than "town-criers." They possessed a valued craft which involved international negotiations and a "ceremonial ministry" requiring exact knowledge of ritual. The ability to perform precise ritual exactly is obviously connected with the possession of a magic art. The herald-function is actually pre-Homeric, and the pre-Homeric herald had an "affinity with the singer or bard." Perhaps the beginnings of song and poetry are to be found in the magical incantations intoned by herald-bards who presided over the execution of ritual. Originally the herald-bard figure is "both the leader in song and the leader in ceremony. . . ." By Homer's time ritual and song are separated and exist apart. But "the two crafts of the herald and the bard seem to have been derived from the single craft of the leader in magic ritual" (26–31).

It is impossible to present in detail Brown's analysis of the Homeric *Hymn to Hermes* (69–105 in his book), but some of its major points should be noted. The poem presents Hermes as thief—his trickster-magician role has practically disappeared—as criminal, but the author expresses no disapproval of his thievery nor does he assert that crime does not pay (74–75). In fact, it is rewarded: Hermes gets to keep the fifty cattle which he has stolen from Apollo and is allowed to mate them with Apollo's bulls. He becomes a co-sharer of Apollo's wealth, in return for which he shares with Apollo his new invention, the lyre, and teaches the god how to play it (90–92).

In Brown's view the author of the *Hymn* portrays Hermes as a "socio-psychological type." That is, the Hermes of the *Hymn* presents an "idealized image of the Greek lower classes, the craftsmen and merchants." For a culture that sought divine sanction or origin for its actions, Hermes embodies the new commercialism of late sixth- and fifth-century B.C. Athens. Hermes justifies the theft of cattle by "the ethical principle of acquisitive individualism." Apollo, by contrast, identifies trade with theft. What we have is the conflict between "traditional patriarchal morality, sustained by the aristocracy, and the new economy of acquisitive individualism." From the traditional aristocratic view, trade is identified with cheating, profit equated with theft. The link between craftsmanship and commerce is found throughout the mythology of Hermes (78–87).

The Homeric *Hymn* contains two new themes which develop the meaning of the myth: the conflict with Apollo and the representation of Hermes as a new-born baby. In the strife between the two gods Hermes is the aggressor: "His ambitious aggressiveness is the mainspring of the whole plot of the *Hymn*." Hermes wants to be equal with Apollo, "the aristocrat of Olympus," this desire showing that they are opposing figures in Greek mythology. Brown's analysis is proto-Marxian: the strife between Hermes and Apollo is a mythical expression of "the insurgence of the Greek lower classes and their demands for equality with the aristocracy."

The incredible accomplishment of a day-old baby who pits himself against the Olympian Establishment—and wins—dramatizes this contrast between power and helplessness, "between the established authority of the aristocracy and the native intelligence of the rising lower classes." Hermes knows what he wants and by the end of the day has gotten it: equality with Apollo. The poet is in fact explaining something about competing cults which stand for the same things, one dominant, the other rising and challenging it. Hermes and Apollo both were gods of music and prophecy, patrons of youth and athletics, guardians of houses and of roads and gods of pastoral life. "Hermes' inroads into Apollo's property [the cattle] imply that the cult of Hermes was actually making inroads into spheres hitherto presided over by Apollo."

The two gods are not only rivals in music, but the poet claims—special pleading—that Hermes is superior to Apollo in music. When Hermes, representing "the aspirations and achievements of the Greek lower classes" becomes Apollo's equal, the inference to be drawn is that the lower classes (now *nouveaux riches*) have made it.

The ideas expressed in the *Hymn*, as analyzed by Brown, met resistance. The aristocratic ideal in art, represented by Apollo, was not to be easily overturned, and Hermes was rejected by Apollo's partisans, including Pindar, Plato, and Callimachus. Since the *Hymn* was controversial the last seventy-eight lines were added by someone wishing to recover the ground won by Hermes and lost by Apollo in the earlier parts of the poem, in fact to make Hermes inferior to and a subordinate of Apollo (87–105).

One or two brief observations may be made about Brown's analysis of the *Hymn*. First, the weapons of the lower classes against the aristocracy in the class conflict in ancient Greece which the *Hymn* represents are craftsmanship and commerce: Ur-capitalism. The aristocrats are anticapitalist and consider commerce thievery. Things are thus topsy-turvy in Marxian terms. One cannot apply in the present discussion a conventional Marxian model to Greece. Second, slavery has been left out of the discussion and obviously must be included in any treatment of the development of the economy of ancient Greece. Brown's analysis is valuable, though, in demonstrating the way mythology can be used in political and economic development. For Roland Barthes, mythology is the means by which the (French) bourgeois establishment "naturalizes" and thus perpetuates itself. (See his *Mythologies* [New York, 1972], the essay entitled "Myth Today," 109–59, especially 137 ff.) The problem, both in the Homeric *Hymn* and in Barthes' description of mythology (and so perhaps with all mythologies), is that myth creates universals from a limited set of particulars, establishing these "universals" as the natural order of things.

Brown notes a relation between Hermes and Heracles, also a mythological figure associated with the lower classes. Both are cattle thieves, the distinction between them being that Heracles robs by force while Hermes thieves by stealth (Brown, *Hermes*, 7), although Heracles is "cleansed," e.g., in Hesiod's *Shield of Heracles*. Furthermore, Hermes is a prodigious worker like Heracles (79). But in his discussion of the infant prodigy who accomplishes so much on his first day of life, Brown ignores Heracles, a similar prodigy who strangled serpents sent by Hera to his crib on his first day of life. (See ch. 5, n. 1, the references to Pindar's *Nem.* 10 and Theocritus' *Idyll* 24.) The similarities between the two figures are significant enough to warrant a closer study of their relation.

7   At 1. 7. 3, 1. 9. 5, and 3. 10. 4 Apollodorus says that Perieres was the son of Aeolus, although he notes at 1. 9. 5 that some considered Perieres the son of Cynortas (*sic*).

8   Ancient authors differed in their opinions as to the mother of Asclepius (see Frazer, *Apollodorus* 2. 13–15), although Hesiod (*scholium* to Pindar *Pyth.* 3. 8), Pindar, the author of the Homeric *Hymn 16, to Asclepius* 1–3, Apollonius Rhodius *Argonautica* 4. 616–17, Ovid, and Pausanias 2. 26. 3–5 considered Coronis his mother. (For Pindar and Ovid, see n. 9.)

9   Pausanias 2. 26. 3–5 says that Coronis, pregnant by Apollo, accompanied her father, Phlegyas, to the Peloponnese and at Epidaurus secretly gave birth to Asclepius. She exposed the baby on a mountain where it was suckled by a goat and guarded by a dog. The goatherd who found Asclepius was reaching down to pick him up when he was suddenly blinded by a great light which shone from the child. Asclepius soon became famous for his power to heal the sick and raise the dead.

Ovid *Met.* 2. 534–47, 598–632 tells the more familiar story of Coronis' infidelity which was reported to Apollo by the raven (then white). The god, stricken (his laurel crown falls from his head, his lyre pick drops from his fingers and he pales), seizes his bow and shoots Coronis through the heart. Bleeding to death she tells him she should have been allowed to give birth to her baby before being punished: "Two of us now die in one body." Apollo too late feels remorse for his punishment. He hates himself for his anger at what he heard, hates the raven, hates his bow and his hand and his arrows. He tries to revive Coronis with his medical arts but cannot. He then prepares her body for burning on a pyre, but cannot endure the thought of his son burning to ashes, and so he snatches him from the womb of his mother amid the flames and carries him to Chiron's cave. He then turns the raven, who expects a reward for his information, black. In Ovid's version we note (1) that Apollo, although he is a god, and the god of healing, cannot restore Coronis to life once she is dead and (2) that the infant Asclepius is snatched from his mother's dead body —from death to life.

Pindar *Pyth.* 3. 1–67 tells the myth of Asclepius in a poem consoling Hieron, tyrant of Syracuse, who was incurably ill and died a few years after the poem was composed. Pindar's version emphasizes the mixture in people of sin and goodness, health and sickness. The healer Asclepius is killed by Zeus for bringing a dead man back to life for money. Money cannot buy life. The poem begins, "I wish Chiron, who is dead, were alive." Thus in the very first line Pindar acknowledges the impossibility of overcoming death, of the dead returning to life.

As for the blood of the Gorgon used by Asclepius, Euripides *Ion* 999–1005 says that Athena gave Erichthonius, an early king of Athens, two drops of the Gorgon's blood in his youth, one of which kills, the other of which heals all diseases.

Apollodorus ignores (or does not know) the myth of plague at Rome, seeking a cure for which Roman envoys went to Delphi and then to Epidaurus to ask the aid of Asclepius, there a god. In the form of a snake he returned with them to Italy and healed the city (Ovid *Met.* 15. 622—744). For discussion of those whom Asclepius raised from the dead, see Frazer, *Apollodorus* 2. 16–18.

10   At Euripides *Alcestis* 1–8 Apollo explains that Zeus killed Asclepius with a thunderbolt and so he killed the Cyclopes (the makers of the thunderbolt) in revenge. For this Zeus compelled him to work for Admetus, whose cattle he tends. See 1. 9. 15 for Apollo's period of service to Admetus during which he enabled him to win his wife, Alcestis, and arranged for a substitute for Admetus when his time came to die.

11   Pausanias 3. 12. 1–2 says that Odysseus won the hand of Penelope in a footrace which took place on Apheta Street in Sparta.

12   The love-making of both Zeus and Tyndareus with Leda, the wife of the latter, resulted in the births of the semidivine Pollux and Helen and the mortal Castor and Clytemnestra. The myth is similar to the story of Zeus and Amphitryon, both of whom made love with Alcmena, the latter's wife, either in the same night or on two consecutive nights, resulting in the near-simultaneous births of the semidivine Heracles and the mortal Iphicles (see 2. 4. 8 and ch. 4, n. 16).

At Euripides *Helen* 17–21 Helen herself says that Tyndareus is her father, but acknowledges a story that Zeus flew to her mother, Leda, in the form of a swan and entered her bed, pretending to flee from an eagle in pursuit of him—if the story is true, she says.

In one account Leda is said to have laid two eggs, from one of which Castor and Pollux were hatched, from the other Helen and Clytemnestra (see Frazer, *Apollodorus* 2. 23–24). Hence the expression "from the twin eggs," in giving the ultimate cause of something (in its original meaning, the cause of the Trojan War).

William Butler Yeats' poem, "Leda and the Swan," is perhaps the finest poetic version of the myth.

13   For this first rape of Helen, see also Epitome 1. 23 which says
that Helen was twelve years old at the time. (Diodorus Siculus 4. 63. 2
says that she was ten.) Theseus was fifty, hence he turned Helen over
to the care of his mother, Aethra (no Humbert Humbert he), until she
became ripe for marriage (Plutarch *Theseus* 31). He chose Aphidnae
for them to live in, a town in Attica fifteen to twenty miles northwest
of Athens, for secrecy, according to Plutarch (loc. cit.), or to keep
from the Athenians' sight a source of great annoyance (Diodorus 4.
63. 3, who does not say precisely why the Athenians were annoyed.
It was probably not due to the age gap between the two but to the
probability of war with Sparta which Theseus' action incurred).

Pausanias 2. 22. 6–7 gives a bit of gossip: He says that Helen was
pregnant when her brothers recovered her, gave birth to a daughter
and entrusted the infant to Clytemnestra, who was by this time married to Agamemnon, to rear as her own. The daughter was Iphigenia.
If this is true, then Iphigenia was sacrificed (see Aeschylus' *Agamemnon*) to recover her own mother—material, it would seem, for a tragic
drama.

Theseus' rape of Helen was apparently told in the *Cypria*, a poem
in the Epic Cycle. See Evelyn-White, *Hesiod*, 501.

14   See Frazer, *Apollodorus* 2. 26–27 for variants in the list of
Helen's suitors.

15   The original intention of the oath taken by Helen's suitors as
we see from Apollodorus' account, was to ensure that none of them
would violate the choice made. A much earlier work, Hesiod *Catalogue
of Women and Eoiae*, frag. 68, lines 89–100 (in Evelyn-White, *Hesiod*,
199), confirms this, adding that Menelaus won Helen because he gave
the most gifts.

Euripides' *Iphigenia in Aulis* spells out Tyndareus' dilemma even
more clearly: Each suitor threatened the others with murder if he did
not win Helen. Tyndareus was at a complete loss whether or not to
offer Helen in marriage until he hit upon the expedient (no mention of
Odysseus) of oaths sworn and right hands clasped, fortified by treaties
made with sacrifices, that the suitors would join in defending whoever
won Helen if someone should take her from her lawful husband, and
that they would undertake an expedition and conquer his city, Greek
or barbarian. When the suitors gave their pledges—and Tyndareus
thought that he had outwitted them—he allowed Helen to choose
whomever she loved and she chose, unfortunately, Menelaus (53–71).

Thucydides 1. 9. cuts smartly through the myth by saying that
Menelaus' brother, Agamemnon, assembled his expedition and led the
suitors of Helen to Troy not so much because of their oaths but because
he was foremost in power at that time.

16   Our interest here lies in the number of children Helen bore (and by whom), not in the number of Menelaus' offspring. In n. 13 we noted (from Pausanias) that Iphigenia was Helen's first born, by Theseus. While Homer affirms only one child (*Iliad* 3. 174–75 and *Odyssey* 4. 12–14, where she is named Hermione), from various authors and commentators of antiquity we can assemble a group of eight children (including Iphigenia) to whom the most beautiful woman of ancient Greece gave birth by at least three and perhaps four men (the fourth, unnamed, would be the father of Aethiolas, who, however, may be Menelaus' son). See Frazer, *Apollodorus* 2. 28–29.

17   Castor and Pollux (= Polydeuces in Greek) are called *Dios kouroi,* "sons of Zeus," in the Homeric *Hymn 33, to the Dioscuri,* 1, whence their joint name, *Dioscuri.* The short hymn celebrates them as saviors of sailors in storms at sea. When a ship is buffeted by the wind and swamped by waves, men pray to them and, flashing through the air on wings of golden light, they come to calm the gale and smooth the frothing sea, fair signs to sailors of release from toil and woe (11–16).

The electrical phenomenon known as St. Elmo's Fire ancient sailors identified as epiphanies of Castor and Pollux, the twin lights considered an omen of safety (J. G. Frazer, *Pausanias's Description of Greece,* 6 vols. [London, 1898], 3. 13–14, comment on Pausanias 2. 1. 9). T. W. Allen, W. R. Halliday and E. E. Sikes, eds., *The Homeric Hymns* (Oxford, 1936), 437, think that they acquired their function as saviors of sailors at sea (their chief one) from their participation in the voyage of the Argo (1. 9. 16 and 1. 9. 20 and ch. 3, n. 5).

At Pindar *Nem.* 10. 55–90 we find the version of the myth of the battle between Castor and Polydeuces and the sons of Aphareus which Apollodorus followed. The dispute was over cattle (no more detail from Pindar than this). Lynceus, with his x-ray vision (see 3. 10. 3), saw the twins hiding in a tree trunk, he and Idas attacked them, and the latter fatally stabbed Castor with his spear. Polydeuces chased them both to the tomb of their father where they together tore the gravestone out of the ground and heaved it at him. He caught the blow in the chest, did not recoil, rather, leaping forward drove his spear deep in Lynceus' side. Zeus then blasted Idas with a thunderbolt.

Polydeuces rushed back to his brother who lay on the ground gasping out his life's last breath. Weeping, Polydeuces prayed to Zeus to allow him to die with Castor, whom alone of men he had trusted to share in the hardship and exhaustion of their labors. Zeus, drawing near to him, said, "You are a son of mine, but he was planted in your mother as mortal seed" (80–82). But the god gives Polydeuces a choice: Immortality for himself on Mount Olympus or, sharing his brother's death, he can breathe the air of the underworld half of the time, live in the golden houses of heaven the other half (in alternation with Castor). Polydeuces decides at once. Castor then opens his eyes and speaks. (But of course they will never be together again.)

The Homer of the *Iliad* either does not know or alters this element of the myth. Helen at the wall of Troy, pointing out the Greek chieftains to the Trojan elders, cannot see her brothers, Castor and Polydeuces, on the field below. She concludes that either they did not come to Troy, or came and have not entered battle, fearing the shame that attaches to her. "Thus she spoke, but the grain-growing earth already held them, there in Lacedaemon, in their beloved fatherland" (3. 236–44).

The Homer of the *Odyssey*, on the other hand, does know the story: "I saw Leda," (in the underworld) Odysseus tells the Phaeacians, "who bore strong-minded sons of Tyndareus, Castor . . . and . . . Polydeuces, both of whom living still the grain-growing earth holds. Even in the underworld they are honored by Zeus, each in turn living every other day, each in turn again, dead" (11. 298–304).

In another version of the myth (Theocritus *Idyll* 22. 137–211), Castor and Polydeuces carry off the two daughters of Leucippus who are bethrothed to Lynceus and Idas, having first bribed the girls' father. The twins are pursued and caught by Lynceus and Idas. Castor kills Lynceus in a duel after rejecting his attempts to settle the matter amicably. Zeus strikes Idas dead with a thunderbolt before he can hurl his father's tombstone at Castor.

While the rape of Leucippus' daughters by the sons of Tyndareus was a favorite subject in art, as Frazer, *Apollodorus* 2. 30–31 points out, citing many references from Pausanias, Theocritus in his ugly version of the myth "seems to go out of his way to place the Dioscuri in an unfavorable light" according to A. S. F. Gow, ed., *Theocritus*, 2 vols. (Cambridge, Eng., 1952), 2. 384. See Gow's discussion of the poem, 2. 382–85. Commenting on the attempt by the Dioscuri to steal the girls by means of bribes Gow says, "The circumstances envisaged by . . . [Theocritus] are obscure and do not correspond to any known version of the story . . ." (comment to 22. 150, 2. 401).

Allen *et al., The Homeric Hymns,* 438, and Frazer, *Apollodorus* 2. 32–33, say that in the Hellenistic and subsequent periods Castor and Pollux were identified with the evening and morning stars, Pollux seen at dawn as the morning star, rising until it fades in the light of day, Castor as the evening star which daily sinks at dusk into the earth.

18   Apollodorus seems to misrepresent the love-making of Iasion and Demeter by calling it rape. Homer at *Odyssey* 5. 125–28 says that Demeter, yielding to Iasion's passion, made love with him in a thrice-

plowed field. Zeus shortly found out and struck Iasion with a thunder-bolt. The context of the passage is Calypso's complaint to Hermes, sent from Zeus to gain Odysseus' release, that male gods begrudge goddesses' taking mortal lovers (whom they kill, e.g., Orion and Iasion), and now the gods begrudge her keeping Odysseus (5. 118–29). Hesiod *Theogony* 969–71 says that Demeter bore Ploutos ("Wealth") to Iasion after making love with him. The expression Hesiod uses for "making love" (970) is a variation of the one Homer uses at *Odyssey* 5. 126. Finally, Hyginus *Fabulae* 270 lists Iasion among "Men Who Were Most Attractive." Rape there was aplenty in the ancient (and mythological) world, but the evidence seems to clear Iasion of the charge.

19   A comparison between the line of descent from Dardanus given by Homer *Iliad* 20. 215–19, 230–40 (Aeneas speaking to Achilles) and that by Apollodorus here shows a discrepancy and yields at least one interesting point. Homer names one Ilus, son of Tros and father of Laomedon (who was in turn father of Priam, father of Hector). Apollodorus names two Iluses: the first a son of Dardanus who died childless; the second a son of Tros (as was Homer's Ilus). Apollodorus here omits Laomedon, son of Ilus, son of Tros (although Homer names him in the passage referred to), picking him up at 3. 12. 13, where he names him (properly) as son of Ilus and lists his offspring, as does Homer in the present passage.

It is interesting to note that Aeneas gives the line of descent from Dardanus to Hector and to himself (seven generations, Dardanus, son of Zeus, the first) without mentioning *one* wife and/or mother or sister and/or daughter. Apollodorus, on the other hand, lists the wives and/or mothers (e.g., Dardanus was son of Zeus by Electra; Dardanus and Batia had Ilus and Erichthonius; Erichthonius and Astyoche had Tros, etc.) and gives the names of sisters and/or daughters (e.g., Ilus, Assaracus, and Ganymede had a sister, Cleopatra; Ilus was the father of Laomedon but also of the girl Themiste; Laomedon had five sons, named by Homer and Apollodorus [3. 12. 13], but the latter names their mother, Strymo [or possibly others] and their three sisters, Hesione, Cilla, and Astyoche).

Obviously the *Iliad* and the *Library* hardly bear comparison. Moreover, the author of the latter seems obsessed with genealogies which, since there was so much intermarriage in Greek mythology, required naming and keeping track of mothers and daughters. Even so, the comparison between the two authors' narration of the same line of descent strikingly reveals the acknowledged male ethos of the *Iliad* in an unlooked for place. Nor can the omission of mothers and daughters in Aeneas' account to Achilles in the *Iliad* be attributed entirely to epic or formulaic economy: He interrupts his genealogy for ten lines (20. 220–29) to tell Achilles that Erichthonius became rich and possessed 3,000 mares. The North Wind fell in love with them, coupled with them, and the mares who conceived bore him twelve colts. These played at the edges of the wheat fields (but did not damage the grain) or ran on the beach along the line of the breaking waves. The lovely lines nicely break up the recitation of family line through seven generations. Still, the absence of women in Homer's account, when compared to Apollodorus', seems striking.

Apollodorus mentions the rape of Ganymede earlier at 2. 5. 9 (see also ch. 5, n. 14) and Homer, in the genealogy just mentioned, says that Ganymedes (the Greek version of the name) was the loveliest of mortal men, and because of his beauty the gods carried him off to live among the immortals and pour wine for Zeus (*Iliad* 20. 232–35).

The Homeric *Hymn 5, to Aphrodite* 202–08 says that Zeus, not the gods, carried off Ganymedes, catching him up in a whirlwind because of his beauty, to live among the immortals in his palace and fill their glasses, ladling the ruby-red nectar from a golden bowl. Between the *Iliad* and the *Hymn* the abductor(s) have changed from "the gods" to "Zeus." Finally, Pindar *Ol.* 1. 40–45 tells us (what we might have suspected) that Zeus stole away Ganymedes because he was in love with him.

Virgil *Aeneid* 5. 252–55 says that Jove's eagle carried off Ganymede while he was hunting on Mount Ida, adding to Juno's grievances against Troy (*Aeneid* 1. 26–30), and presumably to those against Jove for his endless philandering. Ovid *Met.* 10. 155–61 also briefly tells us that Jove, on fire for Ganymede, turned himself into an eagle and carried the boy off to serve nectar, much to Juno's annoyance.

Lucian *Dialogues of the Gods* 4 parodies the myth by characterizing Ganymedes as a simple country bumpkin carried off from Mount Ida where he was tending sheep who, when he and Zeus reach heaven and the latter changes back from eagle to god, first wants to know how he managed the metamorphosis, doubts Zeus' divinity (calling him a kidnapper), finally recognizes him (the source of hail and thunder), asks "Did I do something wrong (to be carried off)?" and worries about the sheep he left untended. He continues to play a role of exaggerated (but sincere) innocence by which Lucian mocks Zeus' sexual interest in him.

For Aphrodite as the mother of Aeneas by Anchises, see Homer *Iliad* 2. 819–21, Hesiod *Theogony* 1008–10. At *Iliad* 5. 311–18 his goddess mother carries Aeneas safely away from the battlefield where his hip was shattered by a stone hurled by Diomedes.

After so much raping of women by men in Apollodorus, Ovid's

Metamorphoses, and elsewhere in ancient mythology, it is startling to
encounter something like the reverse in the Homeric *Hymn 5, to
Aphrodite.* Of course Aphrodite does not physically rape Anchises,
she seduces him.

It all starts because Aphrodite has power to compel passion in gods
and mortals alike, male and female (except for Athena, Artemis, and
Hestia) and even in animals. Zeus, to counterbalance this power, makes
Aphrodite fall in love with a mortal man.

The choice is Anchises (53 ff.), a handsome shepherd on Mount Ida.
When Aphrodite sees him, agonizing desire overwhelms her heart and
she falls passionately in love. Immediately she returns to Cyprus, to
her temple at Paphos, where the Graces, her handmaidens, bathe her
and anoint her with perfumed oil, the sweet aroma of which the gods
always have about them. She puts on beautiful clothing, golden earrings and necklaces and spiralled bracelets of gold, and hurries back
to Troy, to the hut of Anchises on Mount Ida in the afternoon.

She stands before him like a virgin so as not to frighten him.
Astonished by her beauty, her size, her clothing and golden ornaments,
especially by the necklaces which shine upon her tender breasts like
the moon, he falls headlong in love. But he assumes that she is a
goddess and courteously offers to build her an altar and to sacrifice to
her. "Anchises, you beautiful man," she replies, "I'm no goddess. Why
do you compare me to one? I'm human" (108–10, and she names her
"father"). She continues: Hermes brought her to him from a great
distance, telling her repeatedly that in Anchises' bed she would be
called his wedded wife and bear him brilliant babies. "Take me," she
says, "a virgin inexperienced in love, and show me to your father,
mother, brothers. I'll be a good daughter-in-law" (133–36).

She fills him with desire. If you are human and all the rest you say
is true, he says, then you will be called my wife each day from now
on. Nothing can stop me from making love with you, right now! He
takes her hand and Aphrodite, eyes on the ground, shyly sidles to
the bed. Anchises removes her earrings, bracelets and necklaces, un-
does her undergarment and takes off her clothes (putting them on a
silver chair). And then, by the will of the gods, that afternoon he makes
love, a mortal, with an immortal goddess, and does not know it.

In the late afternoon she arises and dresses while Anchises sleeps.
She assumes her divine appearance and then awakens him. "Get up,"
she says, "why are you sleeping? Do I look the same to you now as
when you first saw me?" (177–79). Anchises quickly awakens, and
when he sees her, is terrified and covers his head. "I knew, when I
first saw you, that you were a goddess. But you lied to me. Now at
your knees I beg you in the name of Zeus, don't let me live impotent

among men. For a man who makes love with immortal gods loses his life-giving potency" (185–90).

"Cheer up, Anchises, you beautiful man, you've nothing to fear from the gods. You're our friend. You will have a fine son, a ruler of the Trojans, and his children will have children on and on. His name will be Aineias for I'm terribly (*ainos*) depressed because I fell into bed with a mortal man" (192–99).

"If you were to remain as handsome as you are now, you might be my husband and I wouldn't be depressed. But soon pitiless old age will cover your whole body as it does all humans, ruining, exhausting them—the gods despise it. I shall be in great disgrace among the gods every day from now on because of you" (241–48). Her last words to Anchises: "If you ever tell or boast in foolish pride that you made love with Aphrodite, Zeus in anger will strike you dead with a thunderbolt. That's all I have to say. Keep it in your head, don't mention my name and avoid the gods' wrath" (286–90).

20   Cadmus chose the site of Thebes in a similar way. See 3. 4. 1.

21   Triton, who reared Athena, was god of the river Triton in Libya (Herodotus 4. 180).

At *Iliad* 19. 126–31 Homer says that Zeus threw Ate out of heaven (but makes no mention of the Palladium).

22   See n. 19.

23   In Homer, Dawn arises from the bed of Tithonus to bring light to gods and man (*Iliad* 11. 1–2, *Odyssey* 5. 1–2).

The Homeric *Hymn 5, to Aphrodite* 218–38 narrates the story of Dawn's love for Tithonus: When she carries him off to Mount Olympus she begs Zeus to make him immortal, and he does so. She forgets, however, to ask Zeus to keep him young. When he begins to age she leaves his bed but continues to take care of him. And when old age so enfeebles him that he can hardly move his body, she puts him in a room and closes the doors. He mutters there, endlessly, but has no strength at all in his gnarled old limbs.

Aphrodite tells Anchises this story as a reason for rejecting any further relation with him. He will grow old (like Tithonus), and the gods despise old age (244–46). The interest here lies in the connection between Aphrodite and Dawn. Deborah D. Boedeker, *Aphrodite's Entry into Greek Epic* (Leiden, 1974: *Mnemosyne Supplement* 23), which the author has been unable to see, maintains that Aphrodite originated as the Indo-European Dawn-goddess (within whose sphere lay sexual attraction). In early Greek literature, Boedeker says, Aphrodite evolved beyond this origin and was no longer a Dawn-goddess, although traces of the earlier identity remain.

The Scholiast on Homer *Iliad* 11. 1 says that when Tithonus was old and decrepit Dawn turned him into a grasshopper so that she might hear him singing forever. (At *Iliad* 3. 149–52 Homer describes the Trojan elders, men now too old to fight, yet fine speakers still, like cicadas in trees singing with delicate voices.)

Propertius 2. 18. 7–18 tells a quite different tale: Dawn spurns Tithonus in his old age not at all nor allows him to lie abandoned in their Eastern home. Often when she returns at night she caresses him even before she bathes her horses. Lying quietly in his arms in India, she complains that day returned too soon, and boards the chariot, calling the gods unjust, and unwillingly performs her duty for the world. Her joy in old Tithonus, alive, is greater than her grief at Memnon's death. So beautiful a girl as she is, she feels no shame to sleep with the old man and to kiss his old white head again and again.

24   Ovid *Met.* 11. 749–95 tells the story of Aesacus' metamorphosis into a diver (*mergus*) for grief of Hesperia (as he names Cebren's daughter), whom he loved and whose death he inadvertently caused. Ovid's version follows immediately upon the somewhat similar myth of Ceyx and Alcyone (see 1. 7. 4 and ch. 2, n. 4). Aesacus in his grief jumped from a cliff but Tethys, a sea goddess, out of pity softened his fall into the sea and turned him into a bird, saving his life, though he wished for death. He hates being compelled to live and so as a bird he tries to kill himself, flying high in the air and then diving into the water. But he never succeeds, for his feathers retard his downward plunge. Furious, he dives again, trying endlessly to drown himself. Thus his name, diver.

25   The Roman emperor Tiberius, who had a special interest in mythology, Suetonius tells us, was fond of asking learned men "Who was Hecuba's mother?" (*Tiberius* 70), a question which Frazer *Apollodorus* 2. 45 admits he cannot answer.

26   From Pindar *Paean* 8a (Snell), which is very fragmentary, we learn of a prophecy made before Paris' birth (by whom it is impossible to tell), about "destined suffering" (16) and about a dream Hecuba had while pregnant: "For it seemed that she gave birth to a fire-bearing, hundred-handed [Fury?] . . . and that he cast all Ilium to the ground" (19–23).

Helen, defending herself in Euripides' *Trojan Women*, blames others for Troy's fall: "First, Hecuba gave birth to the origin of the calamity when she bore Paris. Second, Priam destroyed both Troy and me by not killing the baby long ago, a bitter likeness of a burning torch, Alexander" (919–22).

The Chorus in Euripides' *Andromache* cries, "If only his mother had bashed the evil creature's head in before he settled on Mount Ida, at the time when Cassandra cried, 'Kill this horrible infection of Priam's city!' Whom did she not accost? What elder of the city did she not beg, 'Murder the baby'?" (293–300). Cassandra, then, is very likely the source of the prophecy in Pindar's *Paean*. (For Paris as a burning torch see also Virgil *Aeneid* 7. 319–20.)

Hyginus *Fabulae* 91 tells us that Hecuba, pregnant, had a vision that she gave birth to a burning torch from which came forth a multitude of serpents, giving a possible origin in myth to the imagery of fire and serpents which Bernard M. W. Knox sees as intertwined and dominating book 2 of the *Aeneid*, in which Virgil narrates the destruction of Troy. See his "The Serpent and the Flame: The Imagery of the Second Book of the *Aeneid*," *Amer. Journ. of Phil.* 71 (1950), 379–400.

27   Apollodorus follows the account Cassandra gives to the Chorus in Aeschylus *Agamemnon* 1202–12. "I agreed to make love with Apollo, but I lied," she says (1208). Hyginus *Fabulae* 93, however, makes Cassandra entirely blameless: Wearied from playing in Apollo's temple (where apparently she was already a priestess), Cassandra lay down to sleep. Apollo came upon her sleeping and wanted to make love. She refused and the god, to punish her, destroyed the credibility of her true prophecies. For a different story about the way in which Cassandra became a prophetess, see Frazer, *Apollodorus* 2. 48–49.

28   Oenone writes to Paris at Troy during the Trojan War in Ovid *Heroides* 5, but long before he is wounded by Philoctetes. The letter only obliquely alludes to the outcome of the myth told by Apollodorus: Oenone says that Poseidon has given her an herb that will cure anything—anything but her love for Paris (147–49).

29   See 1. 9. 3 and ch. 2, n. 14.

30   Asopus as a god was permanently crippled by Zeus' thunderbolt (Callimachus *Hymn* 4, *to Delos*, 78).

31   According to Ovid *Met.* 7. 517–660 Juno, jealous of Aegina, afflicted the island named for her (and ruled by Aeacus) with a plague of such virulence that nearly all human and animal life there died. Aeacus in despair cried out to Jove to restore his people or kill him as well. He sees a column of ants marching in formation on an old oak tree and prays to Jove to grant him people like them. In a dream the ants on the tree appear to Aeacus to drop to the ground and grow into human shape. He awakens, thinking it was just that, a dream, and despair returns. But suddenly his son Telamon bursts into his bedroom to say that a population has appeared. Aeacus sees the humans newly made from ants with his own eyes and calls them Myrmidons (from *myrmêx*, the Greek word for "ant"). Like ants, they are industrious, thrifty, and have endurance. (Achilles, grandson of Aeacus, takes a contingent of Myrmidons to Troy, e.g., Homer *Iliad* 1. 328, and passim.) Ovid's version of the plague (described at length) seems to follow the

models found in book 6 of Lucretius' *De Rerum Natura* and Virgil *Georgics* 3. 478 ff. See William S. Anderson, ed., *Ovid's Metamorphoses: Books 6–10* (Norman, Okla., 1972), 295–96.

32   Phocus is a masculine form of the Greek feminine noun *phôkê*, "seal," hence the son's name was "Seal."

33   Frazer, *Apollodorus* 2. 56 notes that Apollodorus seems to be the only ancient writer who attributes the drought in Greece to Pelops' murder of Stymphalus.

Plato says that Aeacus was a judge in Hades, along with Minos, Rhadamanthys, and Triptolemus (*Apology* 41a). He had jurisdiction over the souls from Europe, according to Plato *Gorgias* 524a; Rhadamanthys judged souls from Asia; and Minos made up the court of appeal (Triptolemus is not mentioned in this passage).

34   According to Ovid *Met.* 11. 266–81, Pausanias 2. 29. 9–10, and Diodorus Siculus 4. 72. 6–7, it was Peleus, not Telamon, who murdered Phocus (without drawing a lot). Ovid does not say how or why, only that Peleus fled to Trachis and sought refuge with King Ceyx, concealing his crime and lying about the cause of his flight. Ovid does not mention Telamon in this passage.

Pausanias says that Peleus and Telamon challenged Phocus to a pentathlon contest and when it was Peleus' turn to hurl the stone which they were using instead of a discus, he purposely threw it at Phocus, struck, and killed him. Pausanias then says that "they" did this to please their mother, Endeis, who apparently wanted to be rid of her stepson. Both brothers fled, but Telamon later denied his complicity in the murder. Aeacus would not let him set foot on Aeginetan soil to plead his case, but told him that he could present his side from the deck of a ship or from a mound or small islet in the harbor, if he chose to make one. He built the mound, stood on it to argue his case, was judged guilty, reboarded his ship, and sailed back to Salamis to which he had earlier fled.

Diodorus claims that Peleus hurled a discus and accidentally killed Phocus. For this his father banished him and he fled to Phthia. He goes on to say that Telamon fled to Salamis—that and no more.

Pindar, earlier than any of the above mentioned authors, refuses to talk about the murder directly (*Nem.* 5. 11–18), although he attaches guilt both to Peleus and Telamon (as does Hyginus *Fabulae* 14), and says that they left the island, driven out by a *daimôn*.

Most of the evidence for the killing of Phocus has been presented here, but for more detective work on this murder mystery, see Frazer, *Apollodorus* 2. 57–59.

Pindar *Isth.* 6. 35–54 describes Heracles' visit to Telamon to enlist him for his expedition against Troy. He arrives during a banquet and, handed a goblet inlaid with gold, stands, draped in his lion skin, to pour a libation to Zeus. Heracles prays for a brave son to be born to Telamon and Eriboea (as Pindar names Telamon's wife), who will have a nature as unbreakable as the lion skin which he wears. A great eagle, sent by Zeus, descends from the sky in answer to the prayer. Heracles, trembling with joy, speaks as a seer: "You will have the son you ask for, Telamon. Call him by the name of the eagle (*aietos*), Aias (Greek for Ajax), broad in strength and terrible in the labors of the hosts of war" (52–54).

Frazer, *Apollodorus* 2. 61 reports the story that Heracles wrapped Ajax as a baby in his lion skin, making him invulnerable except in the armpit or in the neck (accounts differ). When he tried to commit suicide he could not drive the sword into his body, the blade instead bending back in the shape of a bow. Finally some divinity showed him where to force the sword into himself and he died. Alcibiades in Plato *Symposium* 219e says that Socrates was much more invulnerable to money than Ajax to iron, with this myth probably in mind. For discrepant accounts of Peleus' purification, see Frazer, *Apollodorus* 2. 61–62.

35   For the recurrent mythical motif of a sexual proposition made by an older married woman to a younger man who is in some way indebted to her husband, see 2. 3. 1–2 (Proteus-Bellerophon-Stheneboea) and ch. 4, n. 10.

Pindar *Nem.* 5. 25–34 tells the story briefly, naming Acastus' wife Hippolyta, rather than Astydamia, the name Apollodorus gives her. (See also Pindar *Nem.* 4. 54–61 where he again calls her Hippolyta.)

36   Apollodorus is confused here, marrying Peleus to his own daughter. (See 3. 12. 1–2.) He compounds his confusion by saying that Polydora was a daughter of Perieres. (It was her husband, Borus, who was Perieres' son.) He recovers somewhat by acknowledging that the river Sperchius was the true father of Polydora's son Menesthius, but then errs in saying Peleus was called his father. See Homer (*Iliad* 16. 173–78), who says that Menesthius was the son of the river Sperchius but called the son of Borus (the husband of Polydora originally named by Apollodorus: 3. 13. 1–2).

37   In his version of the marriage of Peleus and Thetis, the grand social occasion of ancient mythology, Apollodorus simplifies a more complex mythical tradition (omitting some of it) in order, perhaps, to present a short, coherent account. He mentions the competition between Zeus and Poseidon for Thetis, which Themis resolves by her piece of vital information. According to Pindar *Isth.* 8. 27–47, who tells this part of the myth, Themis in addition suggests Peleus, the most pious man in Iolcus, as a husband for Thetis, and the two gods give their assent.

This version of the myth ignores the one we find in Aeschylus' *Prometheus Bound*, perhaps the first play of a trilogy: Prometheus, chained on Mount Caucasus by Zeus' minions, reveals that he alone has knowledge of a match Zeus plans to make which will drive him from power in fulfillment of the curse of his father, Cronus. Nothing —no torture nor pain—can force Prometheus to name for Zeus the one fated to overcome him (907–27, 987–96).

Although *Prometheus Unbound*, probably the second play of the trilogy, is lost, from what fragments survive it seems likely that in this play Prometheus divulged his secret: If Zeus has a union with Thetis, she will bear him a son who will overthrow him. In exchange for this information, Prometheus is released from confinement on Mount Caucasus by Heracles. See George Thomson, *Aeschylus and Athens* (London, 1966), 309–15.

There is also conflict in the tradition about Thetis' desire to marry Peleus. (In Pindar's version the question what Thetis wants does not arise.) At Apollonius Rhodius *Argonautica* 4. 790–809, Hera tells Thetis that she reared her and that she loved her because she resisted Zeus' advances. Zeus, however, angered by her rejection of him, has vowed that Thetis will never marry a god. (Apollodorus mentions this version.) He still kept his eye on her, though, until he heard Themis' prophecy, then gave her up. Hera thereupon chose Peleus for Thetis in order to make her a happy bride, and invited all the gods and goddesses to the wedding. Hera herself carried the bridal torch in gratitude for the good will and deference Thetis had shown to her. Apollonius does not say that Thetis embraced Hera's choice, but the implication is that she is happy to marry Peleus. Yet at Homer *Iliad* 18. 432–35 Thetis tells Hephaestus that Zeus forced her alone of the Nereids to marry a mortal and she had to endure such a marriage, against her will. Now Peleus lies in the halls, broken by old age. (Cf. with Aphrodite's reasons for rejecting Anchises in the Homeric *Hymn 5, to Aphrodite* 241–48 and n. 19.)

In Ovid *Met.* 11. 217–65 Thetis wants neither to make love with nor to marry Peleus. In Ovid's version it is Proteus, the sea god, not Themis, who says that Thetis' son is destined to be mightier than his father. Jove, hearing this, kept away from her, but urged Peleus to become her lover. Peleus found Thetis sleeping in a cave by the sea whither she was accustomed to ride nude on the back of a dolphin. He seized her and pleaded with her, but she refused to make love. Peleus was on the point of raping her, but Thetis changed herself into a bird (he held on), into a tree (he held on), into a tigress (he let go and commenced to pray). Proteus (not Chiron, as in Apollodorus' version) in answer to Peleus' prayer advised him how to subdue (or "win") Thetis: By catching her asleep, tying her up tightly, and holding onto her through all her changes until she became herself again. Peleus followed Proteus' instructions and Thetis, finding escape impossible, gave in, they made love and she became pregnant with Achilles.

Pindar *Nem.* 4. 62–65 very briefly recounts Thetis' transformations (into fire, lion's claws, sharp teeth) which Peleus overcame in order to marry her. For the transformations of Nereus, the river Achelous, and Proteus, see 2. 5. 11 (for Nereus); 2. 7. 5 (for Achelous); and ch. 5, n. 22 (for Proteus, and for Achelous in Sophocles' *Women of Trachis*).

The wedding feast, which took place on Mount Pelion, is described as a beautiful and graceful affair in two passages in Greek literature, Pindar *Pyth.* 3. 86–95 and Euripides *Iphigenia in Aulis* 1036–79. (Apollonius Rhodius' detail of Hera's carrying the bridal torch was mentioned above and for Catullus 64 see below.) Gods and goddesses came and sat in golden chairs. Centaurs and the Graces came, the Muses sang, the Nereids (Thetis' sisters) danced, and Ganymedes served as pourer of wine. Chiron prophesied the birth of Achilles and the gods sang the wedding hymn foretelling Achilles' great deeds. In addition to the wedding gifts which Apollodorus mentions, Homer *Iliad* 18. 82–85 says that Peleus also received from the gods on his wedding day the armor that Achilles took to Troy.

Catullus 64, an *epyllion* (little epic) of 408 lines uses the marriage of Peleus and Thetis as an outer frame for the inner story, the elopement of Ariadne with Theseus. For a fine analysis of Catullus' use of the myth, see Leo C. Curran, "Catullus 64 and the Heroic Age," *Yale Classical Studies* 21 (1969), 171–92.

38   Apollonius Rhodius *Argonautica* 4. 866–79, from whom Apollodorus borrows the story of Thetis' attempt to make Achilles immortal, gives important details omitted in Apollodorus' account: Thetis' motive, understandable enough, was to ward off from Achilles hateful old age. At Homer *Iliad* 18. 432–35 she tells Hephaestus that Zeus forced her to marry a mortal (Peleus) and now he is so enfeebled by old age that all he can do is lie about the palace.

Peleus' reaction, though, is equally understandable: He awakened in the middle of the night to see his son gasping in the fire and cried out. Thetis, hearing his cry, snatched up Achilles, threw him screaming to the floor, and disappeared, returning to the sea. There she lives with her father, Nereus (e.g., *Iliad* 1. 357–58).

Apollodorus at 1. 5. 1–2 describes Demeter's similar attempt to make Demophon, the son of Celeus and Metanira, immortal. Metanira, discovering her child in a fire, screams and the baby is burned up. For comment on these stories and on the practice, see Frazer, *Apollodorus* 2. 311–17, appendix 1, "Putting Children on the Fire."

The story that Thetis dipped the infant Achilles in the river Styx, thus making him invulnerable (except at the heel, by which she held him) is alluded to in Statius *Achilleid* 1. 133–34 and 269–70.

39   Peleus thus avenged himself on Astydamia (and Acastus) for their injury to him, described at 3. 13. 3. For a similar story, see Herodotus 7. 27–29, 38–40.

40   In the *Achilleid* by the Roman poet Statius (ca. 45–96 A.D.), Thetis spirits away Achilles from his tutor, the centaur Chiron on Mount Pelion, and takes him to the court of Lycomedes, king of the island of Scyros, to prevent his going to Troy where she knows he is destined to die. Achilles, who much prefers the outdoor life with Chiron and his young hunting companion, Patroclus, resents being dressed as a girl until he sees Deidamia, one of the king's daughters, with whom he immediately falls in love. Thetis introduces Achilles to Lycomedes as his (Achilles') sister and asks the king to rear her until she is ready for marriage (1. 104–362).

Years later, the Greek chieftains, much in need of Achilles at Troy, implore their prophet, Calchas, to locate him for them. Through his seercraft he discovers that Achilles is hidden away on Scyros, and Diomedes and Odysseus are sent to bring him to Troy (1. 467–559).

Odysseus and Diomedes arrive at Lycomedes' palace with gifts for his daughters but also with a shield, spear, and trumpet (ostensibly for Lycomedes). As they distribute the gifts Achilles is drawn to the shield and spear. Odysseus, at his side, whispers that he knows his identity and urges him to come with him. When a blast from the trumpet is sounded by a Greek man-at-arms, Achilles seizes the sword and shield, ready for battle. His girl's clothing falls from him and his true identity is revealed to an amazed Lycomedes, who is further shocked to learn that he has a grandson from Deidamia, the father of whom is Achilles (1. 697–910). See also Hyginus *Fabulae* 96 for a similar but much abbreviated account.

Zeus gave Dionysus to Ino and Athamas to rear as a girl (3. 4. 3).

Homer's account of Phoenix's departure from his father's house and coming to Peleus in Phthia (*Iliad* 9. 438–95) differs in important details from the version of Apollodorus. According to Homer, Phoenix's mother persuaded him to make love with his father's mistress to break up the relationship. His father, learning of it, cursed him with childlessness. Phoenix thought of killing his father, but a god checked his anger. He was placed under a kind of house arrest by relatives for nine days, but escaped on the tenth and came to Phthia, where Peleus received him and loved him as a son, giving him a territory to rule. Achilles, whom he fondled as a baby, became a son to him since he could have no children of his own. Hence Peleus sent Phoenix to Troy with Achilles, to teach him to be a speaker of words and a doer of deeds.

Apollodorus' version of the false accusation of Phoenix by his father's mistress is another example of a mythical motif noted earlier. See 2. 3. 1–2 and ch. 4, n. 10. For further comment on the Phoenix story, the subject of tragedies by Sophocles and Euripides, see Frazer, *Apollodorus* 2. 74–75.

Homer *Iliad* 23. 83–90 relates Patroclus' murder of the son of Amphidamas over a game of dice.

CHAPTER EIGHT

The Kings of Athens
(3. 14. 1–3. 15. 8)

BOOK 3 14 Cecrops, who was born from the earth and had the body of a man and of a snake, was the first king of Attica. The land formerly called Acte he named Cecropia after himself. In his time, they say, the gods decided to assign cities to themselves in which each would receive his own honors. Poseidon came first to Attica. He struck the ground in the middle of the Acropolis with his trident, producing the sea which they now call Erechtheis. Athena came after him and, making Cecrops a witness, took possession of Attica by planting an olive tree which can still be seen in the Pandrosium. When the two of them, Athena and Poseidon, fought over the land, Zeus stopped the fight and appointed the twelve gods as judges, | not Cecrops and Cranaus, as some said, nor Erysichthon. | They decided to award the land to Athena because Cecrops testified that she was the first to plant the olive. Athena therefore called the city Athens after herself. Poseidon in a rage flooded the Thriasian plain and put Attica under water.[1]

2   Cecrops married Agraulus, the daughter of Actaeus, and had a son, Erysichthon, who died childless, and daughters named Agraulus, Herse, and Pandrosus.[2] Agraulus had a daughter Alcippe by Ares. Halirrhothius, the son of Poseidon and a nymph Euryte, tried to rape her, but Ares caught him and killed him. Accused by Poseidon, Ares was tried in the Areopagus before the twelve gods and acquitted.[3]

3   Herse had by Hermes a son Cephalus, with whom Dawn fell in love. She carried him off and, after having intercourse with him in Syria, bore a son, Tithonus, who in turn had a son, Phaethon, the father of Astynous.[4] He in turn had a son Sandocus, who traveled from Syria to Cilicia and there founded Celenderis, married Pharnace, the daughter of Megassares the king of Hyria, and had a son, Cinyras. Cinyras went to Cyprus with people, founded Paphos, and there married

Metharme, the daughter of Pygmalion, the king of the Cyprians. By her he had sons named Oxyporus and Adonis, and daughters named Orsedice, Laogore, and Braesia. They, on account of Aphrodite's wrath, went to bed with foreign men and died in Egypt. Adonis, while still a boy, because of Artemis' anger was gored while hunting a boar and died. | Hesiod says that he was a son of Phoenix and Alphesiboea, but Panyasis says that he was a son of Thias king of Assyria. | Thias had a daughter Smyrna. Because of Aphrodite's anger (for she did not honor the goddess), Smyrna fell in love with her father and with the help of her nurse contrived to go to bed with him for twelve nights without his knowing who she was. When he found out, he drew his sword and chased her. As he began to overtake her, she prayed to the gods to become invisible. Pitying her, they turned her into a tree which they call *smyrna* [myrrh]. Ten months later the tree burst open and Adonis, as he is called, was born. Because of his beauty, while he was still an infant Aphrodite hid him in a chest without the gods' knowledge and entrusted him to Persephone. When Persephone saw him, she refused to give him back. Zeus, being appealed to for a decision, had the year divided into three parts and ordered Adonis to remain by himself for one part, with Persephone for another, and with Aphrodite for the third. Adonis, however, assigned to Aphrodite also his own part. Later, while hunting, he was gored by a boar and died.[5]

5   When Cecrops died, Cranaus, who was born from the earth, became king. During his reign the flood in Deucalion's time is said to have occurred.[6] Cranaus married a Lacedaemonian woman, Pedias, the daughter of Mynes, and by her had daughters named Cranae, Cranaechme, and Atthis. Atthis died while still a young girl and Cranaus called the land after her.

6   Amphictyon expelled Cranaus and became king.[7] | Some say that he was Deucalion's son, others that he was born of earth. | In the twelfth year of his rule Erichthonius in turn expelled him. Some say that Erichthonius was the son of Hephaestus and Cranaus' daughter Atthis, others that he was the son of Hephaestus and Athena. For Athena, it is said, went to Hephaestus wishing to forge weapons. He had been abandoned by Aphrodite. Filled with desire for Athena he chased her, but she ran away. When with great effort he caught up with her (for he was lame), he tried to make love with her. But she, being chaste and a virgin, would not submit to him. He ejaculated on the leg of the goddess and she in disgust wiped off the sperm with a piece of wool and threw it on the ground. Erichthonius was born from the sperm which fell on the ground. She reared him without the knowledge of the other gods, wishing to make him immortal. She

put him in a basket and gave him to Pandrosus, the daughter of Cecrops, forbidding her to open the basket. But the sisters of Pandrosus opened it out of curiosity and saw a snake coiled around the baby. According to some they were killed by the snake itself, but others claim that they were driven insane because of Athena's anger and threw themselves down from the acropolis. Erichthonius was reared in a sacred grove by Athena herself and after expelling Amphictyon became king of Athens. He set up the wooden image of Athena on the acropolis and instituted the Panathenaic festival. He married Praxithea, a river nymph, by whom he had a son Pandion.[8]

7   When Erichthonius died and was buried in the same sacred grove of Athena, Pandion became king. During his reign Demeter and Dionysus came to Attica where they were welcomed, Demeter by Celeus at Eleusis, and Dionysus by Icarius who received from him a cutting of the grape vine and learned how to make wine. Wishing to give the god's gift to men Icarius went to some shepherds who tasted the liquid then drank it greedily, without water, for enjoyment. Thinking that they had been bewitched, they killed Icarius. The next day they regained their senses and buried him. His dog Maera led his daughter Erigone, who was looking for him, to the body. After weeping for her father, she hanged herself.[9]

8   Pandion married Zeuxippe, the sister of his mother, and by her had two daughters, Procne and Philomela, and twin sons, Erechtheus and Butes. When war broke out with Labdacus over land boundaries, Pandion summoned Tereus, the son of Ares, from Thrace as an ally. After winning the war with his help he gave to Tereus his daughter Procne to marry. Tereus had a son, Itys, by her. Tereus fell in love with Philomela and seduced her, saying that Procne, whom he had hidden in the country, was dead. Afterwards he married Philomela and went to bed with her. He also cut out her tongue. But by weaving letters in a robe, Philomela spelled out to Procne the terrible things that had been done to her. After she sought out her sister, Procne killed her son Itys, boiled him, and served him to Tereus without his knowledge. Then she fled at once with Philomela. When Tereus learned what had happened, he seized an axe and pursued them. They were caught at Daulia in Phocis and prayed to the gods to be turned into birds. Procne became a nightingale and Philomela a swallow. Tereus, too, was turned into a bird, becoming a hoopoe.[10]

15 When Pandion died, his sons divided his estate. Erechtheus received the kingship and Butes received the priesthoods of Athena and Poseidon-Erechtheus [sic]. Erechtheus married Praxithea, the daughter of Phrasimus and Diogenia, daughter of Cephisus, and had sons named Cecrops, Pandorus, and Metion, and daughters named Procris,

Creusa, Chthonia, and Orithyia, the last of whom Boreas carried off.[11]

Butes married Chthonia; Xuthus, Creusa; and Cephalus, the son of Deion, Procris. Procris accepted a golden crown from Pteleon, went to bed with him, and when she was found by Cephalus, fled to Minos. He fell in love with her and persuaded her to make love with him. But if a woman made love with Minos it was impossible for her to live afterwards. For his wife Pasiphae, since Minos went to bed with many women, put a spell on him, and after going to bed with a woman he turned wild animals loose on her genitals and she was thus destroyed.

Minos had a swift dog and a javelin that was always accurate, and in return for these Procris went to bed with him, after first giving him tea from Circe's root to drink to prevent his harming her. Afterwards, fearing the wife of Minos, she went to Athens, became reconciled with Cephalus, and went hunting with him, for she liked to hunt. She had chased an animal into a thicket and Cephalus, not knowing she was there, hurled a javelin and struck and killed her. He was tried in the Areopagus and condemned to exile forever.[12]

2   While Orithyia was playing by the Ilissus River, Boreas carried her off and made love with her. She bore him daughters named Cleopatra and Chione, and sons with wings named Zetes and Calais, who sailed with Jason and died in pursuit of the Harpies. | But according to Acusilaus they were killed at Tenos by Heracles. | [13]

3   Phineus married Cleopatra and by her had sons named Plexippus and Pandion. After his sons were born he married Idaea, the daughter of Dardanus. She falsely accused her stepsons to Phineus of seducing her and he, believing her, blinded them. When the Argonauts sailed by with Boreas, they punished him for it.[14]

4   Chione had intercourse with Poseidon and without her father's knowledge gave birth to a son, Eumolpus. In order not to be found out she cast him into the sea, but Poseidon rescued him, brought him to Ethiopia, and gave him to Benthesicyme to rear. She was his daughter by Amphitrite. When Eumolpus was grown, Benthesicyme's husband gave one of his two daughters to him. Because Eumolpus tried to rape his wife's sister, he was exiled and so went with his son Ismarus to Tegyrius, the king of Thrace, who gave Ismarus his daughter in marriage. Eumolpus was later discovered to be plotting against Tegyrius and so fled to the Eleusinians and became friends with them. Later, when Ismarus died, he returned at the summons of Tegyrius and, after settling his old feud with him, succeeded to the kingship. When war was imminent between the Athenians and the Eleusinians, he was summoned by the Eleusinians and fought as their ally with a large force of Thracians.[15]

When Erechtheus asked the oracle how the Athenians could win the war the god replied that they would be successful if he would slaughter one of his daughters. When he slaughtered the youngest, the others also killed themselves, for some say that they had sworn an oath with each other to die together.[16] In the battle which took place after the death of his daughters, Erechtheus killed Eumolpus.

After Poseidon destroyed Erechtheus and his house, Cecrops, the oldest of the sons of Erechtheus, became king.[17] He married Metiadusa, the daughter of Eupalamus, and had a son, Pandion. Pandion became king after Cecrops, but was expelled by Metion's sons because of a revolt. He went to Pylas at Megara and married his daughter Pylia. Later he was also made king of the city, for Pylas, after killing his father's brother Bias, gave Pandion the kingship. He himself went to the Peloponnese with a group of people and founded a city, Pylus.

While Pandion was in Megara he had sons named Aegeus, Pallas, Nisus, and Lycus. Some say that Aegeus was the son of Scyrius, but that Pandion claimed him as his own. After the death of Pandion, his sons made an expedition against Athens, expelled the sons of Metion, and divided the rule into four parts, although Aegeus had all the power. His first wife was Meta, the daughter of Hoples, and his second Chalciope, the daughter of Rhexenor. Since he had no son he feared his brothers, so he went to Pythia and asked the oracle how to get children. The god replied, "Do not open, my good man, the swelling mouth of the wineskin until you come to the height of the Athenians." He was unable to comprehend the oracle and returned to Athens. Traveling through Troezen he stayed as a guest with Pittheus, the son of Pelops, who, since he understood the oracle, got him drunk and made him go to bed with his daughter Aethra. In the same night Poseidon also had intercourse with her. Aegeus ordered Aethra, if she bore a son, to rear him without saying whose he was. He left a sword and sandals under a rock and said that when this son was able to roll it away and pick them up she was to send him away with them.[18]

Aegeus himself went to Athens and held the games of the Panathenaic festival in which Androgeus, the son of Minos, defeated everyone. Aegeus sent him against the bull of Marathon, which killed him. But some say that on the way to Thebes to participate in the games in honor of Laius, Androgeus was ambushed and killed by fellow competitors who were envious of him.[19] Minos was sacrificing to the Graces on Paros when the death was announced to him. He threw away the garland he was wearing and stopped the flute music but completed the sacrifice nonetheless. Because of this men even now sacrifice to the Graces on Paros without flute music and garlands.

Shortly thereafter Minos, having command of the sea, made war on Athens with a naval expedition, captured Megara, of which Nisus, the son of Pandion, was king and killed Megareus, the son of Hip-pomenes, who had come from Onchestus to help Nisus. Nisus also died, through the treachery of his daughter. For he had a purple hair in the middle of his head and an oracle had declared that if it were removed he would die. His daughter Scylla, who had fallen in love with Minos, pulled out the hair. After Minos got control of Megara, he tied the girl by the feet to the stern of a ship and drowned her.[20]

When the war had gone on for some time, Minos, unable to capture Athens, prayed to Zeus for revenge against the Athenians. Thereupon both a famine and a plague fell upon the city. At first the Athenians, in accordance with an old oracle, slaughtered the daughters of Hya-cinth: Antheis, Aegleis, Lytaea, and Orthaea, upon the grave of Geraes-tus the Cyclops. (Their father Hyacinth had come to Athens from Lacedaemon and lived there.) When that had no effect they asked the oracle for deliverance. The god told them to allow Minos to exact whatever vengeance he chose. They then sent a message to Minos and permitted him to ask for satisfaction. Minos ordered them to send seven boys and seven girls without weapons to be fed to the Mino-taur. It was shut up in a labyrinth from which it was impossible for anyone going in to escape. For by means of intricate turnings the exit had been concealed. Daedalus, the son of Alcippe and Eupalamus, the son of Metion, built it, for he was an excellent architect and the in-ventor of statues. He had fled from Athens after throwing down from the acropolis Talos, the son of his sister Perdix. Talos was his pupil and Daedalus was afraid that he would prove superior to himself because of his inventiveness, for Talos had found the jawbone of a snake and with it sawed a thin piece of wood. When the corpse was discovered Daedalus was tried in the Areopagus and, being condemned, fled to Minos.[21]

NOTES

(3. 14. 1–3. 15. 8)

1   The usual story is that Poseidon and Athena competed for pos-session of Attica at the same time on the Acropolis of Athens. Phidias, the great fifth-century B.C. artist, told the story in sculpture on the west pediment of the Parthenon. At Ovid Met. 6. 70–82, Athena weaves it into a tapestry.

The "sea" which Poseidon produced with his trident was a salt water well. Herodotus 8. 55 says that it and the olive tree which Athena created were located in the Temple of Erechtheus on the Acropolis (called the Erechtheum). Frazer, however, agrees with Apollodorus that the olive grew in the Pandrosium, a sacred enclosure just to the west of the Erechtheum, and he thinks that Pausanias saw it there as well. See J. G. Frazer, *Pausanias's Description of Greece*, 6 vols. (London, 1898), 2. 337 (comment on Pausanias 1. 26. 5) and 343–44 (comment on 1. 27. 2).

When Xerxes invaded Athens in 480 B.C. and burned the Acropolis, Athena's original olive tree was also burned. Shortly afterwards, however, the charred trunk put out a shoot eighteen inches long and so the life of the original tree was miraculously preserved (Herotodus 8. 55, reporting the story which the Athenians told him).

Pausanias 1. 26. 5 says that it was possible to see the shape of a trident in the rock forming the salt water well in the Erechtheum and at 1. 27. 2 he implies that the olive tree, regenerated after the Persians burned it, was still living when he visited the Acropolis (sometime in the second century A.D.).

When Apollodorus says, "Zeus . . . appointed the twelve gods as judges" of the competition, he forgets that Zeus, Poseidon, and Athena were three of the twelve.

Themistocles (ca. 528–462 B.C.), the Athenian statesman whose strategies enabled Athens to defeat the Persians in the decisive battle of Salamis in 480, and who then by his political sagacity started Athens on her way to becoming the leading power of Greece, would have given the victory to Poseidon if he had been a judge of the competition between the two gods. For the myth poses the question whether Athens was to thrive by farming or by the sea. Themistocles, Plutarch says (*Themistocles* 19), developed the great natural harbor of the Piraeus and oriented the city toward the sea. Thus he reversed the policy of the ancient kings of Athens. For they, endeavoring to draw citizens away from the sea and to accustom them to live not by sailing but by tilling the soil, gave out the story about Athena's defeat of Poseidon in a competition for the country which she won by producing the olive. Themistocles, Plutarch continues, made the city dependent on the Piraeus and the land on the sea. Through this policy Athens reached the zenith of her political and cultural development in the fifth century.

The Thriasian plain, flooded by Poseidon in his anger, is the plain in which Eleusis is located (Frazer, *Apollodorus* 2. 81).

The myths of the early kings of Attica, complex to begin with, are made more so by Apollodorus' meandering style. Anne Pippin Burnett, trans., *Ion by Euripides* (Englewood Cliffs, N.J., 1970), appendix II: "Athena and Athens," 142–49, sorts out this complexity as clearly as possible and the reader is urged to consult these pages of her book. We may note the origin of the complexity in "the fact that the Athenians made three mutually contradictory claims, one of them itself paradoxical, about their own origins. They said (1) that they were descendants of a legendary mortal, Cecrops; (2) that they were sprung from their own soil; and (3) that they were descendants of Athena, who was nonetheless a virgin divinity" (142).

2   Cecrops' first daughter is named Aglaurus by Pausanias 1. 2. 6, Hyginus *Fabulae* 166, and Ovid *Met.* 2. 739. Apollodorus seems to have transposed letters in naming her Agraulus, and one may suppose that the name of Cecrops' wife should also be Aglaurus.

3   The Areopagus, Greece's oldest and highest court, was established by the gods to try Ares for the murder of Halirrothius. The court first met on a hill subsequently named "hill of Ares" (*Areios pagos*) after the first defendant in a trial before it. See Euripides *Electra* 1258–63, *Iphigenia in Tauris* 945–46, and Pausanias 1. 28. 5.

For additional famous mythological trials on the Areopagus (those of Cephalus, Daedalus, and Orestes) and for a theory that the name means "hill of cursing," see Frazer, *Pausanias's Description of Greece*, 2. 363–64, comment on Pausanias 1. 28. 5.

4   For Dawn's rape of Cephalus, see 1. 9. 4 (where he is called the son of Deion and Diomede), and for her jealousy of Procris, Cephalus' wife, and attempt to wreck their marriage, see Ovid *Met.* 7. 661–758. The Nurse in Euripides' *Hippolytus* 451–58 uses Dawn's passion for Cephalus and abduction of him to heaven as a mythical (and endorsed) example in her attempt to break down Phaedra's resolution not to give in to her passion for Hippolytus. Apollodorus' version of the myth of Cephalus and Procris (3. 15. 1) differs from Ovid's considerably.

Phaethon's parents were variously named, although the Sun is usually considered his father (see Frazer, *Apollodorus* 2. 82–83). Apollodorus omits to tell the myth of the disaster Phaethon suffered when he tried to drive the chariot of his father, the Sun. Phaethon was unable to control the horses, which ran wildly through the heavens, and nearly burned up the earth. To save it Jove struck him from the sky with a thunderbolt and Phaethon fell dead into the river Eridanus. His sisters, mourning him, were turned into poplar trees, but their tears continued to flow, dripping from the trees and hardening into amber (Ovid *Met.* 2. 1–366).

Hyginus *Fabulae* 152 says that the earth caught fire *after* Jupiter struck Phaethon with a thunderbolt, and that the god, having sought an excuse to destroy the human race, flooded the earth ostensibly to put out the fire and destroyed mankind, except for Deucalion and Pyrrha.

Lucretius *De Rerum Natura* 5. 396–406 in a short narration of the myth says that the Sun god caught the sun as Phaethon fell, caught the loose horses, yoked them together, and resumed the course of the sun. That is what the old Greek poets sang, he says, preposterous and untrue, and he proceeds to explain why (407–10). For similar myths, see Frazer, *Apollodorus* 2. 388–94, appendix 11, "Phaethon and the Chariot of the Sun."

5   Apollodorus gives two accounts of Adonis' parentage, birth, and death, his "own" very brief one and that of Panyasis, both of which agree about the way in which Adonis died (a detail Apollodorus repeats). The effect, though, is one of slight confusion. Panyasis' version has been treated as a regular part of the text since it is fuller than that of Apollodorus.

Ovid is the major source for the myth. According to him Adonis is the son of Myrrha by her father, Cinyras. (See Frazer, *Apollodorus* 2. 84–87 for other references.) At *Met.* 10. 298–552, Ovid narrates the story of Myrrha's passion for her father, Cinyras, which she struggles against. In despair, she is on the verge of committing suicide but is saved by her old nurse who wheedles from her the motive, her desire to make love with her father. The nurse makes arrangements (the similarity with Euripides' *Hippolytus* is obvious) and Myrrha finds herself in her father's bed, to which she returns for several glorious nights, conceiving a child in the process. Finally Cinyras, ignorant of her identity and eager to know who is so in love with him, calls for a light, discovers his daughter and horrified, draws his sword. Myrrha flees and for nine months wanders in the desert. Weary, heavy with her child, she prays to be removed both from life and from death. The gods hear her prayer and transform her into a tree. She weeps, nevertheless, her flowing tears the source of the perfume myrrh so valued in antiquity.

At once the baby struggles toward birth, the wood of the tree splits open, and he is born. Wood nymphs lay him on the soft grass and bathe him in his mother's tears of myrrh.

When Adonis becomes a young man Venus falls in love with him, hunts with him, but warns him to be careful of boars and lions. At 10. 708–39 what Venus feared for Adonis comes to pass: He strikes a boar a glancing blow, the beast shakes off the spear, turns, charges, and gores Adonis fatally in the groin. From afar Venus hears him groaning as he lies dying, and rushes to him to find him dead in a pool of blood. In her grief she creates a fitting memorial for him by sprinkling nectar over his blood. At once the slender flower called anemone springs up, too slight to stand for long in the wind from which it takes its name (*anemos*).

6   At 3. 8. 2 Apollodorus says that the flood occurred during the reign of Nyctimus, king of Arcadia.

7   Amphictyon was Cranaus' son-in-law according to Pausanias 1. 2. 6.

8   Euripides *Ion* 265–74 refers to Erichthonius' birth from the earth (without mentioning Hephaestus) from which he was taken by Athena and given to Cecrops' daughters. Athena did not give birth to him, Euripides emphasizes (270), for she was a virgin. They released him from his container and therefore died. At *Ion* 20–26 Euripides says that Athena set two snakes to guard Erichthonius (with the baby in a container of some kind) and gave him to Cecrops' daughters (called Aglaurids, after their mother Aglaurus) for safe-keeping. Whence the Athenian custom of "rearing their children in golden serpents," i.e., with golden circlets in the shape of serpents around their necks or bodies in remembrance of the serpent which guarded Erichthonius, or as amulets.

Ovid *Met.* 2. 547–62, telling the same story, identifies Aglaurus as the culprit who opened it (the other two sisters were faithful to their task), and says that there was one snake in the basket with the baby. Athena found out what Aglaurus had done from a crow which was hidden in the thick foliage of an elm observing the sisters and the basket. Hyginus *Fabulae* 166 says that when Athena heard the story from the crow she drove the girls insane and they threw themselves into the sea.

Hyginus *Astronomica* 2. 13 says that Erichthonius was born a serpent, and that when the daughters of Cecrops opened the container they went insane and hurled themselves from the Acropolis. The serpent slithered under Athena's shield and was reared by her. (Cf. Pausanias 1. 24. 7.) The point of the association, or even identification, of Erichthonius with a snake was to confirm his status as earth born.

The sacred grove in which Athena reared Erichthonius was the Erechtheum, on the Acropolis at Athens. The Athenians in the fifth century believed that a serpent belonging to Athena lived in the Erechtheum as guardian of the Acropolis, and once a month they set out honey cake for it to eat (Herodotus 8. 41; cf. Aristophanes *Lysistrata* 758–59; for a cynical view, see Plutarch *Themistocles* 10).

The wooden image of Athena apparently escaped destruction when the Persians burned the Acropolis in 480 B.C. (Herodotus 8. 54), for Plutarch *Themistocles* 10 clearly implies that the Athenians carried it with them to the island Salamis, to which they fled for refuge when they abandoned the city to the advancing Persian army. For a description of the statue, see Frazer's comment on Pausanias 1. 26. 6 in *Pausanias's Description of Greece*, 2. 340–41.

The Panathenaic festival which celebrated the unity of Attica under Athens (hence Plutarch *Theseus* 24 attributes its founding to Theseus, the mythical unifier of Attica) took place every four years during nine days in July. (This is the "greater" festival; a "lesser" one occurred yearly.) There were musical competitions, a recitation of the complete *Iliad* and *Odyssey* by relays of singers, athletic events, horse and chariot racing, and military competitions. The seventh day ended with torch races in the evening. An all night festival followed these, climaxed by a procession of Athenian citizens representative of the entire population to the Parthenon on the Acropolis, where a newly woven *peplos*, or robe, was presented to Athena as an offering. The procession was the high point of the festival. It is depicted on the Parthenon frieze, a band of relief sculpture 3 feet 5 inches high and 524 feet long which ran around the upper edge of the outer wall of the cella (i.e., the building proper) of the Parthenon. See E. Norman Gardiner, *Greek Athletic Sports and Festivals* (London, 1910), 229–45, and for the Parthenon frieze, J. J. Pollitt, *Art and Experience in Classical Greece* (Cambridge, Eng., 1972), 83–90. N. G. L. Hammond, *A History of Greece* (Oxford, 1963), 165, gives 566 B.C. as the date of the institution of the Panathenaic festival, i.e., he puts its founding in a definitely historical, not mythological time.

9   Diodorus Siculus 1. 29. 1–3 says that Erechtheus, by birth an Egyptian (although he is Pandion's son at 3. 14. 8), brought grain to Attica from Egypt in a time of drought and famine and was made king because he saved the people from starvation. He then instituted the festival of Demeter at Eleusis. From these events the tradition arose that Demeter "came" to Attica (see also 1. 5. 1 and ch. 1, n. 18). The Parian Marble (for which see ch. 2, n. 3) agrees with Diodorus that Demeter came to Attica in the reign of Erechtheus. As Frazer, *Apollodorus* 2. 95 notes, "the advent of Demeter and Dionysus is a mythical expression for the first cultivation of corn and vines in Attica. . . ."

10   The story of Tereus, Procne, and Philomela was the basis for a lost tragedy of Sophocles, entitled *Tereus,* from which most of the surviving versions of the story are probably drawn. In addition to Apollodorus' account of the myth we have Hyginus *Fabulae* 45, short and with a doubtful text in one place; Ovid *Met.* 6. 424–674, the best known version; and a few other narrations of the story (see Frazer, *Apollodorus* 2. 98–100).

Apollodorus' account presents problems. Either he tries somewhat elliptically to integrate two versions (one of which is similar to Ovid's narration) or there are textual difficulties. Editors of the Greek text have tried to make the story here more coherent (at least in terms of Ovid's telling of the myth) by deleting (Hercher) or bracketing as doubtful (Frazer) the lines translated by "saying that Procne . . . was dead. Afterwards he married Philomela and went to bed with her."

(Wagner accepts these lines as valid.) Hyginus *Fabulae* 45, however, says that after Tereus married Procne he returned to Athens to ask Pandion to allow him to marry Philomela, saying that Procne had died. Pandion gave Philomela to him and sent guards with her. Tereus threw them into the sea and captured Philomela who had been found on a mountain (?). On returning to Thrace, Tereus entrusted Philomela to the king, Lynceus. His wife, Lathusa, brought her at once as a concubine (?) to Procne, who was a friend of hers. Procne recognized her sister and Tereus' crime (the Latin is doubtful here) and together they began to plot vengeance. Tereus meanwhile was shown prophetic signs of Itys' death at the hand of a relative. Suspecting his own brother, Dryas, he killed him. Procne killed Itys, served him to his father at a banquet, and fled with Philomela. Pursuit and metamorphoses occurred: Procne was changed into a swallow, Philomela into a nightingale (reversing Apollodorus' transformations; see below). Tereus was changed into a hawk.

In Ovid's version of the myth, Tereus helps Pandion in a war against "barbarians" and is rewarded with marriage to Pandion's daughter, Procne. After living with him in Thrace for five years (during which time Itys was born), Procne longs to see her sister Philomela, and asks Tereus to go to Athens and ask Pandion if Philomela may visit them. On seeing Philomela in Athens Tereus falls passionately in love with her. He can barely keep his hands off her during the journey by ship to Thrace. As soon as they land he drags her to a hut and rapes her. She threatens to expose his crime, he cuts out her tongue with his sword to prevent her from doing so, rapes her again, and leaves her in the hut under guard. Returning to Procne, Tereus tells her that Philomela has died.

Philomela weaves the story of Tereus' crime into a tapestry and manages to send it to her sister. Aghast, Procne rescues Philomela from the hut, brings her to the palace, and together they plan revenge. They kill Itys, cut him up, and serve his flesh to Tereus at a banquet which they say is especially to honor him. Satisfied after a full dinner, Tereus calls for his son. Procne says that he is present. Tereus looks around for him, and at that moment Philomela bursts into the banquet hall still bloody from butchering Itys and flings the child's head at the father. Tereus overturns the table in shock and grief, draws his sword and begins to pursue the sisters. All are turned into birds, Tereus becoming a hoopoe. Ovid does not say what kind of birds Procne and Philomela become, but in the Greek tradition followed by Apollodorus (but later reversed by Roman mythographers), Procne is changed into a nightingale, mourning for her son in her cry "Itu! Itu!," while the tongueless Philomela is turned into a swallow (Frazer, *Apollodorus* 2. 99–100).

The above synopsis does scant justice to one of Ovid's most powerful stories. It begins a distinct section of the work, 6. 401–11. 795 (end), the theme of which is disastrous sexual passion in human beings. See Brooks Otis, *Ovid as an Epic Poet* (Cambridge, Eng., 1970), 83–90.

With Tereus, Procne, and Philomela, Ovid turns "to the impious interrelations of mortals, which lead to . . . the punishment of the guilty and the innocent in the same irrational series of events. . . . Ovid . . . henceforth maintains our interest in the way men and women, without the jealous or irrational intervention of gods, can make their own lives so rich and yet so miserable because of failure to control their passions" (William S. Anderson, ed., *Ovid's Metamorphoses: Books 6–10* [Norman, Okla., 1972], 205–06).

In addition, Ovid brings together here two related motifs found throughout the work to make a forceful (perhaps shocking) statement about his vision of art. The first is the motif of blocked utterance: the inability of a human being to speak to another and its consequences (found, e.g., in the Io, Callisto, and Actaeon episodes). The second is the motif of art *from* pain or *into* pain: art and pain are locked into a cause and effect relationship in which each is now cause, now effect (found, e.g., in the Arachne, Marsyas, and Orpheus episodes, for the last of which see ch. 1, n. 6). Here blocked utterance (the severing of Philomela's tongue) coincides with and adds to incredible pain and they together create art (the tapestry). Art does its work well as it sets in motion revenge, more pain, and the horrible death of the innocent Itys. (For the suggestion that Ovid believed that art could be highly immoral —not a new idea to readers of Pindar or of Plato, *Republic* 10—see ch. 4, n. 11.)

11   For the priesthood of Poseidon-Erechtheus, see Frazer, *Apollodorus* 2. 101–02. Apollodorus expands slightly on the rape of Orithyia by Boreas at 3. 15. 2. Ovid tells the story at *Met.* 6. 682–721, relieving the horror of the Tereus-Procne-Philomela myth which it follows (ending book 6) with a slightly upbeat note: Boreas first tried the normal method of procuring Orithyia as his wife by becoming her suitor and asking for her hand. But as god of the North Wind he was associated with the violent north country of Tereus and so was rejected. Thereupon he resorted to methods more in keeping with his true nature, and after a blustering speech to himself (*Met.* 6. 687–701), carried her off. But Orithyia bore twin sons, Zetes and Calais, to Boreas and the couple seemed to live happily ever after. (Cf. Apollonius Rhodius *Argonautica* 1. 211–18.)

12   Apollodorus mentions the dog Minos gave to Procris at 2. 4. 7. For a summary of and comment on Ovid's version of Cephalus and Procris (*Met*. 7. 661–758), see ch. 2, n. 15. See also 3. 14. 3 and n. 4 (Cephalus and Dawn). Cephalus' trial on the Areopagus was one of several famous mythological trials. See n. 3.

13   The wings of Zetes and Calais fascinated Apollonius Rhodius and Ovid. The former describes the twins rising into the air flapping dusky wings spangled with gold, which grew from each side of their ankles (*Argonautica* 1. 219—21). The latter says that they were born without wings but sprouted them (inherited from their father) in adolescence at the time their beards began to appear (*Met*. 6. 711–18).

Zetes and Calais are listed as members of the Argo's crew at 1. 9. 17. At 1. 9. 21 Apollodorus narrates their pursuit of the Harpies, but makes no explicit mention of their death, although he says that one of them (unnamed) while pursuing the Harpy Ocypete fell with her from the sky out of exhaustion. Apollonius Rhodius *Argonautica* 1. 1298–1308 agrees with Acusilaus that the twins were killed by Heracles at Tenos, because they dissuaded the Argonauts from returning to Mysia to pick up Heracles after they set sail without him. Heracles had gone in search of Hylas who was kidnapped by water nymphs. Heracles made a burial mound for them and erected two pillars on it, one of which sways when their father, the North Wind, blows.

14   At 1. 9. 21 Apollodorus mentions three variants to account for the blinding of Phineus, one of which, that he was blinded by the Argonauts because he had blinded his sons, he gives here as the "orthodox" version. In so doing he forgets that in the earlier passage he describes the Argonauts as Phineus' benefactors, releasing him from the plague of the Harpies in return for directions to Colchis. Phineus, his sons, and Idaea compose one of the many triangles in Mediterranean mythologies in which a son (or younger man) is falsely accused by an older woman, the wife of his father (or benefactor), who has made sexual overtures and been rejected. See 2. 3. 1–2 (and ch. 4, n. 10) and 3. 13. 3 (and ch. 7, n. 35). Sophocles *Antigone* 970–76 says that Phineus' wife herself blinded his sons with weaving pins. Note blinding in an "oedipal" myth, as in the Oedipus myth itself.

15   Eumolpus was commonly believed to have founded the Eleusinian mysteries. Apollodorus implies as much at 2. 5. 12. See also Frazer, *Apollodorus* 2. 108–09. For the Eleusinian mysteries, see ch. 1, n. 18.

16   At 3. 15. 1 Apollodorus names four daughters of Erechtheus. Of these, Orithyia was married to Boreas, and Procris was accidentally killed by her husband, Cephalus. That leaves only two, Chthonia and Creusa, and Euripides *Ion* 277–80 says that Creusa was spared from sacrifice because she was a newly born infant. The tenth-century A.D.

lexicon-encyclopedia entitled the *Suda* (or *Suidas*), however, attributes six daughters to Erechtheus, but says that only the two oldest, Protogonia and Pandora, offered to sacrifice themselves (s. v. *parthenoi*). According to Hyginus *Fabulae* 46, Erechtheus had four daughters who swore an oath among themselves that if one of them met her death, the others would commit suicide. When Eumolpus was killed by the Athenians after the war with the Eleusinians, Poseidon demanded that one of Erechtheus' daughters be sacrificed to him. Chthonia (whom alone Hyginus names) was chosen, and the others killed themselves.

17   Hyginus *Fabulae* 46 says that Zeus struck Erechtheus with a thunderbolt at the request of Poseidon, who wanted to avenge himself on the Athenians for killing his son, Eumolpus.

18   Aegeus might well be puzzled by the deceptively simple oracle (which Plutarch *Theseus* 3 says was a cliché in ancient Greece) since it means "Do not drink wine/Do not make love, until you get home." No doubt he had been doing both at home for years without results. Pittheus, famous for his erudition and wisdom (Plutarch *Theseus* 3), on hearing the oracle understands at once that the king of Athens is potent and fertile. The offspring of Aegeus and his daughter, Aethra, Pittheus probably realizes, would have in his veins the blood of two (perhaps *the* two) great houses of Greece: Those of Pelops and of Erechtheus. Such a pan-Hellene would be a noble creature indeed, and such was Theseus.

In the third episode of Euripides' *Medea*, Aegeus, on his way from Delphi to Troezen, encounters the unhappy heroine (663–758). Aegeus tells her the oracle (679–81) on which she makes no comment but promises to end his childlessness with drugs (708–18).

Aegeus' childlessness was in contrast to the extreme fertility of his brother, Pallas, who had fifty sons. They were potential usurpers, plotting against Aegeus, who feared them, and scorning him for his sterility (Plutarch *Theseus* 3 and Diodorus Siculus 4. 60. 4–5).

19   Several sources referred to by Frazer, *Apollodorus* 2. 116–17, indicate that Androgeus' victories in the Panathenaic festival were the ultimate cause of his death. Minos considered the Athenians responsible, for he went to war against them (3. 15. 8).

20   Nisus with his life-maintaining purple hair is an example of the "external soul," for reference to which (and for other examples), see ch. 2, n. 9. Aeschylus *Choephoroe* 612–22 says that Minos bribed Scylla with a golden necklace to cut her father's magic hair. Virgil *Georgics* 1. 404–09 describes the sea eagle, Nisus', constant pursuit of his daughter, Scylla, changed into a bird. The myth is the subject of the *Ciris*, a poem of 541 lines doubtfully attributed to the young Virgil. The best known version is that of Ovid *Met.* 8. 1–151.

21   The fourteen Athenian youths were sent to Crete every nine years (according to Plutarch *Theseus* 15 and Diodorus Siculus 4. 61. 3). At 3. 1. 3–4 Apollodorus tells of the passion of Pasiphae for the bull from the sea, the birth of the Minotaur, and the labyrinth built by Daedalus in which it was confined.

Talos aroused murderous envy in Daedalus by inventing the potter's wheel and the compass, as well as the saw (applying to iron the idea given by the snake's jawbone; see Diodorus Siculus 4. 76. 4–7). Ovid *Met.* 8. 236–59 follows a different tradition with different details (see Frazer, *Apollodorus* 2.121): The boy makes an iron saw after studying the backbone of a fish; no mention is made of the potter's wheel; and Ovid gives him, rather than Daedalus' sister, the name Perdix ("partridge"), by which he was known before the metamorphosis. As he fell through the air from the Acropolis, Athena caught him and changed him into a bird, but Ovid suggests that Perdix himself invented his transformation while falling: "The force of his swift brilliance was changed into wings and into feet . . ." (254–55).

Daedalus' trial was one of four famous mythological trials on the Areopagus (see n. 3).

CHAPTER NINE

Theseus
(3. 16. 1—Epitome 1)

BOOK 3 16 A son, Theseus, was born to Aegeus by Aethra and when he was grown he pushed aside the rock, took up the sandals and sword, and hurried on foot to Athens.[1] He cleared the road of the robbers besieging it. First, in Epidaurus, he killed Periphetes, the son of Hephaestus and Anticlia. He was nicknamed "Clubber" from the iron club which he carried due to weak ankles and with which he killed

2 passers-by. Theseus took away his club and carried it himself. Second, he killed Sinis, the son of Polypemon and Sylea, daughter of Corinthus, who lived on the Isthmus of Corinth. He was nicknamed "Pine-bender," for he forced passers-by to bend down pine trees. Lacking strength to hold them down indefinitely, they were hurled through the air and died miserably. Theseus killed Sinis in the same way.

Epit. 1 Third, at Crommyon, he killed the sow Phaea, named after the old woman who fed it. | Some say that this sow was the offspring

2 of Echnida and Typhon. | Fourth, he killed Sciron the Corinthian, the son of Pelops, or as some say, of Poseidon. He lived among the rocks in the Megarid, which were called Scironian after him, and forced passers-by to wash his feet. While they were washing them he threw

3 them into the sea as food for a giant turtle. Theseus seized him by the feet and threw him into the sea. Fifth, in Eleusis, he killed Cercyon, the son of Branchus and a nymph Argiope. This man forced passers-by

4 to wrestle with him and killed them. Theseus lifted him up and threw him down on the ground. Sixth, he killed Damastes [Procrustes] whom some call Polypemon. He had a house beside a road and kept two beds made—one small, the other large. Offering passers-by a place to stay he put short men in the large bed and then beat them with a hammer to make them the same length as the bed. Tall men he put in the small bed and sawed off the parts of their bodies extending over it.[2]

5 After freeing the road Theseus came to Athens. Medea was at that

time married to Aegeus and, plotting against Theseus, persuaded
Aegeus to be on his guard against him, alleging that Theseus was
plotting against him. Aegeus, failing to recognize his own son, feared

6 him and sent him against the bull of Marathon. After Theseus killed
it, Aegeus offered him a poison which he had received from Medea
that very day. Just as the drink was being served to him, he gave his
father his sword. Aegeus recognized it and knocked the cup from his
hands. After being recognized by his father and learning of the plot,
Theseus banished Medea.[3]

7 He was included in the third group chosen as tribute for the Mino-
taur, | or as some say, volunteered for it |. The ship had a black sail

8 and Aegeus commanded his son, if he returned alive, to spread a white
sail. When he arrived at Crete, Ariadne, the daughter of Minos, fell in
love with him and offered to help him if he agreed to take her away
to Athens as his wife. After Theseus promised under oath to take her
away, Ariadne asked Daedalus to reveal to her the exit from the

9 labyrinth. At his suggestion she gave Theseus thread when he entered
it. He fastened it to the door and went in letting it out behind him. He
found the Minotaur in the most remote part of the labyrinth, beat it
to death with his fists, and went out again by winding up the thread.
By night he went with Ariadne and the [Athenian] children to Naxos.
There Dionysus, desiring Ariadne, carried her off to Lemnos and had
intercourse with her. She gave birth to Thoas, Staphylus, Oenopion,
and Peparethus.

10 Grieving for Ariadne, Theseus forgot to spread the white sail when
he sailed for home. From the Acropolis, Aegeus saw the ship with a

11 black sail and thinking that Theseus was dead, threw himself down
from the Acropolis and died. Theseus accepted the power at Athens
and killed the fifty sons of Pallas. Moreover, he killed as many as tried
to oppose him and ruled alone.[4]

12 Minos, when he learned of the escape of Theseus and those with
him, confined Daedalus, who was responsible for it, in the labyrinth
with his son Icarus, born to him by Naucrate, a slave of Minos. But
Daedalus made wings for himself and his son. As the boy began to
fly, he warned him neither to fly too high lest the sun melt the glue

13 and the wings come apart, nor to fly near the sea, lest the wings come
unglued because of the moisture. But Icarus ignored his father's commands and, exhilarated, flew higher and higher until the glue melted
and he fell into the sea and died. (It was named Icarian after him.)

14 But Daedalus arrived safely at Camicus in Sicily. Minos pursued him,
carrying a spiral shell. In each country where he looked for Daedalus,
Minos proclaimed that he would give a large reward to the man who
drew a thread through the shell. He thought that in this way he would

find Daedalus. When he came to Camicus in Sicily, to the court of Cocalus where Daedalus was hiding, he showed the spiral shell. Coca-
15 lus took it, announcing that he would thread it, and gave it to Daedalus. He fastened a thread to an ant, bored a hole in the shell, and allowed the ant to go through it. When Minos received back the shell with the thread through it, he knew that Daedalus was with Cocalus and imme- diately demanded him. Cocalus promised to surrender him and asked Minos to be his guest. While being bathed by Cocalus' daughters, he was killed. Some say that he died from being scalded with hot water.[5]
16 Theseus made an expedition against the Amazons with Heracles and carried off Antiope | or as some say, Melanippe; Simonides says Hippo- lyte |. Because of this, the Amazons marched against Athens. They encamped around the Areopagus but were defeated by Theseus and
17 the Athenians.[6] Theseus had a son, Hippolytus, by Antiope, but later received Phaedra, the daughter of Minos, from Deucalion as his wife. During the marriage festival, Theseus' former Amazon wife appeared armed with her sister Amazons and was on the point of killing the wedding guests, but they quickly shut the doors and killed her. | Some,
18 however, say that she was killed by Theseus in battle. | After Phaedra bore Theseus two children, Acamas and Demophon, she fell in love with Hippolytus and begged him to make love with her. But since he hated all women, he refused. Phaedra, fearing that he would slander
19 her to his father, forced open the doors of her bedroom, tore her clothes, and falsely accused Hippolytus of attempting to rape her. Theseus believed her and prayed to Poseidon to destroy Hippolytus. While Hippolytus was driving his chariot beside the sea, the god sent a bull from the surf. The horses were frightened, the chariot was wrecked, and Hippolytus, entangled in the reins, was dragged to death. When Phaedra's passion for him became known, she hanged herself.[7]
20 Ixion desired Hera and tried to rape her. When Hera told Zeus, he, wishing to know if it were really so, shaped a cloud in Hera's likeness and laid it beside him. When he boasted that he had intercourse with Hera, Zeus as punishment tied him to a wheel on which he is carried by winds through the air. The cloud gave birth to Centaur.[8]
21 Theseus allied himself with Pirithous in a battle against the centaurs. For when Pirithous was seeking to marry Hippodamia, he entertained the centaurs who were related to her. Unaccustomed to wine, they drank without restraint and became drunk. When the bride was brought in they tried to rape her. But Pirithous armed himself and fought them with Theseus, who killed many of them.
22 Caeneus was originally a woman, but when Poseidon made love with her she asked to become a man and invulnerable. And so in the battle with the centaurs he was scornful of being wounded and killed many

of them. But others stood around him beating him with fir trees and buried him in the ground.[9]

23   Theseus made an agreement with Pirithous that they would marry daughters of Zeus. With his help he carried off Helen from Sparta for himself when she was twelve years old and then went to Hades to ask Persephone to marry Pirithous. The Dioscuri, with Lacedaemonians and Arcadians, captured Athens, recovered Helen, and took Aethra, the daughter of Pittheus, captive. Demophon and Acamas fled.

24   The Dioscuri also brought Menestheus back from exile and made him the ruler of Athens. Theseus went with Pirithous to Hades where he was the victim of a trick. For Pluto, pretending to offer them food and drink, told them to sit first on the chair of forgetfulness, to which they became attached and were also bound by the coils of snakes. Pirithous remained bound there forever, but Heracles brought up Theseus and sent him to Athens. Driven from there by Menestheus, he went to Lycomedes, who threw him into a pit and killed him.[10]

NOTES

(3. 16. 1–Epitome 1)

1   In addition to his human father, Aegeus, Theseus had a divine father, Poseidon (Diodorus Siculus 4. 59. 1; cf. Plutarch *Theseus* 6). Apollodorus recognizes only the human paternity of Aegeus. He does allow, however, that Poseidon had intercourse with Aethra on the same night as Aegeus (3. 15. 7).

With Poseidon sharing paternity with Aegeus, Theseus was not only a scion of two great houses of Greece, those of Pelops and of Erechtheus (see ch. 8, n. 18), but could claim divine descent as well. In this respect he is like Heracles, son of Zeus and Amphitryon by Alcmena. Theseus and Heracles were also first cousins once removed: Pittheus, the maternal grandfather of the former, was the brother of Lysidice, the maternal grandmother of the latter, both being children of Pelops. (For Theseus as an Athenian parallel to the Dorian Heracles, see n. 2.)

Minos, king of Crete, once called into question Theseus' claim that Poseidon was his father. They were aboard Minos' ship taking the fourteen Athenian youths to be sacrificed to the Minotaur. (Theseus had volunteered to go as one of the intended victims.) Minos threw a golden ring into the sea and challenged Theseus to dive down and bring it up to prove his claim. Immediately he jumped from the ship. Dolphins carried him down to the palace of Poseidon where the god's consort, Amphitrite, placed around his shoulders a crimson cloak and fitted on his head a wreath "dark with roses," a wedding present to her from Aphrodite. Theseus then emerged unwet from the sea by the stern of the ship, wearing the gleaming gifts from the gods and so foiling Minos. The myth is brilliantly told by Bacchylides 17 (see the translation and also the note in Robert Fagles, trans., *Bacchylides: Complete Poems* with Introduction and Notes by Adam M. Parry [New Haven and London, 1961]).

When he came of age in Troezen, Theseus easily lifted the stone, removed the sword and sandals, and left for Athens. A statue on the Acropolis at Athens in bronze, except for the stone, commemorated this first heroic deed of Theseus (Pausanias 1. 27. 8).

2　　The final portion of Apollodorus' work survives only in the form of an "epitome" (pronounced epiTOME), which means "abridgement."

In killing the predators infesting the road from Troezen to Athens, Theseus performed six labors in imitation of the twelve of Heracles (Diodorus Siculus 4. 59). The renown of Heracles' achievement kindled the imagination of Theseus as a child and he idolized the great hero. He was always eager to hear others speak about Heracles and the kind of man he was, especially if they had seen him or witnessed any of his words or deeds (Plutarch *Theseus* 6; cf. 8 and 11). Theseus himself, when he was seven years old, saw Heracles at Troezen on a visit to Pittheus. Heracles, the story goes, had taken off his lion's skin to eat dinner. Some children, including Theseus, came to meet him, but when they saw the skin, thinking it was a living lion, they all ran away except for Theseus. Somewhat frightened, he nevertheless got an axe from a servant and was prepared to fight (Pausanias 1. 27. 7).

The parallels between the two heroes, extending to lineage and to descent from Pelops (which made them cousins: n. 1), gives poignancy to Theseus' reception of Heracles at Athens after he murdered his wife and children. (See Euripides' *Heracles* and ch. 5, n. 6.) The humanity of Theseus as kind receiver of the cast off or broken and defeated is also portrayed in Sophocles' *Oedipus at Colonus* and Euripides' *Suppliants*. Theseus, like Heracles, also experienced the tragedy of killing his own son (Euripides' *Hippolytus*).

For other narrations of Theseus' labors, see Bacchylides 18, Ovid *Met.* 7. 425–52, and Plutarch *Theseus* 8–11. The killing of the bull of Marathon is an "extra" labor, usually separated from the original six (Epitome 1. 5–6; Ovid, above, who places it first; Diodorus 4. 59; and Plutarch *Theseus* 14).

3　　The bull of Marathon which Theseus kills represents the seventh labor of Heracles (2. 5. 7) and so provides a further link between the two heroes.

For Medea's attempt to poison Theseus when he arrives at Athens, see 1. 9. 28 (and ch. 3, n. 13) and Plutarch *Theseus* 12.

4   The bull of Marathon killed by Theseus was also the bull from the sea sent to Minos from Poseidon which aroused passion in Pasiphae and by which she had the Minotaur (3. 1. 3–4). Theseus, therefore, kills both the Minotaur and its father. Is revenge taken for these killings? We may note that Theseus is responsible for the death of his father because he forgets to lower the black sail and raise the white sail as he and his father agreed would be done on the return voyage from Crete if Theseus survived the Minotaur. When he sees the black sail Aegeus, in grief at the supposed loss of Theseus, jumps to his death from the Acropolis at Athens. Why does Theseus forget? Because of grief over the loss of Ariadne (Epitome 1. 10 and Diodorus 4. 61. 6); because Ariadne, whom he abandoned on the island of Dia, curses him (Catullus 64. 188–245)? Either way, Ariadne, daughter of Pasiphae and so half-sister of the Minotaur and sister of Phaedra, whom Theseus later marries, is the cause. (Granted that Ariadne provided Theseus the means to return from the labyrinth.)

Theseus later kills his son, Hippolytus, with a curse because he believed a false suicide note left by Phaedra alleging an attempt by Hippolytus to seduce her. The truth, of course, is that Phaedra was herself afflicted with illicit passion for Hippolytus, as was her mother, Pasiphae, for the bull from the sea sent by Poseidon. Theseus' curse works: Hippolytus, driving his chariot along the shore away from Troezen into exile is killed by another bull from the sea sent by Poseidon (Euripides' *Hippolytus*).

Homer *Odyssey* 11. 321–25 makes a very brief allusion to the myth of Theseus, the Minotaur, Ariadne, and Aegeus. Diodorus Siculus 4. 61. 3–8 and Plutarch *Theseus* 15, 17–20, 22 tell the myth in a more or less straightforward manner. Plutarch *Theseus* 20 notes the many variants, inconsistent with each other, in the Theseus-Ariadne story.

For the Roman poets Catullus and Ovid, Dionysus did not, as Apollodorus says, carry off Ariadne. Rather, Theseus abandoned her on Dia. Catullus gives the finest and fullest poetic rendition of this story in surviving Greek and Latin literature in his poem 64. 52–264. Ovid returns to the myth more than once: see *Heroides* 10, *Ars Amatoria* 1. 525–62, and *Met.* 8. 155–82.

Dionysus transformed Ariadne's crown (she was a princess) into the constellation, the Northern Crown (Diodorus Siculus 4. 61. 5 and Ovid *Met.* 8. 177–82).

5   The myth of Daedalus, the labyrinth, and the Minotaur (and the escape of Daedalus and his son Icarus from Crete) has fascinated (or possessed) the English painter, sculptor, and novelist, Michael Ayrton. For his account of the way in which he became "the dedicated chroni-

cler of a myth," see "The Path to Daedalus" in D. R. Dudley, ed., *Virgil* (London, 1969), 176–201, which includes photographs of his paintings and sculptures of aspects of the myth. In Ayrton's novel, *The Maze Maker* (New York, 1967), Daedalus describes the Minotaur in the labyrinth. He had superhuman strength, but the weight of his head and huge shoulders carried on light legs made his balance uncertain. Moreover, the setting of his eyes in the sides of his bull's head prevented him from focusing them straight ahead. This defect in vision made him uncertain how to attack and gave an opponent an advantage:

" 'Splay-legged, he moved forward again with the waddling motion of a toad, stopped, spun, fell to his knees groping with both hands, seeming to plead for sight of his enemy. He came springing to his feet like a wrestler and suddenly saw me in his right eye. He head dropped and his shoulders and crest rose. His arms went back and I knew on the instant that he would attack in bull form, favouring the right horn, turn, if he missed his charge, and bring his hands into play on the turn. He came at me fast and I threw myself to his left. His momentum carried him on and when he turned, reaching out, he was ten yards away. He came at me again but uncertainly, trying to be bull and man at once, searching for a hold. I ran straight at him and twisting as I ran, I passed to his right, leaving him stock-still. This unexpected manoeuvre left him rooted and he lost me. I was behind him. He picked up a stone the size of his own head and crumbled it to powder between his hands. He screamed, raised both arms and gripped his horns, wrenching and pulling at them. Such was the enormous power of his shoulders that it seemed for a moment that he would tear himself in half. He screamed again, lost his footing and fell rolling and jerking. His mouth sprayed foam, his trunk struck the stony floor, thundering against it like a drum. He made a grotesque leap, stood swaying, fell again and remained heaped where he had fallen in a sudden quiet. He had forgotten me' " (197).

In the novel Daedalus gives the meaning of the labyrinth: " 'All this long burrowing and building, to protect or to imprison, this flight through the sky and tunnelling in the earth, seems to me now to add up to no more than the parts of a single great maze which is my life. This maze for the Maze Maker I made from experience and from circumstance. Its shape identifies me. It has been my gaol and my sanctuary, my journey and its destination' " (319). As Ovid says, *tanta est fallacia tecti*; Daedalus and the Minotaur are one.

Daedalus flew first to Cumae in Italy (near Naples), in a version of the myth told by Virgil (*Aeneid* 6. 14–33) and there built a temple to Apollo as a thank-offering for his safe flight. Virgil's brilliant ecphrasis describes the temple doors of gold into which Daedalus worked a bas-relief narrating the entire Cretan myth, including the passion of Pasiphae, the Minotaur, the labyrinth, the death of Androgeus, and Theseus' successful return from the maze with Ariadne's help. "You, too, Icarus, would have a great part in so grand a work of art, if grief would allow it. Twice the father tried to engrave the boy's death in gold, twice his hands fell" (6. 30–33). Virgil allows a mythical artist in his own narration to relate in a different medium the myth which he, Virgil, wants to tell. For Daedalus, however, it is not a myth, but recent true history. By this device, creating what we might call "emphatic indirection," Virgil conveys something of his feeling about using history as the basis for art, which, of course, he does in the *Aeneid*. If Daedalus represents the artist, his success and his failure, then Virgil is indicating clearly that for him (unlike for Ovid) pain in the real world (here Daedalus' "real world") makes the artist falter, prevents him from finishing his work of art.

Ovid's version of the myth (*Met.* 8. 183–235; cf. the earlier *Ars Amatoria* 2. 19–98) is well known and has been a wellspring for later works of art. Daedalus resolves to devise a way to escape from Minos: *dixit et ignotas animum dimittit in artes* (8. 188, "He spoke and turned his mind toward unknown arts"): the epigraph of James Joyce's *A Portrait of the Artist as a Young Man* (New York, 1916).

He instructs his son carefully to follow him and to fly a middle course. But he weeps as he fits the wings to Icarus' shoulders and his hands tremble. He kisses the boy, not knowing it is for the last time. They rise into the air, Daedalus in the lead but constantly looking back to Icarus and urging him to stay close to him, and continuing to instruct him in "fatal arts" (*damnosas artes*, 215). Far below a fisherman nearly drops his rod, a shepherd leans upon his staff, a plowman rests upon his plow, to gape in amazement at the pair flying over them.

Icarus, enraptured by flying, soars higher, toward the sun, which melts the wax holding the wings together. Suddenly his shoulders are bare, flight turns to dead drop into the sea which closes over his mouth ending his cries for his father. Daedalus calls for his son repeatedly, then sees feathers floating on the water. He curses his handiwork (*suas artes*, 234) and buries the body of his son. Again, as often, Ovid links art and pain in a cause and effect relationship (see ch. 8, n. 10). (Cf. Pieter Brueghel's painting, *Landscape with the Fall of Icarus* and W. H. Auden's poem, "Musée des Beaux Arts.")

The myth of Daedalus and Icarus becomes an informing text for James Joyce in his *Portrait of the Artist*. This myth is melded with the Odysseus-Telemachus myth and continues in Joyce's *Ulysses* (Paris,

1922). For additional works of art drawn from the entire Cretan-Athenian myth, see Philip Mayerson, *Classical Mythology in Literature, Art, and Music* (Waltham, Mass. and Toronto, 1971), 321–22 and 369.

6   The Areopagus derives its name ("hill of Ares") from the Amazons' sacrifice to Ares while encamped upon it, according to Aeschylus *Eumenides* 685–90 (see also ch. 8, n. 3). Plutarch *Theseus* 27, using inference in a way reminiscent of Thucydides, concludes that the Amazons' invasion of Athens was no inferior nor womanish (*sic*) enterprise. For they would have been unable to encamp in the city itself and conduct a battle near the Pnyx and Museion hills unless they had conquered the outlying districts and had entered the city unopposed.

Plutarch is amazed that the Amazons could make the journey by land from their country (near the southern coast of the Black Sea, about two-thirds of the way from the Bosporus to the eastern end of the sea) and that they could cross the frozen Bosporus. After four months of fighting, with neither side winning (contrary to Apollodorus' account), the Athenians and the Amazons made peace.

7   The Deucalion from whom Theseus receives Phaedra is a son of Minos and a brother of Phaedra (3. 1. 2), not the Deucalion in whose time the flood occurred (1. 7. 2).

The Theseus-Hippolytus-Phaedra myth belongs to a type of which there are many instances in Greek and Mediterranean mythologies. See 2. 3. 1–2 (and ch. 4, n. 10) and 3. 13. 3 (and ch. 7, n. 35). For the idea that Theseus suffers revenge for killing the Minotaur and his father (the bull from the sea which Heracles brought to Attica and which wandered to Marathon), see n. 4.

Apollodorus presents a version of the myth which was the basis for the first of Euripides' two plays on the subject, the *Hippolytus Kaluptomenos* ("covering himself"; Hippolytus was said to have covered his head in shame at Phaedra's proposal). This play is lost. The second, *Hippolytus Stephanias* ("crowned," because Hippolytus first appears wearing a garland), survives. In it Euripides has altered the character of Phaedra considerably from the first play (as we know it through fragments). The reader will get good guidance on the legend and the ways in which Sophocles, who wrote a tragedy, *Phaedra* (lost), and Euripides made use of it, from W. S. Barrett, ed., *Euripides: Hippolytos* (Oxford, 1964), Introduction, 1–15. Hazel E. Barnes, "The Myth," in Donald Sutherland, trans., and Hazel Barnes, *Hippolytus in Drama and Myth* (Lincoln, Neb., 1960), 103–23, believes that Hippolytus was originally a consort, then a priest of Artemis. The name, with the feminine, Hippolyta, later referred to male and female attendants of Ar-

temis. Barnes also links the Amazons to an Artemis cult which required sacrifice of genitals (removal of a breast for the woman, emas-
culation for the men).

For general interpretive essays on the play, see Bernard M. W. Knox,
"The Hippolytus of Euripides," *Yale Classical Studies* 13 (1952), 3–31,
and R. P. Winnington-Ingram, "Hippolytus: A Study in Causation"
in *Fondation Hardt pour l'étude de l'antiquité classique entretiens* 6
(Geneva, 1960), 171–91. An excellent recent essay on the play is Robert Bagg's Introduction to his translation of the play (*Euripides: Hippolytus* [Oxford, 1973]).

Seneca's *Phaedra* and Racine's *Phèdre* make use of the myth and de-
rive much from Euripides' *Hippolytus*. Leo Spitzer's essay, "The 'Récit
de Théramène' " (in English) in his *Linguistics and Literary History*
(New York, 1962), 87–134, illumines not only Racine's play but its
Euripidean model as well. See Mayerson, *Classical Mythology*, 371–72
for modern dramatic and literary enactments of the myth. Perhaps the
best known is Eugene O'Neill's *Desire Under the Elms*, first produced
in 1924 and filmed in 1962. Also in 1962 Jules Dassin directed the film
Phaedra with Melina Mercouri and Antony Perkins in the Phaedra and
Hippolytus roles.

8   Since Ixion is the father of Pirithous (1. 8. 2), who next enters
Apollodorus' narrative of the myth of Theseus, it is natural for the
author to insert a paragraph here on this great sinner of Greek myth.
Pindar *Pyth.* 2. 21–48 tells the story of Ixion who was guilty of a second
crime in addition to his attempt to rape Hera: He was the first of
mortal men to commit murder (31–33). Apparently purified of this crime
he received a sweet life with the gods in heaven, but he could not
endure great blessedness (26). Ixion's murder victim was his father-in-
law, Diodorus Siculus 4. 69. 4 tells us, and Ixion killed him by hurling
him into a pit filled with fire.

9   The battle between Centaurs and Lapiths at the wedding of the
Lapiths' king, Pirithous, is narrated at great length by Ovid *Met.* 12.
210–535. The Centaurs not only try to rape Hippodamia (whom Ovid
calls Hippodame) but her attendants as well. The outbreak of savage
fighting at a wedding banquet is the most dramatic expression of the
eruption of the bestial into whatever is communal and benign, hence
civilized. The Centaurs, half-beast to begin with, obviously do not belong at such a banquet, for the elements which make it what it is, the
bride, her attendants, and the wine, are for them a fatal combination,
unleashing wild impulses which they cannot control (*Met.* 12. 219–21).
To add to the ugliness, the battle was fought among relatives, since
Pirithous was a son of Ixion from whom the Centaurs were descended.

There is a correspondence, it may be noted, between Ixion who was out of place in heaven (n. 8) and the Centaurs who were out of place at Pirithous' wedding banquet.

The battle was the subject of the western pediment of the great Temple of Zeus at Olympia, and the sculptures from it which survive may be seen in the museum there. See J. J. Pollitt, *Art and Experience in Classical Greece* (Cambridge, Eng., 1972), 35–36. For additional accounts of the battle, see Diodorus Siculus 4. 70 and Plutarch *Theseus* 30 (who calls Pirithous' wife Deidamia).

Caeneus had the worst of everything: Born a girl named Caenis, she was raped by Poseidon and prayed afterwards that she might become a man so that such violence could never be done to her again. Poseidon granted her prayer (Ovid *Met.* 12. 189–209). In fact, Caeneus is made invulnerable, and so at the battle which breaks up Pirithous' wedding, the Centaurs, unable to kill him, bury him in a heap of trees and stones, the weight of which presses him down into the underworld—although a certain Mopsos saw a bird with golden wings emerge from the heap into the clear air, circle the camp with great whirring of wing-beat, then fly away (*Met.* 12. 459–533). See also Apollonius Rhodius *Argonautica* 1. 57–64. At death Caeneus was changed back into a female (Virgil *Aeneid* 6. 448–49).

10   Apollodorus at 3. 10. 7–8 describes Theseus' rape of Helen and her recovery by her brothers, the Dioscuri, who took Aethra, Theseus' mother, with them to Sparta (see also ch. 7, n. 13). According to Homer *Iliad* 3. 144 Aethra was at Troy with Helen as a servant. She must have gone voluntarily and she must, therefore, have been attached to Helen whom she had cared for since Helen was ten or twelve years old.

The Menestheus whom the Dioscuri placed on the throne of Athens was the son of Peteos (3. 10. 8), who was the son of Orneus, the son of Erechtheus (Plutarch *Theseus* 32; Apollodorus 3. 15. 1 omits Orneus as a son of Erechtheus). As a descendant of Erechtheus he was a member of the royal family and his claim to the throne was legitimate. See also Pausanias 1. 17. 5–6. Menestheus led the Athenian contingent with fifty ships, which joined Agamemnon's expedition against Troy (Epitome 3. 11 and Homer *Iliad* 2. 546–56).

Heracles raised up Theseus from the chair of forgetfulness, but when he tried to raise Pirithous, the earth quaked and he let him go (2. 5. 12; see also ch. 5, n. 27). It is fitting that Theseus should be rescued from death by the hero on whom he modelled himself (n. 2).

Both Plutarch *Theseus* 35 and Pausanias 1. 17. 6 say that Lycomedes, king of Scyros (at whose court the young Achilles, disguised as a girl, was reared: 3. 13. 8), killed Theseus from envy of his greatness. Plutarch adds that Lycomedes led Theseus to the highest point on the island and threw him off a cliff. Thus he died—although involuntarily —in the same manner as his father, Aegeus (Epitome 1. 10–11).

CHAPTER TEN

Pelops' Marriage with Hippodamia; His Sons,
Atreus and Thyestes; Thyestes' Banquet; Aegisthus,
Son of Thyestes; Agamemnon and Menelaus,
Sons of Atreus, and Their Marriages with
Clytemnestra and Helen (Epitome 2)

EPIT. 2 Tantalus is punished in Hades in two ways: A rock hangs over him threatening to fall, and he stands in a lake beside which grow fruit trees with branches extending to his shoulders. The water touches his cheeks, but when he wishes to take a drink, it dries up. Whenever he wishes to eat some of the fruit, the branches rise on winds up to the clouds. He is punished in this way, some say, because he tattled to men the mysteries of the gods and because he shared ambrosia with his friends.[1]

2   Broteas, a hunter, failed to honor Artemis and even claimed that he could not be harmed by fire. He then went insane and hurled himself into a fire.[2]

3   Pelops, who was slaughtered and cooked at the banquet of the gods, was handsomer than before when he was restored to life. Because of his unusual beauty he became Poseidon's lover and received from him a winged chariot which could be driven through the sea without wetting its axles.

4   Oenomaus, king of Pisa, had a daughter, Hippodamia, who remained unmarried | either because her father was in love with her, as some say, or | because he had received an oracle that he would die at the hands of the man who married her. He could not persuade her to make love with him and he killed her suitors. For he had weapons and horses

5   from Ares and had offered marriage with his daughter as a prize to any suitor who could take Hippodamia in a chariot and flee as far as the Isthmus of Corinth. Fully armed, Oenomaus would immediately set off in pursuit, intending to kill the suitor if he caught him. The one who escaped was to have Hippodamia as his wife. In this way he had killed many suitors | or, as some say, twelve | . He had cut off their heads and had nailed them to his house.

6   Pelops also came seeking to marry Hippodamia. When she saw how

handsome he was she fell in love with him and persuaded Oenomaus'
7   charioteer, Myrtilus, the son of Hermes, to help him. Myrtilus was in
love with her and, wishing to gratify her, removed the linchpins from
the hubs of the wheels and so caused Oenomaus to lose the race and,
when the chariot was wrecked, to become entangled in the reins and
so to be dragged to his death. | But according to some he was killed
by Pelops. | Realizing Myrtilus' treachery, he cursed him as he was
dying, praying for him to die at the hand of Pelops.[3]

8   As Pelops, Hippodamia, and Myrtilus traveled together, they stopped
to rest at a certain place, and Pelops went off a short distance to bring
water to his wife, who was thirsty. At this moment Myrtilus tried to
rape her. Learning of this from her, Pelops threw Myrtilus from the
Geraestean promontory into the sea, which was called Myrtoan after
9   him. As he fell he cursed the line of Pelops. Pelops went to the ocean
and was purified by Hephaestus, then returned to Pisa in Elis, where he
succeeded to the kingdom of Oenomaus after subduing Apia and Pelas-
giotis. He afterwards called the land Peloponnese after himself.[4]

10   The sons of Pelops were Pittheus, Atreus, Thyestes, and others.[5]
Atreus' wife was Aerope, the daughter of Catreus, and she was in love
with Thyestes. Atreus had once vowed to sacrifice the finest sheep in
his flocks to Artemis, but when a golden lamb appeared they say that
11   he neglected his vow. Rather, he choked it to death, put it in a chest,
and kept it there. Aerope gave it to Thyestes, who had committed
adultery with her.
        When an oracle instructed the Mycenaeans to choose a son of
Pelops as king, they sent for Atreus and Thyestes. During a discussion
about the kingship, Thyestes announced to the people that the man
who possessed the golden lamb ought to become king. When Atreus
12   assented, Thyestes revealed the lamb and was made king. Zeus sent
Hermes to Atreus and told him to make an agreement with Thyestes
that he, Atreus, was to become king if the sun should travel in the
opposite direction. When Thyestes agreed, the sun set in the east. Now
that the god had witnessed Thyestes' greed, Atreus received the king-
13   ship and banished Thyestes. When he later learned of the adultery
he sent a herald inviting him to be reconciled. Atreus, pretending
friendship at Thyestes' arrival, slaughtered his children Aglaus, Cal-
lileon, and Orchomenus, whom he had by a river nymph, although
they had taken up seats as suppliants at the altar of Zeus. Dismem-
bering and cooking them, he placed them before Thyestes without
their extremities. After Thyestes had eaten his fill, Atreus showed him
14   the extremities and banished him from the land. Intent on punish-
ing Atreus by any means, Thyestes consulted the oracle and was told

to make love with his own daughter and to have a child by her. He did so and had by her Aegisthus, who, when he became a man and learned that he was a son of Thyestes, killed Atreus and restored the kingdom to his father.[6]

15   Agamemnon and Menelaus were taken by their nurse to Polyphides, ruler of Sicyon, who in turn sent them to Oeneus the Aetolian. Shortly afterwards Tyndareus brought them back again. After swearing an oath, they drove out Thyestes, who had taken refuge at Hera's altar,

16   and he went to live in Cytheria. Agamemnon was king of Mycenae and married Tyndareus' daughter Clytemnestra. He had killed her former husband Tantalus, son of Thyestes, as well as his son. By her Agamemnon had a son, Orestes, and daughters, Chrysothemis, Electra, and Iphigenia. Menelaus married Helen and was king of Sparta. (Tyndareus gave the kingship to him.) [7]

NOTES
(Epitome 2)

1   Apollodorus' version of the torment of Tantalus combines the account of Homer *Odyssey* 11. 582–92 which describes the perpetual denial of water and fruit, with that of Pindar *Ol.* 1. 55–58 in which Tantalus is menaced by the imminent fall of a stone. (Cf. Pindar *Isth.* 8. 9–11.)

Pindar rejects the story that Tantalus and the gods cut up, cooked, and ate Pelops, and attributes it to an envious neighbor (*Ol.* 1. 46–51). Pelops disappeared at a banquet Tantalus gave for the gods, Pindar agrees: Poseidon, overcome by desire for Pelops, carried him off to Olympus in his chariot just as Zeus later carried off Ganymedes (36–45). Apollodorus accepts the impious banquet and also Poseidon's love for, if not rape of, Pelops (Epitome 2. 3). He agrees also with Pindar about the cause of Tantalus' punishment: Honored by the gods, Pindar says, "he was unable to digest great blessedness," and he is punished "because he deceived the gods and gave to his friends and companions nectar and ambrosia with which the gods had made him immortal" (54–64).

Tantalus' suffering under the stone was proverbial. See Euripides *Orestes* 4–10, Plato *Cratylus*, 395d–e, and Lucretius *De Rerum Natura* 3. 980–84. The last named makes it clear that Tantalus' torture is endless fear: *cassa formidine torpens* (3. 981), "paralyzed by senseless terror." For Cicero death is the stone of Tantalus which always hangs over men's heads (*De Finibus* 1. 18. 60). Again, for Cicero the stone of

Tantalus symbolizes what we call free-floating, objectless anxiety (*Tusculan Disputations* 4. 16. 35). For other ancient references to Tantalus, see Frazer, *Apollodorus* 2. 154–55.

2   Broteas is a shadowy figure, and it is hard to know what he is doing just here in Apollodorus' text. For what is known about him, see Frazer, *Apollodorus* 2. 156.

3   In *Ol.* 1 (see n. 1) Pindar says that Poseidon fell in love with Pelops when Clotho took him from a pure cauldron fitted with a shoulder of shining ivory (25–27). These lines have been taken to refer to the story that Tantalus did in fact serve Pelops to the gods. The gods recognized the dish (except for Demeter, or Themis, who took a bite from the shoulder). Zeus ordered Hermes to put the flesh back in the cauldron and restore the boy whole (Scholiast on *Ol.* 1. 26). The Scholiast also says that after Demeter took a bite of Pelops' shoulder, Hermes made an ivory shoulder and fitted it on Pelops.

The lines in Pindar are better interpreted as referring to a bath of purification from which Clotho, a birth goddess, took the new-born Pelops, the ivory shoulder then being a birth mark. The problem (aside from ivory birth marks) is that Poseidon falls in love with a new-born baby, an occurrence at variance with Pindar's account at 36–42. See Lewis Richard Farnell, *Critical Commentary to the Works of Pindar* (reprinted Amsterdam, 1962), 6, who says that Pindar's version is not "happy."

Hyginus *Fabulae* 83 says that when Pelops was restored to life by the gods, a piece of shoulder was missing and Demeter (not Hermes) fitted ivory in place of the part that was missing.

When the gods removed Tantalus from Olympus to Hades (Epitome 2. 1 and n. 1 above), they inflicted a milder punishment on Pelops, who was guilty only by association, sending him back to earth, according to Pindar. On reaching manhood Pelops resolved to win marriage with Hippodamia and went along the sea shore at night to pray to Poseidon, asking the god to give him a swift chariot and to thwart Oenomaus. Poseidon heard Pelops' prayer and gave him a golden chariot drawn by winged horses which never grew weary (*Ol.* 1. 65–87).

Apollodorus gives twelve, Pindar (above) thirteen as the number of suitors whom Oenomaus had killed. Pausanias 6. 21. 9–11 names eighteen, to whom as a group Pelops erected a tall monument and sacrificed to them as to heroes yearly (indirectly calling attention to himself who had been able to do what they could not).

There are additional accounts of Pelops' victory, all of which involve the treachery of Myrtilus, Oenomaus' charioteer. (Despite his divine chariot and winged horses Pelops was apparently a cautious man and left nothing to chance.) Diodorus Siculus 4. 73. 5–6 says simply that Pelops bribed Myrtilus and won. When Oenomaus came in second he was so depressed at the thought of impending death (in accordance with the oracle) that he committed suicide (Diodorus Siculus 4. 73. 6).

According to Pausanias 8. 14. 11, Myrtilus had always been in love with Hippodamia himself but was afraid to race Oenomaus, driving for him instead. Pelops swore to Myrtilus that he would let him sleep with Hippodamia for one night if he would betray Oenomaus. He did so, but when he afterwards reminded Pelops of his promise, Pelops killed him.

Yet another account, reported by Frazer, *Apollodorus* 2. 161, says that Myrtilus substituted linchpins of wax (probably hard sealing wax) for linchpins of bronze. This would have the same effect as removing the linchpins (which he does in Apollodorus' version) for they would melt when the axle became heated from the friction of the turning wheels.

Pindar, above all this treachery and plotting, says loftily and tersely, "He took the force of Oenomaus and the maiden as his bride" (*Ol.* 1. 88), the zeugma expressing the contemptuous ease with which he thinks Pelops won the race.

4   Euripides *Orestes* 987–94 describes Myrtilus' death: Pelops, pursuing him, forced his chariot over the precipice of the promontory of Geraestus (the southernmost tip of the island of Euboea) into the pounding surf below. Myrtilus' curse began the horrible destruction in the house down to and ended by Orestes (995–1011). For Apia as the original name of the Peloponnese, see 2. 1. 1.

5   Hippodamia bore Pelops six sons according to Pindar *Ol.* 1. 88–89 (who does not name them). Chrysippus, another son of Pelops, was raped by Laius, the father of Oedipus. Pelops was said to have laid a curse on Laius which was fulfilled in the disasters which ruined the house of Cadmus (see 3. 5. 5 and ch. 6, n. 24).

At Hippodamia's instigation Atreus and Thyestes murdered their half-brother, Chrysippus, according to Hyginus *Fabulae* 85. Pelops exiled Atreus (Thucydides 1. 9) and Hippodamia either fled to Argolis (Pausanias 6. 20. 7) or killed herself when Pelops confronted her with the murder (Hyginus *Fabulae* 85).

6   Several ancient sources agree more or less with each other about the golden lamb but are at variance with Apollodorus. Seneca *Thyestes* 220–35 says that a golden ram (not lamb) was the ancient token of the right of Pelops' house to rule. Whoever possessed it, possessed the power. In order to get the ram from Atreus and so legitimize his claim to the throne, Thyestes seduced Aerope, Atreus' wife. Pausanias 2. 18.

1 agrees (though he calls the animal a lamb), adding that in retaliation Atreus murdered Thyestes' children and served them to him at a banquet.

Euripides *Electra* 699–736 describes the discovery in the flocks of the wondrous golden lamb which was brought to the agora of Mycenae to be shown to the citizens. Thyestes got possession of it by seducing Aerope and exhibited it as a sign of his right to rule. Zeus expressed his displeasure by changing the course of the sun and the stars.

At *Orestes* 807–18 Euripides describes the strife over the lamb as leading directly to Atreus' murder of the sons of Thyestes, whom he serves to their father at a banquet. Later in the play Euripides varies the story slightly (995–1010): The quarrel over the lamb altered the course of the sun and Zeus changed the course of the Pleiades. Next the banquet of Thyestes and Thyestes' seduction of Aerope (in that order) are mentioned. The lines, a choral ode sung by Electra, are not expected to be a straightforward chronicle of events.

The Scholiast on Euripides *Orestes* 998 gives a version more in harmony with that of Apollodorus: Atreus wishing to demonstrate that the kingdom belonged to him, promised that he would exhibit a golden lamb born in his flocks. Thyestes, however, seduced Atreus' wife and stole the lamb. Unable to fulfill his promise, Atreus was going to give up the kingdom (since Thyestes exhibited the lamb), but a wise man said that the people would commit an impious act if they chose Thyestes to be king. As a sign the sun and Pleiades set in the east. Atreus gained the kingship and took vengeance on his brother. The Scholiast concludes by noting that some say that Zeus, to show favor to Atreus, made the sun and the Pleiades rise from the west, having reversed their courses for one day.

The Scholiast on *Orestes* 811 tells substantially the same story as Apollodorus, beginning with Atreus' vow to sacrifice his finest sheep to Artemis and continuing through the exile of Thyestes, where the *scholium* ends. (He omits Apollodorus' detail that Atreus choked the lamb to death before putting it in the chest.) For additional references and discussion, see Frazer, *Apollodorus* 2. 164–67.

Seneca *Thyestes* 682–1034 describes at length and in detail the killing of Thyestes' sons by Atreus: He ties the two boys' hands behind their backs and performs rituals for sacrificing animals. He then plunges his sword up to his hand into the neck of the first, then withdraws it. The boy stands erect, begins to waver, then collapses upon his uncle. Atreus drags the second son to the altar near his fallen brother. He severs his head with a blow from his sword. The body falls; the head rolls away uttering an inaudible murmur (720–29).

Seneca continues in this cinematic way through the preparation and serving of the banquet and Thyestes' recognition afterwards. Revenge will come when Agamemnon is murdered by Clytemnestra and Aegisthus (Epitome 6. 23–24 and ch. 12, n. 11).

Revenge comes sooner according to Hyginus *Fabulae* 88 who tells of Thyestes' incest with his daughter Pelopia at Sicyon. Actually it is rape at night and Thyestes does not know the identity of his victim. She manages to steal his sword. In a rather complicated story Atreus comes to Sicyon looking for Thyestes, whose presence is needed at Mycenae to end barrenness caused by the murder of his sons. He sees Pelopia, supposes her to be the king's daughter, and asks to have her as his wife. The king gives her to him, pregnant with Aegisthus, and when he is born she exposes him. Goatherds find and rear him.

Atreus sends his sons, Agamemnon and Menelaus, to Delphi to inquire about Thyestes' whereabouts. Thyestes, as it happens, has come to ask the oracle how to avenge himself on his brother. The sons of Atreus capture him and take him home where Atreus imprisons him. He summons Aegisthus, who he thinks is his own son (Aegisthus has somehow made his way from the goatherds to Atreus' palace and is there passed off by Pelopia, his mother, as Atreus' son) and sends him to kill Thyestes. Thyestes sees the sword Aegisthus is wearing (his own, taken from him by Pelopia when he raped her), questions him about it, and orders him to call Pelopia. She tells how she took the sword from her nocturnal rapist by whom she conceived Aegisthus. She now snatches it away and plunges it into her breast. Aegisthus removes it from her body and takes it, covered with blood, to Atreus who, thinking that Thyestes has been killed with it, rejoices. Aegisthus then kills him while he is performing sacrifices at the shore and returns with his father, Thyestes, to their ancestral kingdom. Hyginus is believed to have derived this story, which he has not told terribly well, from Sophocles' *Thyestes*, now lost. (See Frazer, *Apollodorus* 2. 168–69.) We may imagine how Sophocles would have handled the recognition scene when Thyestes, Pelopia, and Aegisthus learn each other's true identities.

7   In this brief account of Agamemnon and Menelaus, Apollodorus obviously adheres to a tradition different from that followed by Hyginus *Fabulae* 88 (and Sophocles, if Hyginus derived from him the story of Thyestes' revenge: see n. 6). In Seneca's *Thyestes*, moreover, it is Atreus who kills Thyestes' sons, Tantalus and Plisthenes (717–29), and serves them at a banquet to their father. At Euripides *Iphigenia in Aulis* 1148–50, however, Clytemnestra says that Agamemnon killed her first husband, Tantalus (whom Pausanias 2. 18. 2 identifies as

Thyestes' son; at 2. 22. 3, however, he says that Tantalus was the son of Thyestes or a certain Broteas). The mythological tradition thus has variants inconsistent with each other.

Homer does not know of Electra, the daughter of Agamemnon and Clytemnestra, and the heroine in a surviving play by each of the three tragedians. Nor does he know of the sacrifice of Iphigenia. At *Iliad* 9. 142–45 he names Agamemnon's children as Orestes, Chrysothemis, Laodice, and Iphianassa, all still living at the dramatic date of the poem.

At 3. 11. 2 Apollodorus says that Tyndareus gave his kingdom at Sparta to Menelaus after the Dioscuri joined the gods.

CHAPTER ELEVEN

The Trojan War
(Epitome 3–5)

EPIT. 3 Alexander later carried off Helen in accordance with the will of Zeus, | as some say, so that his daughter might acquire fame
2 when Europe and Asia went to war, or as others say, so that the race of demigods might be exalted. | For one of these reasons Strife tossed an apple among Hera, Athena, and Aphrodite as a prize for beauty, and Zeus ordered Hermes to lead them to Alexander on Mount Ida for him to judge among them. Each promised Alexander gifts if he chose her: Hera, rule over all men; Athena, victory in war; and Aphro-
3 dite, marriage with Helen. He chose Aphrodite and sailed to Sparta in ships built by Phereclus.[1] For nine days he was the guest of Menelaus and on the tenth, when Menelaus went to Crete to bury Catreus, his maternal grandfather, Alexander persuaded Helen to go off with him. She abandoned her nine-year-old daughter Hermione, put most of her
4 property on board, and set sail with him at night. Hera sent a heavy storm upon them which forced them to put in at Sidon. Wary of pursuit, Alexander delayed a long time in Phoenicia and Cyprus. When
5 he was certain that he was not being pursued, he came to Troy with Helen. | Some say that Hermes stole Helen in obedience to Zeus' will, brought her to Egypt, and gave her to Proteus, the king of the Egyptians, to guard, and that Alexander went to Troy with an image of Helen made from clouds. | [2]
6 When Menelaus realized that Helen had been abducted, he went to Agamemnon at Mycenae and begged him to raise an army throughout Greece against Troy. He also sent a herald to each of the kings, to remind them of the oaths they had sworn and to advise each to safeguard his own wife, saying that all Greece shared the insult. Many
7 were enthusiastic about the expedition. Some went to Odysseus in Ithaca, who did not want to go and pretended to be insane. But Palamedes, the son of Nauplius, proved that his insanity was feigned. He

followed Odysseus as he pretended madness and, snatching Telemachus from Penelope's arms, drew his sword as though to kill him. Odysseus, fearing for his son, confessed that the insanity was false and joined the expedition.

8   Odysseus took a Phrygian prisoner and forced him to write a treasonable letter to Palamedes as though from Priam. After burying gold in Palamedes' tent, he planted the letter in his camp. Agamemnon read it, found the gold, and delivered Palamedes to the allies to be stoned as a traitor.[3]

9   Menelaus went with Odysseus and Talthybius to Cinyras on Cyprus and tried to persuade him to join the alliance. Cinyras gave them breastplates for Agamemnon and swore to send fifty ships, but sent only one, which the son of Mygdalion commanded. The rest he molded from earth and launched in the sea.

10   The daughters of Anius, the son of Apollo, Elais, Spermo, and Oeno, are called the wine-makers. Dionysius granted them the ability to make olive oil, grain, and wine from the earth.[4]

11   The expedition against Troy assembled at Aulis. | It was composed of the following: ten commanders from the Boeotians who brought forty ships; from the Orchomenians, four who brought thirty ships; four commanders from the Phocians who brought forty ships; from the Locrians, Ajax, son of Oileus, who brought forty ships; from the Euboeans, Elephenor, son of Chalcodon and Alcyone, who brought forty ships; from the Athenians, Menestheus bringing fifty

12   ships; from the Salaminians, Ajax, son of Telamon, bringing twelve ships; from the Argives, Diomedes, son of Tydeus, and those with him: they brought eighty ships; from the Mycenaeans, Agamemnon, son of Atreus and Aerope, with one hundred ships; from the Lacedaemonians, Menelaus, son of Atreus and Aerope, with sixty ships; from the Pylians, Nestor, son of Neleus and Chloris, with forty ships; from the Arcadians, Agapenor with seven ships; from the Eleans, Amphimachus and those with him with forty ships; from the Dulichians, Meges, the son of Phyleus, with forty ships; from the Cephallenians, Odysseus, son of Laertes and Anticlia, with twelve ships; from the Aetolians, Thoas, son of Andraemon and Gorge,

13   bringing forty ships; from the Cretans, Idomeneus, son of Deucalion, with forty ships; from the Rhodians, Tlepolemus, son of Heracles and Astyoche, with nine ships; from the Symaeans, Nireus, son of Charopus, with three ships; from the Coans, Phidippus and Antiphus, the

14   sons of Thessalus, with thirty ships; from the Myrmidons, Achilles, son of Peleus and Thetis, with fifty ships; from Phylace, Protesilaus, son of Iphiclus, with forty ships; from the Pheraeans, Eumelus, son of Admetus, with eleven ships; from the Olizonians, Philoctetes, son

of Poeas, with seven ships; from the Aenianians, Guneus, son of Ocytus, with twenty-two ships; from the Triccaeans, Podalirius with thirty ships; from the Ormenians, Eurypylus with forty ships; from the Gyrtonians, Polypoetes, son of Pirithous, with thirty ships; from the Magnesians, Prothous, son of Tenthredon, with forty ships. | The total number of ships was one thousand and thirteen; there were forty-three leaders and thirty commands.[5]

15   While the army was at Aulis after the sacrifice to Apollo, a snake darted from the altar to a sparrow's nest in a nearby plane tree. After devouring the mother bird and eight baby sparrows, it was turned to stone. Calchas said that this sign came to them through the will of Zeus, and he interpreted it to mean that Troy was destined to be captured within ten years.[6]

16   They prepared to sail for Troy. Agamemnon was commander of the entire expedition and Achilles, who was fifteen years old, shared the
17   command of the fleet. Ignorant of the course to Troy, they put in at Mysia and sacked it, thinking that it was the Trojan city. Telephus, the son of Heracles, was king of the Mysians. Seeing his country plundered, he armed his subjects, chased the Greeks to their ships, and killed many men, including Thersander, son of Polynices, who stood his ground. When Achilles charged at Telephus, he turned and ran,
18   but while fleeing he became entangled in a grape vine and was wounded in the thigh by a spear. The Greeks left Mysia and put out to sea. A violent storm arose during which they were separated from each other and landed in their own countries.[7]

The war is said to have lasted for twenty years.[8] For they set out on the expedition two years after Helen was carried off, having made their preparations during that time. Eight years after they came back to Greece from Mysia, they returned to Argos and went to Aulis.

19   When they assembled again at Argos after those eight years, they
20   were at a loss as to the way to Troy since they had no commander who knew the course to sail. But Apollo told Telephus, whose wound would not heal, that he would be cured if the man who wounded him were to treat him. So he went from Mysia to Argos dressed in rags and begged Achilles to cure him. After Telephus promised to show the way to Troy, Achilles healed him by applying to the wound rust which he had scraped from his Pelian spear. Now made well, Telephus plotted the course for them, and Calchas confirmed its accuracy by means of his art of divination.[9]

21   When they set sail from Argos and came a second time to Aulis, the fleet was checked by adverse winds. Calchas said that they could not sail unless Agamemnon's most beautiful daughter were offered to Artemis as a sacrifice. The goddess was angry with Agamemnon

because when he had shot a deer he said that not even Artemis could
22   have done it and because Atreus had not sacrificed the golden lamb
to her. After he heard this prophecy Agamemnon sent Odysseus and
Talthybius to Clytemnestra to ask for Iphigenia, saying that he had
promised to give her to Achilles to be his wife as a reward for going
on the expedition. Clytemnestra sent her, and Agamemnon, placing
her beside the altar, was about to slaughter her when Artemis carried
her off to Tauris. There she made her a priestess and substituted a
deer for her at the altar. Some, however, say that Artemis made her
immortal.[10]

23   After setting sail from Aulis they put in at Tenedos, the king of
which was Tenes, son of Cycnus and Proclia | or, as some say, of
24   Apollo. | He had been exiled by his father and had settled there. For
in addition to Tenes, Cycnus had by Proclia, daughter of Laomedon,
a daughter Hemithea, and afterwards married Philonome, daughter of
Tragasus. She fell in love with Tenes but failing to entice him, accused
him falsely to Cycnus of attempting to seduce her, producing as a
25   witness a flute player named Eumolpus. Cycnus believed her, shut
Tenes and his sister up in a chest, and put them out to sea. When the
chest washed ashore on the island of Leucophrys, Tenes got out and
settled there, naming it Tenedos after himself. Cycnus later learned the
truth, stoned the flute player to death, and buried his wife alive in the
earth.[11]

26   Tenes saw the Greeks as they made for Tenedos and tried to hold
them off by throwing rocks at them. He died, however, struck in the
chest by Achilles' sword, although Thetis had warned Achilles not to
27   kill him, for if he did so she said that he would die at Apollo's hands.
While they were performing a sacrifice to Apollo, a water snake came
out from the altar and bit Philoctetes. The wound would not heal
and when it began to stink, the army could not endure the smell. At
Agamemnon's orders, Odysseus left him on the island of Lemnos along
with the bow of Heracles which he had inherited. Isolated there, he
survived by shooting birds.[12]

28   Putting out from Tenedos the Greeks sailed to Troy and sent Odysseus and Menelaus to demand back Helen and the property. In their
29   assembly the Trojans not only refused to return Helen but wanted to
kill the envoys. Antenor, however, saved them, but the Greeks, angered at the barbarians' arrogance, put on their armor and sailed
against them. Thetis ordered Achilles not to be the first to go ashore,
for the one who landed first was to be the first to die. When the
barbarians learned that the fleet was sailing against them, they set
30   out for the sea in armor and tried to prevent the landing by hurling
stones at the Greeks. Protesilaus was the first to disembark from his

ship and, after killing many Trojans, died at Hector's hand. His wife, Laodamia, desired him even after his death and made an image of him with which she had intercourse. The gods pitied her and Hermes brought Protesilaus back from Hades. When Laodamia saw him she thought that he had returned from Troy and rejoiced, but when he was carried back again to Hades she killed herself.[13]

31   After Protesilaus died and Achilles went ashore with the Myrmidons, he struck Cycnus in the head with a stone and killed him. When the barbarians saw him dead they fled into the city, but the Greeks leaped from the ships and filled the plain with bodies. They penned 32 up the Trojans and besieged them. They also drew their ships ashore. Since the barbarians would not venture out, Achilles ambushed and killed Troilus in the temple of the Thymbraean Apollo. At night he entered the city and captured Lycaon.[14] Taking some of the chieftains with him, he also ravaged the countryside and went to Mount Ida to steal cattle belonging to Aeneas. Aeneas fled, and Achilles drove off the 33 cattle after killing the cowherds and Mestor, son of Priam. He also captured Lesbos, Phocaea, then Colophon, Smyrna, Clazomenae, and Cyme, and after them Aegialus and Tenus, the so-called Hundred Cities. Next he captured Adramytium, Side, Endium, Linaeum, and Colone. He also captured Hypoplacian Thebes, Lyrnessus, Antandrus, 34 and many other cities.[15] Allies joined the Trojans in the ninth year at war. | From the neighboring cities came Aeneas, son of Anchises, and with him Archelochus and Acamas, sons of Antenor and Theano, commanders of the Dardanians; from the Thracians, Acamas, son of Eusorus; from the Cicones, Euphemus, son of Troizenus; from the 35 Paeonians, Pyraichmes; from the Paphlagonians, Pylaemenes, son of Bilsates; from Zelia, Pandarus, son of Lycaon; from Adrastia, Adrastus and Amphius, sons of Merops; from Arisbe, Asius, son of Hyrtacus; from Larissa, Hippothous, son of Pelasgus; from Mysia, Chromius and Ennomus, sons of Arsinous; from the Alizones, Odius and Epistrophus, sons of Mecisteus; from the Phrygians, Phorcys and Ascanius, sons of Aretaon; from the Maeonians, Mesthles and Antiphus, sons of Talaemenes; from the Carians, Nastes and Amphimachus, sons of Nomion; from the Lycians, Sarpedon, son of Zeus, and Glaucus, son of Hippolochus. | [16]

   4   Achilles became angry because of Briseis and refused to go into battle.[17] Taking courage, the barbarians came out of the city. Alexander fought individually with Menelaus and was defeated, but Aphrodite rescued him. Pandarus shot an arrow at Menelaus and broke the truce. 2 Fighting bravely, Diomedes wounded Aphrodite as she was giving aid to Aeneas. He encountered Glaucus, remembered the friendship of their fathers, and exchanged arms with him. When Hector challenged

the best warrior to individual combat, many came forward but Ajax was chosen by lot and distinguished himself. When it was night heralds separated them.

3   The Greeks dug a ditch and built a wall to protect their harbor. After a battle on the plain the Trojans drove the Greeks behind the wall. They sent Odysseus, Phoenix, and Ajax as ambassadors to Achilles, begging him to rejoin them and promising him Briseis and other

4   gifts. When night came they sent Odysseus and Diomedes to spy on the Trojans. They killed Dolon, son of Eumelus, and Rhesus the Thracian, who had arrived the day before as a Trojan ally and had not yet entered battle. He had set up camp some distance from the Trojan force and apart from Hector. They also killed twelve men sleeping

5   around him and drove their horses to the ships.[18] In a fierce battle during the day Agamemnon, Diomedes, Odysseus, Eurypylus, and Machaon were wounded, the Greeks were routed, and Hector breached the wall, forced Ajax to retreat, and set the ships on fire.

6   When Achilles saw Protesilaus' ship burning he sent out Patroclus with the Myrmidons, dressed in his own armor and with his own horses. The Trojans, seeing him and thinking that he was Achilles, turned and fled. Patroclus pursued them inside their wall and killed many, including Sarpedon, son of Zeus. He was killed by Hector after

7   first being wounded by Euphorbus. When a battle raged over his corpse Ajax fought bravely and with difficulty recovered the body. Achilles put aside his anger and received back Briseis. He put on armor which was brought to him from Hephaestus and joined the fighting, pursuing the Trojans as far as the river Scamander where he killed many of them, including Asteropaeus, son of Pelegon, who was the son of the Axius River. The Scamander attacked Achilles violently. But Hephaestus pursued it with a great flame and dried it up. Achilles killed Hector in individual combat, fastened him by the ankles to his chariot, and dragged him to the ships. He buried Patroclus and held games in his honor, in which Diomedes won the chariot race, Epeus won in boxing, and Ajax and Odysseus in wrestling. After the games Priam came to Achilles to ransom Hector's body and buried it.[19]

5   Penthesilia, daughter of Otrere and Ares, accidentally killed Hippolyte, and after being purified by Priam, killed many men in battle, including Machaon. Later she died at the hands of Achilles. After her death he fell in love with her and killed Thersites for mocking him.[20]

2   Hippolyte was the mother of Hippolytus and is also called Glauce and Melanippe. At Phaedra's marriage festival she appeared in armor with her Amazons and said that she was going to kill Theseus' guests. She died during the battle that took place, either accidentally at the hands of her ally Penthesilia, or killed by Theseus or the men around

him, who realized the Amazons' intention and quickly shut the doors to trap her inside [Epitome 1. 16–18].

3   Memnon, son of Tithonus and the Dawn, came to Troy with a large force of Ethiopians to oppose the Greeks, killed many of them, including Antilochus, and was killed by Achilles. As he pursued the Trojans,

4   Achilles was shot in the ankle by Alexander and Apollo at the Scaean gates. In the battle to recover his corpse, Ajax killed Glaucus, gave his arms to be taken to the ships and picking up the body, carried it in a rain of arrows through the middle of the enemy while Odysseus fought off his attackers.

5   When Achilles died the army was filled with despair. They buried him with Patroclus on the island of Leuce, mixing their bones together. It is said that after death Achilles lives in the Islands of the Blest with Medea.[21] They held games in his honor in which Eumelus won the chariot race, Diomedes the foot race, Ajax the discus-throw, and Teucer

6   the contest in archery.

    His armor was offered as a prize to the best warrior, and Ajax and Odysseus competed for it. Odysseus was chosen by Trojan judges | or as some say, by allied ones. | Deranged by grief, Ajax planned to attack the army at night, but Athena made him insane. She turned him sword

7 in hand toward the cattle, so that in his madness he slaughtered them and their herdsmen, thinking that they were Achaeans. When he later recovered his sanity, he killed himself. Agamemnon forbade his body to be burned and he alone of those who died at Ilium is buried in a coffin. His grave is at Rhoeteum.[22]

8   When the war had gone on for ten years and the Greeks had lost heart for it, Calchas prophesied that they could not capture Troy without Heracles' bow. Hearing this, Odysseus went with Diomedes to Philoctetes on Lemnos and, getting possession of the bow by trickery, induced him to sail to Troy. When Philoctetes arrived his wound was

9 healed by Podalirius and he shot Alexander.[23] At his death Helenus and Deiphobus quarrelled over which of them was to marry Helen. When Deiphobus was chosen Helenus left Troy and lived on Mount Ida. Calchas said that Helenus knew the oracles protecting the city and

10 so Odysseus lay in wait for him, captured him, and brought him to the camp. He was forced to tell how Ilium could be captured. There were three conditions: First, Pelops' bones must be brought to the Greeks; next, Neoptolemus must fight with them; and third, the Palladium, which had fallen from heaven, must be stolen from Troy. For as long as it remained within the city Troy could not be taken.[24]

11   When they learned these things the Greeks transported Pelops' bones and sent Odysseus and Phoenix to Lycomedes on Scyros. They persuaded him to allow Neoptolemus to go. After he arrived at the camp

and received his father's armor from Odysseus (who gave it to him
12   willingly), he killed many Trojans. Later, Eurypylus, son of Telephus,
came as an ally of the Trojans in command of a large force of Mysians.
13   He distinguished himself in battle but was killed by Neoptolemus.[25]
Odysseus went with Diomedes at night to the city. He left Diomedes
outside while he disheveled himself, put on ragged clothes, and entered
the city disguised as a beggar. Helen recognized him, however, and
with her help he stole the Palladium. After killing many of the sentries,
he brought it to the ships with the help of Diomedes.[26]
14   Later he had the idea of constructing a wooden horse. He suggested
it to Epeus, an architect, who cut up lumber from Mount Ida and built
a horse that was hollow with openings in its sides. Odysseus persuaded
fifty of the best warriors to enter it | or as the author of the *Little Iliad*
says, three thousand | . The rest were to burn their tents at nightfall,
15   then sail away and lie to off Tenedos. At the end of the night they
were to sail back. Persuaded by Odysseus the Greeks ordered the best
fighters to enter the horse, appointed Odysseus their commander, and
inscribed on the horse these words: "The Greeks dedicate this thank-
offering to Athena for their return home." They burned their tents,
left Sinon behind to make a fire signal for them, put to sea by night
and hove to off Tenedos.
16   When it was day the Trojans saw the camp of the Greeks deserted
and believing that they had fled, joyfully dragged the horse inside the
17   city and stationed it at the palace of Priam while they decided what
to do with it. When Cassandra said that there was an armed force
inside it and Laocoon the seer agreed, some thought that they should
burn it while others wanted to throw it off a cliff. The majority, how-
18   ever, decided to leave it as an offering to the goddess and turned to
sacrifice and celebration. But Apollo sent them a sign: Two serpents
19   swam across the sea from the neighboring islands and devoured the
sons of Laocoon.
When it was night and all were asleep, the Greeks sailed back from
Tenedos after Sinon signalled to them with a fire on the grave of
Achilles. Helen walked around the horse and called to the chieftains
imitating the voice of each of their wives. Anticlus wanted to answer
20   but Odysseus held his hand over his mouth. As soon as the enemy
was asleep they opened the horse and emerged with their weapons.
The first, Echion, son of Portheus, was killed when he leaped down,
but the rest slid down a rope, went to the wall, opened the gates and
21   let in those who had sailed back from Tenedos.[27]
Advancing into the city armed, they entered the houses and killed
the sleeping Trojans. Neoptolemus killed Priam, who had taken refuge
at the altar of Zeus of the Courtyard. Odysseus and Menelaus recog-

nized Glaucus, son of Antenor, as he fled into his house, came with a
small group of men and rescued him. Aeneas escaped carrying his
22 father Anchises, for the Greeks let him go because of his piety. Menelaus killed Deiphobus and led Helen to the ships. Theseus' sons, Demo-
phon and Acamas, led away also Aethra, the mother of Theseus. | For
they say that these came to Troy later. | Locrian Ajax saw Cassandra
clinging to a wooden statue of Athena and raped her. Because of this
the statue looks to heaven.[28]

23   After they killed the Trojans, they burned the city and divided the
spoils. Next they sacrificed to all the gods, threw Astyanax down from
the ramparts, and slaughtered Polyxena on the grave of Achilles.
Agamemnon was awarded Cassandra; Neoptolemus, Andromache; and
Odysseus, Hecuba. | Some say that Helenus got Hecuba and crossed
over with her to the Chersonese. There she turned into a bitch and
he buried her at a place now called the Tomb of the Bitch. |

Laodice, the most beautiful of Priam's daughters, was swallowed up
by the earth in full view of everyone. After the Greeks had sacked
Troy and were about to sail away, they were delayed by Calchas who
told them that Athena was angry because of Ajax's impiety. They were
going to kill him but he fled to an altar and they let him go.[29]

NOTES
(Epitome 3–5)

1   Alexander, the second son of Priam and Hecuba, was exposed
at birth because of a dream Hecuba had before he was born. A servant
took up the baby, reared it on his farm, and named it Paris. Later he
was named Alexander. (See 3. 12. 5 and ch. 7, n. 26.) Homer uses both
names for him in the *Iliad*, but uses Alexander far more frequently.
His selection of Aphrodite as winner of the prize for beauty is conven-
tionally called the Judgment of Paris. (He will be referred to as Alexander in the notes.)

The earliest reference to the Judgment of Paris is Homer *Iliad* 24.
22–30: Achilles' continual mutilation of Hector's body, whom he kills
in the tenth year of the war, arouses pity in all the gods, who urge
Hermes to steal it. Hera, Athena, and Poseidon demur. The two goddesses still despise Ilium, Priam, and his people because Alexander
rejected them and chose Aphrodite.

There are two versions of the Judgment of Paris, one of which has
two variants. (Neither version takes precedent over the other as to
"authenticity.") In the version with two variants: (1) Strife comes to
the wedding of Peleus and Thetis and starts an argument among Hera,

Athena, and Aphrodite as to which is the most beautiful. At the command of Zeus, Hermes leads the three to Alexander, now a shepherd on Mount Ida, for him to decide. Enticed (or bribed) by her promise of marriage with Helen, he chooses Aphrodite. See the synopsis of the lost epic, *Cypria,* made by Proclus, in Hugh G. Evelyn-White, ed., *Hesiod, the Homeric Hymns and Homerica* (Cambridge, Mass. and London, 1936), 489, 491. (2) Zeus fails to invite Strife to the marriage of Peleus and Thetis. She comes anyway, but is not admitted to the wedding banquet. From the door she rolls an apple into the midst of the party, saying that the most beautiful woman may pick it up. Hera, Aphrodite, and Athena begin to extol each her own beauty and then to quarrel among themselves for the apple. Zeus commands Hermes to conduct them to Mount Ida and to order Alexander to decide. Hera promises him sovereignty over all lands and outstanding wealth; Athena promises to make him the bravest and wisest of men; and Aphrodite promises him marriage with Helen, the most beautiful woman in the world. Alexander prefers Aphrodite's gift and so judges her the winner of the apple. See Hyginus *Fabulae* 92.

Lucian *Dialogues of the Sea-Gods* 5 tells essentially the same story but alters or adds details for vividness: Strife comes to the wedding banquet unnoticed—easy enough to do since the guests were drinking, dancing and singing—and tosses down an apple of solid gold inscribed "for the fair." It rolls to the feet of Hera, Aphrodite, and Athena. Hermes picks it up, reads the inscription aloud, and the goddesses all reach for it, each insisting that it is for her. Zeus intervenes before they begin to fight, refuses to judge himself, but sends them to Mount Ida to Alexander, a man of taste and a good judge of beauty (Zeus says). Lucian does not tell the outcome but predicts victory for Aphrodite.

The second version of the myth omits Strife and the marriage of Peleus and Thetis. The longest account is given by Lucian *Dialogues of the Gods* 20. Zeus gives Hermes the apple inscribed "for the fair" and sends him and the three goddesses to Mount Ida, where Alexander will decide which of the three is the most beautiful and so deserving of the apple. He cannot judge them with their clothes on, so they disrobe (Hermes looks the other way). Nor can he decide by viewing all three together, so while two retire he carefully examines each one in the nude, Aphrodite last. She tells him to take his time and look at her carefully, calls him the handsomest boy in Phrygia, and promises him marriage with Helen, the most beautiful woman in the world. He gives her the apple.

This version (without, of course, Lucian's embellishment) is alluded to by Euripides in several plays: *Andromache* 274–92, *Trojan Women* 919–32, *Helen* 23–30, and *Iphigenia in Aulis* 1299–1309.

Homer *Iliad* 5. 59–64 notes the sad case of Phereclus who was killed in the war which his ship, built for Alexander's voyage to Sparta for Helen, helped to start.

2   Homer *Iliad* 6. 289–92 mentions the stay of Helen and Alexander in Sidon. Cf. Proclus' synopsis of the lost epic, *Cypria*, in Evelyn-White, *Hesiod*, 491, and Dictys of Crete *The Trojan War* 1. 5.

Hesiod seems to have been the first to say that only a phantom of Helen went to Troy. The lyric poet Stesichorus (ca. 632–ca. 553), Plato tells us (*Phaedrus* 243a-b), slandered Helen in a poem and was struck blind. He then composed another poem, undoing his slander, thus inventing the palinode. The following fragment remains: "The story is not true, / you did not go in the finely equipped ships, / nor did you come to Troy's citadel." The poet thereupon recovered his sight. See D. A. Campbell, ed., *Greek Lyric Poetry: A Selection* (New York, 1967), n. to Stesichorus frag. 192, 258–59.

The story that Helen went to Egypt, not to Troy, was reported (and believed) by Herodotus (2. 112–20) and became the basis for Euripides' *Helen*. Herodotus heard from priests at Memphis in Egypt that Alexander and Helen, on their way to Troy from Sparta, were driven by storm winds to Egypt. Alexander's servants deserted him and accused him to Egyptian authorities of abducting Helen. He was seized and brought before Proteus, king of Egypt. Outraged at Alexander's violation of Menelaus' hospitality, Proteus kept Helen and deported Alexander, whom Egyptian law forbade him to kill. Homer knew this story, Herodotus says, quoting *Iliad* 6. 289–92 and *Odyssey* 4. 227–30, although he did not make use of it. (*Iliad* 3 and and *Odyssey* 4 are good reasons why he did not.)

The priests also told Herodotus that Menelaus went to Troy with an expedition of Greeks to recover Helen. On arrival they sent envoys into the city (one of whom was Menelaus) to demand her back. The Trojans said then that they did not have Helen, and although the Greeks did not believe them and began the war, they kept on saying it for ten years, until the city was captured and the Greeks learned the truth: Helen was indeed not there. Menelaus then went to Egypt and recovered Helen. Herodotus believed the story for he reasoned that the Trojans would have given Helen up rather than suffer as they did for so long, since Alexander was but one of Priam's numerous sons, many of whom, including Hector, Priam's heir, were killed in the course of the long war fought because of Alexander's crime.

In Euripides *Helen* 31–55 (produced in 412 B.C., just a few years after the publication of Herodotus' *Histories*), Helen says that Hera, angry at the outcome of the Judgment of Paris, made a phantom image of her and gave it to Alexander who thought it was the flesh-and-blood woman. Zeus brought war to Greeks and Trojans in Troy who fought for Helen, or rather for her name. For Hermes, at Zeus' command, spirited her to Proteus in Egypt, who kept her safe for Menelaus. He, meanwhile, had gathered an army and went to Troy to track down her captors. Because of her, Helen says, many died at Troy and although she endured much she was cursed and believed to have enmeshed Greece in a great war by betraying her husband (see also 582–88, 669–83). Her statement articulates the theme of the play with its "antinomies, body *versus* name, reality *versus* appearance, . . . pointing to the elusiveness of truth amid ironical webs of ignorance." For the play's "basic antithesis" is the one between "truth and seeming, or, more concretely, . . . the ambiguous situation of Helen herself: she is, in fact, the innocent wife of Menelaus, but the world knows her as an adulteress and the cause of a disastrous war" (Cedric H. Whitman, *Euripides and the Full Circle of Myth* [Cambridge, Mass., 1974], 37, 39).

After the war Menelaus, trying to reach home, arrives in Egypt, shipwrecked and in rags, bringing with him the phantom Helen whom he had taken from Troy. The play turns on his meeting and recognizing the real Helen (the phantom disappears) and their subsequent escape from the son of Proteus (now dead) who wants to marry Helen. The recognition involves the realization that the Trojan War was fought for nothing (706–07).

At *Electra* 1280–83 Euripides' indictment of war (and of Zeus) though brief, is savage: Helen remained in Egypt and did not go to Troy. Rather Zeus sent an image of her to Ilium in order that there might be strife and bloodshed among men.

For Aeschylus the story of the real and phantom Helens (if he knew it) must have seemed meaningless hocus-pocus: "Paris came to the house of the sons of Atreus," he says, "and violated the table of guest-friendship by stealing the woman. She left to her people a thronging with spear and with shield, the arming of sailors. And she stepped lightly through Ilium's gates, bringing to them her dowry, death" (*Agamemnon* 399–408).

3   It was Odysseus, the reader will remember, who suggested to Tyndareus that all Helen's suitors swear an oath to protect her chosen husband, intending by this device to prevent those not chosen from harming him in their disappointment and frustration (3. 10. 9).

Odysseus did not want to go to Troy, Hyginus *Fabulae* 95 tells us, because he learned through an oracle that he would not return home until twenty years had passed and then without his companions. Pretending madness, he put on a hat worn by the insane and yoked a horse with an ox to a plow. Palamedes, aware that the madness was feigned, placed Odysseus' son, Telemachus, in his cradle in front of the plow. Odysseus dropped his pretence and agreed to go, from that moment hating Palamedes. For variants and additional references, see Frazer, *Apollodorus* 2. 176–77.

Palamedes by his stratagem outwitted Odysseus, something Odysseus would not lightly bear. Moreover, when the Greek expedition was stalled at Aulis by contrary winds, and the soldiers were in danger of starving and were fighting among themselves for food, Palamedes taught them to read Phoenician writing and devised a fair way to distribute what food they had. He occupied their idleness by teaching them to play with dice and contrived other benefits which made him famous among the Greeks. The chieftains out of envy intrigued against Palamedes at Troy and planted under his bed gold and a forged letter from Priam urging him to betray the Greeks. They then "discovered" the gold and the letter, and Palamedes, convicted as a traitor, was stoned to death (Scholiast on Euripides *Orestes* 432). The moral seems to be, *Le mieux est l'ennemi du bien* and, alas, *le bien* always wins.

Hyginus *Fabulae* 105 gives a version similar to that of Apollodorus. Dictys of Crete *The Trojan War* 2. 15, however, noting Odysseus' envy of Palamedes' superiority, says that Odysseus and Diomedes told Palamedes that they had found gold in a well and wished to share it with him. They persuaded him to descend into the well and then stoned him to death. Dictys adds that Agamemnon was suspected of complicity in the plot, for Palamedes was very popular with the soldiers, most of whom openly stated their preference for him as commander-in-chief. This story, however, does not speak well of Palamedes' intelligence. Pausanias 10. 31. 2 says that he read in the epic *Cypria* (now lost) that Odysseus and Diomedes drowned Palamedes while he was fishing.

Palamedes' father, Nauplius, sailed to Troy demanding satisfaction from those guilty of his son's murder. He was unsuccessful and so devised a two-pronged revenge which was very effective (Epitome 6. 7–11).

The unprincipled viciousness of Odysseus evidenced in the story of Palamedes is totally absent from Homer's epic. But Homer conducted a great whitewash, as Pindar *Nem.* 7. 20–23 believed: "I imagine the account of Odysseus is greater than what he did, because of the charm of Homer's song. For his winged skill invests his lies with dignity, and his poetic craft deceives us, leading us astray with myths [*muthois*]." The point to be made has little to do with Odysseus' morality or lack of it (one sees an unprincipled Odysseus in Sophocles' *Philoctetes*).

Rather, what is important in these lines of Pindar is the poet's assumption of a greater fluidity in the ancient Greek mythological tradition than many modern handbooks, with their tendency to homogenize myths and present Greek mythology as somewhat monolithic, would lead us to believe. Along with this greater fluidity goes a greater freedom in the imagination of the Greek artist to create what he wants to create and to say what he wants to say.

4   The connection between the daughters of Anius, king of Delos, and the Greek expedition to Troy would, no doubt, have been made clear in Apollodorus' full text, of which the Epitome is an abridgement. The name of each of the daughters is derived from that which she has the power to produce, Elais from *elaia*, "olive"; Spermo from *sperma*, "seed"; and Oeno from oinos, "wine." Anius and his daughters provisioned the Greek army at Aulis, supplying them with grain, wine, and food for the voyage to Troy (Dictys of Crete *The Trojan War* 1. 23).

Ovid *Met*. 13. 632–74 says that Agamemnon requisitioned by force Anius' four (not three) daughters to feed the Greek expedition. They managed to escape, two going to Euboea, and two to Andros, where their brother was king. Threatened with war he gave them up, but as they were about to be bound in chains for their return to the Greeks, they prayed to Dionysus, who changed them to white doves, sacred to Aphrodite.

5   The reader who so desires may compare Apollodorus' catalog of ships and army commanders with that of Homer *Iliad* 2. 494–759, made at Troy. (Homer makes a special invocation to the Muses to aid him, otherwise his memory would fail: 2. 484–92.) The reader may also compare Apollodorus' catalog with those of Euripides *Iphigenia in Aulis* 192–295, made at Aulis; Hyginus *Fabulae* 97, made who knows where; and Dictys of Crete *The Trojan War* 1. 17, made at Aulis. For the catalog as a *tour de force* for the oral poet, see Charles Rowan Beye, *The Iliad, the Odyssey and the Epic Tradition* (Garden City, N.Y., 1966), 89–93.

6   At *Iliad* 2. 299–329 Homer says that Calchas interpreted the portent to mean that the Greeks would fight in Troy for nine years and capture the city in the tenth. See also Ovid *Met*. 12. 11–23.

7   Achilles shared the command of the fleet with Ajax and Phoenix (Dictys of Crete *The Trojan War* 1. 16). Evidently it was not unusual for a Greek ship or fleet to set out upon an expedition without knowing the way. So the Argo set sail for Colchis (stopping at Salmadessus in Thrace to ask directions of Phineus: 1. 9. 9–22).

Dictys of Crete *The Trojan War* 1. 7 narrates the encounter between Greeks and Mysians, altering some of Apollodorus' details. The Greek landing at Mysia was opposed by guards at the shore who told them to wait until they reported their arrival to the king. The Greeks paid them no heed and fighting started. Telephus was pursuing Odysseus in a vineyard when he tripped over a vine and fell. Achilles saw from a distance what had happened (Odysseus presumably kept on running without looking back), hurled his spear, and wounded him. After a day of battle there was a truce for burial of the dead on both sides. During the truce three Greeks who were grandsons of Heracles (Telephus' father) approached the king, identified themselves, explained the purpose of the expedition, and invited his help. Telephus criticized the Greeks for the hostile manner in which they landed and declined to join them since Priam was his father-in-law. But he stopped the fighting and allowed the Greeks to leave. Before they sailed away, however, he wanted to see the descendants of Pelops, to whom he was related. He gave them gifts, and the Greeks supplies. Agamemnon and Menelaus ordered the army physicians, Podalirius and Machaon, sons of Asclepius, to treat Telephus' wound. The Greeks, because of bad weather, returned to Boeotia from which they had set sail. From there they went each to his own kingdom.

Proclus in his synopsis of the lost epic, *Cypria*, however, agrees with Apollodorus that the Greeks were scattered by a storm when they left Mysia, although he does not say where they went, except for Achilles, who, he says, put in at Scyros and married his childhood sweetheart, Deidamia, daughter of King Lycomedes (Evelyn-White, *Hesiod*, 493; for Achilles and Deidamia, see 3. 13. 8 and ch. 7, n. 40).

8   In the tenth year of the fighting at Troy, Helen tells Hector that she has been away from Sparta for twenty years (Homer *Iliad* 24. 765–66).

9   See Frazer, *Apollodorus* 2. 188–89 for works extant and lost which refer to the cure of Telephus' wound by rust from the weapon that caused it. The principle, as Frazer says, is that of sympathetic magic. So Iphiclus, son of Phylacus, is cured of impotence (or sterility) by drinking a mixture containing rust from the blade of a knife used for castrating rams beside which he once sat as a child (1. 9. 12).

10   Artemis' demand that Agamemnon sacrifice his daughter in expiation for an impious statement made against her was also prompted by an earlier act of impiety, as Apollodorus tells us, which was Atreus' refusal to sacrifice the golden lamb to her, as he had promised (Epitome 2. 10–12). The goddess' brutality (for the punishment seems to outweigh the crimes by far) is mitigated by her last minute removal of Iphigenia to Tauris and substitution of a deer at the altar in her place.

The story of Iphigenia's sacrifice (or near sacrifice) was well known and was narrated in the *Cypria* (according to Proclus in his summary of it: see Evelyn-White, *Hesiod*, 493, 495); by Ovid *Met.* 12. 24–38; by Hyginus *Fabulae* 98, who says that the deer Agamemnon boasted of shooting belonged to Artemis; and by Dictys of Crete *The Trojan War* 1. 19–22, who says that the animal was a female goat which Agamemnon heedlessly killed near a grove of Artemis and in which the goddess had taken special pleasure. Despite the emphasis on Agamemnon's sacrilege in Hyginus and Dictys of Crete, the punishment still seems excessive, unless the miracle is accepted as part of the myth.

The best known version is Euripides' *Iphigenia in Aulis*, one of his last plays, probably written in 407 B.C. and produced in 405, after the playwright had died. (See also his *Iphigenia in Tauris* 1–41.) The text of the play is corrupt in many places and the ending, in which a messenger announces the miracle of the substitution of a deer for Iphigenia at the altar (1532–1629), is considered spurious. (See Charles R. Walker's Introduction to his translation of the play in the Chicago series.) The true ending, nevertheless, probably included the saving of Iphigenia by Artemis (D. J. Conacher, *Euripidean Drama: Myth, Theme and Structure* [Toronto, 1967], 249, n. 1). Euripides' emphasis in the play, however, is not upon the miracle by which Iphigenia is saved, but upon her sudden transformation (1368 ff.), before which she is terrified and resists being sacrificed, after which she embraces sacrifice as martyrdom, becoming a Greek Joan of Arc. This transformation, as Conacher says, "gives the play whatever meaning it has" (253). The problem, however, is not just her sudden decision (criticized first by Aristotle *Poetics* 1454a 31–33), but her lack of awareness of the sordid cause for which she martyrs herself (Conacher, *Euripidean Drama*, 264).

The miraculous removal of Iphigenia, who is magically transported to Tauris and there becomes a priestess of Artemis, has some similarity to the miraculous transporting of Helen to Egypt after Alexander's abduction (while he proceeds to Troy with a phantom Helen: Epitome 2. 3–5 and n. 2). The rape of Persephone resonates in the fates of both Helen and Iphigenia in these versions of their myths (see 1. 5 [entire] and ch. 1, n. 18 for Persephone; for the similarity among the three heroines, see Richmond Lattimore, *Story Patterns in Greek Tragedy* [London, 1964], 52–53). Both Aeschylus and Sophocles wrote plays on Iphigenia. Neither survives. Of Aeschylus' we know nothing. Sophocles seems to have followed the story in the *Cypria* (Conacher, *Euripidean Drama*, 251).

A useful comparison from Hebrew mythology is the story of God's command to Abraham to sacrifice his late born son and heir, Isaac. Abraham obeys God, whom he has not offended in any way, proceeds to the place of sacrifice, lying to the boy who asks his father where the animal for sacrifice is—or by his answer ("God will provide") teleologically suspending ethics, according to Søren Kierkegaard's famous essay, *Fear and Trembling* (trans. W. Lowrie [Princeton, 1941]). As he takes the knife in hand to kill his son, God intervenes, satisfied that Abraham's faith is absolute. Abraham looks up, sees a ram caught in a thicket, and sacrifices it (Genesis 22:1–19).

God did provide. The lie in human, finite terms became a truth in the end, by faith.

In Aeschylus' *Agamemnon* (the first play of his trilogy, *Oresteia*), the girl's throat is cut like an animal's at the altar, her blood gushes out upon it, and she dies (104–248, especially 228 ff., the Chorus' description of the sacrifice; also 1377–81, 1412–21, 1431–33 and 1521–29, in which Clytemnestra cites the murder of her daughter as her motive for killing Agamemnon). The reason for the sacrifice in this play seems even more meaningless and savage than in the versions so far considered (in which Iphigenia is saved): In the camp at Aulis twin eagles attack a pregnant hare and devour its unborn young. Artemis in anger sends contrary winds which prevent the fleet from sailing, the delay threatening the disintegration of the expedition. To save it (i.e., to stop the winds), Agamemnon is told that he must sacrifice his daughter. Torn by anguish he "puts on the yoke of necessity" (218). Iphigenia, after pleading in vain with her father, is brought to the altar bound and gagged (so she cannot curse him). Unable to cry out, she shoots a glance of mute appeal from face to face of the men lifting her up to cut her throat above the altar, men for whom as a little girl she used to sing when they were guests at her father's table. Aeschylus deliberately eliminates any act of Agamemnon as a cause for Artemis' anger. Then why such a price—Iphigenia—for the killing of a pregnant hare by two eagles who have nothing to do with Agamemnon? The answer to this question (if indeed it is possible to give a satisfactory one) is central to our understanding of the meaning of the play. See the discussion in ch. 12, n. 11.

For Lucretius the sacrifice of Iphigenia was an instance of crime perpetrated not in the name of religion, but by religion itself. His description of the girl's slaughter, as vivid as Aeschylus', ends with outraged indignation: *tantum religio potuit suadere malorum,* "That religion could urge on so much evil!" (*De Rerum Natura* 1. 82–101).

11   The Cycnus-Tenes-Philonome triangle belongs to a frequently recurring type of story. See 2. 3. 1–2 (and ch. 4, n. 10), 3. 13. 3 (and ch. 7, n. 35) and Epitome 1. 18–19 (and ch. 9, n. 7).

12   For Philoctetes on Lemnos see ch. 3, n. 3. He had received the bow with which he shot birds from Heracles in return for lighting the

hero's funeral pyre (see ch. 5, n. 42; Apollodorus 2. 5. 7, however, says that Poeas, Philoctetes' father, lit the pyre and received the bow). Aeschylus, Sophocles, and Euripides each wrote a play entitled *Philoctetes* (see Frazer, *Apollodorus* 2. 197). Only that of Sophocles, produced in 409 B.C. when the playwright was eighty-seven, survives. For references to it, see ch. 3, n. 3 and ch. 5, n. 1, and for Apollodorus' brief narration of Philoctetes' coming to Troy, see Epitome 5. 8–9.

13   Homer tells of the embassy of Odysseus and Menelaus to Troy in an attempt to recover Helen by diplomacy rather than by war (*Iliad* 3. 203–24).

Thetis' advice to Achilles was common sense, but an oracle nevertheless had declared the same thing: The first Greek ashore would be the first to die (Ovid *Heroides* 13. 93–94, Hyginus *Fabulae* 103). Protesilaus' ship was the first to make the shore against fierce resistance from the Trojans, Dictys of Crete says, during which many were killed, Protesilaus by Aeneas (not by Hector; see *The Trojan War* 2. 11). See also Homer *Iliad* 2. 698–702 who says a "Dardanian man" killed him.

When Laodamia hears of Protesilaus' death (as Hyginus *Fabulae* 103, 104 tells us), she prays in her grief to the gods to be allowed to speak with him for three hours. Hermes brings him to her from the underworld, but when the three hours are up, takes him back down again. This meeting and its parting serve only to increase her grief. She makes a bronze image of Protesilaus which she fondles. A servant bringing her fruit in the morning peers through a crack and sees Laodamia embracing and kissing the effigy. Thinking that she has a living man in her bed the servant runs to tell Laodamia's father. He bursts into the room, sees the image, and to end her torture, orders the figure to be burned on a pyre. Laodamia hurls herself upon it and burns to death. According to Propertius 1. 19. 7–10, death in the underworld could not blot out Protesilaus' equal longing for Laodamia. (For the myth, see also Ovid *Heroides* 13.)

Protesilaus' brief return from the underworld brings to mind the Orpheus and Eurydice myth (1. 3. 2 and ch. 1, n. 6), and Laodamia's image of her beloved reminds us of Pygmalion, who carved an ivory statue of his ideal woman which he caressed and embraced until Aphrodite, in answer to his prayer, brought it to life (told by Orpheus at Ovid *Met.* 10. 243–97).

14   Dictys of Crete *The Trojan War* 2. 12 accuses Cycnus of a sneak attack on the Greeks who were engaged in burying Protesilaus. Achilles comes to the rescue and kills him.

Ovid *Met.* 12. 72–145 in a different version describes a long, exhausting battle between the two heroes, each the son of an immortal (Cycnus, son of Poseidon; Achilles, son of Thetis) and so very nearly invulnerable. Achilles' first spear-cast strikes Cycnus' chest, but dulls the point of the spear head rather than harming him. Cycnus taunts Achilles: "Why are you so surprised? I wear my armor for show, not for protection" (87–90). Achilles hurls another spear which also has no effect. Cycnus, mocking Achilles, stands unprotected, offering himself to Achilles' third spear, which, like the first two, cannot pierce Cycnus' skin. Achilles, enraged like a bull in the arena maddened by the scarlet cape (Ovid says), inspects his spear, doubts his strength, hurls a fourth spear at a certain Menoetes which pierces breastplate and chest and he falls, reassuring Achilles. He draws the spear from the dying Menoetes and hurls it at Cycnus, but it bounces off him as if from a wall or rock. Achilles then leaps from his chariot, attacks Cycnus with his sword, but only blunts its edge against his opponent's body. In a frenzy, he then begins to beat him about the face and temples with his shield and the hilt of his sword until Cycnus gives way, becomes dizzy, and stumbles against a rock. Achilles forces him backwards over the rock with his shield and knees, unfastens Cycnus' helmet-thongs, and strangles him with them. He prepares to strip his armor, but sees that it is empty: Cycnus has changed into a swan (Greek *kyknos*) and flown away.

Virgil *Aeneid* 1. 474–78 describes (in an ecphrasis) the death of Troilus, a son of Hecuba by Apollo (3. 12. 5), carved in relief on the Temple of Juno in Carthage viewed by Aeneas: Fleeing weaponless from Achilles, half in and half out of his chariot hurtling behind horses out of control, Troilus clings to the reins nevertheless, his hair and neck bumping on the ground, his dragging spear inscribing a line in the dust with its point. For other stories of the death of Troilus, see Dictys of Crete *The Trojan War* 4. 9 and Frazer, *Apollodorus* 201–02, who notes the prophecy that Troy could not be taken if Troilus lived to the age of twenty. In later literature the Trojan Troilus was linked with the Greek Cressida in a tragic love affair in works by Boccaccio, Chaucer, and Shakespeare. See Philip Mayerson, *Classical Mythology in Literature, Art, and Music* (Toronto, 1967), 396–97.

Homer *Iliad* 21. 34–127 gives a different account of the death of Lycaon, a son of Priam, twice caught unarmed by Achilles. The first time Achilles sells him into slavery in Lemnos, but he is shortly ransomed and makes his way back to Troy, staying inside the walls for eleven days. On the twelfth he re-enters battle, but in headlong flight from Achilles along with other Trojans, he plunges into the river Xanthus. Emerging weaponless, he encounters Achilles, lusting for blood to avenge the death of Patroclus. Lycaon runs in under Achilles' spear and catches him by the knees with one hand in the suppliant's posture, holds Achilles' spear with the other, and begs for his life.

Achilles gives him some battlefield philosophy: "Nay, friend, die even thou; why do you weep thus? Patroclus died, a better man than you, and do you not see the kind of man I am, so handsome and magnificent? My father is a nobleman, my mother a goddess, but death and iron destiny are waiting even for me. Some day at dawn or in the afternoon or at midday someone will take my life from me in battle with the cast of a spear or an arrow shot from a bowstring" (106–13). Lycaon lets go the spear and sits back, hands outstretched. Achilles draws his sword and plunges it up to the hilt in Lycaon's neck.

15   Achilles captured Briseis when he sacked Lyrnessus (Homer *Iliad* 2. 688–93), and it was the contention for her between him and Agamemnon (who took her from him) which caused Achilles' wrath, the subject of the poem.

16   The reader may compare Apollodorus' list of Trojan allies with that of Homer at *Iliad* 2. 816–77.

17   There is a lacuna in the text after the clause "Achilles . . . Briseis." The phrase which follows "Briseis" ("of the daughter of Chryses"), which must be construed with the missing passage has been omitted.

   Apollodorus from here follows the *Iliad* of Homer in relating the incidents of the Trojan War.

18   The night patrol of Diomedes and Odysseus in which they meet Dolon and kill him after learning of the arrival of Rhesus and the location of his camp (*Iliad* 10) is the basis for the *Rhesus*, attributed to Euripides and the only surviving Greek drama which derives its plot directly from the *Iliad*. For the question of Euripidean authorship, see Richmond Lattimore's Introduction to his translation of the play in the Chicago series. Both Lattimore and G. M. A. Grube, *The Drama of Euripides* (London, 1941), 439–47, accept Euripides as the author. Conacher, *Euripidean Drama*, viii, is not convinced of the play's authenticity, and T. B. L. Webster, *The Tragedies of Euripides* (London, 1967), 6, excludes the play from Euripides' corpus. Lattimore notes that the tragedians, when writing plays about the heroes of the Trojan War, regularly chose episodes either before or after the events of the *Iliad*.

19   It is doubtful that a reader of Epitome 4, an abridgement of Apollodorus' synopsis of the *Iliad*, would be inspired to read that work of art itself. Not merely because Epitome 4 omits references to sublime parts of the poem, e.g., Helen at the wall of Troy (*Iliad* 3), or Hector taking leave of Andromache at the gates of Troy (*Iliad* 6). The plain fact is, we get nothing of the beauty of the poem from what is mentioned in the Epitome: the wrath of Achilles (4.1 = *Iliad* 1), the embassy to Achilles (4. 3–4 = *Iliad* 9), the encounter between Achilles and Priam (4. 7 = *Iliad* 24). Apollodorus has given us the *múthos*, or

"plot" (somewhat incomplete) of the *Iliad*, but we have no sense of the poem itself. Why do we not? What is the relation between myth and work of art? Epitome 4 forces this question upon us more than any part of Apollodorus commented on so far. Can we say that the myth, or plot, "is to literature what an armature of a roughly shaped block is to sculpture—a first shape, a source of ideas?" (Susanne K. Langer, *Feeling and Form* [New York, 1953], 274). If so, then it is hardly anything, to judge by the example here. Articulation, whether in stone or in language, is all, it would seem. The analogy is not completely satisfactory: the stone is the medium with which the sculptor works as he articulates his artifact. What is the medium composing myth, which the literary artist articulates to create literature? Is Epitome 4 a "roughly shaped block" and since it is language, not stone, may we call it a severely retarded articulation of the *Iliad* which is an articulation at the highest level of genius? Perhaps the attempt to separate myth from literature as a skeleton from a body, a rough block of stone from the sculptor's carving, a content from a form, is misguided. Perhaps myth is the dominant, or more easily discerned, pattern of a filigree of words (the work of literature), this filigree a composition of articulations (or *articuli*: see Ferdinand de Saussure, *Course in General Linguistics* [New York, 1966], 111–14; and Roland Barthes, *Elements of Semiology* [Boston, 1970], 56–57).

Adam M. Parry, "Have We Homer's *Iliad*?" *Yale Classical Studies* 20 (1966), 177–216, says of the *Iliad*: "Its excellence is no more mere ... [*mûthos*] than is that of Sophocles' *Oedipus*.... If we should try to define the *Iliad* in a general way, we might think of a long poem dealing critically with the heroic conception of life.... Distinct figures —Agamemnon, Achilles, Odysseus, Paris, Hector—are dramatized for us in crucial situations, and their *attitudes* as they speak and act in conflict with each other constitute the real force of the poem....

"To offer a succession of scenes so comprehensively evaluating the human situation, to present them in a dramatic trajectory which reaches a climax in XXII and ends in the resolution of XXIV, requires an artistic construct of the highest order....

"This construct is in the first place a certain proper order of scenes.... But a scene is not a given block of material.... It is itself made up of parts, and will be more or less effective, ... as these parts are more or less well arranged. The ... [order] of Homeric poetry, then, involves the quality of language as well as the construction of plot....

"... the Homeric descriptions and similes, which are also dramatic scenes, must continually evoke and further define this heroic world. Herein lies 'the golden light' which Homer sheds over the world, and herein is the nobility and strangeness of the language which must be everywhere 'holy and sweet and wonderful' [quoting his father, Milman Parry]" (190–94). See also Adam Parry, ed., *The Making of Homeric Verse: The Collected Papers of Milman Parry* (Oxford, 1971), the Introduction to which (ix–lxii) is probably the single best short essay on the Homeric question in print at this time (1976). See also Maurice Platnauer, ed., *Fifty Years (and Twelve) of Classical Scholarship* (Oxford, 1968), ch. 1, "Homer," with contributions by E. R. Dodds, L. R. Palmer, and Dorothea Gray, 1–49.

20   Thersites, the "ugliest man [*aischistos*: ugliest in appearance and demeanor] to come to Ilium" (Homer *Iliad* 2. 216), who lacks a sense of decorum and the fitness of things (*Iliad* 2. 213, 214), is whipped with a sceptre by Odysseus when he talks out of turn in the Greek assembly (*Iliad* 2. 265–69). Modern readers tend to romanticize Thersites as a prototype of the modern antiheroic, perhaps even proletarian, rebel, but so to view him violates the Homeric narrative. Here his viciousness is plainly exhibited. (See also Proclus' summary of Arctinus' *Aethiopis*, a poem in the Epic Cycle, in Evelyn-White, *Hesiod*, 507.)

Machaon and Podalirius, sons of Asclepius, were physicians to the Greeks. Machaon was said by Pausanias 3. 26. 9–10 and Hyginus *Fabulae* 113 to have been killed by Eurypylus.

21   Achilles could not be hurt by weapons or missiles except in the ankle, by which his mother held him when she dipped him as an infant in the river Styx to make him invulnerable (see Statius *Achilleid* 1. 133–34 and 269–70). Apollodorus earlier followed the version which told of Thetis' attempt to make her baby immortal by burning him in a fire at night, until she was discovered by Peleus, who was horrified (3. 13. 6 and ch. 7, n. 38).

Achilles' death is attributed to Apollo and Alexander at Homer *Iliad* 22. 359–60; cf. 19. 416–17. In other versions Alexander shot the arrow at Achilles which Apollo guided to its mark (Virgil *Aeneid* 6. 56–58, Ovid *Met.* 12. 597–609). Hyginus *Fabulae* 107 says that Apollo in the guise of Alexander shot and killed Achilles, but Homer *Iliad* 21. 277–78 (contradicting other references in the poem) says that Apollo alone will kill him. Finally, Euripides *Andromache* 655 and *Hecuba* 387–88 say that Alexander alone killed him. See Frazer, *Apollodorus* 2. 215 for reference to the story of the treacherous murder of Achilles by Deiphobus and Alexander in a temple of Apollo in Troy, where he had gone under truce to negotiate his marriage with Priam's daughter, Polyxena, which was to end the war.

Agamemnon in the underworld describes Achilles' funeral to him, enabling him, since he could not be present, at least to hear about it from one who was there (Homer *Odyssey* 24. 43–94). The particularity of Agamemnon's description gives a matter-of-fact quality to it which makes the scene seem strange when we remember that it is a dead Agamemnon who is telling this to a dead Achilles.

Apollodorus' statement that Achilles was buried on Leuce disagrees with Homer's version and was perhaps derived from Arctinus' *Aethiopis*, a poem (now lost) in the Epic Cycle. (See Proclus' summary in Evelyn-White, *Hesiod*, 509.)

Hera prophesies to Thetis before Achilles is born that he will live after death in the Elysian Fields, married to Medea (Apollonius Rhodius *Argonautica* 4. 810–15). According to Homer *Odyssey* 11. 471–540 Achilles inhabits the underworld where he strides the field of asphodel (the name of the grass or wild flower which grows in this meadow in Hades).

22   The dispute over the arms of Achilles, known as the Judgment of Arms, presents the ambivalence in the Greek mind about the nature of heroism, an ambivalence depicted in the characters of Ajax and Odysseus. Each was preeminent in one of the two aspects of heroic *aretê* or excellence, Ajax as a doer of deeds, Odysseus as a speaker of words. Achilles combined both of these qualities in himself to the highest degree and thus was the ideal hero—in theory (see Homer *Iliad* 9. 442–43). Significantly, Ajax and Odysseus, offering in combination ideal *aretê*, are sent by Agamemnon to persuade Achilles to rejoin the fighting (*Iliad* 9) after he withdraws from it in anger.

Ajax was considered the best Greek hero after Achilles (*Iliad* 2. 768–69). He is more than once called the "wall of the Achaeans" (*Iliad* 3. 229, 6. 5, 7. 211) and when he leads the battle to defend the Greek ships against Hector and the Trojans, he demonstrates why this epithet is applied to him (15. 674–746).

Odysseus was famous for his eloquence (see *Iliad* 3. 203–24; it should be noted, however, that his eloquence has little effect on Achilles in *Iliad* 9 who is moved more by Ajax's short, blunt speech). Odysseus went to Troy at night in disguise and stole the Palladium (without which Troy could not be conquered: Epitome 5. 10), and it was his idea to construct a hollow wooden horse as a means to introduce Greek warriors into the impregnable city (Epitome 5. 13–14). Ajax and Odysseus represent, in fact, an antithesis between the relative values of action and speech, deeds (*erga*) and words (*logoi*). See ch. 6, n. 23.

Homer refers to the Judgment of Arms at *Odyssey* 11. 543–64, the passage in which Odysseus encounters Ajax in the underworld and seeks to become reconciled with him. His eloquence, however, is met with silence from Ajax who, angry still, turns away from Odysseus while he is still speaking.

The dispute over the arms of Achilles and Ajax's madness and suicide were part of the Epic Cycle: see Proclus' summary of Arctinus' *Aethiopis* and the *testimonium* to Lesches' *Little Iliad* in Evelyn-White, *Hesiod*, 509 and 513 respectively.

For Pindar the outcome of the Judgment of Arms and Ajax's suicide are an indictment both of Homer (who puffed Odysseus beyond his true worth) and the blind folly of the generality of men, skillfully deceived and led astray by *múthoi* (*Nem.* 7. 20–30). He is more out-spoken in another poem (*Nem.* 8. 21–27) in which he sees the "glit-tering lie" as winning the prize while the man inarticulate but valiant in spirit is downed into obscurity. For the Greeks, he says, pandered to Odysseus in secret votes; Ajax was bereft of the golden arms and wrestled with death.

Sophocles based his play *Ajax* on the hero's insanity caused by the Judgment of Arms, his slaughter of livestock, thinking in his madness that they are Agamemnon, Menelaus, Odysseus, and the other chieftains, his recovery of sanity and subsequent suicide. The play represents, in the character of Ajax, the contradictions in the heroic world (and espe-cially in its code: "Help your friends; harm your enemies"), and the fragility of its order. He was wrongfully denied the arms of Achilles and so denied his heroic identity by men who, though friends, by this act became his enemies whom the heroic imperative in which his iden-tity was grounded commanded him to hurt. The conflict is unbearable and results in madness.

Ajax, however, is more than an emblem of the contradiction in and fragility of the heroic world. He recovers his sanity and sees the im-possibility of his position in the world while at the same time achiev-ing a vision of reality which comprehends the role change plays in a coherent order (see Sophocles *Ajax* 646 ff.). Change requires that the old give way, that he remove himself. Ajax has acquired self-knowledge of a difficult kind: His season is past, he must withdraw. And so he commits suicide to bring himself into harmony with the order of things. See the author's "Sophocles' Ajax: His Madness and Transfor-mation," *Arethusa* 2. 1 (1969), 88–103. For a different kind of inter-pretation which, while emphasizing the greatness of Ajax, recognizes the need for (and the humanity of) Odysseus, inheritor of the world for whom Ajax makes way, see Bernard M. W. Knox, "The *Ajax* of Sophocles," *Harv. Stud. in Class. Phil.* 65 (1961), 1–37. Lois V. Hinck-ley, "Ajax and Achilles: Their Literary Relationship from Homer to Sophocles" (Ph.D. diss., University of North Carolina, 1972), sees "Ajax' defeat in the Judgment of Arms and his subsequent death as a replay of Achilles' successful challenge in the *Iliad*. The different ends of the two heroes, however, indicate the difference which Sopho-cles recognizes between the heroic standards of the heroic world and the temper and values of his own fifth-century Athens" (3). See Euripides *Helen* 94–102 for reference to the Judgment of Arms and Ajax's suicide.

In Ovid *Met.* 13. 1–398 Ajax and Odysseus engage in a set debate for the prize of Achilles' arms. Odysseus wins by a shrewd and brilliant speech which proves Pindar's contention mentioned above, and Ajax kills himself.

Contrary to Apollodorus, the Sophoclean Ajax received, or is to receive, the play implies, proper funeral rites which included the burning of the corpse on a pyre. See Sir Richard C. Jebb, ed., *Sophocles: The Ajax* (Cambridge, Eng., 1896, reprinted Amsterdam, 1962), xxix–xxxii.

23   For Philoctetes on Lemnos see ch. 3, n. 3, Epitome 3. 27, and n. 12. For Sophocles' play *Philoctetes*, see ch. 3, n. 3 and ch. 5, n. 1. In that drama it is Helenus, the Trojan seer, not Calchas, who tells the Greeks that Heracles' bow is required for the capture of Troy (604–13, 1337–42). The Greek chieftains send Neoptolemus, rather than Diomedes, with Odysseus to Lemnos to bring the bow (and Philoctetes) to Troy. For the sources for this and other variants of the story of Philoctetes' arrival at Troy, see Frazer, *Apollodorus* 2. 222–23.

24   Homer *Odyssey* 4. 276 seems to imply that Helen and Deiphobus were married. Helen in Euripides *Trojan Women* 959–60 says that Deiphobus forced her to marry him (but the lines may be spurious).

Epitome 5. 8–10 lists four conditions necessary to the capture of Troy. The first is the presence of Heracles' bow which Philoctetes possesses. The other three are named in Epitome 5. 10. According to Apollodorus, Calchas reveals the first condition, although Sophocles' *Philoctetes* attributes its revelation to Helenus (see n. 23). But in Apollodorus' version the capture of Helenus does not occur until Philoctetes has arrived and killed Alexander. When that happens Helenus and Deiphobus vie for Helen; Helenus loses and goes to Mount Ida. Calchas apparently knew only of the condition requiring the presence of Heracles' bow. But there were others—necessarily so, since the presence of Heracles' bow did not bring about the fall of Troy. Calchas knows that Helenus, now exiled, so to speak, from Troy, knows these other conditions which must be met before the city can be captured, and so Odysseus finds him and brings him to the Greek camp to reveal them. For the Palladium, see 3. 12. 3 and ch. 7, n. 21.

25   Lesches, author of the *Little Iliad*, a lost poem of the Epic Cycle, says that Odysseus gave up Achilles' arms to Neoptolemus, with whom Apollodorus thus agrees (see Evelyn-White, *Hesiod*, 511).

Odysseus tells Achilles in the underworld that he brought his son, Neoptolemus, to Troy from Scyros. He goes on to say that Neoptolemus distinguished himself in council and in battle, as a speaker of words and a doer of deeds, displaying the same quality of *aretê* or excellence as his father. Odysseus says that he could not name all those whom Neoptolemus killed in battle, but he singles out the slaying of the hero Eurypylus, son of Telephus, as a special example of his *aretê*. (See Homer *Odyssey* 11. 506–37.)

26   According to Lesches *Little Iliad,* Odysseus made two distinct secret forays into Troy. In the first he entered the city as a spy, was recognized by Helen, and the two of them plotted the capture of the city. Odysseus then killed some of the Trojans and returned to the ships. Helen in the *Odyssey* tells this story to Telemachus and Pisistratus, embroidering it a bit, no doubt, to give herself credit: Odysseus came into the city disguised as a beggar but Helen immediately recognized him. She bathed and dressed him and swore not to betray him. He then divulged the Greeks' war plans to her, killed many Trojans, and left. The Trojan women wept but she rejoiced, for she had long since been ready to return home (*Odyssey* 4. 242–64). Euripides *Hecuba* 239–50 relates that Helen told Hecuba of Odysseus' presence in Troy at this time and he begged the queen for his life. Although he was completely in her power, she let him go. We have no way of knowing whether or not Euripides invented this encounter for his own dramatic purpose in the *Hecuba.*

In the second foray, according to Lesches, Odysseus and Diomedes stole the Palladium (see Evelyn-White, *Hesiod,* 511). Apollodorus has here conflated these two expeditions into one.

Sinon, left behind to deceive the Trojans about the wooden horse built by the Greeks (they have withdrawn to the offshore island of Tenedos), tells Priam that Odysseus and Diomedes polluted the Palladium with bloody hands when they stole it, and that from that moment and for that reason the Greek fortunes fell (Virgil *Aeneid* 2. 162–70). This (and what follows) is, of course, a lie, designed to give credibility to the wooden horse and the reasons the Greeks built it and withdrew. For other versions and variants, see Frazer, *Apollodorus* 2. 226–29 and R. G. Austin, ed., *P. Vergili Maronis Aeneidos Liber Secundus* (Oxford, 1964), 83–85 (n. *ad lineam* 2. 163).

27   The stratagem of the wooden horse built by the Greeks was narrated by Lesches in the *Little Iliad* and by Arctinus in the *Sack of Ilium,* two lost poems from the Epic Cycle (see Evelyn-White, *Hesiod,* 511 and 521). Demodocus, the bard of the Phaeacians, sings the tale of the wooden horse at the request of Odysseus (Homer *Odyssey* 8. 492–515), relating, as do Arctinus and Apollodorus, the debate among the Trojans what to do with it. In the *Odyssey,* Demodocus' song of the deception and concealment originally engineered by Odysseus leads

directly to the end of Odysseus' concealment of his identity from the Phaeacians (8. 547–586; 9. 1–20).

Apollodorus attributes to the *Little Iliad* the absurd number of 3,000 soldiers who entered the Trojan horse, but the surviving fragments of the summary of the *Little Iliad* say only that the Greeks put "the best men" into the wooden horse (the phrase used twice by Apollodorus; cf. *Odyssey* 4. 272, 8. 512) without giving a number (see Evelyn-White, *Hesiod*, 511). Homer names five men who were in the horse: Odysseus, Menelaus, Diomedes, Anticlus, and Neoptolemus (*Odyssey* 4. 269–88 and 11. 523–32), although in both passages he implies that there were many more. Virgil *Aeneid* 2. 259–64 names nine among whom two of Homer's five (Diomedes and Anticlus) are absent.

Euripides *Trojan Women* 511–67 in a haunting choral lyric describes after the fact the joy the Trojans felt when they went down to bring the horse into the city—the description undercut by references to the true nature of the sinister device. But at the time, while they hauled the image on wheels in the dead of night to Athena's temple, the Trojans gaily played the lyre and sang, girls danced around the horse, all homes were lit with lamps, all were awake, rejoicing.

Later in the night when all were asleep, a bloodcurdling cry pierced the city, making children clutch their mother's gowns in fright. Then the bloody slaughter began.

The account surpassing all others in Greek and Latin literature of the Trojan Horse, its entry into Troy, the death of Laocoon and his sons (not just his sons, as Apollodorus says), and the destruction of Troy is the second book of Virgil's *Aeneid*. Comment on this part of Virgil's poem is beyond the scope of these notes. Readers who know Latin (and perhaps those who do not) will benefit enormously from Austin's great commentary on book 2 in *Aeneidos Liber Secundus*. Bernard M. W. Knox's "The Serpent and the Flame: The Imagery of the Second Book of the *Aeneid*," *Amer. Journ. of Phil.* 71 (1950), 379–400, remains one of the best literary analyses of book 2.

On the horrible death of Laocoon and his two sons as narrated by Virgil (*Aeneid* 2. 201–27), see Austin's masterly short essay prefacing his comment to lines 199–227 (*Aeneidos Liber Secundus*, 94–97), e.g.: "His [Virgil's] treatment of the actual calamity is in the high vein of Greek tragedy; its brilliance, and its restraint, may be realized if it is compared with Eur. *Hipp.* 1210 ff. (the sea-monster), Eur. *Bacch.* 1122 ff. (the tearing of Pentheus), Soph. *OT* 1268 ff. (the blinding of Oedipus), or Soph. *Trach.* 772 ff. (Heracles' poisoned garment). . . . Virgil has fashioned the Greek myth into something entirely Roman, in making the fate of Troy so closely and so directly shaped by a prodigy [i.e., the twin serpents from Tenedos which slaughter Laocoon and his children], the kind of thing that can often be seen in Roman historical writing . . . : myth has become history in the Roman manner" (95–96).

Austin reminds us that we must not read Virgil's narrative here without considering the marble statuary known as the *Laocoon Group*, now in the Vatican, photographs of which can be seen in M. Bieber, *Laocoon, The Influence of the Group Since Its Recovery* (New York, 1942) and in other works listed by Austin (*Aeneidos Liber Secundus*, 98). In addition, the reader is directed to the famous eighteenth-century essay, *Laocoon*, by G. E. Lessing (trans. Edward A. McCormick [Indianapolis and New York, 1962]) on the difference between poetry and sculpture which he observed in the quite different ways Virgil and the sculptor of the Laocoon Group rendered Laocoon's expression of pain as he and his children were killed by the serpents.

Menelaus, by way of praising Odysseus' control of the soldiers in the horse, describes Helen's attempt to trick them into betraying their presence inside by calling to individual warriors by name, imitating the voices of their wives. Although sorely tempted to respond, the Greeks controlled themselves and kept quiet, except for Anticlus, who wanted to answer back. Odysseus was forced to clap his hand over his mouth to keep him quiet (Homer *Odyssey* 4. 271–89). According to a later tradition Odysseus inadvertently smothered Anticlus by the force of his hand over his mouth. See Austin, *Aeneidos Liber Secundus*, 123, n. to *Aeneid* 2. 261. Menelaus thus counters with this story of Helen's treachery her earlier one portraying her loyalty (*Odyssey* 4. 242–64 and n. 26).

Odysseus tells Achilles in the underworld that his son, Neoptolemus, was the only soldier in the horse (besides himself, we assume) who was not pale, weeping, and trembling. Neoptolemus, rather, kept begging Odysseus to let him out of the horse and was continually reaching for his sword and spear in his eagerness to kill Trojans.

Ronald A. Knox imagines a letter composed by Odysseus to Penelope from within the Trojan horse, imitating Ovid's *Heroides*, letters of forlorn heroines to absent lovers (quoted in Austin, *Aeneidos Liber Secundus*, Appendix B, 295).

A version of Knox's Latin poem might run something like this:

Odysseus to Penelope

I send this letter to you, dear, from the Trojan shore,
from a jerry-built contraption where I'm sitting on the floor.
I know my writing's crooked and the line goes up and down;
my elbow keeps on bumping into neighbor Demophon.
The ink is made from blood, but please don't pay it any heed:

I got it making his leg, not one of mine, to bleed.
Epeus built the damnedest thing in which I've ever ridden:
A hollow wooden horse on wheels: it's that in which I'm hidden.
We chose by lot the men to come—fair, but not particular,
and wouldn't you know that everyone is lean and hard and
    angular.
We're squeezed in here like sardines in a very narrow jar.
How could I ever think this was a way to win a war!
The crest of Thoas' helmet is ti-tickling my no-nose,
and in my side Thessander's arrows, sharpened for his foes.
We're lurching now from side to side, rolling into the town.
I'm such a wretched sailor. I hope. I keep. My breakfast down.
Now someone's hurling spears into the belly of the horse.
They're sure to stick in someone's—ouch! one stuck *me* in the
    arse!
Penelope, farewell. If fate lets me out of here,
My own feet are the only way I'll travel anywhere.

28   Hecuba watches Neoptolemus cut the old king's throat at the altar (Euripides *Trojan Women* 481–83; cf. *Hecuba* 23–24). At Virgil *Aeneid* 2. 526–58 Priam's son Polites, wounded by Neoptolemus and then pursued by him, runs down a long colonnade trying to escape. Neoptolemus is close behind and jabbing at him with his spear. Polites crosses a hall and falls dead at the feet of his parents. Rage rises up in Priam; old and weak though he is, he curses Neoptolemus for killing his son before the eyes of his father and feebly casts his spear at him. Neoptolemus tells him to take his complaints to Achilles in the underworld. He drags the old man, slipping in the blood of his son, to the altar, twines his hair in one hand, and with the other plunges his sword up to the hilt in Priam's side. He cuts off the head and throws the trunk out upon the Trojan shore unburied.

Neoptolemus is himself slain at Delphi by the Altar of Apollo (see Epitome 6. 14 and ch. 12, n. 4) in retribution for the death of Priam (Pausanias 4. 17. 4).

Menelaus and Odysseus spare Glaucus, son of Antenor, because of ties of guest-friendship with his father (Homer *Iliad* 3. 203–07). Antenor had also advocated in the Trojan assembly that Helen and her possessions be returned to the Greeks (*Iliad* 7. 347–53), although the Greeks would not necessarily have known this.

Livy begins his history of Rome (*Ab Urbe Condita* 1. 1) with the statement that when Troy was captured, although the Greeks dealt savagely with the other Trojans, they refrained from exercising the rights of war against Aeneas and Antenor because of the ancient law of guest-friendship and because these two were ever advocates of peace and of returning Helen.

Menelaus killed Deiphobus whom Helen had married (or with whom she had a liaison) after the death of Alexander: Epitome 5. 22.

Aethra, the mother of Theseus, first took care of Helen when Theseus abducted her as a little girl. She was taken to Sparta by Castor and Pollux when they recovered Helen from Attica, and voluntarily went with Helen to Troy with Alexander where she served as one of her attendants (Homer *Iliad* 3. 144). See 3. 10. 7–8, ch. 7, n. 13, and Epitome 1. 23.

Both Locrian Ajax and the returning fleet suffer punishment for his rape of Cassandra. See Epitome 6. 5–7 and ch. 12, n. 2.

29   Euripides' *Trojan Women* (produced in 415 B.C.) presents in the starkest manner the savagery of the Greeks toward the Trojans after the city was captured, savagery, Euripides says, senseless but endemic to war. In the play the women are awarded to the various chieftains as Apollodorus says that they were. (He may have followed Euripides.) Polyxena is slaughtered on Achilles' grave. Cassandra, crazed by rape by Locrian Ajax, comes on stage dressed for marriage, carrying a wedding torch and singing a hymn. But she also tells the uncomprehending women that she will be the cause of Agamemnon's death and prophesies Odysseus' suffering before he reaches home. Astyanax, the son of Hector, is thrown down from the walls of Troy by order of Odysseus so that the royal Trojan line may be extirpated. The central character of the play is the aged Hecuba, mother of unspeakable sorrow, whose sons were killed in the war one by one and whose husband, old Priam, was killed most brutally before her eyes by Neoptolemus at an altar in the palace. The queen of Troy will be Odysseus' slave. But the final, numbing blow for her is the killing of her grandson, Astyanax. In a cynical juxtaposition Euripides uses the taking away of the boy to his death and the return of the broken body to Hecuba to frame the scene in which Helen defends her life against Hecuba's accusation with Menelaus as judge. His original intention was to kill his former wife. She appears before him carefully dressed in beautiful clothing. Her argument (if such it can be called) begins by putting the blame for all the woe of war on Hecuba, who gave birth to Alexander in the first place. To conclude her defense she drops to her knees before Menelaus, embracing his legs and begging for her life. He mutters something about maybe killing her when they get back home and they exit from the stage.

Talthybius, the Greek herald, then brings the body of Astyanax on a shield to Hecuba. He is a gentle man who loathes this duty. Out of

feeling for Hecuba he stopped to wash the blood from the corpse before giving it to her. "O Greeks," she cries, "what were you afraid of
when you killed this child?" (1159–60). As she arranges the broken
limbs on the shield she speaks to the boy, to herself, or to no one at
all, remembering Astyanax alive as she looks at the ringlets on his
crushed head, his little hands now broken at the wrists. Her grief
drives her down upon the ground to beat it uselessly with her weak
old fists. Troy is burning to the ground and soldiers come to lead the
women away. She drags herself to her feet: "Shaking limbs, bear my
steps," she says; "move on, wretched woman, into a life of slavery
from this day" (1328–30).

Seneca also wrote a play which he called the *Trojan Women*, influenced by Euripides' tragedy, but quite different from it both in details
of plot and in mood. Ovid *Met.* 13. 399–575 narrates the aftermath of
Troy's fall, including the killing of Astyanax, and describes at length
the sacrifice of Polyxena at Achilles' tomb (demanded by Achilles'
ghost). He also relates Hecuba's metamorphosis into a bitch. It follows
upon her revenge on Polymestor, king of the Bistones in Thrace, across
the Hellespont from Troy, to whom she and Priam sent their young
son Polydorus for safekeeping at the outbreak of the war. Priam also
sent a large sum of gold to Polymestor at the same time. When Troy
fell Polymestor stabbed Polydorus to death, threw his body into the
sea, and it washed ashore at Troy. The Trojan women scream in horror
when they see it, but Hecuba makes not a sound: Grief has silenced
her voice and dried her eyes. Unmoving like a rock she stares now
at the ground, now at the sky, now at the face of Polydorus lying in
the water, now at his wounds, carefully at his wounds, and fortifies
herself with rage. She goes to Polymestor's palace, asks for an audience, and tells him that she has gold hidden away which she wants him
to give her son. He eagerly follows her to a secret place and there,
with Trojan women holding him, she gouges out his eyes with her
fingers, digging and scraping the empty sockets after the eyes are gone,
spattering herself with his blood. The Thracians chase her, hurling
spears and stones at her, but she bites at the rocks with a growling
sound, tries to speak, but barks instead.

On the sacrifice of Polyxena and Hecuba's revenge against Polymestor for the murder of Polydorus, see also Euripides' *Hecuba*, which
puts these two actions apparently lacking causal connection into one
play. One critic of the play sees its unity in the transformation of
Hecuba which the two disparate sections, so juxtaposed, present:
Hecuba accepts the sacrifice of Polyxena demanded by Achilles' ghost
with resignation, but then is transformed into a "fiend of vengeance"
at the death of Polydorus. See Conacher, *Euripidean Drama*, 152–53.

Although Conacher disagrees with this interpretation (which he has cited), his own is but a modification of it. For him the "moral disintegration" of Hecuba is best seen in her use and misuse of rhetoric (with which she argues for punishment for Polymestor). Hecuba, he says, "avenges one child by betraying the other," that is, by becoming the debased opposite of her noble daughter, Polyxena (Conacher, 164–65). More simply (and less cerebrally), one may say that Hecuba reaches the breaking point and breaks.

Dares the Phrygian *The Fall of Troy* 43 is one of those noted by Apollodorus who say that Helenus took Hecuba across the Chersonese. For other references to the aftermath of the defeat of Troy, see Frazer, *Apollodorus* 2. 240–41.

Odysseus advised the Greeks to stone Locrian Ajax to death for raping Cassandra (Pausanias 10. 31. 2), advice which, if followed, might have saved the Greeks from death and loss on the sea returning home (see Epitome 6. 5–7 and ch. 12, n. 2).

CHAPTER TWELVE

The Returns, Including Agamemnon's Death
and the Return of Menelaus
(Epitome 6)

EPIT. 6 After these things, Agamemnon and Menelaus quarrelled in the assembly, Menelaus maintaining that they should sail away while Agamemnon insisted that they remain and sacrifice to Athena. Diomedes, Nestor, and Menelaus all set sail at the same time. Diomedes and Nestor had a safe voyage, but Menelaus ran into a storm and lost all of his ships except five with which he arrived in Egypt.[1]

2 Amphilochus, Calchas, Leonteus, Podalirius, and Polypoetes left their ships in Ilium and traveled by land to Colophon. There they buried Calchas the seer. For it had been foretold that he would die if
3 he met a seer wiser than himself. They were guests of Mopsus, son of Apollo and Manto, who engaged in a contest with Calchas in the art of divination. When Calchas asked him how many figs were growing on a wild fig tree nearby, Mopsus answered, "Ten thousand and
4 a bushel and one fig over," and the answer turned out to be correct. Mopsus then asked Calchas how many pigs a pregnant sow was carrying in her womb and when was she due to give birth to them. When Calchas answered eight, Mopsus smiled and said, "Calchas, you fall short of true prophecy but I, who am the son of Apollo and Manto, have a wealth of keen vision. I say that there are not eight, as Calchas says, but nine in the womb, all males, and that they will be born tomorrow exactly at the sixth hour." When it turned out to be so, Calchas died of a broken heart and was buried at Notium.

5 After making a sacrifice, Agamemnon sailed away and put in at Tenedos. Thetis came and persuaded Neoptolemus to wait for two days and to make a sacrifice. He obeyed her, but the others set sail. They ran into a storm at Tenos which Athena begged Zeus to send upon
6 the Greeks, and many ships were lost. Athena also hurled a thunderbolt at Ajax's ship. As it broke into pieces he climbed on a rock and claimed that he had been saved despite Athena's intention. But Posei-

don split the rock with his trident and Ajax fell into the sea and drowned. When his body washed ashore at Myconos, Thetis buried it.[2]

7   The others were driven at night to Euboea.

Nauplius lit a fire signal on Mount Caphereus, and thinking that it was from some of those who had been saved, they put in for the shore and wrecked their ships on the Capherian rocks. Many men were

8   drowned. The reason for Nauplius' action was that Palamedes, his son by Clymene, daughter of Catreus, had been stoned to death through the plotting of Odysseus. When he learned this Nauplius sailed to the

9   Greeks and demanded recompense for the death of his son. But he came away without it, for they all refused him in order to gratify King Agamemnon, with whose help Odysseus killed Palamedes. Nauplius then sailed along the coast of Greece and persuaded the wives of the Greeks to commit adultery, Clytemnestra with Aegisthus, Aegialia

10   with Cometes, son of Sthenelus, and Meda, the wife of Idomeneus, with Leucus. (But Leucus killed her along with her daughter Clisithyra although she had taken refuge in a temple, and having caused ten cities

11   on Crete to revolt, became tyrant of them. When Idomeneus landed at Crete after the Trojan war, Leucus drove him out.) Nauplius had plotted all of this earlier and, learning later of the return of the Greeks to their native lands, he lit the signal fire on Mount Caphereus (now called Xylophagus). There the Greeks perished, making for shore in the belief that there was a harbor.[3]

12   Neoptolemus remained on Tenedos for two days at the suggestion of Thetis, then traveled by land to the country of the Molossians with Helenus. Phoenix died on the way and Neoptolemus buried him. He defeated the Molossians in battle and became their king. By Andro-

13   mache he had a son, Molossus. Helenus built a city in Molossia in which he lived and Neoptolemus gave him his mother Deidamia for a wife. When Peleus was banished from Phthia by the sons of Acastus

14   and died, Neoptolemus inherited his father's kingdom. After Orestes went insane Neoptolemus carried off his wife, Hermione, who had previously been betrothed to him at Troy. For this reason he was killed by Orestes at Delphi. | Some say, however, that he went to Delphi to demand recompense for his father's death from Apollo, stole offerings dedicated there, set the temple on fire, and was killed for this act by Machaereus the Phocian. | [4]

15   After their wanderings the Greeks sailed to and settled in various lands: Libya, Italy, Sicily, the islands near Spain and along the Sangarius River. There are also some who settled on Cyprus. Those who were shipwrecked at Caphereus were scattered in different directions: Guneus came to Libya; Antiphus, son of Thessalus, came to the land of the Pelasgians, which he gained control of and called Thessaly, and

Philoctetes came to the land of the Campanians in Italy. Phidippus settled with the Coans in Andrus, Agapenor on Cyprus, and others elsewhere.[5]

15a   Apollodorus and the rest say the following: In Libya, Guneus left his ships and went to the Cinyps River to live. Meges and Prothous lost their lives at Caphereus in Euboea with many others.[6] When Prothous was shipwrecked at Caphereus, the Magnesians with him were carried to Crete and settled there.

15b   After the sack of Ilium, Menestheus, Phidippus, and Antiphus, Elephenor's people, and Philoctetes all sailed together as far as Mimas. Menestheus then went to Melos and became king after Polyanax, the king there, died. Antiphus, son of Thessalus, came to the land of the Pelasgians which he took control of and called Thessaly. Phidippus with the Coans was driven first to Andros and then settled on Cyprus. Elephenor died at Troy and his people were shipwrecked in the Ionian Gulf and settled at Apollonia in Epirus. Tlepolemus' people put in at Crete, then were driven by winds to the islands of Spain and settled there.[7] The people of Protesilaus were castaways on Pellene near the plain of Canastrum. Philoctetes was driven to Campania in Italy and, after making war on the Lucanians, settled at Crimissa near Croton and Thurium. After he ceased wandering he built a temple to Apollo the Wanderer | to whom he also dedicated his bow, according to Euphorion | .

15c   The Navaethus is a river in Italy. It was so named, according to Apollodorus and the rest, because after the capture of Ilium, the daughters of Laomedon (who were sisters of Priam), Aethylla, Astyoche, and Medesicaste, being in that part of Italy with the rest of the female prisoners from the war and fearing slavery in Greece, set fire to the ships. As a result the river was called Navaethus ["Burning Ship"] and the women were called Nauprestides ["Ship-burners"]. The Greeks with them, having lost their ships, settled there.[8]

16   Demophon put in with a few ships at the land of the Thracian Bisaltians. Phyllis, the daughter of the king, fell in love with him and was given to him in marriage by her father with the kingdom as her dowry. But he wished to go away to his own country and, after much pleading and swearing to return, he departed.

    Phyllis accompanied him as far as the place called the Nine Roads and gave him a basket which she said contained an object sacred to

17   Mother Rhea. He was not to open it until he had given up hope of returning to her. Demophon went to Cyprus and settled there. When the time appointed for his return had passed Phyllis cursed Demophon and killed herself. Demophon opened the basket and was overcome with fear. He mounted his horse and spurred it on so violently that

the horse stumbled. He was thrown and fell upon his sword and so lost his life. Those with him settled on Cyprus.

18   Podalirius came to Delphi and asked the oracle where he might live. The god said that he should settle in a city where he would suffer no harm if the sky around it fell. He then settled in a region of the Carian Chersonese [southern Asia Minor] which is surrounded by a ring of mountains.

19   Amphilochus, son of Alcmaeon, who, according to some, arrived later at Troy, was driven by a storm to the home of Mopsus. Some say they fought in individual combat over the kingdom and killed each other.[9]

20   The Locrians returned to their own country with difficulty and, when Locris was afflicted by a plague three years later, they received an oracle telling them to propitiate Athena at Ilium and to send as suppliants two young girls each year for a thousand years. The first ones,
21   chosen by lot, were Periboea and Cleopatra. When they arrived at Troy, they were pursued by the inhabitants and ran into the temple. They did not approach the image of the goddess but swept the temple and sprinkled water on the floor. They did not go out of the temple
22   but had their hair cut off, wore only tunics, and went barefoot. When the first two died, the Locrians sent others. They entered the city at night in order not to be killed, as they would be if they were seen outside of the sacred area. The Locrians later sent babies with their nurses. They stopped sending the suppliants after a thousand years had passed and after the Phocian War.[10]

23   When Agamemnon arrived back in Mycenae with Cassandra, he was killed by Aegisthus and Clytemnestra. She gave him a tunic without sleeves or neck and murdered him while he was trying to put it on.
24   Aegisthus became king of Mycenae. They also killed Cassandra. Electra, one of Agamemnon's daughters, stole away her brother Orestes and gave him to Strophius the Phocian to rear. He brought him up with his son Pylades. When he was grown Orestes went to Delphi and asked the god if he should avenge himself on the murderers of his
25   father. The god gave him permission, so he went to Mycenae secretly and killed both his mother and Aegisthus. Shortly thereafter, afflicted with madness and pursued by the Furies, he came to Athens and was put on trial in the Areopagus | by the Furies, according to some, or by Tyndareus, as others say, or by Erigone daughter of Aegisthus and Clytemnestra, according to still others | . Since the votes at the trial were evenly divided he was acquitted.[11]

26   When Orestes asked the oracle how to be freed from his disease, the god replied that he could be healed if he went to the land of the Taurians and brought back from there the wooden image. The Tau-

rians were a part of the Scythians and they murdered strangers and cast their bodies into a sacred fire. This fire was in a sacred grove and was carried up from Hades through a rock. Orestes, therefore, went to the land of the Taurians with Pylades. They were discovered, caught, and led bound to Thoas the king, who sent both of them to the priestess. Recognized by his sister [Iphigenia] who was the priestess among the Taurians, Orestes carried away the wooden image and fled with her. He brought it to Athens, where it is now called the image of Tauropolus.[12] But some say that Orestes was carried by a storm to the island of Rhodes and that the image was enshrined in a wall in accordance with an oracle.[13] He went to Mycenae and there married his sister Electra to Pylades, while he himself married Hermione | or as some say, Erigone | and had a son, Tisamenus. He was bitten by a snake and died at Oresteum in Arcadia.[14]

Menelaus and five ships put in at Sunium, a promontory of Attica. Driven from there to Crete, he was again carried a great distance by winds and wandered through Libya, Phoenicia, Cyprus, and Egypt, collecting great sums of money as he went. | According to some he discovered Helen at the court of Proteus, king of Egypt. Until that time Menelaus possessed only an image of her made from clouds. | After wandering for eight years, he sailed home to Mycenae and found Orestes who had avenged his father's murder. He then went to Sparta and regained possession of his kingdom. He was made immortal by Hera and went with Helen to the Elysian Fields.[15]

NOTES
(Epitome 6)

1   The title of the chapter repeats that of the work in five books by Agias (or Hagias) of Troezen known as the *Nostoi* or *Returns*, which was part of the Epic Cycle. Proclus' very brief summary of the poem along with *testimonia* from various sources can be found in Hugh G. Evelyn-White, ed., *Hesiod, the Homeric Hymns and Homerica* (Cambridge, Mass. and London, 1936), 525, 527, 529. The genre was known to the Homer of the *Odyssey* (and that poem belongs to it), for the bard at Odysseus' palace sings of the "disastrous return of the Achaeans" (1. 326–27).

Nestor tells Telemachus at *Odyssey* 3. 130–94 that Athena was responsible for the quarrel between Agamemnon and Menelaus, who assembled the chieftains at the unheard of time of sunset when many were drunk. Menelaus wanted to sail at once, Agamemnon to sacrifice to Athena before sailing in order to placate Athena's wrath. The assembly split over the issue and the two sides quarrelled through the night. At dawn, half of the army stayed with Agamemnon; the other half, including Nestor, Menelaus, Diomedes, and Odysseus, put out to sea. They sailed to Tenedos where Odysseus turned around and took his fleet back to Agamemnon on the Trojan shore. Nestor, Diomedes, and Menelaus continued on. Diomedes reached Argos in four days, and Nestor sailed with a continuing fair wind to Pylos. He later heard, Nestor says, that Achilles' men, Philoctetes, Idomeneus, and Agamemnon, all arrived safely home, although Agamemnon's homecoming was hardly safe for him.

Nestor has no information about Odysseus but tells Telemachus (3. 276–300) that Menelaus lost his helmsman off Cape Sunium and stopped with his fleet to bury him. Back on board their ships and underway again, Menelaus and his crew ran into a storm off Malea (the promontory at the tip of the finger of the Peloponnese which forms the eastern coast of the Laconian Bay). The fleet was divided: Part was driven to Crete while Menelaus arrived with some ships in Egypt.

2   Two chieftains were lost at sea, Proteus tells Menelaus in Egypt (Homer *Odyssey* 4. 496–511), one of whom lives on somewhere (Odysseus), the other, Locrian Ajax, was driven by Poseidon (not Athena) onto the rocks of Gyrae (variously located off Myconos, Tenos, or southeast Euboea; see W. B. Stanford, ed., *The Odyssey of Homer*, 2 vols. [London and New York, 1959], 1. 281–82, comment on 4. 500–01). Despite Athena's hatred for him as the rapist of Cassandra, Locrian Ajax would have been saved but for his arrogant boasting. For Poseidon heard him and split with his trident the rock on which Ajax had found refuge. The part on which he was perched fell into the sea, carrying him with it, and he drowned.

Virgil *Aeneid* 1. 36–45 gives a version of the death of Locrian Ajax which agrees with Apollodorus'. Juno complains that she is forbidden to keep the Trojans from Italy while Pallas (i.e., Athena) burned up the Argive fleet and drowned the men because of the criminal lust of Ajax. Athena herself (Juno says) hurled one of Jove's thunderbolts, split their ships, and whipped up the sea with gale winds. Ajax she carried off in a whirlwind and impaled on a sharp rock where he gasped out flame from his pierced breast. (His death was thus a kind of rape and so a fitting punishment for his crime.)

Aeschylus created one of his most striking images in the herald's description of the violent storm which attacked the heroes returning from Troy: After a night of crashing waves, stormwind, and driving rain, the ships spinning out of control in darkness, those who survived saw in the morning sun the Aegean sea blossoming with corpses of

Achaeans and floating bits of ships (*Agamemnon* 648–60). See Frazer, *Apollodorus* 2. 246–47 for additional references to the death of Locrian Ajax.

3   Apollodorus first refers to Nauplius at 2. 1. 5. For the death of his son Palamedes, for which Nauplius sought vengeance, see Epitome 3. 6–8 and ch. 11, n. 3. Hyginus *Fabulae* 116 tells us that Nauplius killed any Greeks who made it to shore after their ships were wrecked on the rocks to which his treacherous beacon had lured them. Odysseus, alas, was carried by wind to Marathon (Hyginus says). In Euripides *Helen* 766–67 Menelaus mentions Nauplius' beacons as one of the hazards of the return from Troy. See also Seneca *Agamemnon* 557–78.

For another version of Idomeneus' return to Crete from Troy, see Frazer, *Apollodorus* 2. 394–404, appendix 12, "The Vow of Idomeneus."

4   After Alexander's death Helenus and Deiphobus contended for marriage with Helen. She chose Deiphobus and Helenus exiled himself to Mount Ida. He was captured by Odysseus and brought to the Greek camp in order to reveal the oracles which Calchas said he knew, the fulfillment of which was necessary for Troy's capture. One of them required Neoptolemus to join the Greek forces (Epitome 5. 9–10). Servius on *Aeneid* 2. 166 implies that Helenus was happy to betray the Trojans—concerning the Palladium at least—for he hated them because he was denied Helen. Apollodorus follows Agias, *Returns*, in saying that Thetis warned Neoptolemus to return home by land (see Evelyn-White, *Hesiod*, 527). But Servius (again on *Aeneid* 2. 166) says that Helenus warned Neoptolemus of the shipwreck at sea awaiting the returning Greeks because of their desecration of the Palladium and urged him to travel home overland.

Neoptolemus was awarded Andromache after the fall of Troy (Epitome 5. 23). She then accompanied Helenus and Neoptolemus on the latter's homeward journey. At Virgil *Aeneid* 3. 294–336 Aeneas finds, much to his surprise, that Helenus is married to Andromache and rules the Greek city Buthrotum (in northwest Greece on the coast of Epirus, opposite modern Corfu; the area was also known as the land of the Molossians, the way by which Apollodorus refers to it). Andromache tells Aeneas how this strange state of affairs came about: After she gave birth to Neoptolemus' child, as his slave, not his wife, he left her and went to steal away Hermione from Orestes, putting her (Andromache) in the hands of Helenus, also his slave. Orestes killed Neoptolemus out of jealousy and maddened by the Furies (for the murder of his mother) at Achilles' altar at Delphi (see Servius on *Aeneid* 3. 332). At Neoptolemus' death Helenus acquired a part of his kingdom. But Servius on *Aeneid* 3. 297 begins further back than

Andromache does, saying that Neoptolemus, dying at Delphi at the hands of Orestes, willed Andromache and his kingdom to Helenus in gratitude for the earlier warning Helenus gave him to return from Troy by land and not by sea.

The marriage of Helenus to Deidamia, Neoptolemus' mother (3. 13. 8), hardly makes sense and, as Frazer, *Apollodorus* 2. 251 notes, was apparently not mentioned by any other writer.

The feud between Peleus and the family of Acastus may have originated in Astydamia's false accusation of him to her husband, Acastus, when Peleus rebuffed her advances. A particularly nasty woman, Astydamia told Peleus' wife that her husband was going to marry a daughter of Acastus, hearing which the poor woman hanged herself (3. 13. 3; see also ch. 7, n. 35). Euripides *Trojan Women* 1126–30 says that Neoptolemus left Troy hurriedly for home, taking Andromache with him, because he had received word that Acastus had exiled Peleus.

See Dictys of Crete *The Trojan War* 6. 7–9 for a much longer version of this story.

The story of the marriage of Hermione, first to Orestes and then to Neoptolemus, and the death of the latter, is somewhat tangled. Virgil's narration of these marriages (in *Aeneid* 3) was described above, although Virgil omits the detail, given by Apollodorus, that Hermione was betrothed to Neoptolemus while the latter was at Troy. See also Ovid *Heroides* 8, Hermione to Orestes, begging him to rescue her from Neoptolemus who has carried her off.

Homer *Odyssey* 4. 1–9 relates that Menelaus betrothed Hermione to Neoptolemus at Troy and conducted their wedding when he returned to Sparta. At Euripides *Andromache* 966–81, Orestes tells Hermione that Menelaus promised her to him before he went to Troy, but while there he promised her to Neoptolemus if he would capture Troy. When Neoptolemus returned Orestes begged him, he says, to give up his claim to Hermione and let him marry her, since his mental and social condition (due to his matricide) made marriage with someone outside the family difficult. Neoptolemus insulted him for the murder of his mother and mocked his madness. Beaten down, suffering, yet he endured and went away against his will without her. Later at Delphi, however (1085–1165), he persuades the Delphians to kill Neoptolemus who, he tells them, has come to rob the temple. (He had in fact come to make restitution to Apollo for earlier demanding recompense from the god for his father's death. See also 49–55 and Euripides *Orestes* 1654–57.) At the altar of the god a band of men attacks him, he fights furiously, but a Delphian man (not Orestes) finally kills him.

Pindar, writing some sixty years before Euripides' *Andromache*, gives a version of Neoptolemus' death in one poem which he "cleanses" in another. In *Paean* 6. 109–20 the poet says that Apollo swore that Neoptolemus would never arrive happily home from Troy, nor live to old age, because he murdered Priam at the altar in his courtyard (see Epitome 5. 21 and ch. 11, n. 28). The god killed him while he was wrangling with attendants over proper dues to be paid, in his (Apollo's) own precinct beside the *omphalos* ("navel" of the earth). Pindar apparently offended the Aeginetans with his poem, for Neoptolemus, a great-grandson of Aeacus, was one of their heroes. In *Nem.* 7, written for an Aeginetan victor and possibly to be dated to 485 B.C., Pindar includes a "passage intended as a palinode to soothe their [the Aeginetans'] feelings" (Lewis Richard Farnell, *Critical Commentary to the Works of Pindar* [Amsterdam, 1965], 294): Neoptolemus came to Delphi with good will—and lies buried there—after he sacked Priam's city. He went there to sacrifice to the god the first fruits of the spoils from Troy. There he got involved in a fight over the flesh of the sacrifice and a man drove his sword in him. The hospitable Delphians were deeply saddened. But his death there was proper, for it was fated that a descendant of Aeacus be within the ancient grove beside the temple and there dwell as a divine overseer of processions and sacrifices to heroes (33–47).

These accounts of Neoptolemus' death at Delphi should serve to emphasize once again the freedom Greek and Roman authors used in drawing upon their mythology.

For variants and additional details about Neoptolemus' return from Troy to his death, see the very full notes in Frazer, *Apollodorus* 2. 250–57.

5   Epitome 6. 15 a–c do not occur in the text of the Epitome but are taken from the *Scholia on Lycophron* (902, 911 and 921 respectively) by Johannes Tzetzes, the twelfth-century A.D. Byzantine polymath. These paragraphs narrate more fully the wanderings described in Epitome 6. 15 which precedes them, and Frazer, *Apollodorus* 2. 257 conjectures that Tzetzes drew upon the full text of Apollodorus rather than upon the Epitome.

6   There is a lacuna in Tzetzes' text after the sentence, "Meges . . . others." Meges, Prothous, and the others (unnamed) who lost their lives at Capbereus were, no doubt, lured on to the rocks there by the beacon of Nauplius (Epitome 6. 7–11).

7   Menestheus, the Athenian chieftain (Epitome 3. 11), took no share of the spoils of Troy, having come with Acamas and Demophon, sons of Theseus, for the sole purpose of recovering Theseus' mother, Aethra, if we may believe Arctinus of Miletus, author of the *Sack of Ilium* (a poem in the Epic Cycle), or rather the Scholiast on Euripides

Trojan Women 31, who quotes him (see Evelyn-White, *Hesiod*, 523).
Aethra went to Troy with Helen (see ch. 9, n. 10). Demophon and
Acamas did in fact take away their grandmother after the capture of
Troy (Epitome 5. 22). But Menestheus, Apollodorus here tells us, after
the war went to the island of Melos and became king. Why did he
not return to Athens? Demophon went to Cyprus (Epitome 6. 16–17).
It was then left to Acamas to escort his grandmother back to Athens.
The "returns" of the Greek chieftains, with the exception of the more
important ones, sound more like a Diaspora in the Apollodorus-Tzetzes
account. Such a resettling of Greeks in the Mediterranean world after
the Trojan War (if such in fact happened) would have helped to lay
the groundwork for the national Greek consciousness which arose
centuries later.

There is a lacuna in Tzetzes' text after the sentence, "Tlepolemus'
. . . there."

8   An incident similar to the ship-burning of the captive Trojan
women occurs in the *Aeneid* (5. 604–771) while Aeneas and the men
celebrate in Sicily the anniversary of the death of his father, Anchises.
Instigated by Juno and weary of endless voyaging, the Trojan women
set fire to the ships, all but four of which are burned up. Since there
are too few vessels for all to sail in, a decision is made that those who
wish may stay behind and some do so, as here in the Apollodorus-
Tzetzes text.

9   At Epitome 6. 2–3 Apollodorus says that Amphilochus and others
traveled by land from Troy to Colophon where they were guests of
the seer Mopsus. Colophon is near the coast of Asia Minor, north and
slightly east of the island of Samos. In a note to the present passage
Frazer, *Apollodorus* 2. 265–67, refers to the tradition that Amphilochus
and Mopsus went to Cilicia where they founded the town of Mallus
(in the northeast corner of the Mediterranean). Pausanias 1. 34. 3
confirms this tradition by saying that the oracle of Amphilochus at
Mallus was the most infallible one of his time (second century A.D.).
Frazer, *Apollodorus* 2. 265–67, discusses the controversy over which
of the two Amphilochi was the oracular one.

10   The Locrian plague was probably due to Locrian Ajax who, at
the time of the capture of Troy, pulled Cassandra from a statue of
Athena to which she was clinging and raped her (Epitome 5. 22). Ajax
died for this crime (Epitome 6. 5–7 and n. 2), but the Locrians apparently continued to pay for it.

11   The story of the return of Agamemnon, his murder, Orestes'
revenge and its aftermath is incorporated in or the subject of more
surviving Greek literature than any other myth. It was told in Agias'

Returns, a poem in the Epic Cycle (lost, but summarized by Proclus; see Evelyn-White, *Hesiod,* 527).

As a theme in counterpoint to the events of Homer's *Odyssey* and announced by Zeus at the very beginning of the poem (1. 28–43), the tragic return of Agamemnon both creates much of the poem's dramatic tension and gives immediacy to it. For as it appears in the *Odyssey,* it is a completed action which is known to the major characters (for whom it has different meanings) and against which the return of Odysseus unfolds. Odysseus-Agamemnon, Penelope-Clytemnestra, Telemachus-Orestes and the suitors-Aegisthus are the pairs whose members are or ought to be like or unlike each other: Telemachus should be like Orestes and do to the suitors what Orestes did to Aegisthus (*Odyssey* 1. 298–302; 3. 193–200, 247–310; cf. 4. 514–37). Penelope is no Clytemnestra, the ghost of Agamemnon tells Odysseus on his journey to the underworld, or at least he hopes for his sake that she is not: One can never be too careful (11. 385–456).

The suitors both are and are not like Aegisthus: They are only potential usurpers. No one of them can get past Odysseus' banquet hall and into Penelope's bed, as Aegisthus got into Clytemnestra's bed, because of Penelope's fidelity to the absent Odysseus. But neither does Penelope have the hatred for Odysseus which Clytemnestra has for Agamemnon because of the murder of their daughter Iphigenia (see ch. 11, n. 10). The suitors have no particular grudge against Odysseus except perhaps for his absence and the deaths of their relatives in the Trojan War. Aegisthus, however, sought vengeance against Agamemnon for the horrible murder of his brothers by Agamemnon's father, Atreus, who served the children as a meal to their (and Aegisthus') father, Thyestes (Epitome 2. 10–14, ch. 10, n. 6, and Aeschylus *Agamemnon* 1577–1611). Finally, Odysseus proves himself to be unlike Agamemnon by returning secretly to his palace disguised as a beggar rather than openly and in pomp (Aeschylus *Agamemnon* 782/3–957), kills the usurpers, re-establishes himself in his kingdom, and puts it in order (*Odyssey* 22–24). His triumph, in fact, lends a happy outcome to the return of Agamemnon long after the fact, for Agamemnon is gladdened when the suitors arrive in Hades and he hears the cause of their death. He momentarily forgets his own treacherous murder as he vicariously enjoys Odysseus' victory over the men who had sought to murder him. Even his faith in women is partially restored because of Penelope (*Odyssey* 24. 98–202). The account here given of the Agamemnon theme in the *Odyssey* is only a sketch and by no means conveys the skill with which Homer has orchestrated it into his poem.

Pindar *Pyth.* 11. 17–37 gives a compact rendition of the myth in twenty-one lines (of a sixty-four line poem): Orestes' nurse, Arsinoë, snatched him from death at the very moment Clytemnestra was murdering Agamemnon and Cassandra with an axe. The poet asks: Was it the sacrifice of Iphigenia which gnawed at her and incited such wrath, or did the nights she spent yielding and docile in another man's bed lead her astray? (He does not answer the question, at least not directly.) Agamemnon, returning home victorious, died and also caused the death of Cassandra, after he had burned and plundered Troy for Helen. But Orestes came to Strophius, who lived at the foot of Parnassus, and in time killed his mother and Aegisthus. Pindar gives no more. The relation of the myth to the poem has been much discussed, but most ably and correctly by David C. Young, *Three Odes of Pindar* (Leiden, 1968), 1–26.

Aeschylus' *Oresteia*, produced in 458 B.C. and the only dramatic trilogy to survive antiquity, presents the most complex literary version of the myth extant. In the first play, the *Agamemnon*, Agamemnon returns victorious from Troy and is killed by Clytemnestra with the complicity of her lover, Aegisthus. Her motive is his sacrifice of their daughter Iphigenia at Aulis ten years earlier to appease Artemis and end contrary winds preventing the expedition from sailing to Troy (see Epitome 3. 21–22 and ch. 11, n. 10). Aegisthus' motive is vengeance for the banquet which Agamemnon's father, Atreus, served to his father, Thyestes, and which consisted of the flesh of Thyestes' children, Aegisthus' brothers (see Epitome 2. 10–14, ch. 10, n. 6, and Aeschylus *Agamemnon* 1577–1611).

In the second play, the *Choephoroe* ("*Libation Bearers*"), Orestes returns to Argos from Phocis where he was taken as a child to Strophius to be reared (Apollodorus here, Pindar *Pyth.* 11. 34–37, and Aeschylus *Agamemnon* 877–86). Apollo has commanded him to avenge his father's death by killing Aegisthus and Clytemnestra (*Choephoroe* 269–305, 555–59, 900–02, 1029–32) which he does (in that order) and is almost at once set upon by Furies, both avengers of matricide and other shedding of kindred blood and symbols of madness (1048–62).

In the third play, the *Eumenides* ("*Kindly-Minded Ones*"), Orestes has taken refuge from the Furies (who form the Chorus of the play) at the Altar of Apollo at Delphi, although they remain close by. Apollo puts them to sleep, enabling him to escape from them, and instructs him to go to Athens where he will be tried on the Areopagus for matricide. The ghost of Clytemnestra awakens the Furies, who find Orestes gone and quarrel with Apollo. He defends Orestes for the matricide which has brought the Furies upon him, since he was avenging Clytemnestra's murder of her husband. (That murder was not the shedding of kindred blood and so does not interest the Furies.) At 235 the scene changes to Athens where Orestes is tried for murder. The Furies prosecute; Apollo defends. Judges and jury are twelve Athenians (following the Athenian practice of combining these two functions). The trial initiates Athens' highest court, the Areopagus, meeting on the "hill of Ares" (681–710; but see ch. 8, n. 3 for a different tradition of the origin of the Areopagus). Athena votes with the jury and since she is male-born (from Zeus) she casts her vote, she says, for the male, for she is male-oriented in everything except marriage, and to her, Clytemnestra's murder of Agamemnon is a more serious crime than Orestes' murder of Clytemnestra (734–43). Since the twelve jurors are evenly divided (752–53), Athena's vote for Orestes decides the case.

The Furies, whose rights have been overridden, threaten vengeance until Athena persuades them to become Eumenides, "Kindly-Minded Ones," goddesses of Persuasion, and promises them the power to make Athenian households flourish (895) and in general to mediate peace and prosperity to Athens (902–1020).

This simple synopsis does not convey the interweaving of themes and imagery, interdependent and interacting throughout the trilogy, to form a web of literature as complex and difficult as any other in extant Greek literature. A list of themes would include love versus hate; conflict between male and female and between Olympian (patriarchal) and native or earlier earth (chthonic) divinities (matriarchal); conflict between right and right; learning by suffering; the transformation of passionate, family vendetta into public, communal, and dispassionate justice; the progressive evolution of (Athenian) society into a more humane form; and celebration of Athens. The image which informs the work (and which is also a theme) is that of a sacrifice, according to Anne Lebeck, *The Oresteia* (Cambridge, Mass., 1971), 7 and *passim*. A good place for the Greekless reader to begin is Richmond Lattimore's Introduction to his translation of the *Oresteia* in the Chicago series.

The synopsis also does not touch upon two major problems of interpretation which, most simply stated, are the cause(s) of the events in the trilogy (presented in the *Agamemnon*) and the resolution of those events (presented in the *Eumenides*). Aeschylus is a brilliant poet and was famous in antiquity for his spectacular dramaturgy. But as a theologian attempting to justify god's ways to men—and most critics agree that the subject of the trilogy is human justice derived from Zeus—he fails. He fails because being Greek he viewed "reality" (the sum of his perceptions) as definable in terms of cause and effect relations. His thought system (the Greek language) presented and articulated reality as a system of cause and effect. As Lebeck says in *The Oresteia*, "The first drama of the trilogy is marked by a concern with causality. It attempts to dispel the darkness that surrounds events, making them appear a series of unrelated points rather than a line whose course is as unswerving as it is predictable. When the moment of retribution comes at the end of the drama, every causal factor falls into place and is seen as part of a divine plan" (25). The "concern with causality" is indeed there. But, alas, "every causal factor" does not ". . . [fall] into place." Surely every reader of the plays will agree that Aeschylus saw the problem as deeply as his thought system allowed him to: Cause and effect are the basis for the nature of things. Break the relation between cause and effect and chaos results. Yet conflict arises between human beings, not conflict of right against wrong, but of power against power, right against right (*Choephoroe* 461). Continue the cause and effect relation in these conflicts in an eye-for-an-eye and a tooth-for-a-tooth mode ("the principle of like for like," Lebeck, *The Oresteia*, 14) and soon everyone is eyeless and toothless. Interrupt the cause and effect relationship, however, and the world, physical, social, moral, will fall into chaos. But Aeschylus could not resolve the issue. He could have resolved it with the concepts of grace and faith ("For by grace are ye saved through faith") as St. Paul resolved it: see the book of Romans in the *New Testament* (the quotation is from Ephesians 2:8). But Aeschylus could not adopt these concepts because they were not part of his intellectual and/or religious tradition and because to do so would have meant throwing cause and effect out the window.

The problem is brought into sharpest focus in the description of the sacrifice of Iphigenia in the *parodos* ("first choral ode") of the *Agamemnon*. Analysis of it begins with the attempt to determine the reason(s) for the sacrifice. The description of it is preceded by a simile of vultures wheeling above their robbed nest, screaming for their stolen young, and then by reference to an event which occurred at Aulis: Twin eagles in sight of the army swooped down upon a pregnant hare and devoured her and her unborn young. That event is read as an omen by the seer Calchas. It angers the goddess Artemis who in return changes the winds to detain at Aulis the Greek expedition bound for Troy to recover Helen. It is on the point of disintegrating when Calchas then divines the solution: Artemis will be appeased if Agamemnon's daughter, Iphigenia, is sacrificed to expiate the crime of the eagles. (Artemis is the goddess of animals and of the young and is thus revolted by such animal savagery—although it occurs constantly in the natural world.)

If Aeschylus had written the *parodos* simply thus we would question his intelligence (as Denys Page has done in his Introduction to John Dewar Denniston and Denys Page, eds., *Aeschylus: Agamemnon* [Oxford, 1957], xv: "... the faculty of acute or profound thought is not among his [Aeschylus'] gifts"). But Aeschylus is much more complex: past, present, and future seem to be linked in the *parodos* by cause and effect, but not in a conventional, chronological way. It is here, though, that one questions him most seriously. Lebeck, perhaps the most brilliant American critic of the *Oresteia*, attempts to elucidate simile, omen, and the sacrifice of Iphigenia but with only partial success. The vulture simile "reflects the paradox of right and wrong that runs throughout the trilogy. Paris is guilty of stealing Helen; Agamemnon is no less guilty" (9), i.e., because he has taken a child (Iphigenia) from its parent. But the crimes of Paris and Agamemnon cannot be equated or placed side by side in parataxis: The first was freely committed for the benefit of its perpetrator and made him happy (if only temporarily); the second was caused by the first and grimly carried out with great personal loss after much agonizing.

"The simile and the omen showed that just vengeance can become unjust transgression. They also illustrated the principle of like for like" (Lebeck, *The Oresteia*, 14). Whose transgression (in addition to Paris')? Agamemnon's? It has not as yet occurred. "An omen of eagles devouring a helpless creature stood for Agamemnon's vengeance and transgression" (15). If the omen is a symbol for Agamemnon's future transgressions (the deaths of Iphigenia and of innocents at Troy) can it at the same time be a cause for the death of Iphigenia, which becomes punishment in advance of Agamemnon's later crimes at Troy? This makes no sense. Lebeck's acknowledgement of Aeschylus' concern with causality was noted above. But something has gone wrong. Richness of imagery can obscure incoherence of thought, but it cannot serve as a substitute for coherence of thought.

Again, "In Calchas' prophecy Artemis requires payment for a transgression of which the omen is a symbol (135–137, 144). . . . By demanding the sacrifice of Iphigenia she brings about the sacrifice of Agamemnon . . ." (Lebeck, *The Oresteia*, 22). And again, one must ask, what is the transgression "of which the omen is a symbol" and why must Agamemnon be sacrificed? He dies because of Iphigenia's death—or so his murderess, Clytemnestra, says (*Agamemnon* 1377–81, 1412–21, 1431–33, 1521–29)—which was itself *caused* by an omen which is a *symbol* of his transgression before it happens.

A clue comes: "In the *Oresteia* man's fate is determined by two principles: first, like for like, and second, the belief that an impious father begets a son destined to commit a kindred impiety. . . . Thus on the level of imagery Agamemnon's death duplicates the two crimes for which he is responsible" (Lebeck, *The Oresteia*, 33). What two crimes? The answer is that "In the simile and omen of the *parodos*, the child victims of Agamemnon and Atreus are simultaneously evoked.... Through the image of mourning for lost young, the wrong which Agamemnon suffers (theft of Helen) calls up both the wrong which he inflicts on Clytemnestra (murder of Iphigenia) and that which his father inflicted upon the children of Thyestes. The simile is a prelude to the omen" (Lebeck, *The Oresteia*, 33). (But to repeat: The wrong which Agamemnon "inflicts on Clytemnestra" is caused by the omen.) To continue: "The death of the hare and her unborn young symbolizes first the destruction of Troy and all within it.... Thus the omen includes not only the destruction of Troy and the sacrifice of Iphigenia but the banquet served Thyestes as well. This is the three-fold significance of the murdered young" (33–34). Finally, Calchas sees that the omen means "that Artemis is angered by the crime of Atreus, that by this crime the normal course of nature was disturbed[.] In order that Agamemnon atone for the guilt of his father she demands 'another sacrifice' and renders him guilty of his father's crime" (35).

It is true that the banquet of Thyestes weighs as a cause of doom in the *Agamemnon*, in lines spoken by Cassandra (1090–92, 1095–97, 1183–97, and 1217–26), by the Chorus (1242–45, in response to Cassandra's insistent revelation of her knowledge of the past crimes of the house of Atreus), by Clytemnestra (1500–04), and by Aegisthus (1577–1611), for whom Agamemnon's murder (which he did not perform) avenges that monstrous banquet. But these lines, it should be observed, are far from the *parodos* where the simile, omen, and sacrifice of Iphigenia, which set the trilogy in motion, are described.

Thus in a trilogy "marked by a concern with causality" (Lebeck, *The Oresteia*, 25) what we have is this: Zeus (= justice in the order of things) and Artemis (fitted somehow into justice in the order of things) punish Agamemnon (1) for his father's crime (this is sufficiently ortho-dox Greek theology); and (2) for the sacrifice of Iphigenia and for the deaths of innocents at Troy. But the sacrifice of Iphigenia is caused by Artemis' anger at eagles killing and eating a pregnant hare. Taken literally, this equates the life of a hare with the life of a human being. This concept of deity (which is man-made in every culture under the sun) is crazy. Taken symbolically, the omen of the eagles in Lebeck's interpretation refers to Atreus' crime for which Agamemnon shall pay. This is fair enough, if true; but a symbol which justifies a punishment for a crime causes that crime (Iphigenia's death). At the same time the symbol (the omen of the eagles) stands for crimes-to-come at Troy, as punishment for which Iphigenia's death is demanded in advance.

Lebeck, it should be said, is representing Aeschylus faithfully, and with extreme penetration, except, perhaps, in her insistence that the omen of the eagles is to be linked to the banquet of Thystes. The problems lie with Aeschylus.

Eduard Fraenkel, ed., *Aeschylus: Agamemnon*, 3 vols. (Oxford, 1950), seems to have assessed the problem correctly (see 2. 96–99): "... we are not told anywhere in the ode [*parodos*] why the wrath of Artemis is directed against the Atridae [= Agamemnon and Menelaus, sons of Atreus]." He repeats what every classicist knows: "... the poet does not want us to take into account any feature of a tradition which he does not mention" (97). "Aeschylus ... makes it clear [in the *parodos*] that all the evil that is to befall Agamemnon has its first origin in his own arbitrary decision" (99). No payment for Atreus' crime here, all mention of which Fraenkel omits (including Atreus' refusal to sacrifice to Artemis the golden lamb: Epitome 2. 10–12). Aeschylus solves the problem (which is that the *parodos* gives no indication why Artemis is angry with the Atridae) by boldly overriding coherence with high-flown poetry (99).

The problem of the resolution (the freeing of Orestes) in the *Eumenides* is that it is arbitrary. Apollo's argument that Orestes did not kill his parent because the true parent is the father (657–66), although he can point to Athena as living proof, is still specious. Athena breaks the jurors' tie in favor of Orestes because she favors the male (734–43). Thus the foundation of justice in Athens in the court of the Areopagus.

Aeschylus in the *Oresteia* used a myth to create a myth for Athens. His myth had the task all myth has, "... of giving an historical intention a natural justification, and making contingency appear eternal. ... What the world supplies to myth is an historical reality, defined ... by the way in which men have produced or used it; and what myth gives in return is a *natural* image of this reality" (Roland Barthes, the essay entitled "Myth Today" in *Mythologies* [New York, 1972], 142). The Athenian audience no doubt returned home from viewing the *Oresteia* confirmed in the belief, as many have often been confirmed, that the *ad hoc*, random particulars of their history were part of a system, divinely ordained.

Euripides and Sophocles both wrote plays entitled *Electra*, the basis for their plots being the return of Orestes to Argos to avenge the death of his father. Euripides' *Electra* is thought to have been written and produced prior to Sophocles' *Electra*, the former dated ca. 418, the latter ca. 413 (see J. H. Kells, ed., *Sophocles: Electra* [Cambridge, Eng., 1973], 1, n. 2, in agreement with T. B. L. Webster, whom he cites). The issue is by no means closed, however, and D. J. Conacher, *Eurip-*

idean Drama: Myth, Theme and Structure (Toronto, 1967), 202, n. 9 thinks that Sophocles' play was prior to Euripides'.

From their titles it is obvious that both playwrights have sought to focus attention on the sister of Orestes who has remained near (Euripides) or at (Sophocles) home for many years, waiting for Orestes' return and longing to avenge their father's murder.

Other plays using the Agamemnon myth: Euripides' *Orestes*, his *Andromache* (touching tangentially on it: Orestes rescues Andromache from the clutches of Menelaus) and Seneca's *Agamemnon*.

In the twentieth century the myth has particularly attracted playwrights, *viz.*, Eugene O'Neill, *Mourning Becomes Electra*; T. S. Eliot, *The Family Reunion*; Jean Giraudoux, *Electre*; and Jean Paul Sartre, *The Flies*. (See Philip Mayerson, *Classical Mythology in Literature, Art, and Music* [Waltham, Mass. and Toronto, 1971], 433–36 for other works.) Michael Cacoyannis filmed a version of Euripides' *Electra* in 1963 with Irene Pappas in the title role.

12   Orestes' final release from the Furies, gained by bringing the wooden image of Artemis from the land of the Taurians (in the Crimea), is the subject of Euripides' *Iphigenia in Tauris*. In Aeschylus' *Eumenides* Orestes was acquitted of his mother's murder in a trial on the Areopagus. Euripides produced a kind of harmony between his own and Aeschylus' earlier version of the myth by making the divided Athenian jurors of the *Eumenides* the Furies themselves. Those who did not accept the verdict continue to pursue him (*Iphigenia in Tauris* 939–75; see Cedric H. Whitman, *Euripides and the Full Circle of Myth* [Cambridge, Mass., 1974], 26–27).

In one version of the myth of Iphigenia she was not sacrificed at Aulis but magically carried to Tauris by Artemis where she became the goddess' priestess (see Epitome 3. 21–22 and ch. 11, n. 10). As such in Euripides' play she presides over the sacrifice of all strangers who come to the land of the Taurians. Orestes and Pylades arrive there to retrieve the image of the goddess (kept in the temple where Iphigenia serves the goddess and where the human sacrifices occur), are captured by Taurian herdsmen, and brought to Iphigenia to be sacrificed. An elaborate recognition scene between brother and sister, each of whom supposed the other dead, occupies the middle third of the play (*Iphigenia in Tauris*, 472–935). In the final third (979 to the end) Orestes, Iphigenia and Pylades by a ruse remove the image of Artemis from the temple to the seashore and then escape from Tauris.

Anne Pippin Burnett, *Catastrophe Survived* (Oxford, 1971), 48, observes that the play "tells a story of two fraternal pairs, one divine and one mortal, a group of four who have so assorted themselves that the brother god, Apollo, is the patron of the mortal brother, Orestes, while his sister, Artemis, stands in the same relation to the mortal sister, Iphigeneia. The final achievement of the play is double, as each brother rescues his sister in a mirroring pair of actions that are simultaneous and interdependent. . . ."

The fine writing on this play continues in Cedric H. Whitman's comment that it is "a tale of divine power roused and active, but somehow stayed; of tragedy suffered, but rounded into peace" (*Euripides and the Full Circle of Myth* [Cambridge, Mass., 1974], 2–3).

13   There is a lacuna in the text after the clause, "But . . . Rhodes."

14   For the marriage of Pylades to Electra, see Euripides *Electra* 1249–50; *Iphigenia in Tauris* 695–99, 716–18, 915, 922; and *Orestes* 1658–59. As to the marriage of Orestes and Hermione, see Epitome 6. 14 and n. 4.

The body of Orestes was buried at Tegea in Arcadia. The Spartans were once told by an oracle that in order to be victorious in war with the Tegeans they must recover Orestes' bones. A certain Spartan named Lichas discovered that they were buried in a blacksmith's shop. The blacksmith told Lichas that in digging a well in his shop he had dug up a coffin ten feet long. When he opened it he learned, to his surprise, that the body had been ten feet long, too (Herodotus 1. 67–68).

15   Menelaus sailed in company with Nestor as far as Sunium (the tip of Attica) where his helmsman suddenly died. Menelaus stopped to bury him and Nestor sailed on. Back at sea after the funeral, Menelaus and his fleet were driven by storm winds to Crete where all but five ships were wrecked on reefs. Those five sailed on and eventually came to Egypt where Menelaus made a large fortune and wandered (probably trading) among foreigners. So Nestor tells Telemachus (Homer *Odyssey* 3. 276–302).

For Menelaus' discovery of Helen at the court of Proteus in Egypt (the subject of Euripides' *Helen*), see Epitome 3. 5 and ch. 11, n. 2. Homer *Odyssey* 3. 303–12 says that Aegisthus ruled Mycenae for seven years after he (*sic*) killed Agamemnon. In the eighth year Orestes came back from Athens and killed Aegisthus. (In the tragedians Orestes returns from Phocis.) On the very day that Orestes held a funeral-feast for Aegisthus and Clytemnestra (Homer has omitted direct reference to Orestes' matricide), Menelaus returned, ships laden with riches.

The sea god Proteus in Egypt prophesies to Menelaus that he is fated not to die in Argos. Rather, the gods will send him to the Elysian Fields where there is no snow, but winters mild and rainstorms never. There soft zephyr-winds from the ocean blow continually to refresh mankind. This life is Menelaus' because he married Helen and thus is Zeus' son-in-law (Homer *Odyssey* 4. 561–69). Notice that Homer does not mention Helen as Menelaus' companion in the Elysian Fields. Euripides *Helen* 1666–77 is ambiguous: The Dioscuri, Helen's brothers, say that she will be called a goddess and will share with them men's libations and hospitality. The gods have destined wandering Menelaus to dwell in the Island of the Blessed.

CHAPTER THIRTEEN

The Return and Death of Odysseus
(Epitome 7)

EPIT. 7 | Odysseus, as some say, wandered through Libya, or as others say, through Sicily, or as yet others say, over the ocean or over the Tyrrhenian Sea. |

2   After he sailed from Ilium he put in at Ismaṛus, a city of the Cicones, captured it in a battle and plundered it, sparing only Maro, a priest of Apollo.[1] The Cicones living on the mainland learned of this and came

3   in arms against him. After losing six men from each ship, he put to sea and fled. He landed in the country of the Lotus-eaters and sent some of the crew to learn about the inhabitants. A pleasant fruit called lotus grew in the land which made anyone who tasted it forget everything. After tasting the lotus the men stayed there. When Odysseus realized what had happened, he made the rest of his men wait and forced those who had tasted the lotus to return to the ships. He then sailed away to the land of the Cyclopes.[2]

4   Leaving the other ships at the island nearby, he approached the land of the Cyclopes in his own and went ashore with twelve companions. They entered a cave near the water, taking with them a skin full of wine, which Maro had given to Odysseus. The cave was inhabited by Polyphemus, son of Poseidon and a nymph Thoosa, a huge

5   wild cannibal with one eye in his forehead. They started a fire, sacrificed several of the kids, and ate them. The Cyclops returned, driving his flock into the cave, and put a huge stone over the entrance. When

6   he saw the men he ate some of them. Odysseus gave him a taste of Maro's wine. After he drank he asked for more and, after drinking a second time, he asked Odysseus his name. When he said that his name was Nobody, Polyphemus threatened to eat them all and Nobody last of all, that being the guest-gift he promised him. But he became drunk

7   from the wine and fell asleep. Odysseus found a stake lying in the cave and with four companions sharpened one end of it, heated it in

the fire, and blinded the Cyclops. When Polyphemus cried out, the neighboring Cyclopes came and asked who was harming him. He said "Nobody," and they, thinking that he meant that he was being harmed
8 by nobody, went away. When the sheep sought their usual pastures, Polyphemus opened the cave and, positioning himself at the entrance, spread out his hands and felt over them. But Odysseus tied three rams together, hid underneath the belly of the middle one and passed out of the cave with the flock. He then released his companions from the other sheep and drove the animals to the ships. As he sailed away, he shouted to the Cyclops that he was Odysseus and that he had
9 escaped out of his hands. A seer had foretold to the Cyclops that he would be blinded by Odysseus and, hearing the name, he grabbed up rocks and hurled them into the sea. The ship barely escaped them. From that time on Poseidon was enraged at Odysseus.[3]

10 Putting out to sea with all of his ships Odysseus came to the island of Aeolia, the king of which was Aeolus. Zeus had given him charge of the winds, both to restrain them and to release them. He received Odysseus as his guest and gave him a bag made of cowhide in which he had confined winds, showing him the ones to use when he sailed and tying the bag tightly in the ship. By using the proper winds Odysseus was sailing along well, but after he had come near Ithaca
11 and had seen the smoke rising from the city, he went to sleep. His companions, thinking that there was gold in the bag, untied it and let the winds go. They caught up the ships and drove them back the way they had come. Odysseus returned to Aeolus and asked for a favorable wind, but he expelled him from the island, saying that he could not save him since the gods were working against him.

12 Sailing away, then, he came to the land of the Laestrygonians and anchored his own ship last.[4] The Laestrygonians were cannibals and their king was Antiphates. Wishing to learn who the inhabitants were Odysseus sent some of his men to find out. The king's daughter met
13 them and led them to her father. He seized one and devoured him and chased the rest, shouting and calling the other Laestrygonians. They came to the sea, smashed the ships with rocks, and ate the men. Odysseus chopped through the cable holding his ship and put to sea, but the rest of the ships were lost together with their crews.

14 He arrived with one ship at the island of Aeaea, where Circe, daughter of the Sun and Perse, and sister of Aeetes, lived. She had knowledge of all kinds of drugs. Odysseus divided his crew and then was chosen by lot to stay by the ship with one group while Eurylochus made his
15 way to Circe with twenty-two men. At her invitation they entered her house, except for Eurylochus. She gave each man a cup filled with a

mixture of cheese, honey, barley, and wine, to which she had added a drug. After they drank it, she touched them with a wand and changed some of them into wolves, some into pigs, some into asses, and some into lions.[5] Eurylochus watched this and reported it to Odysseus.

16

Odysseus got moly from Hermes and went to Circe. He put the moly among her drugs and when he drank the mixture was the only one not bewitched. He drew his sword and threatened to kill her, but she calmed his anger and restored his companions. After exacting an oath from her that she would do him no harm, Odysseus went to bed with her and by her had a child Telegonus. He stayed with her for a year.[6] Then having sailed the ocean and sacrificed to the souls of the dead, he followed Circe's advice and consulted the seer Tiresias.[7] He beheld the souls of the heroes and heroines and also saw his mother Anticlia, and Elpenor, who had died of a fall in Circe's house.

17

18

He returned to Circe who sent him off again. Putting out to sea he sailed by the island of the Sirens, Pisinoe, Aglaope, and Thelxiepia, daughters of Achelous and the Muse Melpomene. One of them played the lyre, another sang, and the third played the flute, and through their music they tried to lure those who sailed by to linger with them. From the thighs down they were shaped like birds. Odysseus wished to hear their song when he sailed past them and so, following Circe's suggestion, he stuffed wax in the ears of his crew and ordered them to tie him to the mast. Lured by the Sirens to stay with them, he begged to be untied, but they only tied him tighter and so he sailed by. The Sirens had received a prophecy that they would die if a ship sailed past them. Therefore they now died.[8]

19

20

After the Sirens, Odysseus faced two possible ways to sail. One way went by the Wandering Rocks and the other past two huge cliffs. On one cliff was Scylla, the daughter of Crataeis and Trienus (or Phorcus), with the face and chest of a woman and with six heads and twelve dogs' feet from her flanks down. On the other cliff was Charybdis, who three times a day sucked in water and spewed it out again. Following Circe's advice, he avoided sailing by the Wandering Rocks and went instead past the cliff of Scylla, while standing armed at the stern. Scylla appeared, snatched up six companions, and devoured them.

21

22

From there he came to Thrinacia, an island of the Sun, where cattle were grazing. Held by unfavorable winds he remained there. When his crew slaughtered some of the cattle and ate them because they were without food, the Sun reported it to Zeus. After Odysseus put out to sea Zeus struck his ship with a thunderbolt. When the ship broke up Odysseus held on to the mast and drifted to Charybdis.

23

Charybdis swallowed the mast and Odysseus grabbed a branch of an overhanging wild fig tree. He waited until he saw it shoot up again, then climbed upon it and was carried to the island of Ogygia. There Calypso, the daughter of Atlas, welcomed him and after going to bed with him bore him a son, Latinus. He stayed with her for five years, then made a raft and sailed away.[9] This was broken up in the sea because of Poseidon's wrath and Odysseus was cast naked on the shore of the Phaeacians. Nausicaa, the daughter of king Alcinous, was washing clothes when Odysseus sought her protection. She brought him to Alcinous who made him his guest and, after giving him gifts, sent him with an escort to his own country. In anger at the Phaeacians, Poseidon turned the ship to stone and hid the city by surrounding it with a mountain.

When Odysseus returned to his country he found his household ruined. For suitors, thinking that he was dead, were paying court to Penelope. | From Dulichium came fifty-seven: Amphinomous, Thoas, Demoptolemus, Amphimachus, Euryalus, Paralus, Evenorides, Clytius, Agenor, Eurypylus, Pylaemenes, Acamas, Thersilochus, Hagius, Clymenus, Philodemus, Meneptolemus, Damastor, Bias, Telmius, Polyidus, Astylochus, Schedius, Antigonus, Marpsius, Iphidamas, Argius, Glaucus, Calydoneus, Echion, Lamas, Andraemon, Agerochus, Medon, Agrius, Promus, Ctesius, Acarnan, Cycnus, Pseras, Hellanicus, Periphron, Megasthenes, Thrasymedes, Ormenius, Diopithes, Mecisteus, Antimachus, Ptolemaeus, Lestorides, Nicomachus, Polypoetes, and Ceraus. [Apollodorus only names fifty-three.]

There were twenty-three from Same: Agelaus, Pisander, Elatus, Ctesippus, Hippodochus, Eurystratus, Archemolus, Ithacus, Pisenor, Hyperenor, Pheroetes, Antisthenes, Cerberus, Perimedes, Cynnus, Thriasus, Eteoneus, Clytius, Prothous, Lycaethus, Eumelus, Itanus, and Lyammus.

Forty-four came from Zacynthos: Eurylochus, Laomedes, Molebus, Phrenius, Indius, Minis, Liocritus, Pronomus, Nisas, Daëmon, Archestratus, Hippomachus, Euryalus, Periallus, Evenorides, Clytius, Agenor, Polybus, Polydorus, Thadytius, Stratius, Phrenius, Indius, Daesenor, Laomedon, Laodicus, Halius, Magnes, Oleotrochus, Barthas, Theophron, Nissaeus, Alcarops, Periclymenus, Antenor, Pellas, Celtus, Periphas, Ormenus, Polybus, and Andromedes. [Apollodorus only names forty-one.]

From Ithaca itself there were twelve suitors: Antinous, Pronous, Liodes, Eurynomus, Amphimachus, Amphialus, Promachus, Amphimedon, Aristratus, Helenus, Dulicheus, and Ctesippus. | [10]

They came to the palace and exhausted Odysseus' herds in feasting.

Penelope promised under pressure to marry when the shroud for Laertes was finished, and for three years she wove it by day and
32 unravelled it by night. In this way Penelope deceived the suitors until she was found out. When Odysseus learned of the situation at home, he came disguised as a beggar to his servant Eumaeus, was recognized by Telemachus, and entered the city. Melanthius the goatherd, who was a servant, encountered them and abused them. When Odysseus came to the palace, he asked the suitors for food. Finding a beggar there named Irus he wrestled with him.[11] He revealed himself to Eumaeus and Philoetius and, with these and Telemachus, plotted against the suitors.

33 Penelope gave to the suitors the bow which Odysseus had received from Iphitus and said that she would marry the one who strung it. When no one was able to do so, Odysseus took it and shot down the suitors with the help of Eumaeus, Philoetius, and Telemachus. He also killed Melanthius and the maidservants who were sleeping with the suitors and revealed his identity to his wife and his father.[12]

34 After sacrificing to Hades, Persephone and Tiresias, he traveled on foot through Epirus and came to Thesprotia, where he made a sacrifice according to Tiresias' directions and propitiated Poseidon.[13] Callidice,
35 the queen of the Thesprotians at that time, asked him to stay and offered him the kingdom. After making love with him she bore him a son, Polypoetes. Odysseus married Callidice, became king of the Thesprotians and, in a battle, defeated the neighboring people who attacked him. When Callidice died, he turned the kingdom over to Polypoetes and returned to Ithaca, where he found a son, Poliporthes, born to him by Penelope.

36 When Telegonus learned from Circe that he was Odysseus' son, he sailed in search of him. Coming to the island of Ithaca he drove away some of the cattle. When Odysseus came to rescue them, Telegonus wounded him with his spear which was tipped with the tail
37 of a sting-ray, and Odysseus died. After he recognized him, Telegonus wept bitterly, brought the corpse and Penelope to Circe, and there married Penelope. Circe sent them both to the Islands of the Blest.[14]

38 | Some, however, say that Penelope, after being seduced by Antinous, was sent to her father, Icarius, by Odysseus, and that while she was
39 in Mantinea in Arcadia she bore Pan to Hermes. Others say that she died at the hands of Odysseus himself, because she was seduced by
40 Amphinomus. There are some who say that Odysseus, being prosecuted by the relatives of the dead, made Neoptolemus, king of the islands off Epirus, his judge. He thought that with Odysseus out of the way he could occupy Cephallenia and so condemned him to exile.

Odysseus then went to Aetolia, to Thoas, son of Andraemon, married his daughter, and died an old man, leaving behind a son by her named Leontophonus. | [15]

NOTES
(Epitome 7)

1   Epitome 7. 2–23 gives an abridged synopsis of Homer's narration in the *Odyssey* of the adventures of Odysseus as he returned from Troy to his home on the island of Ithaca; his entry, disguised as a beggar, into his palace; his revelation of his identity to and slaughter of a group of barbarous (even murderous) men of Ithaca who had for years plundered his possessions under the guise of wooing his wife, Penelope; and his revelation of his identity to a dubious Penelope and to his father. The adventures, with which Apollodorus begins, occupy books 9. 37–13. 125 of the *Odyssey* (Cicones to Phaeacians). Homer uses ring composition: In book 5 Odysseus leaves Calypso on the island of Ogygia and reaches the shore of the island of Scherie, the home of the Phaeacians, at the end of the book. In books 6–8 he goes to the palace of Alcinous, the Phaeacian king, and is hospitably received. He narrates his adventures up to his arrival there in books 9–12, ending them (and book 12) with his arrival and sojourn on Ogygia. In book 13 he bids farewell to his Phaeacian hosts and a crew of Phaeacian sailors convey him by ship to Ithaca.

Apollodorus occasionally adds details not found in Homer and he obviously omits many. Most striking is the absence of reference to the *Telemacheia*, so called (books 1–4), with which the poem begins and which presents the declining state of Odysseus' household and Telemachus' resolve to rid himself of the suitors. Thus the poem of Odysseus' return begins with his absence from the place to which he will return and the bad effects of that absence. His character (or self) is strongly felt by means of the vacuum which his absence has created, a vacuum which is partially filled (or increased?) by stories about him told to Telemachus by people who knew him (especially in books 1, 3, and 4). Odysseus' appearance in the poem (in book 5) is thus carefully and dramatically prepared for in the first four books of the poem. Along with this preparation (and part of it) is Telemachus' coming of age, characterized, as noted above, by his decision to rid the palace of the suitors. Prompted by Athena, who is disguised as a family friend named Mentes, Telemachus decides to go in search of news of his father as a first step, to determine whether he is alive or dead. He travels first to Pylos where he listens to Nestor and obtains some information (book 3), and then to Sparta where he hears Helen and Menelaus and learns more (book 4). From there he returns to Pylos and his ships and sails back to Ithaca. The suitors, meanwhile, have decided to murder Telemachus and set out to waylay him at sea on his return (book 4, end). "Homer designed his poem," H. D. F. Kitto says, "in what musicians call ternary form, A-B-A: Ithaca, with his son seeking news of his father—the whole story of Odysseus' wanderings—Ithaca, and the triumph of father and son" (*Poiesis* [Berkeley and Los Angeles, 1966], 123).

The plot (*mûthos*) hardly does justice to the work of art itself and forces us to consider the question: What is the relation between myth and the narrative art (verbal or visual) in which it occurs? (See ch. 11, n. 19.) The suggestion was made in that note that perhaps myth cannot be separated from literature as a skeleton from a body or a form from a content.

Adam Parry's comment on the *Iliad* quoted in n. 19 to ch. 11 may be repeated with reference to the *Odyssey*: "To offer a succession of scenes so comprehensively evaluating the human situation, to present them in a dramatic trajectory ... requires an artistic construct of the highest order" ("Have We Homer's *Iliad*?" *Yale Classical Studies* 20 [1966], 193). The implication is clear: The total poem, all its words, all its lines, creates its essence. Myth (or plot) and narrative surface, form and content, surface and deep structures are artificial divisions (or attempts at division) of what cannot be divided. The poem, its meaning, and its language are a unity. That language happens to be ancient Greek and the difference between the original and a translation (let it be said) is the difference between the real Helen and the phantom Helen.

2   One might call the lotus the marijuana of ancient myth. Not that the Greeks did not know about the real stuff (cannabis), too, through Herodotus 4. 74–75, but apparently did not use it for pleasure, as did the Scythians.

3   Odysseus' encounter with and deception of the Cyclops Polyphemus, narrated in book 9 of the *Odyssey*, has thematic significance for the entire poem. For the importance of "Nobody" which Odysseus gives as his name to Polyphemus, see Norman Austin, "Name Magic in the Odyssey," *Calif. Stud. in Class. Antiquity* 5 (1972), 1–19 and the author's "*Odyssey* 9: Symmetry and Paradox in *Outis*," *Class. Journ.* 68 (1972), 22–25.

The Cyclops episode is the basis for a satyr play (the fourth play after a trilogy, for comic relief of a sort) by Euripides entitled *Cyclops*. A very short play (709 lines), it follows closely the Homeric version of the tale. The humor lies not only in the buffoonery of the play but in the incongruity of the portrayal of Polyphemus, who is as bestial as ever, but also possessed of wit and capable of sophistry equal to that of his opponent, Odysseus. See D. J. Conacher, *Euripidean Drama: Myth, Theme and Structure* (Toronto, 1967), 317–26.

Polyphemus is characterized differently in the pastoral poetry of Theocritus. In *Idyll* 11, yet unblinded, he is lovesick for Galatea who rejects him because of his grotesque appearance. He consoles himself by singing, his song a hopeless plea to Galatea to come to him. She does not, but he feels better, for poetry is the remedy for unrequited love. (See also *Idyll* 6.)

At Virgil *Aeneid* 3. 588–683 Aeneas and his crew anchor off the island of the Cyclopes (i.e., Sicily) unknowing and go ashore. There they meet a half-crazed creature, Achemenides, a Greek somehow left behind by Odysseus when he and the remainder of his men escaped from Polyphemus' cave. He tells the story of their encounter with the Cyclops, a reworking of Homer's story (*Odyssey* 9) because, as R. D. Williams says, Virgil was fascinated by Odysseus' sea adventures in the *Odyssey* and "wished to introduce something of this atmosphere into Aeneas' voyage" (*P. Vergili Maronis Aeneidos Liber Tertius* [Oxford, 1962], 181, comment to lines 588–89).

After Achemenides finishes his story Polyphemus himself appears, heading for the shore with a pine trunk for a cane, where he laves his unhealed eye socket with salt water and grinds his teeth at the pain. He hears the Trojans (who have now boarded their ships) frantically rowing away, but unable to catch them, he lets out a bellow which echoes and reverberates through the trembling sea and the terrified land of Italy and caves of Aetna. See also Ovid *Met.* 14. 160–220 for an elaboration perhaps based on Virgil's version.

In a quite different kind of treatment Ovid *Met.* 13. 740–869 describes Polyphemus in love with Galatea (making use of the Hellenistic pastoral tradition). The savage giant pursues her endlessly, although she despises him. On fire with passion for her he neglects his herds and attends to his appearance, combing his hair with a rake, trimming his beard with a sickle and inspecting the results in a pool of water. His love of killing, his savagery, his thirst for blood, have all apparently disappeared. Warned by Telemus that Odysseus will take away his eye he laughs: "You're wrong, you stupid seer, for another has caught my eye." Sitting on a hill near his cave he plays a huge set of pipes made with a hundred reeds which echoes over the mountains and the sea. Then he sings, and Galatea, far away in the arms of her lover, Acis, cannot avoid hearing his song. He compares her beauty (and her obstinacy) to almost every animal, vegetable, and mineral under the sun (and to that, too). By this endless string of metaphorical comparisons (and perhaps by the episode), Ovid mocks pastoral poetry.

Polyphemus offers to Galatea a part of a mountain, caves, and the wealth of nature: Apples, grapes, strawberries, cherries, plums, chestnuts, wild strawberries, cattle too many to count, with small udders, lambs, kids, and milk, some for drinking, some for cheese. And as for pets, no deer, rabbits, goats, doves or birds for her, but bear cubs! He knows what his appearance is like (he saw himself in a pool), but he is *big*. Lots of hair, true, but trees have leaves; horses, manes; birds, feathers; sheep, wool. Beards and hairy bodies make men more handsome. As for his one eye like a great shield in the middle of his brow, well, the sun is the sky's one great eye and can see all things.

His song leads him inevitably to question why Galatea loves Acis rather than him. Let Acis love himself! We begin to hear the sound of gnashing teeth: Would that Acis could feel his strength. He would tear out his living guts, pull him apart, and scatter the pieces over land and sea. For fire burns in his injured heart like the fire in Mount Aetna. But it makes no difference to Galatea.... Unlike Theocritus' Polyphemus, he finds no remedy for his love in song.

4   There is a lacuna in the text after the clause, "Sailing . . . and."

5   In Homer *Odyssey* 10. 237–43 Circe turns the companions of Odysseus into pigs only, although when the men arrived at her house in the woods they saw tamed wolves and mountain lions which were formerly men. These strangely mild animals fawned on them and stayed near the house to hear Circe's singing (10. 210–23).

6   The magical plant moly (Greek *môlu*) had a black root and a milk-white flower. It was difficult for mortals to uproot, but easy for gods (Homer *Odyssey* 10. 302–06).

Ovid *Met.* 14. 223–440 gives shortened versions of Odysseus' and his companions' encounters with Aeolus, the Laestrygonians, and Circe in the words of Macareus, a Greek at Cumae, who relates these adventures to his old acquaintance Achemenides when the latter arrives there (traveling with the Trojans since they rescued him from the island of the Cyclopes; see n. 3).

Homer does not mention Telegonus, the son of Odysseus and Circe. Hesiod *Theogony* 1014 says that Circe bore Telegonus to Odysseus, but the line is considered spurious. Agias, author of *Returns* (a poem in the Epic Cycle), refers to Circe's son, Telegonus (Hugh G. Evelyn-White, ed., *Hesiod, the Homeric Hymns and Homerica* [Cambridge, Mass. and London, 1936], 529), and the *Telegony*, composed by Eugammon and also belonging to the the Epic Cycle, has as its subject the deeds of this son of Odysseus by Circe. (For Proclus' summary, see Evelyn-White, *Hesiod*, 531.) The author of the *Telegony* was also said to have made Telegonus (or Teledamus) a son of Odysseus by Calypso (Evelyn-White, *Hesiod*, 533).

7 Tiresias first appears in Apollodorus at 2. 4. 8. How he was blinded and became a seer is related at 3. 6. 7 (see also ch. 6, n. 33) and his death at 3. 7. 3.

8 Although Homer uses the dual number (which English lacks) twice when referring to the Sirens (*Odyssey* 12. 52 and 167), elsewhere he uses the plural for them (e.g., 12. 39, 42, 44, 158, 198). W. B. Stanford, ed., *The Odyssey of Homer*, 2 vols. (New York and London, 1959), 1. 407, comment to 12. 51–2, suggests that the dual was retained by Ionian rhapsodists for metrical purposes and used indiscriminately with the plural. Thus we may accept Apollodorus' three Sirens.

Apollonius Rhodius *Argonautica* 4. 891–99 names the island which the Sirens inhabit as Anthemoessa. Their mother, Apollonius says, was the Muse Terpsichore (although Apollodorus says in the present passage and at 1. 3. 4 that they were the daughters of Achelous and the Muse Melpomene; at 1. 7. 10 he names their parents as Achelous and Sterope). The Sirens, Apollonius says, once were attendants of Persephone and used to sing to her. At that time, too, they were part bird and part maiden.

Ovid *Met.* 5. 552–63 provides more information: The Sirens were companions of Persephone when she used to go picking Spring flowers. When she disappeared they sought for her over the entire world in vain. They longed for wings to continue their search over the water and the gods gave them wings. But lest their singing voices, born to soothe the breezes, lose their lovely sound, their young girls' faces and human voices remained. Here in Ovid the human voice (*humana vox*, 563) is preserved, rather than lost, when metamorphosis, which usually blocks utterance, occurs. But in the case of the Sirens, whose beautiful singing is deadly, would it not have been better if they had lost their voices?

Through Persephone the Sirens are connected, one may suggest, with the underworld. As they flew over land and sea, looking for the lost girl, they hoped that the sound of their voices calling her might enable them to find her. But she was in Hades and unable to return to her forlorn friends, whether or not she heard them. We may note that in Apollonius Rhodius *Argonautica* 4. 903–09 the Argo's crew is saved from anchoring on the Sirens' island to listen to them (and die) by Orpheus, whose song defeated death in the underworld, and who here snatches up a lyre, plays a song, and successfully drowns them out.

9   Homer says nothing about a child born to Odysseus by Calypso, although Eugammon in his *Telegony* attributed Telegonus to Odysseus by Circe and by Calypso (see n. 6). Hesiod *Theogony* 1011–13 says that Circe (not Calypso) bore Agrius and Latinus to Odysseus. According to *Odyssey* 7. 259 Odysseus stayed with Calypso for seven years.

10   Homer says that there were 108 suitors (*Odyssey* 16. 247–51). Apollodorus gives numbers which add up to 136, but he only names 129. Homer never lists the suitors by name, mentioning only the more notorious ones.

11   In Homer *Odyssey* 18. 1–99 Odysseus boxes, not wrestles, with Irus.

12   So Apollodorus ends that part of his account of the myth of Odysseus which he drew from Homer's *Odyssey*. Two ancient critics are said to have rejected 23. 297–372 (end) and 24 as spurious. One of these critics additionally singled out 24. 1–204 as spurious (apparently his convictions about spuriousness were of varying intensity with regard to varying portions of the text). See Stanford, *Odyssey* 2. 404–06 (comment on 23. 296 ff.) and 2. 409–10 (a note on the rejection of 24. 1–204). Stanford accepts 23. 297–24. 548, as genuine. Apollodorus did as well: He mentions Odysseus' revelation of his identity to his father, Laertes (occurring at *Odyssey* 24. 205–412, within the portion of the text considered spurious by the ancient critics referred to). Odysseus proposes his visit to Laertes and leaves to visit him at 23. 359–72 (also within the portion of the text considered spurious). So far so good. But Apollodorus omits reference to the very end of the poem, the aftermath of the killing of the suitors: The Ithacans' anger, their decision for war against Odysseus, family and servants, the confrontation between the two groups, Athena's starting and then stopping of hostilities and the peace that her intervention, ratified by Zeus, brings about (24. 413–548 [end]). The reason for this omission, of course, no one knows.

Odysseus home, grievances redressed, and peace established in Ithaca, however, provide a fitting end to the poem, book 1 of which describes the precarious state of the absent Odysseus' household and the suitors' bellicose arrogance. Moreover, a conference in heaven with Zeus and Athena as the two speakers opens the work and is nicely balanced by the intervention of Athena (with Zeus' approval) at the end.

The *Odyssey* has obviously been much written about: see the bibliography of Stanford, *Odyssey*, 2. 428–432. Howard Porter's Introduction to George H. Palmer, trans., *The Odyssey of Homer* (New York, 1962), published since Stanford's edition, is probably the best short essay on the *Odyssey* in English: Ideal for students and the non-classicist and rich with ideas for the classicist. Norman Austin's "The One and the Many in the Homeric Cosmos," *Arion* N. S. 1/2 (1973/ 1974), 219–74, the second chapter of his *Archery at the Dark of the Moon: Paratactic Esthetics in the Odyssey*, forthcoming from the University of California Press, promises a fine work which aims "toward a definition of Homeric poiesis" (268 n. 1).

The influence of the Odyssey on subsequent Western literature is enormous and cannot be discussed here. The poem "Ithaka" by C. P. Cavafy is worth quoting, however, both for its own sake and because it expresses a modern Greek poet's response to a work of art created at the beginning of the literary tradition of his own language and culture:

Ithaka

As you set out for Ithaka
hope your road is a long one,
full of adventure, full of discovery.
Laistrygonians, Cyclops,
angry Poseidon—don't be afraid of them:
you'll never find things like that on your way
as long as you keep your thoughts raised high,
as long as a rare excitement
stirs your spirit and your body.
Laistrygonians, Cyclops,
wild Poseidon—you won't encounter them
unless you bring them along inside your soul,
unless your soul sets them up in front of you.

Hope your road is a long one.
May there be many summer mornings when,
with what pleasure, what joy,
you enter harbors you're seeing for the first time;
may you stop at Phoenician trading stations
to buy fine things,
mother of pearl and coral, amber and ebony,
sensual perfume of every kind—
as many sensual perfumes as you can;
and may you visit many Egyptian cities
to learn and go on learning from their scholars.

Keep Ithaka always in your mind.
Arriving there is what you're destined for.
But don't hurry the journey at all.
Better if it lasts for years,

so you're old by the time you reach the island,
wealthy with all you've gained on the way,
not expecting Ithaka to make you rich.
Ithaka gave you the marvelous journey.
Without her you wouldn't have set out.
She has nothing left to give you now.

And if you find her poor, Ithaka won't have fooled you.
Wise as you will have become, so full of experience,
you'll have understood by then what these Ithakas mean.

(C. P. Cavafy, *Collected Poems*, trans. by Edmund Keeley and Philip Sherrard, ed. by George Savidis [Princeton, 1975], 35–36.)

13   Odysseus went to the underworld for the express purpose of consulting Tiresias (Homer *Odyssey* 10. 487–95 and 561–65). The seer directs him, after he kills the suitors, to travel inland carrying an oar until he meets people who do not know the sea, nor eat food from the sea, people who do not know ships with purple prows nor flat blade oars, the wings of ships. When he meets a stranger who takes the oar on his shoulder for a winnowing fan, then and there he must plant it in the ground, sacrifice to Poseidon, return home, and sacrifice to all the immortal gods. Then death will drift gently to him from the sea, when he is exhausted by the fullness of old age (*Odyssey* 11. 119–36).

14   Apollodorus seems to follow the *Telegony* by Eugammon, a lost poem in the Epic Cycle, in relating Odysseus' sojourn with Callidice, his return to Ithaca, and his death at the hands of Telegonus, his son by Circe. In Proclus' summary of the *Telegony* (Evelyn-White, *Hesiod*, 531), Telegonus transports the body of Odysseus, and Penelope and Telemachus to Circe's island. She makes Odysseus' original wife and son immortal, Telegonus marries Penelope, and Telemachus, Circe. This end of the Odysseus myth should well serve the psychoanalytic critic of myth and perhaps offers the ideal resolution to the oedipal triangle, if the father happens to have two wife-figures and a son by each. Then one son can kill his father, marry the wife-figure who is not his mother, and the other son can marry the other wife-figure, who is also not his mother. Although patricide is involved, incest does not occur. (In Sophocles' *Oedipus Tyrannus*, Oedipus is undone more by learning of his incest with Jocasta than by finding out that he killed Laius.)

For additional references to Odysseus' death at the hands of his son, Telegonus, see Frazer, *Apollodorus* 2. 303–05. Frazer observes that Odysseus' death from a wound by a sting-ray fulfills Tiresias' prophecy to him in the underworld that his death would come from the sea (see n. 13), although this kind of death hardly seems to be what Tiresias had in mind.

15   For references to Penelope's faithlessness and Odysseus' exile, all postclassical (and non-Homeric), see Frazer, *Apollodorus* 2. 305–07. These stories, which are both offensive and gratuitous, lead one to suggest an image of a garden for the relation of mythology to literature. In this garden, which is the work or works of art, growing from the aesthetic consciousness of a person, persons, or a culture, all kinds of plants grow, are tended, shaped, and arranged. Weeds can grow there, too. Perhaps these additions to the myth of Odysseus not found in Homer can be considered weed-myths.

The continuing influence of Homer's *Odyssey*, where the myth of Odysseus is best cultivated, has been well described by W. B. Stanford, *The Ulysses Theme* (Ann Arbor, 1968). Stanford examines the Odysseus figure from its pre-Homeric origins, through the enormous literature which draws upon both Odysseus and the *Odyssey* (including the Greek tragedians, Virgil, Dante and Tennyson), up to James Joyce's *Ulysses* and Nikos Kazantzakis' *The Odyssey: A Modern Sequel*.

Apollodorus begins his book of Greek mythology with the creation of the physical, nonhuman universe, the elements of which, however, are described as humanized deities: Sky, Earth and their offspring. He faithfully reflects the Greek view of an anthropocentric universe. Apollodorus ends his work with the myth of the most human of all Greek heroes, Odysseus, the Western example of mankind's intelligence, complexity, his good, and his evil. It seems an orderly progression, free from mystery, with man at the center and clearly defined. But the Greeks knew better. Hear Pindar:

> Creatures changing day by day: What is a man, or isn't he?
> The dream of a shadow: mankind.
> But when Zeus-given brilliance comes, light
> plays on men and smoothes their lives.
>
> (*Pyth.* 8. 95–97)

SELECTED BIBLIOGRAPHY

Allen, T. W.; Halliday, W. R.; and Sikes, E. E., eds. *The Homeric Hymns.* 2d ed. Oxford: Oxford University Press, 1936.

Anderson, William S., ed. *Ovid's Metamorphoses: Book 6–10.* Norman: University of Oklahoma Press, 1972.

Barthes, Roland. *Mythologies.* Translated by Annette Lavers. New York: Hill and Wang, 1972. Essay entitled "Myth Today," pp. 109–59.

Cohen, Percy. "Theories of Myth." *Man* N. S. 4 (1969): 337–53.

Evelyn-White, Hugh G., ed. and trans. *Hesiod, The Homeric Hymns and Homerica.* Cambridge, Mass.: Harvard University Press, and London: William Heinemann, Ltd., 1936.

Feder, Lillian. *Ancient Myth in Modern Poetry.* Princeton: Princeton University Press, 1971.

Frazer, Sir James George, ed. and trans. *Apollodorus: The Library.* Two volumes. Cambridge, Mass.: Harvard University Press and London: William Heinemann, Ltd., 1921.

Frye, Northrop. *Fables of Identity.* New York: Harcourt, Brace and World, Inc., 1963. Essays entitled "The Archetypes of Literature" and "Myth, Fiction, and Displacement," pp. 7–38.

Huizinga, J. *Homo Ludens: A Study of the Play Element in Culture.* Boston: Beacon Press, 1955.

Kirk, G. S. *Myth: Its Meaning and Functions in Ancient and Other Cultures.* Cambridge, Eng.: Cambridge University Press, and Berkeley and Los Angeles: University of California Press, 1970.

Kirk, Geoffrey S. "Aetiology, Ritual, Charter: Three Equivocal Terms in the Study of Myths." *Yale Classical Studies* 22 (1972): 83–102.

Leach, Edmund. *Claude Lévi-Strauss.* New York: The Viking Press, 1970.

Lesky, Albin. *A History of Greek Literature.* 2d ed. Translated by James Willis and Cornelis de Heer. New York: Thomas Y. Crowell Company, 1966.

Lévi-Strauss, Claude. *Structural Anthropology.* Translated by Claire Jacobson and Brooke Grundfest Schoepf. Garden City, New York: Doubleday and Company, Inc., 1967. Ch. 11, "The Structural Study of Myth," pp. 202–28.

Lévi-Strauss, Claude. *The Savage Mind.* Chicago: The University of Chicago Press, 1966. Ch. 1, "The Science of the Concrete," pp. 1–33.

Lévi-Strauss, Claude. *The Raw and the Cooked: Introduction to a Science of Mythology: 1.* Translated by John and Doreen Weightman. New York and Evanston: Harper and Row, 1969. "Overture," pp. 1–32.

Mayerson, Philip. *Classical Mythology in Literature, Art, and Music.* Waltham, Mass. and Toronto: Xerox Publishing Company, 1971.

Nilsson, Martin P. *The Mycenean Origin of Greek Mythology.* A New Introduction and Bibliography by Emily Vermeule. Berkeley, Los Angeles, London: University of California Press, 1972.

Otis, Brooks. *Ovid as an Epic Poet.* 2d ed. Cambridge, Eng.: Cambridge University Press, 1970.

Peradotto, John. *Classical Mythology: An Annotated Bibliographical Survey.* Urbana: The American Philological Association, 1973.

Slater, Philip E. *The Glory of Hera.* Boston: Beacon Press, 1968.

Tripp, Edward. *The Meridian Handbook of Classical Mythology.* New York: New American Library, 1974.

Whitman, Cedric H. *Euripides and the Full Circle of Myth.* Cambridge, Mass.: Harvard University Press, 1974.

Index of Proper Names
(from the text of the *Library*)

Acknowledgments

Part of "Frost and Stone," by Archibald MacLeish, from the fall 1963 special issue of the *Amherst Alumni News*, is reprinted by permission of the *Amherst Alumni News* and Mr. MacLeish.

"Ithaka" and part of "Epitaph of Antiochus, King of Kommagini," in *C. P. Cavafy Collected Poems*, translated by Edmund Keeley and Philip Sherrard and ed. by George Savidis, translation © 1975 by Edmund Keeley and Philip Sherrard, Greek text of the "Unpublished Poems" © 1963, 1968 by Kyveli Singopoulou, published by the Hogarth Press Ltd. and Princeton University Press, pp. 67–68 and 237, are reprinted by permission of the Hogarth Press Ltd. and Princeton University Press.

An excerpt from *The Maze Maker*, by Michael Ayrton, copyright © 1967 by Michael Ayrton, is reprinted by permission of Holt, Rinehart and Winston, Publishers, and the Longman Group Ltd.

Excerpts from *Report to Greco* and *The Odyssey*, by Nikos Kazantzakis, copyright © 1965 and 1958 by Simon and Schuster, Inc., are reprinted by permission of Helen N. Kazantzakis and Simon and Schuster, Inc.

Excerpts from *The New Golden Bough*, ed. by Theodor H. Gaster, copyright © 1959 by S. G. Phillips, Inc., are reprinted by permission of S. G. Phillips, Inc.

Library of Congress Cataloging in Publication Data

Apollodorus, of Athens.
   God and heroes of the Greeks.
   Translation of Bibliotheca.
   Bibliography: p.
   Includes index.
   1. Mythology, Greek. I. Simpson, Michael,
1934–   II. Baskin, Leonard, 1922–
I. Title.
PA3870.A75 1976   292'.2'11   75–32489
ISBN 0–87023–206–1 pbk.